GW00359639

Prem Mahadevan is a Senior Researcher at the Center for Security Studies, ETH Zurich. His responsibilities cover the study of intelligence agencies, sub-state conflict and organised crime. He has an undergraduate degree in War Studies and postgraduate and doctoral degrees in Intelligence Studies from King's College, London. This book is based on research conducted at King's College for his doctorate. In addition to publishing in academic and policy journals, he has engaged in strategic analysis and political risk assessment for UK business interests in South Asia.

THE POLITICS OF COUNTERTERRORISM IN INDIA

Strategic Intelligence and National Security in South Asia

Prem Mahadevan

I.B. TAURIS
LONDON · NEW YORK

Published in 2012 by I.B.Tauris & Co Ltd
6 Salem Road, London W2 4BU
175 Fifth Avenue, New York NY 10010
www.ibtauris.com

Distributed in the United States and Canada
Exclusively by Palgrave Macmillan
175 Fifth Avenue, New York NY 10010

International Library of Security Studies, vol. 2

ISBN 978 1 84885 775 9

A full CIP record for this book is available from the British Library
A full CIP record for this book is available from the Library of Congress

Library of Congress catalog card: available

Typeset by Newgen Publishers, Chennai
Printed and bound by CPI Group (UK) Ltd, Croydon CRO 4YY

CONTENTS

FOREWORD

Most studies of terrorism have tended to focus on the 'stimulant side' of the phenomenon like its genesis and cause of growth, the various organisations and structures, their political goals and ideologies, resources and linkages etc. The 'response side', analysing the factors that have led to the demise of different terrorist groups, the impact of governmental policies and strategies, the strengths and limitations of counter terrorist instrumentalities like intelligence, armed forces, police, etc. has, however, remained relatively neglected. For creating appropriate solutions, it is important to analyse empirical data to identify those policy initiatives that hit the terrorists most, those initiatives that failed to deliver the intended results, actions that proved counterproductive or entailed unacceptable costs in terms of men and material, and techniques and methods that forced terrorists to change their intentions or those which led to a degradation of their capabilities.

Terrorism's demise is seldom a simple and straightforward phenomenon that can be achieved by marshalling enough force to kill, capture or otherwise decimate their ranks. There is considerable evidence to indicate that governments have often fallen prey to the classical terrorist strategy of provocation. The subsequent government overreaction frames the government as the aggressors, enabling terrorists to gain people's sympathy and support – a key ingredient of their success. Exclusive dependence on force has often led to the consolidation of fragmented or dissenting terrorist ranks and heavy collateral damage, which swells the ranks of new recruits. A scientific and objective study of the cause-and-effect relationships between the steps taken by governments and the results they produce in an empirical framework is thus necessary to draw the right inferences and learn the right lessons.

The answer as to why the response side of terrorism has remained less studied by scholars is not difficult to find. Both of the domains where the really important data lies are difficult territories for academicians to access. The terrorists, while hungry for publicity, are extremely careful not to let the enemy know their vulnerabilities and which actions of the government may have hurt them. Often they capitalise more on the mistakes committed by the government than on their own achievements. On the other hand, governmental bureaucracies are still reticent, and consider it almost blasphemous to allow any independent scientific and objective analysis of their policies and actions. This book commendably cuts through these barriers and provides a scholar's viewpoint of the role of intelligence in the most formidable area to penetrate: counterterrorism in a South Asian setting. It is the first substantial academic work of its kind and provides a rare insight into this complex phenomenon – demolishing many myths and bringing new findings to light.

Terrorism is essentially a 'covert action' by non-state actors, aimed at achieving a high level of surprise, lethality and secrecy in its operations. This brings the role of intelligence agencies, as the primary providers of knowledge support, to the centre stage and raises demands and expectations from them that have little relation to ground realities. Episodically, these demands are accentuated when losses become unaffordable and public clamouring becomes politically inconvenient for the government to bear. Whenever things go wrong it is presumed to be on account of intelligence failures – premised on two questionable assumptions: that appropriate actions automatically follow availability of good intelligence and that the intelligence apparatus, if alert and efficient, can know and predict the future – under all circumstances. These questionable assumptions are reinforced by the silence of intelligence agencies who, for broader security considerations, can ill afford the luxury of engaging in public debates to defend themselves.

Decision making in governments is a highly diffuse and complex phenomenon and, though intelligence agencies do have a vital role to play, there are many other factors and forces concurrently at work that influence decision making. Governments or their executive agencies do not always have the choice of exercising the options that on hindsight may appear to be the best. The apportioning of all the blame to the intelligence agencies whenever governments are surprised, or face unexpected situations, is tantamount to making the wrong diagnosis and consequently, leads to prescription of the wrong treatment. There has been very little academic effort to analyse and understand this complex phenomenon in a holistic manner, to objectively evaluate the role of intelligence agencies and suggest improvements where they are really called for.

What makes such studies rare and difficult is, however, not hard to fathom. Firstly, intelligence agencies practise near opaqueness, particularly with regard to covert operations, making it difficult for academics to access basic data. Even within the security and intelligence agencies, only few are privy to such information and very little is on record. Secondly, disclosure of information can endanger the safety and lives of people engaged in such operations and the revealed information can benefit the terrorists. Thirdly, there exists the possibility of irresponsible and motivated distortions by vested interests or 'conflict entrepreneurs' who create doubts about the legitimacy and credibility both of the intelligence agencies and the government, an objective that terrorists assiduously pursue.

Here, the author critically examines Indian intelligence systems and processes, evaluating their role in handling Sikh militancy, the Kashmir separatist movement and pan-Islamic jihadism, the three most virulent forms of terrorism faced by India. He examines the operational doctrines and actions of Indian terrorist groups and evaluates how adequate, or otherwise, the response has been. The author, having a long academic grounding and real insight into the functioning of intelligence systems and processes, has been able to use his expertise to his best advantage in dealing with a difficult subject. He underlines that no matter how much Indian intelligence agencies are criticised for under performance or even negligence, the institutional strength and basic soundness of their systems and operational capabilities are amply borne out by objective assessment of their role. This holistic perspective has eluded government commissions of enquiry, both in the West and India, which primarily focus on affixing institutional or individual responsibilities for failure in an episodic context.

The Indian experience of counterterrorism is relevant for any serious analyst of counterterrorism for variety of reasons. Firstly, the global epicentres of terrorism – Pakistan and Afghanistan – happen to be in India's backyard and India has suffered from a most virulent form of state-sponsored cross-border terrorism; suffering more casualties and fighting the battle longer than any other country in the world. Emboldened by its capacity for nuclear brinkmanship, Pakistan seems to consider terrorism as a low-cost option against its bigger adversary and, we believe, continues to pursue it as an integral part of its state policy. Secondly, India has faced and tackled terrorism of various varieties – religious (Sikh and Jihadi terrorism), ideological (left extremism) and ethnic (tribal insurgencies in the North-East) – without conceding to any political demands, and successfully terminating many of them. Lastly, India has fought terrorism within the framework of the rule of law, upholding democratic freedoms and the constitutional rights of the people. It has steadfastly resisted the temptation of using excessive force and has carried out counterterrorist operations within the matrix of legitimate police action. Even where military assistance has been sought, troops have been used in the police role and the army has refrained from using tactics, weapons and doctrines of war. Even in the face of grave provocations and losses, it has, by and large, refrained from using area weapons, gunships, artillery, etc. This largely explains the success of India in denying the support of people to the terrorists, on whose behalf the latter claim to have taken to the gun. Another central feature of Indian counterterrorist doctrine has been to use the coercive power of the state only to neutralise the terrorists and degrade their capabilities, as against using force in retaliatory punitive action or as a display of superior fire power to overawe and deter.

This approach has necessitated making counterterrorist operations in India intelligence-driven – targeting the actual terrorists, their camps, armed caches, etc. as against force-driven operations aimed at capturing and controlling territory. The superior knowledge this strategy requires has been sought primarily through the intelligence agencies, complemented by the efforts of the security forces, a widely-spread administrative infrastructure and information provided by the local population. This approach has underlined the centricity of intelligence in counterterrorism in India and the Intelligence Bureau has been officially designated as the nation's nodal agency for combating terrorism, insurgencies and other violent internal security threats. It is noteworthy that besides the proactive and preventive role of intelligence agencies against physical terrorist targets, their strategic operations can play a seminal role in decimating and hampering terrorist movements. These operations are aimed at forcing the terrorists to change their intentions, creating dissension and confusion in their ranks, creating vested interests in abjuring violence and intervening in the 'politics of terrorism', which often contributes to the demise of terrorist groups. As a case study the book successfully demolishes the commonly held view that Khalistani militancy was defeated by force alone and underlines the seminal role of covert maneuvering by India's Intelligence Bureau, which deftly exploited strategic mistakes made by the ISI.

I would like to compliment the author for this outstanding work – intense in its research and wide in its conceptual sweep. Considering that the book draws mainly from open sources, the effort is commendable. The author has successfully taken intelligence concepts developed by Western scholars and tried to test their veracity in the South-Asian context. The book is thus an exercise in inter-regional knowledge transfer which is unprecedented, since so few scholars have had the luxury of studying intelligence as a purely academic subject for long years in the West. His painstaking research into how the Indian establishment engaged and countered terrorism in India has added considerable empirical value to the work. I am sure scholars, security experts and people at large will find it interesting and useful reading.

Ajit Doval, KC
Former Director Intelligence Bureau
Government of India
New Delhi

ACKNOWLEDGEMENTS

The completion of this book would not have been possible without the support and encouragement that I received from respected colleagues and close friends. Many of those whose experiences were instrumental in the formation of my ideas wish to remain anonymous. In some cases, their reticence is due to modesty and in others, due to legitimate concerns over professional and/or personal security. To these individuals, I can only acknowledge that I remain in their debt. Their willingness to participate in research of no direct benefit to them is testimony to their inquisitiveness and intellectual courage.

I would like to thank my doctoral supervisors at King's College London, Professor MLR Smith and Dr. Mike Goodman. Their engaging lectures would banish even the worst Monday morning hangover. Professor Mats Berdal, who always found time to accommodate my meeting requests and Dr. Ahron Bregman, who took a keen interest in my work, both provided me with much-appreciated support and advice. Dr. David Betz and Professor Christopher Dandeker showed exemplary patience with my abrupt requests for assistance. I am also indebted to Dr. Joe Maiolo, Dr. Peter Neumann, Dr. Susan Martin, Professor Wyn Bowen and Professor Alice Hills for their constructive criticism of my research efforts. Without the benefit of their advice, I would not have finished this book.

Of the practitioners whom I am at liberty to name, I would like to thank Mr. KPS Gill, Lieutenant General (Retd) VK Nayyar, Mr. AS Dulat, Mr. K Shankaran Nair, Mr. DC Pathak, Mr. DC Nath, Mr. Kalyan Mitra, Mr. RK Raghavan and Mr. PKH Hormese Tharakan. Special mention needs to be made of Mr. R Swaminathan and Mr. Sanjay Vir Singh, both of whom tragically passed away before this book could come out. Also, the knowledge of Mr. Praveen Swami, Dr. Bidanda Chengappa and Dr. Bhashyam Kasturi substantially enriched my intellectual landscape. Dr. Ajai Sahni gave me tremendous assistance and shared his insights with me, during my numerous visits to Delhi. Students of contemporary South Asian security are unlikely to find a more knowledgeable teacher.

Two other scholars contributed immeasurably to my understanding of intelligence and terrorism studies. Without studying their pioneering work over many years, I might not have been motivated to research on a topic that has already been much commented upon. I would therefore like to acknowledge my gratitude to Professor Loch Johnson and Brian Michael Jenkins for their intellectual guidance and gracious encouragement. These two gentlemen showed me that the greatest experts do not let ego interfere with inquiry – a lesson that I intend to retain throughout my career.

At I.B.Tauris, my thanks go out to Tomasz Hoskins and Maria Marsh, who were an absolute pleasure to work with. Maria's prompt responses to my queries, always filled with courtesy, made the process of re drafting seem much less of a pain than it really was. Thanks also to Joanna Godfrey for her positive response to my initial manuscript pitch. I am also grateful for the work done by Debasree Bhattacharjee, my copy-editor. Her newly-established firm *Idea Inks* delivered as promised, and with a thoroughness that belied its youth.

Some of those colleagues and practitioners whom I hold in high regard are likely to disagree with the arguments made in this book; that does not alter my respect for them. I consider myself fortunate to have had the opportunity of learning from these individuals and studying their work. I hope that they will see in any intellectual disagreement grounds for further debate on topics that interest us all. Should this book fail to stir any reaction, positive or negative, from such knowledgeable experts, I would be somewhat disappointed.

TIMELINE OF MAJOR EVENTS

1887 Central Special Branch set up in British India to coordinate surveillance of political and inter-regional criminal activities by provincial Special Branches.

1903 Central Special Branch expanded and renamed Department of Criminal Intelligence.

1920 Department of Criminal Intelligence made exclusively responsible for political surveillance, renamed Intelligence Bureau (IB).

1947 India becomes independent of British Empire, fights first war with Pakistan over status of Kashmir.

1951 IB given responsibility for foreign intelligence collection, in addition to domestic intelligence.

1962 India defeated in war with China.

1965 India attacked by Pakistan, fights second war over status of Kashmir.

1968 IB relieved of responsibility for foreign intelligence. New agency created under direct control of Prime Minister – the Research & Analysis Wing (R&AW).

1971 R&AW distinguishes itself prior to and during third Indo-Pakistani war. India liberates the eastern half of Pakistan and creates a new nation, Bangladesh.

1975 Prime Minister Indira Gandhi declares a National Emergency to stall charges of electoral malpractice against her.

1977 State of Emergency lifted. Mrs Gandhi defeated in general elections and her arch-nemesis Morarji Desai becomes Prime Minister. R&AW suffers severe cuts in funding.

1980 Mrs Gandhi re-elected as Prime Minister. Pakistani Inter Services Intelligence (ISI) begins supporting extremist elements in the Sikh diaspora, with the intention of destabilizing her government.

1981 First terrorist incidents take place in the state of Punjab. Awareness spreads of the existence of a Sikh separatist movement. Mrs Gandhi's party meanwhile, provides tacit support to a radical Sikh preacher named Jarnail Singh Bhindranwale.

1984 Bhindranwale's base in the Golden Temple stormed by Indian Army after suspicions that he made contact with the ISI-backed separatists. Many killed in the attack. Some months later, Indira Gandhi shot dead by two of her Sikh bodyguards.

1987 Elections held to the Legislative Assembly of Jammu and Kashmir state. Create widespread resentment as they are perceived to have been rigged in favour of ruling political dispensation.

1990 Massive revolt breaks out in Jammu and Kashmir, with full support from Pakistani government.

1991 ISI formulates Plan K2M, aimed at instigating a nation-wide, synchronized terrorist offensive across India by Sikh and Kashmiri separatists and Pan-Islamist jihadists.

1992 Multi-force crackdown in Punjab, featuring heavy involvement of Indian Army. Sikh separatist movement wiped out.

1993 ISI uses a smuggling syndicate to carry out eleven simultaneous bombings in Mumbai.

1994 Pakistan left isolated at the United Nations High Commissioner for Human Rights Conference in Geneva. India begins to improve its human rights record in Kashmir.

1998 India and Pakistan carry out nuclear tests.

1999 Pakistani troops launch an incursion into Indian territory in the Kargil sector of Jammu and Kashmir. Forced to withdraw but succeed in disrupting Indian counterterrorist grid. Separatist violence escalates after a lull over the previous two years.

2000 Abortive ceasefire between largest Kashmiri separatist group (the Hizb-ul Mujahiddin) and Indian government. Efforts made to split the Hizb from Pakistani and Afghan mercenaries contracted by the ISI to fight in Kashmir.

2001 9/11 attacks in the United States followed by jihadist assault on Indian Parliament.

2002 Military stand-off between India and Pakistan. Under heavy US pressure, Pakistan cuts back support for terrorist infiltration across the Line of Control in Kashmir.

2004 General elections lead to a change of government in New Delhi. The incoming political leadership is inclined to be soft on jihadism for fear of alienating religious minorities.

2006	Indian Prime Minister agrees to establishment of a joint counterterrorism mechanism with Pakistan. Jihadist bomb attacks on the Indian heartland start to occur with greater frequency.
2008	Three-day gunbattle in Mumbai between ten Pakistani terrorists and Indian security forces. Widely perceived as the result of a flawed or non-existent counterterrorist strategy.
2009	Dialogue between India and Pakistan stalled as a result of Mumbai attacks. Lull in jihadist attacks against India.
2010	Foreign governments pressure New Delhi to hold talks with Islamabad. ISI begins using Pakistani terrorists to target Indian aid workers in Afghanistan, shifts to promoting pro-Pakistani activism within India through propaganda and subversion.
February 2011	Under international pressure, India agrees to restart talks with Pakistan.

INTRODUCTION

On 26 November 2008, ten Pakistani gunmen rampaged through the streets of Mumbai, shooting civilians at random. The resultant carnage was labelled as 'India's 9/11'. Melodramatic though the comparison might be, it was not wholly accurate. Unlike the Al Qaeda attacks of September 2001, Mumbai was not an unprecedented operation mounted by free agents. Rather, it represented the continuation of a long-standing covert war being waged, in the view of many analysts, by the Pakistani army and its spy wing, the Inter Services Intelligence (ISI), against India using terrorist proxies. The attacks themselves had been seventeen years in the making.

As early as 1991, the ISI had made a strategic decision to foster terrorism in India's urban heartland – its perceived soft underbelly. It is believed that among the many operational plans drawn up by the agency was one for a commando-style assault on Mumbai (then called Bombay). The plan called for 90 Kashmiri gunmen to sail from Karachi to Mumbai and carry out a shooting spree in the city's streets. The resultant chaos, it was hoped, would undermine India's efforts to attract foreign investment. Over time, a series of such attacks would force the country to choose between surrendering Kashmir, or relinquishing its ambitions of becoming a superpower.

Implementation of this scheme was temporarily shelved because no Kashmiri terrorists were prepared to embark on a suicidal mission. Over the next 17 years however, three politico-strategic trends converged in favour of its enactment. First, the ISI inducted Pakistani mercenaries into Kashmir, thereby blurring the boundaries between indigenous and foreign-born terrorists. Second, Hindu extremists in India began attacking innocent members of the Muslim minority, radicalising some of its members. Lastly, successive Indian governments passively watched these developments unfold, notwithstanding strong words to the contrary. The result was an attack by Pakistani jihadists, aided by radicalised Indian Muslims and launched even as New Delhi enthusiastically pursued peace talks with Pakistan.

Even the Indian response to the attacks cannot compare with the American reaction to 9/11, unless going into an impulsive sulk constitutes a 'response'. Halting bilateral dialogue and demanding that the attack masterminds be brought to justice might have been sensible – if justice were not being demanded from those who perpetrated the crime in the first place. Since 2008, Indian policy statements on counterterrorism have only become louder not better, reiterating vacuous promises of decisive action in the event of another '26/11'. In substantive terms however, Indian counterterrorism remains defensively oriented, relying on intelligence agencies to succeed where politicians, diplomats, soldiers and policemen have failed: in the prevention of terrorist attacks.

Terrorism and Intelligence

This book investigates whether Indian counterterrorist failures are failures of intelligence, or failures to act on intelligence. It concludes that they are the latter. Specifically, they are failures to act on long-term warnings or *strategic* intelligence. Such inaction stems from four factors, two of which are political and two operational. The factors are: a lack of political consistency and consensus, and a lack of operational capacity and coordination. Between them, these constraints ensure that decision-makers in the Indian political and security establishments fail to act on initial warnings provided by intelligence agencies.

Poor responsiveness on the part of decision-makers (also called 'intelligence consumers') creates a knowledge gap between strategic intelligence and short-term or *tactical* intelligence. While Indian intelligence agencies can predict broad shifts in terrorist strategy at the national level, they cannot provide specific details of terrorist plans. Without the latter, terrorist attacks cannot be prevented. Only local security forces can acquire such 'actionable' information, since they are structured and equipped to gather ground-level intelligence. They, and not the national-level intelligence agencies, should play the lead role in combating terrorism.

There is a lacuna of books and academic treatises in India and the Anglo-American world, on the limitations of national-intelligence agencies in counterterrorism. Considering that almost every terrorist attack is followed by proclamations that 'we need better intelligence', this state of events is surprising.[1] Few writers have even bothered to ask: what kind of intelligence is lacking – strategic or tactical? Without answering this question, one cannot prescribe remedies to counterterrorist failure. Ongoing efforts to reform intelligence agencies do not take into account the dichotomy between strategic and tactical intelligence. Consequently, they will not improve counterterrorist performance.

Anecdotal evidence has long indicated that a knowledge gap exists between strategic intelligence (which aims to *predict*) and tactical intelligence (which aims to *prevent*). For decades, counterterrorist campaigns have been dogged by the inability of desk-bound intelligence analysts to progress from generic to specific knowledge of terrorist plans. British forces grappled with the problem in Palestine during 1947–48.[2] Fifty years later, the Russians faced it while combating Chechen separatism.[3] Even the US intelligence community, for all its technical sophistry and analytical talent, has struggled to provide the tactical support demanded by security forces in the War on Terror.[4]

We will see in this book how intelligence agencies face significant limitations when operating against terrorist groups. Their role is mainly confined to educating decision-makers about the nature of a terrorist threat, and predicting its future trajectory. By themselves, such agencies very rarely deliver spectacular results at the local level of counterterrorism. That is the job of security forces, which need to be empowered and authorised to gather information on their own.

By highlighting the differences between strategic and tactical intelligence, this book disputes the wisdom of current efforts to enhance counterterrorism effectiveness. It challenges the dominant presumption that counterterrorist failures are caused by organizational weaknesses within intelligence agencies. It suggests that rather than looking at why these agencies do not produce specific warnings, researchers should examine why decision-makers do not act on generic warnings.

This book demonstrates how terrorist groups surround themselves with counterintelligence defences to prevent leakage of their plans. The four constraints – lack of political consistency, political consensus, operational capacity and operational coordination – are grouped into an analytical model that tests the responsiveness of governments to strategic intelligence. Wherever security forces are permitted to take offensive action upon receipt of initial warnings from intelligence agencies, they can penetrate terrorist groups and thus obtain more detailed information.

A Focus on Indian Counterterrorism

Indian counterterrorist experience is rich with examples where security forces have been employed offensively, and those where they have not. The two sets of examples demonstrate the secondary role of intelligence agencies in counterterrorism, relative to security forces.

The Politics of Counterterrorism in India applies the 'four constraints' model to three terrorist movements – the Sikh separatist movement, the Kashmiri separatist movement and pan-Islamist jihadism. Between them, these movements have been primarily responsible for acts of terrorism and large-scale violence in India. What becomes apparent is that while the organisational deficiencies of Indian intelligence agencies have not varied across time and space, the results of counterterrorism have. These results fluctuate with the operational posture adopted by security forces – the more defensive such postures are, the more dependent they grow on intelligence agencies and the more likely they are to lead to counterterrorist failures.

Such a dynamic explains why, despite their considerable experience in counterterrorism, the Indian security forces have been unable to contain the spread of jihadist terrorism across India. Although they were permitted by the policy-making elite to take an offensive stance against Sikh separatism and, to a lesser extent, against Kashmiri separatism, no offensive action has been taken against jihadism. As a result, the intelligence agencies have been entrusted with dual responsibility for strategic and tactical intelligence – a commitment their finite resources cannot meet.

A Note on Terminology

Before proceeding further, let us briefly examine certain key terms used frequently throughout the book.

Intelligence

'Intelligence' has been conceptualised here as a distinct type of *activity* aimed at increasing one's knowledge of an opponent, as well as the *data* generated by such activity.[5] This usage has been adapted from Thomas Troy, who defines intelligence as 'knowledge of the enemy'.[6] For an activity to qualify as intelligence, it must necessarily involve a well-defined opponent, and the penetration of that opponent's security system. This is because the main characteristic that distinguishes intelligence from other kinds of information-related tasks is the higher level of difficulty involved in data collection. If information on a subject is readily obtainable, then its acquisition does not encompass what is traditionally meant by 'intelligence'.[7]

Strategic and Tactical Intelligence

Broadly speaking, intelligence efforts against terrorism may be divided into two categories, depending on the level at which they are conducted:

Strategic intelligence involves long-term assessment of the threat that an opponent poses to national security. In the context of counterterrorism, it requires analysis of past and present trends in terrorist activity. The purpose of strategic intelligence is to alert policy makers to changes in the nature and trajectory of a terrorist threat, thus helping them formulate timely policy responses. In addition, it also provides a focus for tactical intelligence efforts.[8] Given that such intelligence is not necessarily time-sensitive, responsibility for its production primarily rests with professional intelligence agencies at the national level of government.[9] In some democratic states such as India, such agencies operate without the benefit of arrest powers. This severely reduces their ability to progress from strategic intelligence to tactical intelligence independently, without involving their consumers ie., decision makers.

Tactical intelligence on the other hand, is the acquisition of highly perishable information for consumption by local security forces. In the context in which the term will be used here, the primary purpose of tactical intelligence is to identify and locate terrorist cadres so that these can be neutralised by direct action.[10] Although intelligence agencies often attempt to engage in tactical intelligence, the security forces themselves are best suited to handle it.[11] Beat-level policemen in particular, enjoy key advantages in firepower, legal authority and area-specific knowledge that are unavailable to operatives of national-level agencies.[12] Moreover, they are best placed to identify gaps in local intelligence coverage and devise plans for plugging these.

Between strategic and tactical intelligence, lies an important divider that isolates the two types of activity from each other. This is the element of risk posed by terrorist security systems (also known as *counterintelligence* systems) to the operatives of intelligence agencies. Security forces personnel, with their entitlement to carry arms openly when moving amongst hostile populations, do not face the same level of risk. Moreover, unlike covert operatives, security forces move in large groups and can thus resort to concentrated offensive action as a means of gathering information. Although this point is discussed later, it is important to assert at the outset that strategic intelligence has its own dynamics, which are different from those of tactical intelligence. The former is a task for professional intelligence agencies operating at the national level, the latter for (often) uniformed security forces – specifically, local police personnel.

Terrorism

Terrorism, as the term is used in this book, signifies the generation of fear for political ends, characterised primarily by the use of violence for exemplary effect. Fear serves as an instrument through which control over society is sought. Terrorism is basically a tactic; its long-term strategic effects are conditional on the appropriateness and sophistication of the government's response. By itself, terrorism is just a method of signalling, with the signal delivered through deeds rather than through words.[13] Its purpose is to use the threat of violence to influence individuals' behaviour and/or government policy.[14] The effectiveness of this tactic is however, subject to a paradox: it can only influence governmental decisions if practised on a massive scale, but the larger the scale of terrorist violence, the more likely it is to invite a coercive (as opposed to conciliatory) policy response.[15] Such a response is called 'counterterrorism'.

Counterterrorism

Following on from the above point, counterterrorism is the process by which the government responds to terrorists' signalling. Since the terrorists use violence, so must the government.[16] Counterterrorism must not be confused with conflict resolution. Its objective is not to accommodate a rebellious group, but to eliminate the risk that it poses to non-combatant lives. There is no room for winning hearts and minds (as normally prescribed by writers on counterinsurgency).[17] Dialogue and amicable discussions serve only as tools with which the government can split a terrorist movement into moderate and extremist factions and focus its security apparatus onto the latter. By making conciliatory gestures, it can shore up its own legitimacy and isolate extremists from popular support prior to neutralising them. Eventually, however, the use of violence against those who insist on practising terrorism is inescapable. All that matters is to ensure that such violence is as surgical as possible. TE Lawrence once observed that 'while opinions were arguable, convictions needed shooting to be cured'.[18] Helping the government distinguish between those who hold opinions and those who hold convictions is one of the key tasks of counterterrorism intelligence.[19]

Counterterrorist Success and Failure

The terms counterterrorist 'success' and 'failure' may also be defined at two levels. At one level, counterterrorist failure represents the inability of a government to control the intensity of terrorist violence within a given area, and at another level, an inability to control its geographic spread.

Intensity of terrorist violence: Counterterrorist success is defined as a situation in which the government succeeds in lowering the level of terrorist violence from that of previous years, as measured in terms of non-combatant fatalities within a region. A decrease in the annual number of non-combatant deaths from terrorist attacks is thus a counterterrorist success. Conversely, an *increase* in the annual number of such deaths represents a counterterrorist *failure*.[20] Obviously, such a definition gives a higher weightage to relativity, comparing each year's fatalities with those of previous years. Thus levels of counterterrorist success can be either partial or total: they are partial if the violence only falls to a level below that of previous years, they are total if it ceases completely.

Geographic spread of terrorist violence: However, there is also another definition of the term 'counterterrorist failure'. When security forces and/or intelligence agencies fail to prevent a specific attack by armed militants operating far from their home territory, then too counterterrorism might be said to have failed. This is because a successful deep-penetration strike indicates that the government has failed to contain the geographic spread of violence. Even whilst operating amongst what may be a generally unsympathetic population, terrorists still need a modicum of local support in order to procure weapons, safe houses, funds and transportation.[21] Failure to prevent the geographic expansion of their support network is as much a counterterrorist failure as is a failure to de-escalate their activities within a given region. Conversely, the prevention of a terrorist attack in a region far from the terrorists' home base constitutes a counterterrorist 'success'.

Intelligence Failure Versus Action Failure

Lastly, the difference between 'intelligence failure' and 'action failure' needs to be spelt out. This book uses the definition of intelligence failure advanced by Abram Shulsky and Gary Schmitt in their 1991 book *Silent Warfare*:

> An intelligence failure is essentially a misunderstanding of the situation that leads a government (or its military forces) to take actions that are inappropriate and counterproductive to its own interests. Whether it is subjectively surprised by what happens is less important than the fact that the government or the military is doing or continues to do the wrong thing.[22]

For a situation to qualify as a failure of intelligence, it must feature the government taking actions that are later on found to be incompatible with its interests. A failure to *act* on intelligence however, is qualitatively different in that the government either does not take any action, or does so in insufficient measure to forestall events. Rather than being misdirected and therefore, fundamentally counterproductive, its policy response is inadequate relative to the dictates of the situation. Thus, the government acts along correct lines but with insufficient vigour and so cannot prevent the emergence of a crisis, only managing to mitigate its effects. Needless to say, a failure to act on intelligence, while having serious short and long-term consequences, is not as serious as a failure of the intelligence itself. The latter signifies a basic inability to perceive the larger context surrounding national security issues, and suggests that policy making has become divorced from reality.

'Intelligence failure' as the term is used in this book, encompasses only the failures of intelligence agencies. It does not cover failures of the intelligence process as a whole. This is an important point to remember. Many commentators tend to confuse intelligence failures with action failures simply because the end product is the same: inability to prevent an adverse development from occurring.[23] They do not distinguish between failure to *predict* the development and failure thereafter, to *prevent* it through timely counter-action.[24] As per this book's argument, only predictive failures are truly 'intelligence failures', since they imply that intelligence agencies have not correctly mapped out the dynamics of a conflict.

In distinguishing between intelligence failure and action failure, the book draws upon terminology crafted by the British scholar Michael Herman. Herman argues that the essence of the term 'intelligence' covers only those government organisations that conduct intelligence activities on a full-time basis.[25] It does not include organisations that produce secret information as a by-product of their primary function, for example, the diplomatic corps and the security forces. In effect therefore, a mere lack of tactical intelligence does not qualify as an intelligence failure, if accurate and timely strategic warning has been previously provided by national intelligence agencies.

Based on the above definitions, let us now examine the underlying hypothesis adopted in *The Politics of Counterterrorism in India*.

Hypothesis: Counterterrorist Failures Caused by Intelligence Failures

Counterterrorist failures in India are caused by the poor responsiveness of decision makers (that is, intelligence consumers) to strategic intelligence. Instead of recognising the challenges faced by intelligence agencies, decision makers expect them to provide highly specific information before taking follow-up action. Using security forces in an offensive role, to fill in gaps in the intelligence picture provided by the agencies, is either politically unattractive or operationally unviable as an option (the reasons for this will be discussed shortly).

Yet, offensive counterterrorist operations are crucial to bridging the divide between strategic and tactical intelligence, for three reasons: firstly, they help overcome the 'chilling' effect of terrorist counterintelligence on potential informants within the community from which the terrorists come. By removing or reducing fear of terrorist reprisals, offensive security operations create a safer environment for members of the public to volunteer information.[26] Secondly, such operations provide the security forces with leverage to recruit informers within a locality, by allowing them to dictate the pattern of daily life. Once individuals are subjected to raw demonstrations of governmental power in the form of movement controls and general harassment, they become vulnerable to recruitment.[27] Information can thus be purchased from full-time local informers in exchange for relatively minor concessions.[28]

Lastly, offensive operations also directly generate intelligence, thereby reducing the workload placed on intelligence agencies.[29] Such operations help make security forces self-sufficient in meeting their intelligence requirements. By pursuing terrorists and neutralising them, security personnel come into possession of 'battlefield intelligence', i.e., intelligence obtained directly as a result of combat.[30] In the case of arrested terrorists, such intelligence is obtained mainly through interrogation. In the case of deceased terrorists, it is acquired through analysis of documents and correspondence recovered from their persons.

By allowing security forces to meet their own informational requirements through offensive action, political leaders assist the intelligence effort against terrorism in two ways. Firstly, the resources of intelligence agencies are freed from short-term missions, and can focus on long-term assessment. Given their massive capacity for data collation, storage and retrieval, intelligence agencies possess a comparative advantage over security forces in strategic analysis.[31] When politicians allow the agencies to focus on such analysis, they ensure that the efficiency of these agencies is maximised.

Secondly, using security forces offensively as intelligence-gatherers also cuts down the transmission times of tactical intelligence. While intelligence agencies invariably take time to pass on information to the end-user, local commanders can react much faster on their own intelligence. Turnaround time on intelligence inputs is thus minimised when responsibility for tactical collection is devolved to local security forces. Moreover, such practice sits well with the theory advanced by the Israeli scholar Amos Kovacs, that intelligence is most useful at the level at which it is produced.[32]

The ideal situation in counterterrorism therefore, would be to let intelligence agencies focus on strategic intelligence, while empowering security forces to acquire and act on tactical intelligence. Strategic intelligence would serve primarily to optimise counterterrorist policy so as to further the government's long-term goals. Eventually however, it is tactical intelligence that will produce counterterrorist success, by helping the government systematically wear down terrorist groups through attrition.[33]

In practice, a balance between strategic and tactical intelligence is difficult to achieve, due to the intervention of partisan politics and operational handicaps. In India, successive central (federal) governments have been prevented from acting on strategic intelligence by four major constraints. Consequently, total counterterrorist success remains elusive, while partial successes only occur in the aftermath of major failures to prevent the escalation and/or expansion of terrorist violence. These four constraints can be grouped as:

A Lack of Political Consistency – Indian counterterrorist policy vacillates between coercive and conciliatory (i.e., hard and soft) stances on a purely ad hoc, reflexive basis.[34] The absence of a clear-cut offensive strategy that sets out unambiguous goals for the security forces is a key weakness. Offensive counterterrorist operations get suspended midway, in the belief that the government can negotiate for a political settlement from a position of strength. In the process, terrorist movements acquire a breathing space to regroup and adapt, thereby posing an even tougher intelligence challenge to the security forces when offensive actions need to be renewed.

A Lack of Political Consensus – even when the central government opts for an offensive strategy, its effectiveness is reduced by lack of support, both domestically and internationally. Popular alienation within terrorism-affected regions by poor governance and/or denial of political rights creates resentment, which is subsequently fuelled by local politicians for partisan ends.[35] Foreign governments, for their part, either actively sponsor terrorist movements or remain uncooperative in combating their international support networks. In this situation, New Delhi is compelled to considerably water down the quantum of force employed against terrorists, such that the objective of counterterrorist efforts remains just containment of violence, not its eradication.

A Lack of Operational Capacity – poor local intelligence capabilities, in the form of under-funded and overworked state police forces, severely restrict the quantum of tactical intelligence. Inadequate manpower, firepower, transportation and communication facilities mean that local policemen, as representatives of governmental authority closest to the terrorist problem, cannot counter terrorism aggressively.[36] In this situation, tremendous importance is conferred (by default) on the quality of strategic intelligence. Warnings issued by national-level intelligence agencies play a key role in helping the government mobilise the will and resources needed to expand local policing infrastructure.

A Lack of Operational Coordination – the inadequate capabilities of the police lead to prolonged deployment of central military and paramilitary forces in terrorism-affected regions. These subsequently become producers of tactical intelligence in their own right. However, inter-agency rivalries and the absence of a centralised analysis and assessment machinery at the operational level hampers information-sharing.[37] Terrorist groups take advantage of the lack of coordination endemic to Indian counterterrorist efforts by staging attacks across law-enforcement jurisdictions. Particularly when combating transnational terrorism, lack of coordination in tandem with the deficiencies already mentioned leads to counterterrorist failures.

The four constraints outlined above are symptomatic of a disconnect that exists between strategic and tactical intelligence efforts in Indian counterterrorism. Despite receiving accurate predictive assessments from intelligence agencies, consumers fail to assume the responsibility of acting on them. Instead of recognising that tactical intelligence is basically a security forces responsibility, they expect national intelligence agencies to focus on it.[38] Consequently, early warnings of a terrorist threat do not automatically translate into an ability to prevent its actualisation. Only by eliminating the 'four constraints' can strategic and tactical intelligence achieve synergy. Until this is done, counterterrorist efforts in India will remain hostage to whimsical politics, resource limitations and turf warfare.

To summarise, this book uses the 'four constraints' paradigm to demonstrate why counterterrorist failures in India are not failures of intelligence per se. Rather, they are the result of decision-makers' failure to develop strategic intelligence into tactical intelligence through taking timely follow-up action.

Alternative Hypothesis

The logical riposte to the hypothesis advanced above is that it is too charitable to the Indian intelligence agencies. Instead of poor follow-up on strategic intelligence, counterterrorist failures in India might arise from the poor quality of such intelligence in the first place. Absence of an independent body to monitor the intelligence agencies, coupled with their heavy bias towards recruiting police personnel, might have hampered their professionalism. Instead of evolving to meet the threat of transnational terrorism, Indian intelligence might just be a hidebound bureaucracy more focused on preserving organisational interests and winning the favour of political elites.

Such views are strongly held by both Indian and Western academics. One of these, Vinod Anand, has summarised the weaknesses of the Indian intelligence community as follows:

> The Indian intelligence system suffers from a lack of checks and balances and the consumer hardly gets the required intelligence product. The politicization of some of the agencies has led to reduction of their efficiency. At times, intelligence agencies even tend to take upon themselves the task of decision-making rather than restricting themselves to the advisory role. The bane of intelligence agencies has been lack of focus and direction, turf-battles, poor coordination, uncorroborated reports and lack of professionalism and motivation.[39]

Anand's assessment is supported by the writings of other distinguished scholars such as Desmond Ball, Bruce Vaughn, Manoj Joshi, Bhashyam Kasturi and K Subrahmanyam. All of them have touched on at least some of the points listed by Anand in their critiques of Indian Intelligence. Ball and Kasturi, for instance, argue that wastage and inefficient use of existing intelligence resources are a bigger problem than lack of resources per se.[40] Vaughn and Joshi assert that partisan use of national intelligence agencies by whichever government happens to be in power in Delhi detracts from their effectiveness against genuine security threats.[41] Subrahmanyam and Kasturi both criticise the frequent turf wars between agencies, citing them as a major cause of poor strategic assessment.[42]

Notwithstanding the undoubted expertise of the above writers, the overall impression left by their analysis is misleading. Going by the summary quoted earlier, Indian intelligence agencies seemingly suffer from every managerial problem under the sun. Therefore, it is rather puzzling that they should manage to meet with any success whatsoever. Yet, for all their politicisation and lack of a dedicated cadre, India's intelligence agencies have pulled off some impressive coups. The victory in the 1971 Indo–Pakistani War and the successful counterintelligence program that preceded India's 1974 and 1998 nuclear tests are two of the more obvious successes on the external security front.

Even more relevant to this book are successes in the maintenance of internal security. Two of India's most violent rebellions since Independence, the Mizo and the Sikh separatist movements, have been comprehensively defeated. Moreover, separatism in Kashmir and the north-eastern region of India has been contained, with violence levels either de-escalating steadily or continuing to remain low. Throughout this period (roughly 1966 to the present day), the same intelligence community, with all its inherent faults, has continued to serve Indian policy makers. Yet, the effectiveness of Indian counterterrorism has varied from region to region and movement to movement. Obviously, there is something besides the quality of strategic intelligence that more fundamentally determines the degree of success achieved in counterterrorism.

In other words, there is no demonstrable correlation between Indian counterterrorist performance and purely organisational factors that affects national intelligence agencies. The weaknesses of the Indian intelligence system as identified by Anand have remained constant, while the levels of counterterrorist success attained across time and space have varied. Prior to defeating separatist terrorism in Punjab and Mizoram, New Delhi failed to contain the escalation of violence in these theatres. Ironically, inability to contain terrorism through existing intelligence and law enforcement mechanisms forced New Delhi to opt for an aggressive, militarised response to both movements. Violence levels thus rose sharply before they were brought down by a determined security forces offensive. From Punjab and Mizoram, one can conclude that either national intelligence agencies suddenly grew very competent, or that their role in counterterrorism was a secondary one to begin with. This book leans towards the latter argument.

Indian counterterrorist experience suggests that the action taken on strategic intelligence is more important than the quality of the intelligence itself.[43] Currently, Indian intelligence agencies are being pilloried for failing to meet responsibilities that are strictly speaking not theirs. In reality, the blame for failing to generate tactical intelligence rests with the political establishment and the security forces. Merely assuming that a causal link exists between organisational inadequacies in intelligence agencies and poor counterterrorist performance, does not mean such is the case.

In fact, recent evidence indicates just the opposite. A 2007 study by the American private intelligence firm STRATFOR found the Indian security service – the Intelligence Bureau – to be one of the five most efficient intelligence agencies worldwide.[44] The study's conclusions surprised many Indians, who had dismissed the IB as a bunch of 'semi-competent flatfoots'.[45] Although the Indian external intelligence service, the Research and Analysis Wing (R&AW) did not get comparable grades, it is still quite effective on core issues like Pakistan.[46] While both these agencies may well suffer from the organisational problems attributed to them, scholars need to conduct empirical research before they can suggest that the problems hamper overall performance.

To conclude, while academic and journalistic criticism of India's national intelligence apparatus might not be misplaced, it is far from certain that removing the targets of such criticism would result in improved counterterrorist performance. To understand the relationship between intelligence and counterterrorism, it is necessary to look at the larger context within which the two interact. In studying the political and operational variables that feature in the background of any counterterrorist campaign, this book hopes to take scholarship beyond focusing only on 'intelligence failures'.

Scope of Research

The Politics of Counterterrorism in India focuses on Indian counterterrorist experience for three reasons. Firstly, India has witnessed very high levels of terrorist violence, second only to Iraq, in recent years. Between January 2004 and March 2007, 3,674 Indians were killed in terrorist attacks, more than fatalities in the Americas, Europe and Eurasia combined.[47] Secondly, India's counterterrorist experience dates back to at least 1981, which gives the book a great deal of empirical data on which to base its analysis.[48] Lastly, terrorism in India is a curious hybrid of both domestic and international terrorism, in that it features massive foreign sponsorship of indigenous militants. This book suggests that Indian counterterrorism can offer valuable insights into the difficulties that transnational terrorists pose for intelligence agencies, including in the West.[49]

Within India, the book studies three terrorist movements – the Sikh separatist or 'Khalistan' movement, the Kashmiri separatist movement, and pan-Islamist jihadism in major cities. All three have a number of factors in common. Firstly, each has enjoyed a measure of local support at some stage in its trajectory. Without widespread alienation arising from poor governance and perceived repression, terrorist ideologues could not have gained a following within their respective communities. Secondly, all three movements have been the recipients of material aid from the Pakistani intelligence agency – the Inter Services Intelligence (ISI) Directorate. Thirdly, all three movements have a religious character, even if two of them (Punjab and Kashmir) primarily espouse a political objective, i.e. secession from India.

The Indian counterterrorist campaign in Punjab was the only one of the three that attained total success. Between 1981 and 1991, Indian policy makers and security forces struggled vainly to contain terrorist violence, whilst avoiding the use of excessive force. From 1992 onwards, they affected a paradigm shift towards a highly offensive, militarised counterterrorist response that focused only on wiping out militancy. The result was dramatic: Sikh separatist terrorism disappeared from India's political map in 18 months, never to re-emerge as a serious political movement.

India's counterterrorist offensive in Punjab in 1992–93, which began as an army-led area domination exercise codenamed Operation Rakshak II, thus offers an idealised model.[50] It featured a prodigious amount of operational activity by ground-level security forces who, by sheer force of arms, broke the separatists' psychological stranglehold over Punjab. During the offensive, for the first and only time in the history of Indian counterterrorism, political consistency and consensus was firm, while operational capacity and coordination were high. All of the four constraints listed above as obstacles to the exploitation of strategic intelligence were removed. Hence, the Indian government was able to bridge the gap between strategic and tactical intelligence and achieve total counterterrorist success in Punjab.

In Kashmir and while fighting the pan-Islamist threat however, New Delhi has not been able to overcome the debilitating effect of at least some of the constraints. Counterterrorist operations have thus only yielded partial success in Kashmir, by incrementally lowering terrorist violence levels over the years. Moreover, such success has been preceded by major failures to prevent the escalation of terrorist activity in the first place, despite ample intelligence warnings. Meanwhile, jihadist forays into the Indian heartland have grown more frequent and sophisticated, indicating an outright failure on the part of successive central governments to contain pan-Islamist radicalism.[51]

The fact that all three of these movements overlapped to some degree (in terms of lifespan) makes the variance of counterterrorist results all the more intriguing. Kashmir began to drift inexorably towards militancy from 1987 onwards, at which time violence in Punjab had not yet reached its peak. The comprehensive defeat of Sikh separatism in 1993 did not prevent a massive escalation of violence in Kashmir in 1999 – a trend that was only reversed in 2002. Moreover, while India was eventually able to achieve total counterterrorist success in Punjab and partial success in Kashmir, it failed to contain the spread of pan-Islamist jihadism in its urban heartland from 1993 onwards. Since it was the same intelligence community that combated all three movements, what could explain the difference in results achieved?

This book holds that the above variations in Indian counterterrorist effectiveness can be explained by studying the quantum of offensive action undertaken by security forces. Since offensive operations were at their most intense in Punjab during 1992–93, it is argued that they are crucial to achieving total counterterrorist success. Heavy dependence on intelligence agencies by weak political leaders and resource-strapped security forces only hampers the generation of battlefield intelligence. As a result, the gap between strategic and tactical intelligence, which is maintained by the strength of the terrorists' own counterintelligence regime, cannot be narrowed. Until intelligence consumers assume responsibility for acting on the essentially incomplete warnings issued by intelligence agencies, they cannot rollback terrorist violence.

Literature Review

This book identifies three schools within intelligence studies literature that are relevant to its topic. For the sake of simplicity, they have been described as the 'organisational failure' school, the 'response failure' school and the 'intelligence fusion' school. The first two have an argumentative tone, while the third is value-neutral.

The Organizational Failure School

Since the 11 September 2001 attacks in the United States, the organisational failure school has been in the ascendant. This is because it has contoured itself to explaining why the attacks occurred. The school suggests that weaknesses within national intelligence agencies led to a lack of 'actionable' information on the 9/11 plot. Without specific details on what was going to happen, all the warnings that had been issued on Al Qaeda's activities were worthless. Specifically, it identifies two organisational deficiencies as the main causes of counterterrorist failure: inadequate information sharing and poor strategic analysis.

Amy Zegart's book *Spying Blind* is the foremost treatise from this school. Zegart writes that during the 1990s the Central Intelligence Agency (CIA) and Federal Bureau of Investigation (FBI) had deemed counterterrorism a priority task. However, they were unable to adapt to it, owing to entrenched bureaucratic resistance to reform.[52] Her assertions are backed by strong empirical evidence. Significantly, she does not suggest that the intelligence agencies were basically incompetent, but that structural flaws in the way they operated prevented them from meeting the Al Qaeda threat.

In addition to their intrinsic academic rigour, Zegart's arguments gain credibility from the findings of the *National Commission on Terrorist Attacks upon the United States*. The commission's final report, released in 2004, 'fed a pervasive impression of institutional rot within the intelligence community'.[53] It dwelt on the fact that although the CIA chief nominally controls the entire US intelligence community, his authority in practice is limited to the CIA. To remedy this shortfall between the chief's hypothetical power and his actual power, the report recommended that a new post of National Intelligence Director be created to coordinate intelligence activities.[54]

Since the 9/11 Report was made public, there has been a widespread tendency to equate 'intelligence failure' with failures to share information. Much significance has been attached to the fact that, prior to the attacks, CIA files contained the names of two of the conspirators. Proponents of organisational failure suggest that had this information been passed on to the FBI, the two men could have been arrested and interrogated. Their interrogation in turn, would have revealed further information about the plot. Such reasoning is based on a presumption that all the raw information needed to thwart the attacks was already available with intelligence agencies. It only needed to be brought together so that analysts could discern the underlying pattern that indicated an imminent terrorist threat.[55]

This leads to the second weakness identified by the organisational failure school: insufficient attention to strategic analysis. According to Zegart, the CIA's internal policies lent privilege to current intelligence over long-term assessment. Greater priority was given to supporting counterterrorist operations, such that few resources were focused on monitoring broad trends. Over time, this led to atrophy in strategic intelligence.[56] John Diamond, in his book *The CIA and the Culture of Failure* provides evidence that supports such reasoning. He points out that before the 11 September attacks, there had been no substantial body of intelligence assessments relating to Al Qaeda.[57]

According to writers like Diamond and Calvert Jones, inadequate emphasis on strategic analysis is a bigger problem than lack of information sharing per se.[58] One explanation for this perceived neglect of analysis is provided by George Friedman, the chairman of STRATFOR. Friedman argues that US intelligence agencies are 'hardwired' to focus on collecting information rather than analysing it. This leads to a failure to tease out the nuances of available data and appreciate its full implications. While the CIA can provide information on specific issues, it cannot map out underlying trends and get ahead of them to produce an anticipatory assessment.[59]

Due to these factors (insufficient information sharing and neglect of long-term analysis), the organisational failure school believes that tactical intelligence failures derive from strategic intelligence failures. Weak performance in strategic intelligence provides a shaky informational base upon which decision makers can take action. Unless national intelligence agencies implement reforms to increase information sharing and improve analytical rigour, they will fail to provide actionable warnings.

The Response Failure School

As the name suggests, this school takes a diametrically opposite view to that of the organisational failure school. It suggests that the real cause of counterterrorist failures like 9/11, and indeed other cases of preventive failure outside counterterrorism, is the inability or unwillingness of decision makers to follow up on generic warnings. The response failure school rejects the proposition that tactical-intelligence failures have their origins in bad strategic-intelligence performance.

Rather, it suggests that vague initial warnings of an emerging threat must first lead to a policy decision. The decision will then translate into action and the action in turn, will produce more specific information on the threat. If there are no decisions or actions taken in response to the initial warning provided by intelligence agencies, the information chain gets broken. Consequently, there will be no specific warning of an oncoming attack, even if strategic intelligence has predicted it.

The response failure school has one serious drawback: none of its proponents have produced an empirical analysis that supports their claims. Instead, they have only highlighted the key methodological flaws of the organisational failure school. Richard Betts lists three such flaws:

> One is a focus on the problem of warning, and how to improve intelligence collection, rather than the more difficult problem of how to improve political response to ample warning indicators. Another is a common view of surprise as an absolute or dichotomous problem rather than as a matter of degree. Third is the prevalent derivation of theories from single cases rather than from comparative studies.[60]

Betts argues that very few surprise attacks can qualify as genuine bolts-from-the-blue. Most are preceded by *some* measure of intelligence warning. The problem is that policy makers prefer to wait for the warning to attain greater specificity before ordering counteraction. Mindful of the political, financial and diplomatic costs of pre-emption, they force intelligence agencies to assume tactical responsibilities that lie beyond their capabilities.[61] In the process, as pointed out by Bruce Berkowitz, policy makers gradually abdicate their own responsibility as leaders and fail to take timely decisions.[62]

Former CIA analyst Paul Pillar lists a fourth weakness in the organisational-failure thesis, with reference to the 9/11 attacks. He points out that it is based on a superficial understanding of how terrorist networks operate. Pillar disputes the claim made by the 9/11 Commission that Al Qaeda had a long history of attacking American interests prior to 2001. As a former counterterrorism analyst, he asserts that much of the pan-Islamist threat consisted then (as it does now) of jihadists with no links to Osama Bin Laden. According to Pillar, the Commission airbrushed this fact because it wanted to create an impression that the US intelligence community had missed out on a long-term threat.[63]

Pillar ridicules the demand for intelligence reform, describing it as 'a kind of mood music'.[64] He claims that whatever changes could be implemented within US intelligence agencies to improve counterterrorism performance have already been carried out. Further adaptation is impractical and in any case would not address the deeper issue of getting politicians to take better cognisance of intelligence warnings. Pillar's argument is supported by former CIA operative Harold P Ford, who writes that more than better producers of intelligence, we 'need better consumers of intelligence'.[65]

Amos Kovacs summarises the viewpoint of the response failure school when he asserts that '[m]any "intelligence failures" are not so much failures of intelligence *per se*, but rather failures to use intelligence'.[66] He attributes the blame for non-use to factors that influence decision-making. Among them are: lack of consumer confidence in the accuracy of intelligence data, unwillingness to take action due to overriding political considerations, concerns about compromising sources, and perceptual bias.

Kovacs believes that closer relations between intelligence agencies and decision makers would mitigate the problem of non-use, though not eliminate it. He overlooks the opposite argument: that close relations might foster a culture of dependence on intelligence reports. Decision makers can become so reliant on intelligence agencies to tell them what is happening that, in the absence of detailed information, they feel unable to act. Acknowledging this problem, writers such as John Hollister Headley and Ralph Peters suggest that intelligence consumers be sensitised about the limitations of strategic intelligence.[67] Only then can such intelligence play a meaningful role in decision making.

The Intelligence Fusion School

This school does not attempt to fix blame for past instances of preventive failure. Instead, it focuses on understanding the unique dynamics of counterterrorism intelligence. Like the organisational failure school, it argues the need for better information sharing. Where it differs however is on the level at which such sharing should occur. While the organisational failure school believes that sharing needs to occur at the national level, the intelligence fusion school suggests that it occur at the local level. According to followers of this school, terrorist groups need to be fought through a network of fusion centres, which pool together available information and disseminate it to first responders.

The school has one drawback in that it does not explicitly delineate the respective roles of national intelligence agencies and local security forces in running fusion centres. Consequently, the boundaries between strategic and tactical intelligence are blurred. Yet, as Michael Herman points out, they still exist. According to Herman, counterterrorism intelligence operates 'on twin tracks of timeliness: on one track the long-term research and source development characteristic of "difficult" targets, and speedy reaction on the other track'.[68] The intelligence fusion school does not examine where these two tracks converge, or in fact whether they converge at all.

Nevertheless, the school makes a valuable contribution to intelligence studies literature by emphasising the particularities of counterterrorism intelligence. It has been spurred in this venture by the 9/11 attacks and the search that subsequently ensued for an intelligence system optimised to monitor hostile non-state actors. Such a system, according to Charles Cogan, would feature intelligence operatives working as '*hunters* not *gatherers*. They will not simply sit back and gather information that comes in, analyse it and then decide what to do about it. Rather, they will have to go and hunt out intelligence that will enable them to track down or kill terrorists'.[69]

Cogan's view of intelligence acquisition is somewhat simplistic. He advocates snatch operations in friendly countries, in some cases without the support of the host government. He does not consider the damage that such operations could do to intelligence-liaison channels. However, his basic idea is important since it acknowledges that peacetime methods of intelligence collection do not yield the whole picture on terrorist groups. They need to be supplemented by proactive, militarised efforts to seek out additional information in the field. Cogan advocates integrating national intelligence operatives with special operations units to achieve this militarisation of intelligence gathering.[70]

Jennifer Sims takes a different perspective, pointing out that counterterrorism intelligence is as much a bottom-up process as it is a top-down process. While national intelligence agencies make efforts to increase the data inflow from human and technical sources, it is local law enforcement which most needs to adapt to the counterterrorism mission. First responders not only require intelligence after a terrorist attack, they are also in the best position to gather and collate such intelligence *before* the attack. Sims notes that while attempts by national intelligence agencies to spy on the public provoke an outcry, similar activities are deemed acceptable if carried out by local police forces.[71] More than any other writer from the intelligence fusion school, she comes closest to defining counterterrorism as a tactical intelligence problem rather than a strategic intelligence one.

The British scholar Frank Gregory, in a study of intelligence-led counterterrorism within the United Kingdom, highlights two additional facets of this type of activity. One, it places an enormous strain on the finite resources of national intelligence agencies, tying up as many as 40 operatives per surveillance operation. If national-level agencies like Britain's MI5 are to focus completely on counterterrorism, their coverage of other threats like hostile intelligence services will inevitably slip.[72] Policy makers should consider this before they pressure intelligence chiefs to deliver better results in counterterrorism.

Second, Gregory touches upon an issue not often examined by intelligence studies scholars: the need for legally-admissible evidence to support counterterrorism prosecutions. Not only do intelligence agencies have to gather information that a particular individual is involved in terrorist activity, but in democracies they also have to make that information stand up in court. In cases of pre-emptive arrest, when a person is apprehended on suspicion of being a terrorist, a mistake can do serious damage to the agency's credibility. Gregory points out that this is a continuing problem for MI5, notwithstanding its considerable experience in counterterrorism.[73]

Why Apply American and British Intelligence Studies Discourse to India?

There are three reasons for using Anglo–American concepts to study Indian intelligence performance. First, no indigenous body of literature exists on the subject. Whatever has been published on Indian intelligence is narrative-descriptive work, bereft of analysis. To resist the temptation of passing off impressionistic work as academic research, this book uses American intelligence studies literature as its theoretical foundation. Second, the Indian intelligence community is heavily modelled on its British and American counterparts, thus making a comparison viable. Lastly, this book aims to address criticism of the intelligence agencies that has been levelled by a rough equivalent of the organisational failure school in India. Over the past decade, there has been a tendency to deem every instance of preventive failure as an 'intelligence failure'.[74] In particular, it is felt that counterterrorist failures occur because Indian intelligence agencies refuse to share information with each other. The agencies are perceived to be poorly run, and a general belief pervades both academic and public discourse that organisational reforms are necessary.[75]

Contemporary views of Indian intelligence derive from the Kargil crisis of May–June 1999. The crisis began when Indian forces accidentally discovered that Pakistani troops had occupied a number of hilltops on the Indian side of the Kashmir border. After heavy fighting, the intruders were evicted. However, anger soon focused on the intelligence agencies, which were accused of not providing specific warning of Pakistani plans. In response to political pressure, the government established a four-man committee to study the circumstances leading up to the crisis. The published version of the committee's final report blamed intelligence agencies for not consolidating their reports into a common threat assessment, which could have provided a basis for preventive action.[76]

Much like the *9/11 Commission Report* in the United States, the *Kargil Review Committee Report* created an impression that tactical intelligence failure stemmed from strategic intelligence failure. Both reports suggested that better information sharing and an emphasis on long-term analysis would improve intelligence performance. Both also triggered off attempts at intelligence reform, which soon stalled. Thus, scholars such as James Burch have argued that the American and Indian experiences of intelligence management might offer common lessons.[77] This book endeavours to outline the limitations of strategic intelligence in counterterrorism, with a view to informing both Indian and American debates on the subject.

CHAPTER 1

STRATEGIC INTELLIGENCE IN INDIA

There are two premier intelligence agencies in India – the Intelligence Bureau (IB) and the Research & Analysis Wing (R&AW). Both agencies play a large role in Indian counterterrorism and are 'strategic' in nature, with a focus on guiding national-level policy decisions. Unfortunately, the performance of these two agencies has been negatively impacted by inflated demands from their intelligence consumers in the political and military establishments. These demands create a gap between the agencies' resources, and the requirements they are asked to fulfill. Interestingly, it is the latter which form the standard by which intelligence performance is measured.[1] Thus, high expectations from consumers, when disappointed, automatically generate convenient charges of 'intelligence failure'.

Any evaluation of intelligence performance needs to take into account the limited resources of national-level agencies. Given the defensive nature of Indian security policy, the IB and R&AW have performed fairly well. As the American scholar David Kahn has noted, defensive policies place more demands on intelligence than offensive ones. Consequently, they are also more likely to fall victim to 'intelligence failures', since information requirements cannot always be met.[2] The history of Indian intelligence is replete with examples where the IB and R&AW have been accused of not providing *detailed* information. Few have paused to consider whether that is in fact their core mission.

To understand the role of the IB and R&AW, it is necessary to understand the nature of Indian national-security policy. The major problems in the management of Indian intelligence agencies can be grouped into three categories: organisational, systemic and external. Organisational shortcomings are those that pertain to the in-house policies of intelligence agencies. Systemic shortcomings deal with inter-organisational issues, primarily intelligence assessment. External shortcomings relate to the difficulties posed by partisan politics.

Role of Intelligence in Ensuring Indian National Security

One point must be made clear at the outset: Indian national-security policy is overwhelmingly threat-reactive.[3] It relies on intelligence to guide not only strategic decisions, but tactical ones as well. Intelligence is viewed as a substitute for force, rather than a complement to it. The main reason for this is India's 'selective' poverty, wherein government expenditure is prioritised towards developmental rather than security needs.[4] Such a policy has limited the country's willingness to use force in pursuit of its interests. A resistance to 'wasteful' defence spending precludes the government from keeping the security forces in a high state of readiness. Since scarce resources have to be expended even to keep existing capabilities operational, there is very little scope for undertaking pre-emptive deployments. This is borne out by the historical fact that on no occasion have the Indian Armed Forces been prepared for immediate pre-emptive or even retaliatory action.[5]

Between 1947 (the year India attained independence) and 1962 (the year it lost a war to China), Indian policymakers have relied on diplomatic activism to safeguard the country. Jawaharlal Nehru, the first Prime Minister of India, wanted Indian security policy to be non-militaristic. He exhibited a well-pronounced trait of Indian leaders, showing a keener grasp of diplomatic affairs than military ones.[6] While seeking secret intelligence on India's two biggest neighbours, Pakistan and China, Nehru interpreted this through an exclusively politico–diplomatic perspective.[7] By remaining non-aligned in the cold war, he hoped to build up goodwill with both the United States and the Soviet Union. Nehru thought that either or both of these countries would deter China and Pakistan from attacking India. Time would prove how wrong he was.[8]

Defeat in the 1962 Sino–Indian war shattered Nehru's faith in Gandhian pacifism, which he had previously touted with an evangelistic zeal. Three years later, Pakistan launched a military incursion into the Indian state (province) of Jammu and Kashmir, over which it claimed sovereignty. Although the attack was repulsed, it partially discredited the Nehruvian thesis that an idealistic foreign policy would safeguard Indian security interests.[9] The 1962 and 1965 wars hardened the political mood in New Delhi. They allowed Nehru's daughter Indira Gandhi to adopt a more aggressive national security posture when she became the Prime Minister in 1966. By the time civil war erupted in East Pakistan (now Bangladesh), the Indian policymaking establishment had fewer qualms about using force. It first provided covert support to the East Pakistani rebels, and then intervened militarily on their behalf. The result was a spectacular military victory in December 1971 and the break-up of Pakistan.

Post 1971, India became the hegemon of South Asia. Confident in its power, the country returned to its non-militarist moorings.[10] Although it built up a formidable military capability, this was intended only for territorial defence.[11] Meanwhile, stung by its defeat, Pakistan escalated support to separatist movements in India as a covert form of retaliation (it had already been funding and arming these since the 1950s). The Pakistani military also acquired new equipment and developed a nuclear-weapons programme.[12] Over time, Indian military supremacy in South Asia was whittled down.[13] The country was compelled once again to adopt a defensive security policy, focusing only on the preservation of its borders.[14] Such a policy placed a premium on intelligence, which would be needed to provide advance warning of aggressive action by Pakistan or China.

Genesis of Indian Intelligence

Contemporary Indian strategic intelligence has its roots in the policing systems created to sustain British colonial rule. It combines professionalism with partisanship, and is inextricably linked with the country's politics. The origins of the Intelligence Bureau and those of the Research & Analysis Wing bear this out. Since 1968, the former has been responsible for domestic intelligence and the latter for foreign intelligence. It was only for a brief period prior to that (1951–1968), that both functions were vested in the IB.

The Intelligence Bureau

Described as the oldest intelligence agency in the world, the IB has a mixed reputation.[15] On the one hand, its efficiency has earned it high praise from Western intelligence services.[16] On the other, the agency faces a credibility deficit with its consumers. It is regarded as better at monitoring opposition politicians rather than (genuine) threats to national security.[17] Such views harshly ignore the agency's historical role in Indian politics. The IB has always had a partisan character, but this does not automatically make it incompetent.

Ever since its creation on 23 December 1887, the IB has functioned as a political police without arrest powers. Its particular responsibilities make it a status quo actor, dedicated to preserving the established order. Originally named the Central Special Branch, it coordinated the activities of provincial Special Branches across British India. These branches handled the day-to-day task of performing surveillance on Indian political parties and religious movements.[18] Their reports were consolidated into finished assessments by the Central Branch, which renamed itself the Department of Criminal Intelligence in 1903 and finally adopted the name 'Intelligence Bureau' in 1920.

With the end of British rule in 1947, the subcontinent was divided into India and Pakistan. The IB faced a crippling loss of trained manpower, as British officers who had completely dominated intelligence management, left India.[19] Moreover, they destroyed or shipped to England all sensitive files compiled by the agency. Muslim personnel who had served in the IB carted off any remaining documents to Pakistan.[20] This meant that the agency, which until mid 1947 had no Hindu officers in its senior ranks, was left totally bereft of resources when India became independent.[21] It had to ingratiate itself with the new political order, while simultaneously rebuilding its shattered infrastructure. Having previously served under an unpopular colonial regime, this was not an easy task.

Under its first two chiefs post-independence, the IB reinvented itself as a custodian of Indian democracy. This role allowed it to retain its professionalism while remaining close to any political party that acquired power legitimately.[22] The first Indian Director of the Intelligence Bureau (DIB – as the chief is called), TG Sanjeevi Pillai, regarded the US Central Intelligence Agency as a model to be emulated.[23] His preference stemmed from the fact that the IB was being given responsibility for foreign intelligence in addition to its existing domestic intelligence mandate. Pillai's successor, Bhola Nath Mullik, further strengthened the agency's commitment to democratic rule. Mullik was known among his subordinates as 'the Colossus' and is still revered for being the 'Father of Indian Intelligence'.[24] He established the precedent of obtaining direct access to the Prime Minister and not losing it, come what may. In doing so, Mullik ensured that intelligence reports received attention from the highest level in the policymaking hierarchy.[25]

Mullik's foresight and acumen in bringing about this arrangement meant that chances of an intelligence failure occurring due to a lack of high-level dissemination were reduced. Today, whenever policy makers are surprised by events, they cannot in all honesty claim that intelligence reports have not reached them. (We shall see instances of this in the successive chapters of this book.) Instead, what usually happens is that the IB provides all relevant data to policy makers but leaves its finished assessments open-ended, to suit their agendas.[26] It thus doubly insures itself: first, against charges of selective or biased reporting, and also against the PM's displeasure, if the facts do not agree with his or her preconceived views.[27]

The Research & Analysis Wing (R&AW)

Following the 1965 Indo–Pakistani War, the Indian military complained about the IB's performance in both strategic and tactical intelligence. Coming just three years after the disastrous Sino–Indian War, the military's criticisms carried weight with the government.[28] (The military's own leadership failures had been covered up, ostensibly to preserve public morale.) Accordingly, a proposal was drawn up to create a specialised foreign intelligence agency to focus on strategic intelligence. Originally, this organisation was supposed to be under military orders, but prime minister Indira Gandhi decided to place it in the Cabinet Secretariat – under her personal control.[29]

Thus, on 21 September 1968, the Research & Analysis Wing (R&AW) was created, with Rameshwar Nath Kao as its first chief. Kao and virtually all of the 250-odd staff who formed the original core of R&AW were ex-IB personnel. The new agency itself had been formed by splitting the IB from its external intelligence departments. Unsurprisingly, this division of resources generated some hostility between the R&AW and the now greatly weakened Intelligence Bureau. Rivalries between the two organisations had started and persist to this day in a subdued form. It is generally believed that these rivalries hamper overall intelligence effectiveness.

The R&AW's rise to predominance in the Indian intelligence community was due to its proximity to Indira Gandhi. During 1969 her political party, the Congress (I), went through a period of intense turmoil as rivals conspired to undermine her influence. Kao provided her with information about their machinations, which helped consolidate her power base. Having demonstrated his loyalty, Kao gained Mrs Gandhi's complete trust and his organisation began to wield considerable influence. During this period, the

IB's stature was diminished and a relatively junior police officer was made its Director.[30]

Between 1969 and 1974, the R&AW gained a reputation as a highly efficient intelligence service. It also however had the disadvantage of being saddled with the responsibility for Mrs Gandhi's political errors of judgement. Prominent among these was her decision to declare a National Emergency in June 1975, in order to forestall charges of election malpractices that were being levelled against her. Although it is known that the IB was opposed to her decision, doubts persist about the stand taken by the R&AW.[31] In any case, the duration of the Emergency (1975–77) marked a period during which both agencies were seen as little more than secret police forces that did her bidding.[32] This perception later damaged their effectiveness far more than the agencies' own flaws did. How this happened shall be explained later on in the chapter; let us first examine the structure and problems of the agencies themselves.

Organisational Shortcomings of Indian Intelligence

The in-house problems of the IB and R&AW derive from two maladies: *ad hoc* selection procedures and poor human resource management. To understand these, it is necessary to understand the agencies' rank structure.

At the very top of the IB's organisational pyramid is the Director of the Intelligence Bureau (DIB). Beneath him in the hierarchy are three officers with the rank of Additional Director. (Owing to seniority issues, some among these are usually elevated to the rank of Special Director). Below them are about 25 Joint Directors, who in turn control 50–60 Deputy Directors. The Deputy Directors coordinate and monitor the activities of 150–200 Assistant Directors.[33] All of the above are Class One employees of the Government of India, which makes them gazetted officers.

At the next level come the Class Two operatives. They are ranked as follows: Deputy Central Intelligence Officer, Assistant Central Intelligence Officer (Grade 1 and 2) and Junior Central Intelligence Officer (Grade 1 and 2). Security Assistants (the IB equivalent of police constables) make up the lowest layer.[34]

The R&AW is similarly structured, except that the chief is designated Secretary (Research) and usually has two Special Secretaries working under him. (On the basis of lobbying between various interest groups, one of these is chosen to be groomed as a potential successor to the chief.) Reporting to them are eight or nine Additional Secretaries.[35] Thereafter, come Joint

Secretaries, Deputy Secretaries and Assistant Secretaries, in descending order of rank. Their numbers are kept confidential and are thus unknown.

Despite this formal hierarchy, R&AW and IB depend for their laurels on a small core of sterling operatives. Much of these organisations' manpower consists of deadweight. Like intelligence systems in pre-colonial India, their effectiveness (or lack of it) is derived from key personalities, not larger institutions.[36] Failure to recruit and retain personnel of high calibre has contributed to their poor reputation. (That is not to say manpower issues lie at the heart of their performance, since 'reputations' are subject to biases).[37]

Organisational shortcomings of Indian Intelligence can be broadly categorised as:

1. Chaotic selection of personnel
2. Poor human resource management

Let us examine both these shortcomings:

Chaotic Selection of Personnel

A unique problem facing R&AW is its chaotic personnel-selection policy. Unlike the IB, whose senior ranks are staffed exclusively by officers from the Indian Police Service (IPS), the R&AW recruits from all government services: this has led to the creation of factions and petty rivalry between IPS and non-IPS cadres in the organisation. For a long period, further complications were caused by the recruitment of university graduates to Class One (i.e., officer-rank) posts after 1971.[38] Many of these graduates, though not all, were the academically inept progeny of senior government bureaucrats. Their induction led to the agency being caustically referred to as the 'Relatives and Associates Wing'.

Direct recruitment to the R&AW officer cadre was conducted in a highly ad hoc manner. Initially, it was based on a rigorous program of intellectual and psychological tests, but this was diluted after the 1970s.[39] Class Two employees of the agency, who were also university graduates, began to question the objectivity of the selection process. Owing to their criticism, as well as the limited usefulness of directly recruited officers, the process was stopped in 1997. At present, most of the approximately 300 Class One officer employees of the agency are of the IPS cadre.[40] Tensions, however, persist between them and their colleagues from non-IPS cadres.

The IB is slightly better off, as the homogeneity of its officer cadre promotes a strong sense of camaraderie.[41] Even so, since the late 1980s there has been a decline in the quality of officer applying to the agency. During its initial years after Independence, the IB relied on an Ear-marking Scheme (EMS) to recruit Class One employees. The top ten officers of each year's IPS batch were monitored for a few years, and if judged to be of high calibre, were ordered to join the Bureau. Refusal to comply was not an option in those days.[42] Many of the IB's best operatives were products of the EMS. However, the scheme was gradually discontinued owing to a combination of vested interests.[43] Basically, certain elements within the IPS argued that the IB officer cadre were monopolising access to the top political leadership and creating a virtual aristocracy. They pushed for a dilution of entry requirements, with the result that selection to the agency started to be influenced more by patronage than by merit.

One of the main reasons for the scheme's demise lay in the lack of positive incentives for officers to join. Unlike service in the uniformed police, an IB tenure offered few perquisites such as a large household staff or even opportunities to make money by corrupt means.[44] By the mid 1980s, 50 per cent of senior posts in the agency were lying vacant because bright and talented IPS officers were not interested in a career in intelligence, and their choice could now be exercised.[45] Thereafter, the agency came to be staffed by a floating population of generalists.

As a result of these selection and staffing procedures, neither the R&AW nor IB has a well-developed institutional memory. Many officers are on deputation, serving stints of varying length, depending on the promotional avenues open to them outside the agencies.[46] Few have the time or inclination to develop in-depth expertise on intelligence topics.[47] Arguments have thus been voiced for introducing a CIA-style recruitment process, which would allow both agencies to recruit the best analytical talent from the open market. Given that even the CIA's analyses are reputed to be of dubious quality however, it is unlikely such a step would make a meaningful difference.[48]

Poor Human Resource Management

Failure to efficiently manage human resources is the bigger organisational weakness of Indian intelligence. Caught between a not-too-attractive set of employment conditions, and rampant nepotism, the agencies have been plagued by welfare grievances. Unlike their eighteenth- and nineteenth-century colonial predecessors, today's Indian intelligence operatives are not driven by a zest for imperial conquest. There are no disproportionately huge rewards for risk-taking and seizing the initiative. Consequently, the agencies face difficulties in extracting the most out of a manpower pool that is not highly motivated.

During the 1970s, when India was still a socialist country, R&AW analysts earned almost double the salaries available in the private sector, not counting perquisites.[49] With the liberalisation of the Indian economy post 1991, the desirability of a government job has diminished considerably. Today, middle-rank IB and R&AW officers are vulnerable to enticement by well-funded foreign intelligence agencies – a factor which has constrained counterterrorism cooperation post 9/11.[50] Fearful that the CIA might use counterterrorism meetings to recruit Indian intelligence personnel, New Delhi has restricted agency-to-agency contacts with Washington.

Its concerns are not altogether unfounded, since there have been at least two cases of CIA penetration into the R&AW since 2001.[51] Also, at least nine R&AW officers have gone absent without leave since the agency's creation in 1968. Most defected while posted in Western Europe or North America, in pursuit of a more comfortable lifestyle. Subsequent investigations revealed that they had been recruited by Western intelligence agencies prior to their defection, and had functioned as agents-in-place for some time. Particularly damaging among these cases was the defection of Sikander Lal Malik, a personal aide to R&AW chief Rameshwar Nath Kao. Malik defected during the 1970s while posted to the United States and is alleged to have taken extremely sensitive information with him.[52]

Not that discontentment over pay and lifestyle has always led to treason. It has however reduced motivation levels to the bare minimum expected of government bureaucrats in India. Anger over welfare and promotion policies led to the emergence of an Intelligence Bureau Employees Association in June 1979. Eight months later, a similar employees' union was set up at the R&AW. The senior management of both agencies had to divert resources from traditional intelligence targets towards monitoring the union leaders.[53] An agitation by R&AW junior staff in November 1980 resulted in the suspension of 90 employees.[54] Eventually, unionisation within the intelligence community was banned by law in 1985. There is at present no means of knowing whether the specific issues raised in 1979–1985 by the intelligence unions have been addressed.

Systemic Shortcomings of Indian Intelligence

It has been alleged that turf warfare has prevented intelligence agencies from sharing information. Since all available data is not brought together for evaluation and assessment, knowledge gaps are left unidentified and unfilled.[55] Proponents of such views suggest that strengthening the authority of the Joint Intelligence Committee (JIC) can improve performance in strategic intelligence.[56]

After India obtained independence in 1947, the JIC was created as a subordinate wing of the military Chief of Staff's Committee (COSC). It was the closest that India ever came to establishing an institution dedicated to strategic intelligence. The JIC was responsible for producing long-term assessments based on political, military and economic data provided by collection agencies, which at that point in time basically meant the IB.[57] Until the Sino–Indian War of 1962, it was chaired by a Joint Secretary from the Ministry of External Affairs. After the war, the JIC was placed under the Cabinet Secretariat and the post of its chairman was elevated to Additional Secretary.[58]

Poor Institutional Focus on Long-term Security Challenges

Removing the JIC from the COSC's purview may have been a retrograde step, as it led to a loss of focus. Once the JIC was placed directly under civilian political control, it tended to focus more on matters that interested the civilian leadership. These were essentially transient concerns involving crisis management, and did not pay adequate attention to long-term threats.[59] To correct the imbalance, the JIC was bifurcated into foreign and domestic intelligence wings in 1983. The split was later reversed on the grounds that Indian terrorist movements drew sustenance from overseas and so could not be assessed in isolation. Former R&AW officer B Raman now argues that the bifurcated JIC needs to be revived, given the sheer scale and complexity of terrorism within the country.[60] However, it is unlikely that such a step would make a tangible difference to counterterrorism.

Criticisms of Indian strategic intelligence make great play of the fact that the R&AW and IB have downgraded the importance of the JIC. Such criticisms argue that in their eagerness to rush reports directly to the Prime Minister, both agencies neglect to share information with the Committee. This has reduced its ability to provide timely strategic warning, and the 1999 Kargil crisis is held up as a prime example.[61] An official inquiry into the crisis concluded that poor information sharing had undermined strategic analysis, though it was careful not to assert that better information sharing could have averted the crisis. Instead, the post-mortem made a strong case for re-establishing the authority of the JIC over intelligence assessment.[62] There is no evidence to suggest that such criticisms as were made in the specific context of Kargil, even if justified, are universally applicable to other instances of surprise attack.

Questionable Value of Intelligence Assessments

There is no assurance that more terrorist incidents would be prevented if the JIC were given sole responsibility for strategic assessment within the intelligence community. While it is logical to assume that lack of information-sharing hampers threat assessment, it does not necessarily follow that the threat itself can be forestalled. From the experience of the 1993 Mumbai blasts, which killed 257 people, it appears that even excellent strategic analysis might fail to prevent catastrophic damage. Prediction of a threat does not lead to its prevention, unless strategic intelligence can be developed into tactical intelligence.

The 1993 blasts were predicted in a loose sense, since the R&AW had obtained information that Pakistan-trained terrorists were planning attacks in Indian cities. This information was discussed at a JIC meeting on 20 January 1993. It was then disseminated by the IB to police forces in cities that were assessed to be most at risk. Mumbai (then called Bombay) was one of these cities.[63] Yet, no Indian agency had knowledge of the targets, technique and timing of the attacks – all of which were essential to foiling the conspiracy. Without the three Ts that would have converted the R&AW/JIC's strategic assessment into 'actionable' tactical-level information, the Mumbai Police were unable to prevent the blasts, which occurred on 12 March 1993.[64]

Another example of how the JIC by itself is no solution to preventive failures is provided by the March 1966 insurrection in Mizoram province in north-eastern India. At that time, there was no R&AW and so this agency cannot be blamed for undermining the JIC's authority (which it has since been accused of).[65] Yet, with just the IB as its main supplier of raw data, the JIC still underestimated the seriousness of the Mizo situation. An assessment prepared on 16 February 1966 predicted that rebellious groups might grow violent after one year. This forecast was based on the local electoral cycle, according to which district elections were to be held across Mizoram in March 1967. As it turned out, the Mizo underground launched their military campaign against the Indian government on 1 March 1966 – two weeks after the assessment was compiled.[66]

Lack of Consumer Interest in Strategic Assessments

It is also highly questionable whether policy makers in India value the JIC's assessments. Over the years, the post of JIC chairman has been perceived as a 'consolation prize' for senior intelligence officers who have been marginalised as a result of political vendettas.[67] K Subrahmanyam argues that the Indian intelligence community is not geared towards producing long-term assessments, and nor are its consumers interested in receiving any. Immediate informational requirements dominate the workload of intelligence agencies, which have no option but to support decision-makers in the task of perpetual fire fighting.[68] Blaming R&AW and IB for failing to share their reports with the JIC is a little facile in this situation. Even if such reports were made available, they would only be consolidated into strategic assessments that policy makers would probably not read.

All that can be argued with certainty is that strengthening the JIC cannot do any harm. It might not do much good either, but the currently fragmented nature of intelligence assessment leaves knowledge gaps unidentified. If the JIC can establish what the intelligence agencies do not and cannot be expected to know, it can reduce the critical gap between consumer expectations and producer resources. By doing so, it will also reduce the number of times bogus accusations of 'intelligence failure' are made. The JIC itself however, can only provide insights to policy makers, not additional information. This raises the issue of how policy makers have tended to employ intelligence agencies in the first place.

External Shortcomings of Indian Intelligence

We have seen how Indian strategic intelligence is closely connected with Indian politics. This inter-relationship has a strong and possibly decisive impact on the effectiveness of intelligence agencies. For instance, it determines whether Heads of Government (HoGs) are sympathetic to the agencies' limitations, or even aware of them. Should HoGs adopt a policy that places heavy dependence on intelligence warnings, such as a defensive strategic posture, they increase the gap between expectations and resources. When such policies are accompanied by a cutback on intelligence funding, the seeds are sown for a future surprise attack.

This is exactly what happened after 1977, when Indira Gandhi was voted out of power and a pacifist named Morarji Desai became prime minister. Desai was one of Mrs Gandhi's bitterest political opponents, and was determined to shut down R&AW.[69] Unlike the IB, which swiftly changed loyalties and mounted surveillance on Mrs Gandhi to please the new PM, the R&AW was less opportunistic.[70] Suspecting that the agency's leadership still supported Mrs Gandhi, Desai forced some of its most distinguished officers into retirement. During the two years that he was Prime Minister, the head of the organization, or Secretary, reportedly met with him just thrice.[71] In contrast, Mrs Gandhi had met with the agency chief every day when she was Prime Minister.[72]

The Desai premiership (1977–1979) marked the nadir of R&AW. Upon the PM's orders, the agency stopped hiring new recruits and cut its strength back by one-third. Its offices in the north Indian towns of Chandigarh and Jaipur were shut down.[73] As part of a cost-cutting exercise, agent networks inside Pakistan were deactivated. Some of these were in the Northern Areas of Pakistan Occupied Kashmir (PoK), and were never rebuilt. It was from this region that the Pakistani army launched its intrusion into the adjoining Kargil sector in 1999.[74] Desai also showed remarkable indiscretion on intelligence matters. During a conversation with the Pakistani President in 1978, he let slip that R&AW had penetrated the Pakistani nuclear plant at Kahuta. The Indian agent on-site was identified and eliminated.[75]

Upon returning to power in 1980, Indira Gandhi reversed the intelligence agencies' fortunes. Now it was the IB's turn to suffer and that of the R&AW to prosper. Proposals were floated to consolidate all intelligence activities under the aegis of the latter agency.[76] To protect its turf, the IB went overboard in seeking to regain favour with Mrs Gandhi, who had not forgotten how its leadership had abandoned her in 1977. The agency devoted 70 per cent of its field operatives and 90 per cent of its headquarters staff to monitoring her political opponents.[77] Its coverage of national security threats dropped as a result. According to one estimate, the agency's effectiveness fell by 40 per cent during the early 1980s.[78] Although this would suggest a complete lack of professionalism on the part of top IB officials, an argument can be made that they were only acting in the agency's larger interests.

High Consumer Expectations and Limited Collection Capabilities

Since the prime minister is the most important policy maker in India, he or she ultimately controls the finances that are integral to intelligence work. For this reason, it is vital for intelligence chiefs to remain on good terms with the political leadership, even if that means spying on the opposition. They have no alternative, as the intelligence collection capabilities of IB and

R&AW have always lagged behind consumer requirements. If the expectations placed upon intelligence agencies are not reduced, the only alternative is for politicians to increase the agencies' resources. That is to say, if policy makers want intelligence agencies to produce highly specific information, they must increase intelligence funding proportionately.

Indian intelligence resources have never been plentiful. Until 1935, the colonial IB did not even have a countrywide agent network and depended heavily on local police forces for its raw data. With the emergence of provincial governments dominated by Indians, the agency decided to set up an independent information collection system. This was intended to insure against the possibility of local politicians shutting off the flow of information to Delhi. Accordingly, six Central Intelligence Offices were set up across India.[79]

With the coming of Indian independence in 1947, the IB not only had to rebuild its fledgling collection apparatus, but also adapt to the rapid proliferation of regional governments. Each state (province) within the Indian Union was assigned a Subsidiary Intelligence Bureau (SIB). These were manned by a combination of local police personnel, and IB operatives from other states. Depending on the importance of a particular state, its SIB would by headed by a Deputy Director or a Joint Director.[80]

Until the 1962 Sino–Indian War, the IB made do with very basic infrastructure for the collection and transmission of foreign intelligence.[81] Only after the Indian defeat in that war did the government release funds for strengthening the IB's technical collection capabilities. This was done because the harsh terrain along the Sino–Indian border impeded human intelligence (HUMINT) efforts. The newly acquired capabilities were transferred wholesale to the R&AW in 1968. Thereafter, the IB went back to being a producer of domestic intelligence through human sources.

The quality of its information has since tended to be low, owing to the fact that IB operatives mostly handle 'fringe' human sources. High-level information is rarely obtained, since the counterintelligence methods adopted by the agency's targets are quite rigorous.[82] Infiltrating into jihadist networks has proven nearly impossible because of the very low number of Muslims serving in Indian Intelligence. The R&AW does not have a single Muslim in its 10,000-strong manpower pool while the IB has a small number of Muslim operatives.[83] These operatives did a sterling job of raising new informer networks in Jammu and Kashmir during the 1990s, when terrorist groups were wreaking havoc in the state. Despite their performance however, the IB and R&AW remain averse to employing Muslims, preferring to invest in technical collection.[84]

Increasing New Collection Capabilities

Upgrades of technical-collection systems have had limited effect due to financial constraints. While Morarji Desai downsized the R&AW out of spite, Prime Minister Narasimha Rao did so in 1993 for reasons of economy. India was desperately short of foreign exchange at the time, and could not afford to pay for expensive technical collection platforms such as communications interception equipment. During the 1993–94 fiscal year, the R&AW budget was slashed by 10 per cent. As a result, the agency was denied two reconnaissance aircraft which were urgently needed. The following year, the Indian Finance Ministry further jeopardised intelligence activities by implementing another 20 per cent cut in funding.[85]

Attempts to economize have taken a toll on counterterrorist efforts. When in 1995 Pakistani mercenaries abducted five Western tourists (including an American) in the state of Jammu and Kashmir, no Indian agency had a clue as to their whereabouts. US officials who flew in to assist rescue operations asked for imagery intelligence (IMINT) of the search area but were told the Indians had none. They then supplied their own imagery and Indian agencies were shocked at the high quality of the pictures.[86]

Following the surprise created by Pakistan's military incursion into Kashmir in 1999, the Indian government allocated additional funds to intelligence. Both agencies used the additional funds to enhance tried-and-tested systems of collecting intelligence even as the responsibilities placed upon them multiplied. A sizeable portion of their effort was devoted to upgrading electronic surveillance.

Poor HUMINT Coverage

Indian intelligence agencies have gradually become dependent on technical collection, and begun to neglect traditional espionage. Reports are now based largely on communications intercepts or data culled from news agencies. Human assets, which can be used both for intelligence collection and covert operations, are viewed as too risky to run. At present, most Indian HUMINT efforts against Pakistan and China are carried out from friendly third countries, such as the United Kingdom or Germany.[87] Owing to the Indian policy-making establishment's keenness to appear 'responsible' and non-aggressive, R&AW is reluctant to post officers abroad under non-official cover. Its personnel have therefore become accustomed to operating from the safety and comfort of diplomatic premises.[88] Over time, their cover identities start to wear thin and they remain content with merely keeping up the pretence of being bona fide diplomats.[89] Their concerns whilst abroad are limited to getting the maximum material benefit from a posting, and not being declared *persona non grata* by the host government.

During the 1980s, R&AW foreign postings were divided into 'A' and 'B' categories. Instead of regional capitals in South Asia, the more coveted category 'A' list was headed by Geneva, New York, Paris and Rome, in that order.[90] Even today, jostling for postings in the West remains the primary concern for agency personnel, both at Class One and Class Two levels.[91] (Ironically, much the same goes on in Western agencies, whose operatives compete for foreign postings that offer low living costs and a large 'hardship' allowance – such as India.)

Within Indian Intelligence, embezzlement of Secret Service (SS) funds intended for agent payment is allegedly not uncommon.[92] Though again, this also happens elsewhere: in the late 1990s, the Israeli Mossad was rocked by an embezzlement scandal involving one of its most distinguished field operatives. Given the nature of intelligence work, misuse of agency resources for personal benefit is virtually unavoidable in large bureaucracies.[93] Although in India it is customary to assume that such activities are exclusively the preserve of mercenary-minded civilians, army officers seconded to R&AW are not above them. In fact, they might well be among the worst offenders. An example is provided by the illicit activities concerning officers attached to the agency's Special Frontier Force (SFF).

The SFF is a highly secret paramilitary organization intended for special operations within Tibet and covert counterterrorist action. It is dominated by army officers and has enormous logistical backing. During the 1980s, the force was plagued by scandals involving sexual exploitation of female operatives by their superiors, as well as illegal logging.[94] The degeneration of what had once been a highly professional force occurred because of a metamorphosis in the SFF's manpower profile. Over the years, it became a repository for superseded and retired military personnel. These professional has-beens were more interested in feathering their after-service retirement nests than training for covert operations.[95] Their story is a microcosm of the larger maladies affecting R&AW, where field postings are seen primarily as opportunities for personal enrichment. Unimpressive fieldwork only creates pressure on analysts to squeeze the most meaning out of a limited data set.

Strategic Intelligence and Military Operations

With these limitations, it is not surprising that intelligence agencies, particularly R&AW, are targets of criticism from their consumers. Much of this criticism originates from the Armed Forces, although not all of it is justified. In some cases, the military has blamed intelligence agencies principally to cover up its own blunders. In other cases, an objective conclusion can be reached that the agencies performed poorly, and let their consumers down. Finally, a third possibility exists, which is that genuine confusion prevails as to where the intelligence agencies' responsibility ends, and that of field commanders begins.

Intelligence as a Scapegoat for Military Incompetence

Two examples of the intelligence agencies being unfairly blamed are: the fall of Sela Pass to Chinese forces in 1962, and the breaching of the Ichogil Canal by Pakistan in 1965. Sela Pass was a formidable Indian defensive position in the Eastern Himalayas. The Indian Army had intended to confront any Chinese military offensive at this point – a sort of Maginot Line strategy. Instead, the Sela position just folded up after a key commander lost his nerve, abandoned his troops and fled. Previously, the same officer had disregarded IB reports that the Chinese were preparing to outflank his defences.[96] The resulting rout thus occurred due to a failure of leadership rather than of intelligence.[97] Instead of facing up to this fact, the Indian Army chose to bury it and portray the cowardly officer as a war hero.[98]

The Ichogil Canal episode, which took place during the 1965 Indo-Pakistani War, was another occasion when the IB was slandered to cover up military incompetence. The army was caught unawares when Pakistani forces thwarted an Indian offensive by breaching a large irrigation canal in Punjab.[99] Army officers accused the IB of failing to provide information on Pakistani operational plans. In response, the Bureau cited approximately fifty reports that it had dispatched to the army over the preceding year, about the enemy's likely use of the canal. A neutral enquiry later established that the military's own intelligence staff had failed to convey this information down to units in the field.[100]

Inaccurate Reporting and Operational Mismanagement by Intelligence Agencies

There have however, also been instances when the intelligence agencies were themselves guilty of blunders. One example was the IB's incorrect assessment about Naga insurgents from the north-eastern region of India receiving military training in China. Initially, the agency dismissed agent reports that came in during 1967 about a large group of rebels that was preparing for travel to China.[101] When these reports were later confirmed, the agency went to the opposite extreme and overestimated the number of insurgents who had gone across. Naturally, its credibility with the Indian Army suffered on both counts, particularly since the latter had a better grasp of the ground situation through its own local-intelligence network.[102]

Far more serious was the R&AW's failure in the 1980s to penetrate the Liberation Tigers of Tamil Eelam (LTTE), a terrorist group based in Sri Lanka. Initially, the agency supported the LTTE and even provided it with military ordnance, as a way of gaining leverage over the Sri Lankan government. None of this earned any gratitude from the group's leadership, which stubbornly refused to toe the line prescribed by New Delhi.[103] Eventually, Indian troops were sent to Sri Lanka in 1987 to curb the terrorists' activities, which had started to threaten India's own interests. They ended up fighting an extremely bitter jungle war against the LTTE. What made R&AW responsible for this debacle was that its functionaries had previously worked closely with the LTTE top leadership. Instead of using the latter, they had ended up being used by it.[104]

Poor Consumer Understanding of the Difference Between Strategic and Tactical Intelligence

A final point needs to be made: sometimes problems arise in intelligence-military relations due to differing perceptions of 'strategic' and 'tactical' intelligence. Most operational-level army officers make no distinction between the two functions, seeing them as exclusively the responsibility of intelligence agencies.[105] According to these officers, any situation wherein security forces lack actionable intelligence becomes an 'intelligence failure' by definition. Even soldiers who have served in the intelligence agencies and should have a better understanding of their limitations hold such views. To quote a former major general who served for two years in the R&AW:

> Intelligence agencies are numerous and lack coordination and unity of purpose. These are neither integrated nor geared to meet our immediate requirements; an unhealthy rivalry exists and the agents make money for the same information from more than one agency. Intelligence being the main key to counter-insurgency operations, the units of the security forces are faced with the problem of organizing their own intelligence in large measure.[106]

While most counterinsurgency theorists deem intelligence vital to success, they do not stipulate that it must be provided by national-level agencies. On the contrary, writers like Frank Kitson explicitly state that security forces personnel at the ground level must assume responsibility for tactical intelligence.[107] The above-cited criticism of Indian intelligence thus reflects the perennial problem of overly-high expectations among intelligence consumers. Controlling such demands has been one of the priorities of Indian strategic intelligence, particularly with regard to internal security operations.

Strategic Intelligence and Counterinsurgency

Ever since its creation, the IB has had to work around the fact that it was originally set up to do political surveillance. Its organisation and infrastructure as envisaged by the colonial authorities was geared towards this task. During the British Raj, provincial Special Branches supplied the agency with the bulk of its raw data.[108] Their intrinsic efficiency reduced the need for a large intelligence bureaucracy. However, as the Indian nationalist movement gained momentum, the IB expanded its network of informers. Since Indian political parties were urban-based, almost all of the agency's collection apparatus was confined to monitoring events within towns and cities. Rural intelligence remained a police responsibility.

This factor meant that the IB had (and still has) very limited capability for tactical intelligence outside of population centres. Since the Indian independence movement remained non-violent and did not develop into an insurgency, the Bureau's deficiencies in rural coverage were not of serious consequence to the British. The same did not apply to the security situation in post-colonial India, particularly as insurgencies erupted across the country's remote north-eastern region. This began to happen as early as 1956.

Nehru was adamant that insurgencies in the north-east needed to be defeated through redress of grievance and that use of military force was to be minimised.[109] As an admirer of the ancient Indian political philosopher Kautilya, he advocated a mix of 'hard' and 'soft' measures, with great emphasis being placed on the strategy of divide-and-rule.[110] His model for managing internal conflicts was to focus on bringing about a negotiated settlement with moderate factions of rebel groups. Towards this, he was prepared to use concessions, bribes, intrigues and force – in that order.

The advantage with this approach was that it took a long-term view of conflict resolution. Rather than conquer, the objective of Indian internal security policy was to co-opt alienated populations and induce them to join the national mainstream. From the IB's perspective, such an approach was ideal, as it did not require the agency to provide massive intelligence support to the Armed Forces during counterinsurgency operations.[111] While the military focused on meeting its own intelligence requirements, the IB could study the political dynamics of an insurgency and examine the prospects for negotiation.

An Emphasis on Strategic Analysis

Starting in the 1950s and continuing into the 1960s, the agency developed a counterinsurgency doctrine that was uniquely suited to Indian conditions.[112] Although the specifics of this doctrine remain a closely guarded secret, a broad outline is discernible. Basically, it follows the Kautilyan model of conflict management preferred by Nehru: initiate negotiations to weaken the resolve of rebellious groups and sharpen ideological differences between them. Once factional disputes have erupted within the armed underground, moderate rebels are to be co-opted through bribery, and military operations focused on the most intractable groups. Resort to armed force is to be minimised, so as to avoid strengthening the mass base of the rebellion.[113]

The last principle was in all probability derived from lessons learnt during the colonial era, when the IB underestimated the strength of Indian nationalist sentiment. Having focused on providing tactical-intelligence support to law-enforcement agencies, IB analysts grew disconnected from popular opinion across the country.[114] The colonial regime's tendency to view dissension as a purely law-and-order problem meant that it did not perceive the independence movement as a political phenomenon. Instead of conducting long-term studies of the militancy that was developing among the native population, the IB remained fixated with monitoring individual nationalist leaders. Eventually, like the East German Stasi in 1989, it was swamped under a tidal wave of useless trivia and unable to prevent regime change.[115] Over-emphasis on tactical intelligence, caused by consumer demands, had led to a neglect of strategic intelligence.

Since 1947 therefore, the IB has striven to remain focused on the 'big picture' while dealing with subversive movements, and has relegated tactical intelligence to a secondary priority. Towards this, it has resisted incessant pressure from state police forces to devote more time and resources to meeting their demands for 'actionable intelligence'.[116] Although relations between the agency and its operational-level consumers have suffered as a result, it is for this reason that the mistakes of the colonial regime have so far not been repeated, and no separatist movement within India has succeeded. Strategic analysis to support policy making remains the Bureau's primary task, although, as this book shall demonstrate, the progressive degeneration of police intelligence systems is foisting new and unwanted responsibilities upon it.

Net Assessment of Indian Intelligence

There is no denying that strategic intelligence in India has been afflicted by serious problems. Many of these originate from the strong dependence which policy makers place upon secret information, both in managing domestic politics and in crafting foreign policy. National-security management as a whole rests heavily on raw facts provided by the IB and the R&AW. Both of these agencies lack the human and technical resources required to meet such high consumer expectations. Yet, as this section shall argue, they have still managed to produce successes in cases where their role was limited and clear policy guidance was provided.[117]

Intelligence Successes

For instance, the intelligence agencies can justifiably claim credit for keeping India free from the spillover of militancy elsewhere in the world. Despite its long-standing official sympathy for the Palestinians, New Delhi ensured that their activities on Indian soil did not turn violent.[118] India never saw anti-Israeli terrorism of the kind that pockmarked Western Europe during the 1970s. Similarly, in the years following the Iranian Revolution, the IB and R&AW worked together in rounding up and deporting dozens of Iranian and Iraqi terrorists intent on killing each other on Indian territory.[119] It helped that in both these cases, the nature of the security threat offered Indian politicians little electoral incentive to perpetuate its existence. Consequently, the intelligence agencies could carry out their work in peace, without fear of political interference.

The IB also deserves credit for its successes in neutralising the threat from foreign intelligence agencies. Approximately 30 counterintelligence units of the agency are dedicated to surveillance of major diplomatic missions and their personnel.[120] Naturally, the highest priority goes towards neutralising the efforts of the Pakistani ISI. In connection with this, the IB has scored significant successes, some of which have been described by former agency officers in their memoirs.

As a general rule, Indian counterintelligence prefers to monitor foreign espionage networks and manipulate them, instead of just shutting down their operations. Such a policy not only avoids the embarrassment of diplomatic expulsions but also yields invaluable knowledge about the hostile service's tradecraft.[121] While dealing with the ISI, manipulation has been used to considerable effect in neutralising a highly aggressive espionage effort.

One example is the case of Brigadier Zaheer-ul Islam Abbasi, the ISI station chief in New Delhi in 1988. Abbasi was an ambitious but unskilled operative, whose expulsion for purchasing military secrets ensured him a hero's welcome in Pakistan. Only much later did it emerge that virtually all his intelligence 'coups' had been IB plants, and that his expulsion was engineered to lend credibility to them.[122] In another case, during mid 2002 the SIB in Rajasthan state neutralised a Pakistani spy whose activities it had tracked for two months. War between India and Pakistan seemed imminent at the time, and the Pakistani operative was likely to sabotage missile launches from forward areas.[123]

Even the R&AW has achieved some spectacular intelligence coups, notwithstanding all its personnel problems. The agency's finest hour came in December 1971, when it provided accurate tactical warning of a Pakistani pre-emptive air strike on Indian airbases.[124] Had the attack succeeded, it could have paralysed Indian air and ground forces just as the Israeli Air Force had done to the Egyptians and Syrians in June 1967. During the 1970s, R&AW was also able to tap the telephone of Pakistani Prime Minister Zulfikar Ali Bhutto in Islamabad. (However, this success was tempered by the fact that the agency could only hear his end of the conversation and had to guess what the other party was saying.)[125]

Inadequacy of Intelligence Resources, Relative to Requirements

Given that intelligence agencies in India have a wide mandate, it appears that their resource base, though considerable, is barely able to match requirements.[126] The IB has three main responsibilities, which it fulfils on a continuous basis: political intelligence, counterintelligence and the protection of Very Important Persons (VIPs).[127] Added to this are special duties entrusted to the agency by policy makers, such as covert negotiations with terrorist leaders and monitoring the quality of governance.[128] For example, in February 1997, the agency was asked to identify food-grain hoarders across the country. Despite a good harvest over the previous months, food prices had continued to rise. Suspicious that local distributors were driving up prices by hoarding grain, the Prime Minister's Office asked for IB assistance. Within a short while, the Bureau returned with detailed lists of the worst offenders in eight states, complete with a locality-wise breakup of distributors against whom action could be taken.[129]

A proper appreciation of the sheer magnitude of the IB's responsibilities requires examination of the internal-security situation as a whole. Not for nothing has VS Naipaul famously described India as the land of 'a million mutinies'.[130] Over a third of the country's land area is affected by political violence of sufficient intensity as to be termed 'terrorism'.[131] Added to this are: a disintegrating law-enforcement apparatus and the active complicity of Pakistani Intelligence in sponsoring terrorist movements. All that the agency can do in such circumstances is focus on getting the big picture right, and leave it to local security forces to ferret out the details.

Summary: Look Beyond Organizational Factors for Intelligence Performance Evaluation

The problems facing strategic intelligence in India are of a long-term structural nature. By themselves, they do not explain variations in intelligence performance. As early as 1981, a report submitted to prime minister Indira Gandhi identified the main flaws of Indian Intelligence as:

> Large gaps in intelligence coverage,
> Poor evaluation of available intelligence,
> Overlapping collection mandates,
> Lack of long-term planning for resource management,
> Excessive compartmentalisation, hindering internal communications, and
> Slow transmission of intelligence reports to the end-user.[132]

It is the contention of this book that such flaws have existed through periods of both success and failure in the history of Indian intelligence. To understand fluctuations in the performance of intelligence agencies against terrorism, it is necessary to move beyond organisational studies, and look at the relationship between intelligence agencies and the counterintelligence capabilities of terrorist groups. We shall do this in the next chapter.

CHAPTER 2

THE STRENGTH OF TERRORIST COUNTERINTELLIGENCE

Terrorist movements in India possess four attributes, which reduce their vulnerability to intelligence penetration. These attributes constitute the 'four pillars of terrorist counterintelligence'. Foremost among them is the sympathy which sections of the Indian population have for terrorist groups; local support often screens terrorists from the national intelligence agencies. Combined with the terrorists' willingness to eliminate suspected informers, their tight control over operational security and ability to conduct transnational operations, this greatly limits the effectiveness of intelligence agencies.

Consequently, generic warnings about planned terrorist activities cannot be developed to an actionable standard of detail. The government is confronted with a knowledge gap between strategic and tactical intelligence. Bridging this gap requires the offensive use of security forces. By 'fighting for intelligence' the latter fill in the micro-details in the larger strategic assessments that are prepared by intelligence agencies.[1] Reluctance, or inability to make offensive use of security forces on the other hand, allows the knowledge gap to persist. Thus, even if strategic intelligence predicts a terrorist attack, there will be no tactical intelligence to help prevent it.

To understand the context of events described here, let us consider, in brief, each of the three terrorist movements examined in this book.

The Sikh Separatist Movement

The Sikh separatist movement originated in the early 1980s out of a convergence of interests between Pakistani Intelligence, radical Sikhs based in Europe and North America, and Sikh fundamentalists within Punjab. During 1978–81, the latter received support from the Congress (I), the biggest political party in India. The Congress had wanted to undermine the popularity of its main rival in Punjab, the Akali Dal party, by replicating the latter's religiously-defined approach to politics. However, in 1980–81, Pakistani spies linked up with the fundamentalists supported by the Congress. Under their influence, the fundamentalists began making demands for 'Khalistan', an independent Sikh homeland.[2] During 1981–84, several terrorist attacks occurred in Punjab, forcing the Indian government to send in the army in June 1984.

The army crackdown alienated many Sikhs, whose sense of resentment was propounded by communal riots that took place across northern India in October 1984. Over the following years, New Delhi tried to negotiate with prominent Sikh leaders to come to an amicable settlement. It hoped to replicate the success of its 1986 peace accord in Mizoram, wherein the rebel leadership gave up armed struggle in return for being allowed to form the local government.

However, continuing Pakistani support for Sikh separatist groups hardened the latter's negotiating stance.[3] Whenever New Delhi succeeded in buying off one separatist faction, the others intensified their operations and destroyed any prospect of a negotiated settlement. Eventually, in 1988, the Indian government suspended peace talks and ordered the Punjab Police to begin offensive operations against the terrorists. Led by the highly-respected police chief Kanwar Pal Singh Gill, or KPS Gill as he is commonly known, the force soon had the terrorists on the run and non-combatant deaths declined sharply.

A change of government in New Delhi in December 1989 interrupted the police offensive. Convinced that the terrorists could be won over with concessions, the new political leadership restarted peace talks. For another two years, sporadic negotiations continued between New Delhi and Sikh separatist leaders, even as terrorist violence in Punjab rose massively. Only in late 1991, when the violence threatened to become uncontrollable, did Indian policy makers once again revert to a hard-line stance. The army was re-inducted into Punjab (it had been withdrawn from counterterrorist duties in 1985). Operating jointly with the state police, who provided local-intelligence support, the army crushed the Sikh separatist movement decisively in an eighteen-month offensive.

The Kashmiri Separatist Movement

Terrorism in Jammu and Kashmir (a term used to describe the Indian-administered portion of the Kashmir region) began in 1988. The previous year, an election to the State Legislative Assembly had been rigged by local politicians, who were coalition partners of the then ruling government in New Delhi – the Congress (I). Sporadic attacks on government offices were followed by a massive uprising in December 1989, when terrorists kidnapped the daughter of a senior Indian minister and traded her for the release of some jailed separatist leaders. The uprising was however, confined to the Muslim-dominated Valley of Kashmir, the smallest and most densely populated part of the state.

Pakistan, which had a long history of supporting Kashmiri separatist groups, soon became involved in the rebellion. From 1990 onwards, it provided massive quantities of arms and explosives, as well as paramilitary training to Kashmiri youths.[4] The extent of Pakistani involvement forced New Delhi to permanently deploy the Indian Army in a counterterrorist role in Jammu and Kashmir. During 1990–96, violence in the state continued to escalate (with one short-lived pause during 1991) as the army and Kashmiri separatist groups slugged it out.

Realising that India had a decisive advantage in the conflict due to its enormous military might, Pakistan began dispatching large numbers of foreign mercenaries into Indian territory.[5] These individuals were a motley collection of Pakistani, Afghan and Arab jihadists who had previously fought the Red Army in Afghanistan. Their presence in Jammu and Kashmir sustained violence levels after 1998, when the indigenous Kashmiri separatists began to consider compromising with New Delhi.

After 1998, terrorist violence in Kashmir was dominated by foreign mercenaries. Locally-recruited terrorists meanwhile grew wary of these individuals, whose religious fanaticism did not make them popular among the larger Kashmiri population. Taking advantage of this, Indian Intelligence exploited ideological and ethnic rifts within the separatist movement by reaching out to the indigenous terrorists and marginalising the mercenaries. The Indian government also sought to isolate Pakistan internationally by emphasising commonalities between the mercenary groups and Al Qaeda.

Following the 9/11 attacks on the US, the Indian diplomatic offensive yielded results and Pakistan was compelled by Washington to scale down its support for Kashmiri separatism. Indian security forces meanwhile continued to wear down terrorist groups through a process of attrition. Owing to lack of reinforcements from Pakistan, as well as improved operational capacity and coordination on the part of Indian security forces, the Kashmiri separatist rebellion was greatly weakened.

The Pan-Islamist Threat to India

Pan-Islamist terrorism in India is mainly a foreign threat, originating from across the country's western border. It is part of a strategic thrust conceptualised by Pakistani Intelligence in 1991 and first put into effect in 1993. The aim is to stretch Indian law enforcement capabilities to unsustainable levels by conducting coordinated attacks across the length and breadth of the country. The jihadists and their Pakistani-state patrons hope that such operations will deter foreign investment and fatally damage India's ability to finance its security operations in Kashmir.[6] Their plans have been facilitated by religious riots across India, which have radicalised a small number of Indian Muslims. Believing that the Indian polity has abandoned them to Hindu vigilante terrorism, some Muslims have begun to support jihadist groups in self-defence.

Beginning in 1993, terrorists have carried out a number of attacks in cities across the Indian heartland, with implicit support from Pakistani Intelligence.[7] The majority of these attacks have been directed against unprotected or 'soft' targets. Initially, the jihadists limited themselves to bomb attacks but from 2000, they also began to carry out commando-style assaults using firearms. This was partly due to their demographic profile, which changed in tandem with the violence in Kashmir. During the mid 1990s, it was mostly Kashmiri separatists who carried out expeditionary attacks in Indian cities, with logistical support provided by Pakistan-based criminal syndicates. However, since 2000, the majority of jihadist attacks have been carried out by Pakistani mercenaries, of which the 2008 Mumbai massacre is only the most infamous example. The fact that these mercenaries have managed to create support networks within India despite being foreigners, speaks very poorly of Indian counterterrorist efforts.

Against the backdrop of these three terrorist movements, this book analyses why Indian intelligence agencies cannot produce 'actionable' information on terrorist groups. It examines the four major obstacles that prevent strategic intelligence from being automatically converted into tactical intelligence. Together, these obstacles constitute the 'four pillars of terrorist counterintelligence'.

The First Pillar: Public Sympathy

Indian politics is often characterised by the cynical exploitation of regional and communal (i.e. religious extremist) sentiments. Owing to poor governance, identity groups across the country have developed a sense of political vulnerability.[8] Eager to foment inter-group hostility and then cash in on the electoral benefits of acting as a mediator or protector, mainstream political parties have contributed towards factionalism in the Indian polity. While doing so, they have employed the same tactics used by Third World politicians elsewhere, particularly in post-colonial Africa.[9] Societal polarisation is actively promoted in order to politicise otherwise inert masses of people, turning them into electoral assets which can be fought over. This dynamic has an unfortunate side-effect: it creates firewalls between communities and impedes the free flow of information among them. Should a particular ethnic, linguistic or religious group dominate the security establishment, its members are cut off from the knowledge pools of other identity groups.[10] Furthermore, inter-group hostilities within the establishment can lead to counterterrorist efforts themselves being compromised.

Communal Polarization in Punjab

Separatist terrorism in Punjab began in the early 1980s. Its objective was to establish an independent Sikh nation to be called Khalistan. Initially, counterterrorist operations were hampered by betrayals from within the Sikh-dominated state police.[11] Elements within the force sympathized with the terrorists on the basis of religious solidarity. They provided tip-offs about impending police raids and compromised intelligence operations against the Khalistanis.[12] Occasionally, they also provided the latter with hideouts and allowed them rights of safe passage.[13] During 1984–86, 29 junior police officials were dismissed for providing material and informational support to terrorist groups. Up to one hundred officials were removed from active duty on the basis of similar charges.[14]

Subversion of the local administration and the police remained a problem in Punjab almost till the very end of the separatist movement. In

March 1991, the Indian Army's Military Intelligence Directorate warned that several government servants in the state had pro-separatist sympathies. It also attributed the continuation of terrorist violence to a collapse of governance. Since mainstream political parties were not prepared to unequivocally oppose the demand for Khalistan, separatist groups enjoyed a free run.[15]

This dynamic was only broken when the Punjab Police was suitably armed, equipped, expanded and motivated for its role as the lead agency in counterterrorism. The police was given absolute authority to deal with the terrorist movement, with no interference from the political leadership. Once Sikh policemen began pro-actively hunting down Sikh terrorists, the separatist movement lost its ideological character and rationale. By de-communalising the counterterrorist apparatus, policy makers gradually deprived the Khalistanis of their local support base.

Communalisation and Political Fraud In Jammu and Kashmir

In the case of Jammu and Kashmir, communalisation significantly contributed towards the growth of separatist sentiment among Kashmiri Muslims during the mid 1980s. This was ignited into a full-fledged rebellion after the state government allegedly rigged an election to the State Legislative Assembly in April 1987. The election results were seen as a humiliation for the Islamist-dominated political opposition. An overwhelming majority of the first wave of separatist militants were former activists of opposition parties. Not only were they motivated to take up arms as a result of the rigged election, but also apolitical Kashmiris grew antipathetic to the incumbent administration. Consequently they were inclined to withhold information on preparations for a terrorist campaign. During 1987–90, though the Jammu and Kashmir Police learnt through its informer network that a rebellion was brewing in the state, it was unable to obtain more specific information that could help pre-empt it. Undercover officers either could not or would not provide information on the movements of subversive individuals, leaving the force unable to apprehend them.[16]

Popular hostility towards the government created a counterintelligence wall around the Kashmiri separatist movement, which allowed it to gain critical mass and become viable. Although the state police soon identified the six most influential separatist leaders, it could not locate them because of lack of information.[17] Existing human sources clammed up, and desertions took place within the police force itself. In such a situation, the national intelligence agencies were almost blinded, since their strategic assessments drew heavily on ground-level data sourced through the police. The IB estimated that approximately 1,000 members of the 270,000-strong civil bureaucracy actively supported the terrorist groups. In 1994, the agency compiled a list of suspected 'hardcore' terrorist sympathisers in the state government, which included 59 senior officials.[18] Owing to absence of any systematic effort to remove these officials, counterterrorist operations in the state continued to be vulnerable to betrayal.

Jihadism and Communal Tension

Communalism was also the major factor that allowed pan-Islamist jihadism to establish a following within the Indian Muslim community.[19] Since the early 1980s, tension had been steadily mounting between the Hindus (who constitute 80.5 per cent of India's population) and Muslims (13.4 per cent).[20] Originally, these had focused on the issue of religious conversions, but gradually developed into larger disputes over the status of religious shrines. Furthermore, the Hindus grew insecure and militant as a result of communal massacres by Khalistani terrorists in Punjab and anti-Hindu riots in Jammu and Kashmir. The Muslims in turn were uneasy at the efforts of the Indian government to introduce amendments to the Muslim personal law. Attempts by Hindu fundamentalists to have the Quran officially banned exacerbated their unease.[21]

By 1986, the differences had hardened and both sides began forming vigilante groups to target the other. Given that the Indian police is overwhelmingly Hindu-dominated, this meant that local intelligence flows from the Muslim community began to dry up.[22] One example of how such communal polarisation could benefit jihadism came in November 1993, when police raided a terrorist hideout in the south Indian town of Coimbatore. Although the raid was executed flawlessly and on the basis of specific intelligence, local Muslims refused to cooperate with subsequent police investigations. Some even carried out arson attacks and stoned public transport in reprisal for the police action. Moderate Muslim leaders who counselled restraint were threatened by the hardliners.[23] Such vigilantism sprang from a basic sense of physical insecurity which Indian policy makers failed to address. While it would be incorrect to assert that ordinary Muslims knowingly held back information on terrorist plots, they did retreat behind a wall of seclusion which hampered intelligence activities.[24]

The Second Pillar: Demonstrative Killings

When popular sympathy for a terrorist movement dwindles, the movement does not automatically go out of business. Instead, it earns its 'terrorist' label by eliminating anyone who potentially poses a threat to its existence. Assassination of enemies is the instrument through which terrorist groups remain viable even when popular support for them starts to decline.[25] Such disciplinary campaigns follow a pattern. During the initial stage of their operations, terrorist groups opt for a narrow target range of government officials and collaborators to demonstrate their power. Over time however, this widens to include all those who dissent from the terrorists' worldview or express less than complete support.

From Targeted to Untargeted Killings in Punjab

The emergence of terrorist violence in Punjab during the early 1980s was marked by a systematic assault on the police intelligence system.[26] Since the state police had no prior experience of counterterrorism, the killings of senior and middle-ranking officials paralysed its operations. Starting in April 1983, when a Deputy Inspector General of Police was gunned down, information channels on Khalistani groups began to implode. Any officer who showed commitment in investigating terrorist incidents was killed as a warning to others. In one instance, a Deputy Superintendent of Police was shot dead along with his wife, two children and six other policemen for having interrogated a prominent separatist leader.[27]

The effect of such killings was to generate a culture of risk aversion among the Punjab Police. Interrogations of terrorist suspects had to be carried out by senior officers, since lower ranks feared for their lives. An interim solution was found in late 1984 when men from the Punjab Armed Police, who were less vulnerable to reprisals, assumed responsibility for collating intelligence. Gradually, under the tutelage of the then head of Police Operations and Intelligence, KPS Gill, informer networks were reactivated. Police officers were encouraged to take risks and their successes in counterterrorism were publicised, in order to commit them to an anti-Khalistani stance.[28]

From 1985 onwards, Sikh separatist terrorists alternated between communal massacres of Punjabi Hindus, targeted killings of police informers, and indiscriminate slaughter of any Sikhs who did not support them enthusiastically enough.[29] Upon coming under pressure from the police in 1986, they focused on identifying and eliminating likely spies within their ranks, as well as killing senior police officers.[30] When support for their struggle began to dwindle in 1987, they initially put up posters requesting fellow Sikhs to continue sheltering them.[31] These measures soon gave way to a more direct approach: those who wavered were eliminated. Gradually, terrorist counter-intelligence in Punjab grew less reliant on anti-government sentiment, and more on demonstrative killings that aimed to suppress any dissension before it could gain momentum.

Rise of Indiscriminate Killings in Jammu and Kashmir

The outbreak of terrorism in Jammu and Kashmir was accompanied by a well-coordinated assault on the IB's human intelligence system. Between 3 January and 12 February 1990, four key operatives of the state Subsidiary Intelligence Bureau (SIB) were assassinated.[32] Their deaths led to a near-total collapse of the central government's intelligence network in Jammu and Kashmir, which had never before faced a threat of such intensity. Since none of those killed were carrying firearms, their elimination took the form of public executions.[33] Of the remaining 32 IB operatives in the Kashmir Valley (the epicentre of the rebellion), 26 faced a high risk of assassination, since they lacked even basic physical security.[34] Accordingly, they were immediately withdrawn and for a year thereafter, the SIB could only muster enough resources to rebuild its capacity for strategic intelligence.[35] It was not until 1994 that the IB could start providing tactical support to security forces.

Part of the reason for this delay was the separatists' success in expelling virtually all Hindus from the Kashmir Valley. Hitherto, it had been the Kashmiri Hindus who worked as sources for the IB, not the Muslims.[36] When large-scale violence broke out in late 1989, there were 300,000 Hindus in the Valley. Over a thousand of them were killed over the following years and the homes of a further 30,000 gutted.[37] Eventually, the entire community fled to the Jammu region, which forms the southern parts of Jammu and Kashmir state.

Having crippled the government's intelligence machinery, terrorist groups switched to ensuring that the local population did not waver from supporting them. During 1989–2000, 75 per cent of those killed by terrorist violence in the state were non-combatants.[38] Almost 90 per cent of these non-combatant victims were Muslims: co-religionists of the terrorists themselves.[39] Seen from the terrorists' perspective, such killings were necessary because popular support for the separatist movement had begun to dwindle in 1990–96.[40] The election of a popular state government in 1996 further deprived the separatist movement of credibility. As violence levels began to fall in Jammu and Kashmir, large numbers of Pakistani and Afghan mercenaries entered the conflict at the behest of Pakistan's Inter Services Intelligence (ISI). Originally intended to reinforce indigenous Kashmiri separatist groups, these mercenaries introduced a new degree of barbarism into terrorist counterintelligence.[41]

Many of these mercenaries were battle-hardened veterans of the Soviet-Afghan War and the subsequent Afghan civil war. As fundamentalists from the Wahhabi school of Islam, they had no respect for the mystic and tolerant Sufi traditions of Kashmiri Muslims.[42] Punishments for suspected government agents grew increasingly medieval.[43] These included mutilation and evisceration while alive, with death usually occurring through beheading.[44] The mercenaries occasionally executed whole families, including children, in public through such methods, with the aim of horrifying Kashmiri villagers into submission.[45]

Jihadism and Targeted Assassination

A curious aspect of the pan-Islamist threat facing India is that its roots and support networks are overwhelmingly based in Pakistan. Among the most prominent targets of jihadist groups therefore have been Pakistani leaders who could potentially threaten these networks, such as former President Pervez Musharraf and the late political leader, Benazir Bhutto.[46] However, this is not to suggest that Pakistan-based jihadists have not carried out demonstrative killings in India. The November 2008 commando-style attack on Mumbai, for example, killed the chief of the city police's Anti-Terrorist Squad, along with two other senior officers. Terrorists and their handlers in Pakistan especially hailed the news of these officers' deaths as representing a great operational success.[47]

Overall though, it appears that the counterintelligence value of demonstrative killings is primarily felt in Pakistan. Pan-Islamist groups retain the ability, through sympathisers in the ISI and Pakistan army, to eliminate anyone with a connection to hostile intelligence agencies. The entrapment and murder of the American journalist Daniel Pearl is a prime example. Pearl was regarded with suspicion because he was based in India, which implied to some ISI officials that he was an Indian asset.[48] His attempts to meet lower-rung terrorist leaders, who were allegedly involved in attacks against the US and UK, made him vulnerable to elimination. The manner of his death (ritual beheading) has since become commonplace in the north-western region of Pakistan, which is a sanctuary for militant groups ranging from Al Qaeda to the Taliban. Public executions of potential spies have made this region a 'denied territory' for intelligence agencies attempting to track down Al Qaeda leaders.[49]

The Third Pillar: Operational Security

A strong sense of operational security is crucial to the survival of any terrorist group.[50] Indian intelligence activities against separatist terrorism in Punjab and Kashmir, as well as Pan-Islamist jihadism, have produced varying levels of success. This was partly because security-awareness levels varied for each of these movements.

Amateur Trade Craft in Punjab

Khalistani terrorists had a poorer sense of operational security than their Kashmiri and jihadist successors. Prior to carrying out an operation, they would brag about it to friends and relatives. This meant that Indian intelligence agencies did not have to penetrate the core membership of a terrorist group in order to obtain specific information. Merely raising a 'fringe' source was enough.[51] During the late 1980s, the agencies also invested in new technical-collection systems, which yielded a windfall of data about terrorist plans.[52] Belatedly, terrorist groups attempted to counter technical penetration by adopting coded language. For instance, field-level Khalistani cadres were instructed to write the telephone numbers of their contacts in reverse order, or in the English alphabet. Large towns in north India like Ghaziabad, Jalandhar, Ludhiana and Chandigarh were respectively referred to as 'Transport Company', 'Sports Shop', 'Hosiery Shop' and 'University'.[53] These efforts at communication security were fairly amateurish and did not pose any serious problem for Indian Intelligence.[54]

Good Communications Security in Jammu and Kashmir

Learning from the mistakes made by the Sikh separatists, the ISI subsequently primed Kashmiri terrorist groups with a high degree of awareness about operational security. It provided them with sophisticated encryption equipment that surpassed what the Indian security forces possessed.[55]

During 1990–98, only 20 per cent of all intercepted terrorist messages could be decrypted. To gather inside knowledge of terrorist attack plans, the security forces needed to triangulate, locate and seize a hostile transmitter, complete with its codes.[56] Occasionally, this could be done, particularly if a terrorist cell grew complacent and began transmitting frequently or for long periods. For the rest of the time, traffic analysis of intercepted messages was all that was feasible. This did not yield 'actionable intelligence' on terrorist activities. It did however help in mapping out the call signs and identities of key functionaries within the terrorist command-and-control system.[57] A detailed profile of the separatist movement could thus be built up and constantly updated. Constant surveillance was maintained on the radio networks of three major terrorist groups: the Lashkar-e-Toiba and Harkat-ul Ansar (both dominated by Pakistani mercenaries) and the Hizb-ul Mujahiddin (dominated by local Kashmiris).[58]

Operational Security and Jihadist Cells in India

Like the Kashmiri separatists, jihadist networks in the Indian heartland owed their survival partly to good ISI training.[59] For example, one terrorist who was captured in the state of Gujarat in June 1996 was pressured to make contact with his Pakistani handlers. Unknown to the Gujarat Police, the fax that he sent under their supervision contained an extra word which alerted the ISI to his arrest. The agency promptly ordered all his contacts within India to go underground and so minimised the damage which would otherwise have been caused to that particular terrorist network.[60]

Members of jihadist organisations within India currently keep in contact with their Pakistani mentors through a 'hub and spokes' system.[61] According to this, only a single individual in a terrorist cell of seven or eight knows the identities of all the cell members, and is the contact point with the ISI.[62] Information is transmitted through email 'drafts' folders. The cell leader writes a message and stores it as a draft in an email account. His handlers in Pakistan possess the account password; they read the message, type in a fresh draft in response, and delete the original draft. Since no messages are actually dispatched, Indian agencies cannot penetrate this channel unless they too have the account password.[63]

Such operational security measures do not pose a qualitative challenge for Indian Intelligence, but they cumulatively form a quantitative one. A former Indian Deputy National Security Advisor claimed that, as of 2005, approximately 300 jihadist cells had been neutralised by security forces.[64] While this figure indicates that terrorist tradecraft does not pose an insurmountable obstacle to the IB, it almost certainly complicates the overall task of intelligence collection. Scarce resources have to be divided between countering Pakistan's conventional espionage activities, and countering the activities of jihadist networks as well. Over time, one can anticipate a scenario where Indian tactical-intelligence capabilities get over stretched through monitoring multiple threats.

The Fourth Pillar: Transnational Networks

Transnational support networks of terrorist groups have made foreign-intelligence operations and border control integral to Indian counterterrorism. The prime sponsor of these networks has been the ISI.[65] Dating from the early 1980s, Pakistani support of Khalistani, Kashmiri and jihadist terrorism has sustained these movements through significant operational setbacks. It includes paramilitary training, target selection, financial assistance and inter-group coordination between different terrorist organisations.[66] Along with communalism in India, the ISI is a common link between the three terrorist movements discussed in this book. A 1998 IB assessment calculated that Pakistan-backed militants had inflicted total damage to the tune of INR 645 billion over the past decade.[67] With the collapse of the Khalistan movement, damage costs for 1998–2008 would almost certainly be lower, but still high by objective standards.

The ISI's Offensive Against R&AW

Since it deals with foreign intelligence, the R&AW could have mounted penetration operations against Pakistan-based terrorist groups. This it has failed to do in any substantial measure, owing to the counterintelligence support which the ISI extends to terrorist groups. For nearly three decades, the Pakistani agency has shielded Khalistani, Kashmiri and jihadist terrorists from Indian intelligence. Its counterintelligence division has made the R&AW station in Islamabad defunct, through sustained harassment of Indian embassy officials.[68] In the process, it has ensured that Indian human intelligence (HUMINT) coverage within Pakistan remains patchy and incapable of producing specific information on terrorist activities. The result is that R&AW can contribute little in developing strategic intelligence into tactical intelligence.[69]

During 1991, the ISI realised that merely supporting regionally-confined Indian terrorist groups would not yield long-term results.[70] All New Delhi had to do in response was systematically rotate its enormous security forces through terrorism-affected regions. Given the sheer size disparity between the manpower base available to the Indian government on one hand, and the Sikh and Kashmiri separatist groups on the other, it was a foregone conclusion as to which side would win. To stretch India's counterterrorist machinery beyond breaking point, the ISI decided to encourage joint operations in major metropolises by Khalistani, Kashmiri and Pan-Islamist terrorists.[71] Accordingly, it developed a scheme which became known in the Indian security establishment as Plan K2M (short for 'Khalistan, Kashmir and Muslim Militancy').

To frustrate the R&AW's efforts to monitor Plan K2M, the ISI's counterintelligence staff dramatically escalated harassment of Indian diplomats in Islamabad. The latter were already subject to close surveillance and occasional manhandling. However, the physicality of Pakistani counterintelligence tactics from 1991 onwards was of a totally different magnitude, and posed new risks. That year, the wife of an Indian diplomat was abducted while shopping and brutally interrogated about her husband's activities.[72] The following April, a senior official of the Indian High Commission in Islamabad was abducted and tortured with electrical shocks. Although Amnesty International demanded an explanation for the incident, the ISI brazenly continued with its counterintelligence offensive. A month later, in May 1992, it kidnapped and tortured another Indian diplomat.

These were not isolated incidents; they were part of a focused ISI effort that has continued from the early 1990s to the present day.[73] The Pakistani agency had set out to paralyse the R&AW as far as embassy-based espionage was concerned. It was successful owing to the unwillingness of Indian policy makers to sanction retaliatory attacks on ISI personnel in the Pakistan High Commission in New Delhi.[74] Between January and August 1994, there were 154 reported incidents of harassment against Indian diplomats and their families in Pakistan. This can be contrasted with Islamabad's claim that the IB harassed Pakistani diplomats in New Delhi on 13 occasions during 1987–94.[75] Differences in the two countries' counterintelligence methods are also indicated by another measure: during 1991–94, 35 out of 110 diplomats in the Pakistan High Commission had served in Delhi for over three years. In contrast, only three out of 110 Indian diplomats based in Islamabad were allowed to remain in-country over the same period.[76]

Through sustained attacks on R&AW, the ISI ensured that the rival agency could not penetrate terrorist groups based in Pakistan.

Porous Borders

While foreign-intelligence collection was enormously hampered by ISI counter-espionage, lax border security remained another problem. By operating across national boundaries the Khalistani, Kashmiri and jihadist terrorists reduced their dependence on support networks within India. It thus became difficult for the IB to prepare a composite picture of terrorist activities, because of the constant cross-border movement of senior terrorist leaders.[77] The result was wastage of efforts: enormous resources were poured into hunting down individuals who, upon capture, turned out to be strategically insignificant to the trajectory of terrorist violence in India.

For example, nearly 250 IB and Delhi Police personnel were assigned to track down the notorious Khalistani terrorist Harjinder Singh alias 'Jinda' in 1987.[78] When he was eventually caught, interrogators found that instead of being a mastermind, he was just a low-level gunman with a penchant for derring-do.[79] Similarly, security forces had hoped that by apprehending the Kashmiri separatist ideologue Shabir Shah, they could deal a powerful blow to militancy in Jammu and Kashmir. Shah's arrest in September 1989 dashed this optimistic projection, as it became clear that he was not orchestrating terrorist attacks in the state. Instead, ISI operatives based in Pakistan Occupied Kashmir (PoK), who remained in direct contact with the armed separatist cadres, enacted that role.[80]

This cross-border dimension to Indian terrorist movements has made terrorist infiltration rates into India a vital component of strategic analysis. Along the Line of Control (which divides the Indian state of Jammu and Kashmir from Pakistan Occupied Kashmir), infiltration is computed by taking into account five variables. These are: 1) the number of engagements fought between the security forces and terrorists in border areas 2) the number of terrorists killed within the interiors of the state 3) agent reports from villages located along known infiltration routes 4) interrogation reports and 5) communications intercepts.[81] Such indicators provide only a rough estimate of the number of terrorists entering Jammu and Kashmir at any time of the year. Since the ISI has compartmentalised the Kashmiri separatist movement into a number of independently operating factions, even a high-level penetration does not yield very precise information.[82]

Terrorist Counterintelligence Results: Vague Threat Assessments by Intelligence Agencies

The four pillars of terrorist counterintelligence described above limit the usefulness of strategic intelligence. Thus, much of the output from IB and R&AW consists of 'observational' intelligence.[83] This is information obtained from sources which lie outside the decision-making loop of a terrorist conspiracy. Such sources can only monitor preparations for a terrorist attack, but cannot explain the rationale for them.[84] The raw information they feed their handlers is passed up the chain of command until it is collated and analysed at headquarters. It is at the level of HQ analysts that a pattern might be discerned in terrorist activity, but this too would only form the basis for a general warning.[85] A caricatured 'observational' intelligence report is shown here:

Source: Sage Stossel, The Atlantic.com[86]

A frequent complaint made by intelligence consumers in India is that IB and R&AW warnings with regard to counterterrorism are extremely vague. According to officers of the Special Protection Group (SPG), which is responsible for the security of Very, Very Important Persons, intelligence assessments keep reiterating: 'the possibility of these VVIPs being targeted by assassins cannot be ruled out'.[87] Such generic warnings are likened to 'astrological forecasts, suitably vague about the specifics and frequently issued as bureaucratic ploys to cover all eventualities'.[88]

Indian Intelligence cannot escape this charge of 'vagueness', but it raises the question of just where the intelligence agencies' responsibilities end and those of their consumers begin. Usually, available information on a terrorist plot includes one of the three Ts that together form 'actionable' intelligence – either the target, technique, or time of an attack is known.[89] Problems arise in trying to ascertain the other two Ts through follow-up on the initial lead of the first T. Intelligence agencies are expected to provide this additional information while constantly racing against the clock. The only situation where they can do so is when an intelligence source is directly involved in planning the terrorist attack.[90] Such happy coincidences almost never occur. Frequently, this gives the police an alibi for failing to take intelligence reports seriously on the grounds that they are 'not actionable'.

Intelligence Agencies Burdened by Lackadaisical Attitude towards Security Drills

When police forces neglect basic security drills, owing to lack of intelligence warning, they allow terrorist threats to advance toward their targets. In the process, a greater dependence is placed upon intelligence agencies to provide specific warnings. An example of this dynamic is the assassination of prime minister Indira Gandhi by members of her personal bodyguard in October 1984.

In June 1984, the Indian Army had stormed the Golden Temple (the Sikhs' holiest shrine) on the orders of Mrs Gandhi. Its task had been to flush out Khalistani terrorists who were using the Temple as a sanctuary. During the assault, the Temple had suffered considerable damage as a result of fierce resistance put up by the terrorists. The IB subsequently assessed that many Sikhs would hold Mrs Gandhi responsible for the devastation caused. It warned that she faced a serious threat from her Sikh bodyguards.[91] Upon the agency's advice, all nine Sikhs in her 400-strong security detail were posted to other duties. However, Mrs Gandhi viewed this action as an affront to

Indian secularism and ordered that they be promptly reinstated.[92] Although hers was a principled stand, it also placed a massive new responsibility on the IB. The agency now had to devise an unobtrusive method to keep the suspect bodyguards under surveillance, while allowing them close proximity to the PM. It was still trying to reconcile these two fundamentally opposite requirements when she was assassinated five months later.[93]

Mrs Gandhi's assassination was facilitated by the Delhi Police's failure to follow elementary security procedures while tasking her bodyguards.[94] Two of the Sikh policemen in her security detail went on leave in the fall of 1984, and upon their return were immediately assigned to the innermost perimeter of her official compound. This was a violation of the established protocol, according to which they should have first been posted in the outermost and then the intermediate perimeter before being allowed back to proximate security duties. It was specifically these two individuals who went on to shoot Mrs Gandhi.[95]

Poor Consumer Responsiveness to Warnings

When, as in the above case, analysts do not have information on specific terrorist plots, they can do little more than reiterate the need for continued vigilance. This is done through issuing Unofficial Orders (called UOs in IB parlance) on a relatively frequent basis. Such notes have the unfortunate side effect of de-sensitising consumers to intelligence warnings, and lead to a decline in the agencies' credibility.[96] It was in precisely such a context that in 1986 the Delhi Police failed to take seriously an R&AW warning about a threat to the then Prime Minister Rajiv Gandhi (son of Indira Gandhi).[97] Prior to a public function on 2 October 1986, R&AW operatives in Punjab had obtained specific information that a gunman would attempt to hide in the shrubbery around the function venue. The PM was scheduled to attend, and so would be exposed to a sniper attack.[98] Since R&AW had previously given similar warnings, the Delhi Police did not take the information seriously this time.[99] When the assassination attempt did actually take place, it was not prompt police responses but sheer bungling by the would-be assassin that caused it to fail.

Absence of Actionable Intelligence Due to Lack of Follow-up

Sensational claims that intelligence agencies fail to share information that could potentially save lives are exaggerated.[100] Prior to dissemination, each source report is carefully studied for the purpose of evaluating its sensitivity.[101] Since most of the information obtained by intelligence agencies about terrorist groups is not very sensitive to begin with, it can be disseminated without serious risk of compromise. An example is the July 2000 threat assessment prepared by the Subsidiary Intelligence Bureau in Jammu and Kashmir.[102] The assessment warned that Pakistani mercenaries were likely to launch an attack on the Amarnath Yatra (a yearly Hindu pilgrimage in rural Kashmir). It summarised the latest agent reports and communications intercepts, as well as open-source intelligence derived from analysis of terrorist propaganda. A near-simultaneous input from the R&AW confirmed the IB's warning and identified the terrorist group most likely to carry out the attack.

Less than three weeks later, on 1 August, two Kalashnikov-wielding terrorists gunned down 22 pilgrims and 13 local bystanders at one of the pilgrimage sites. Security forces officials later admitted they had received intelligence warnings about a terrorist attack, but claimed they lacked the manpower to enhance security as had been recommended.[103] Since neither the IB nor R&AW possessed information as to the chosen date, place and method of attack, they had no actionable information to pass on to the security forces. Moreover, under a ceasefire arrangement that came into effect between the time these two agencies disseminated their reports and the terrorist attack, the security forces were constrained from going on the offensive. Instead of taking pre-emptive action to hunt down the terrorists, they had to adopt a defensive posture and wait for the latter to strike first. All that the intelligence agencies could do in this situation was to list the likely attack scenarios (which they did), and urge the security forces to 'maintain a higher level of vigil'. With neither the intelligence agencies nor the security forces able to procure additional details of terrorist plans, the attack could not be stopped.

Overcoming Terrorist Counterintelligence

Agencies such as the IB and R&AW are bureaucratic institutions that are built to operate on a lengthy timescale. Their primary function is to collect information of long-term or 'strategic' value. This means that their products are rarely time-sensitive, while those required for the prevention of terrorist attacks are by definition, extremely time-sensitive. The security forces alone can produce such operational-grade information, through gathering intelligence whilst out in the field.[104]

Intelligence *Collection* versus Intelligence *Gathering*

The difference between intelligence 'collection' and intelligence 'gathering' is that the former is a national-level function carried out in a planned manner by professional agencies such as the IB and R&AW in complete secrecy. The latter, on the other hand, is a local function performed in an ad hoc manner by units of the security forces. It has both overt and covert components.[105]

Intelligence gathering plays a key role in undermining the effectiveness of terrorist counterintelligence. Its output depends on prisoner interrogations, paid informers, unpaid informants, document seizures and field-level communications interception. It allows for the rapid development of strategic intelligence into tactical intelligence. Furthermore, this output, when passed up to the level of national-intelligence agencies, forms a crucial component of the raw data that goes into strategic analysis. Thus, the quality of strategic intelligence is always partly dependent on the quality of tactical intelligence.[106]

Offensive Action Vital to Penetrate Terrorist Counterintelligence

In the short-term, even a highly determined effort by national-intelligence agencies cannot break through strong terrorist-counterintelligence systems. Intelligence gathering through offensive use of security forces thus becomes a vital adjunct to intelligence collection. This was amply demonstrated in the months prior to Operation Bluestar, the June 1984 army assault on the Golden Temple, in the city of Amritsar.

Contrary to popular belief, the IB in 1983–84 actually did a very good job of tracking the stockpiling of arms by Khalistani terrorists within the Temple complex.[107] Its sources reported in considerable detail on the modus operandi of the terrorists' suppliers, who were based in Pakistan.[108] While the agency could provide such strategic information, which was not time-sensitive, it faced a much bigger challenge in trying to obtain real-time information from within the Temple.[109] After 11 undercover policemen were detected by the terrorists and tortured to death, other sources just focused on survival.[110] Informational flows dried up, not because there were no intelligence assets within the Temple, but because they could not run the risk of contacting their handlers.[111]

Eventually, it took a division-level assault by the army, backed up with tanks and artillery, to break the counterintelligence ring that the terrorists had created around the Golden Temple.[112] A Sikh officer, who did a pre-operational reconnaissance of the Temple in mufti, confirmed that the terrorists' vigilance had made spying almost suicidal.[113] Following the assault, which took place on the night of 5–6 June 1984, the army seized all documentation that had been maintained by the terrorists. The total quantity of the material captured amounted to two truckloads. Consisting mostly of personal diaries and financial records, the material helped identify those in the Punjab government who were secretly supporting the Khalistani terrorists.[114] Until then, this information had eluded the IB.

Long-term Benefits of Intelligence Collection by National Agencies

When speedy analysis and dissemination is not a priority, national intelligence agencies can render invaluable support to their consumers. Over a period of roughly a year (1983–84), Indian intelligence succeeded in infiltrating Khalistani training camps in Pakistan. R&AW compiled a detailed report in 1984 of the ISI's involvement in Punjab, much of which was subsequently verified during interrogations of captured terrorists. Meanwhile, IB assets were dispatched across the border to acquire details of terrorist plans.[115] These agents reported back that ISI operatives were advising the Khalistanis to carry out massacres of Hindus in Punjab.[116] Their information was crucial in helping the Indian government fashion a counterterrorist response that placed high priority on preventing Hindu–Sikh communal violence. By learning of the ISI/Khalistanis' larger objective and working to frustrate this, New Delhi was able to avoid being manoeuvred into a position where Sikh alienation from India would increase.[117]

Intelligence efforts to identify the strategic drivers behind Sikh separatism also dispelled the notion that Pakistan's military dictatorship wanted to improve bilateral relations.[118] For years, Islamabad had been advocating the idea of an Indo–Pakistani 'no war pact'. Its purpose in doing so was to narrow New Delhi's policy options in responding to its proxy war in Punjab. As long as ISI involvement in the Khalistan movement remained unproven, Indian politicians were receptive to the idea. However, as evidence of Pakistani support for anti-Indian terrorism started to mount, a discernible change of mood took hold in Delhi. On 11 July 1984, India permanently broke off negotiations on the farcical 'no war pact' and the 'friendship treaty' that had also been proposed.[119]

Indian agents continued to infiltrate ISI training camps for Khalistani terrorists until March 1995, because of lax security. The highest returns from these operations came between 1992 and 1995, when Khalistani groups turned to the Sikh diaspora in the West in search of new recruits. Many Sikh youths from Europe and North America travelled to Pakistan for arms training. Upon completion, these youths simply returned to their home countries. Not only did they refuse to go into action against Indian targets, but many also subsequently briefed Indian Intelligence about their experiences. Fed up with being used as an adventure-tourism agency by thrill seekers, the ISI tightened vetting procedures for Khalistani recruits. After March 1995, it demanded that all Sikh trainees surrender their passports upon arrival in Pakistan. Moreover, they were required to provide information on close family members, so that the agency could wield leverage over them if they tried to back out of terrorist attacks against India. With this regime in place, it became much harder for R&AW to acquire information on the ISI's training programs for Khalistani groups.[120]

Role of Intelligence Agencies in Undermining Terrorist Counterintelligence

In order to undermine terrorist counterintelligence, Indian intelligence agencies create conditions whereby local-security forces can penetrate terrorist groups at their own level, without always taking recourse to offensive action. Thus, while intelligence gathering retains an overt component, covert methods can also be employed under the right circumstances.[121] Since covert intelligence gathering (principally, recruitment of informers) interferes less with the daily lives of non-combatants than overt measures (house searches, census-taking etc.), its use represents a more sophisticated counterterrorist policy.[122] A balance can thus be achieved between strategic and tactical intelligence, with the former remaining a national-level responsibility and the latter being a local-level one.

Criminalisation of Terrorism in Punjab

Of the three terrorist movements studied in this book, the one with the weakest counterintelligence defence was the Sikh separatist movement. Right from the early 1980s, the concept of an independent Sikh state received little popular support (although as individuals, the terrorists themselves enjoyed initial public sympathy). Moreover, their operational security was steadily undermined as a result of progressive factionalism and criminalisation, which hijacked the movement.[123] Finally, their cross-border mobility was severely hampered by improvements in border-policing infrastructure. It was only in their readiness to eliminate potential informers (and indeed, anyone who defied them) that the terrorists enjoyed a long-term counterintelligence advantage.

Credit goes to the IB for gradually weakening the Khalistanis' operational security through a sustained campaign of high-level bribery.[124] The agency bought off senior functionaries in the Khalistan movement. By floating its own pseudo-terrorist groups around 'domesticated' Khalistani ideologues, the IB diluted the political content of the movement.[125] Gradually, the manpower base of Sikh separatist groups was widened from the upper caste (Jats), to include all castes. With this change in recruitment patterns came a change in the character of violence. Terrorist actions were no longer inspired by ideals of political rebellion, but were simply gang murders. Rape of Jat Sikh women by lower-caste terrorists and abductions for ransom became commonplace, contributing to the government's efforts to discredit the movement.[126]

Criminalisation of the Khalistan movement led to a complete loss of support from the Sikh peasantry, while factionalism prevented the ISI from gaining control over it.[127] The Pakistani agency itself had started the process of splitting terrorist groups into extremist and ultra-extremist factions in 1986.[128] It hoped that by doing so, it could thwart New Delhi's efforts to bring about a negotiated peace settlement in Punjab. This was a serious miscalculation. All the IB had to do thereafter was accelerate this trend, to the point where not even the ISI could prevent the Khalistan movement from descending into internecine warfare.[129] When the ISI subsequently sought to reintroduce a sense of political unity and organisational discipline into the Khalistani groups, it was too late. Senior terrorist leaders had sensed that the separatist movement had slipped out of their control and began to negotiate with the Indian government for their personal safety.

One the most important coups achieved by the IB was the infiltration of the so-called 'Panthic Committee' – an apex body set up to coordinate all Khalistani terrorist activity in Punjab. Using long-term deep penetration agents, the IB fractured the unity of the Committee, eventually leading to the creation of four rival Panthic Committees. Each of these claimed the exclusive right to lead the people of Khalistan to glorious 'liberation' and denounced all the other committees as fraudulent. Internecine warfare led to large amounts of intelligence, both strategic and tactical, flowing to the Punjab Police and the IB. This situation was singularly engineered by the IB's operations directorate, as part of a program of strategic counter-subversion. The program aimed to combat terrorism not on an event-specific basis, but as a long-term problem requiring a long-term solution. The deep cover agents used had long gestation periods while they steadily and unobtrusively climbed the ranks of terrorist groups, eventually entering the highest decision-making echelons.

Factionalism between Indigenous and Foreign Terrorism in Jammu and Kashmir

Less than a decade later, similar methods did not produce the same level of success in the state of Jammu and Kashmir, partly because the ISI had learnt the right lessons and kept a tighter control over terrorism in Kashmir.[130] One innovation of the ISI was in introducing foreign mercenaries into the region to offset any attempt by Indian Intelligence to co-opt indigenous separatist groups; this tactic worked. All that the R&AW and the IB could do was monitor relations between indigenous Kashmiri separatist groups and the mercenaries, and exploit any rifts that appeared.[131] This the agencies have tried to do, with limited results.

During the mid 1990s the IB floated a pro-negotiations faction within the indigenous separatist movement. Led by four reformed terrorist leaders, this faction failed to have any impact.[132] A more successful effort in 2000 led to a two-week ceasefire between the Indian government and the Hizb-ul Mujahiddin – the largest terrorist group in Jammu and Kashmir. The Hizb, dominated by ethnic Kashmiris, was relatively moderate compared to mercenary-dominated organisations like the Lashkar-e-Toiba (LeT) and Harkat-ul Mujahiddin. Alarmed at the prospect of the Hizb leadership compromising with New Delhi, the ISI pressured it to abrogate the ceasefire arrangement. Although this peace initiative failed, it firmly established that the ISI and mercenary groups like LeT would act as spoilers even if the indigenous Kashmiri separatists showed willingness to compromise.

Counterterrorist policy in Jammu and Kashmir was thus framed accordingly: while locally-recruited terrorists were to be shown leniency if captured, foreign terrorists could expect no mercy.[133] This approach by the Indian government went some way in weakening the resolve of the indigenous Kashmiri separatists while also poisoning their ties with Pakistan. For instance, the Hizb-ul Mujahiddin split into hard line and moderate factions in 2000, as a direct result of the abortive ceasefire. When Abdul Majid Dar, the leader of the moderate faction, was assassinated by hardliners in 2003, his supporters promptly retaliated by leaking information to Indian security forces. Their tip-offs led to the elimination of senior pro-Pakistan Hizb activists, further polarising the indigenous separatist movement.[134]

Bridging the Gap between Strategic and Tactical Intelligence

Strategic intelligence identifies the long-term influences acting on a terrorist movement, while tactical intelligence merely identifies targets for the security forces to eliminate. Both types of intelligence activity occur in independent spheres, which are kept apart by strong terrorist counterintelligence. The four pillars discussed earlier in this chapter ensure that national intelligence agencies rarely produce 'actionable' information. They create a trade-off between the timeliness and specificity of intelligence reports.[135] Either national agencies issue vague warnings and leave it to the security forces to develop these further, or they wait for their sources to bring in specific information. By that time, it is usually too late to prevent a terrorist attack from occurring.

The only way to go from predicting terrorist activities to preventing them is to empower security forces to meet their own informational requirements. With aggressive follow-up on leads provided by national agencies, security forces can fill in knowledge gaps in the larger intelligence canvas. While doing so however, they need to avoid strengthening public sympathy for the terrorists. Therefore, the government can only crack down on terrorist groups once the latter have already been discredited among their supporters. Bringing this state of events to pass is the objective of strategic intelligence.

Use of Strategic Intelligence for Conflict Resolution

Here, the IB's counterinsurgency doctrine plays a key role. With its emphasis on first understanding the larger strategic context before moving on to minor details, it helps Indian policy makers identify the principal drivers behind a terrorist movement. These key influences are then worked upon and gradually manipulated. The idea is to ensure that they cannot represent a cohesive, long-term threat to Indian internal security. In effect, the primary use to which Indian intelligence agencies are put while fighting terrorism is not prevention of terrorist attacks, but long-term trend analysis.

It was through such analysis that the intelligence agencies were able to identify the power centres of the Mizo rebellion, and neutralise them. A small number of highly skilled intelligence officers gained the confidence of rebel leaders and studied their personal weaknesses.[136] One by one, the latter were bought off by the Indian government. Eventually, the remaining rebels decided to make a virtue of necessity and their overall chief, Pu Laldenga, signed a peace settlement with the Indian government in 1986.[137]

While the counterinsurgency success in Mizoram was an impressive achievement for Indian Intelligence, there was a problem with it: terrorist attacks had continued to occur even as peace talks were on. Despite enjoying the R&AW's hospitality for a number of years in New Delhi, Laldenga used terrorism to strengthen his bargaining position.[138] Even at that time, the Indian government found this unpalatable, and given the virulence of subsequent terrorist movements in Punjab and Kashmir, it is highly unlikely that the Mizoram model can be replicated.[139] In realisation of this, the IB in 2006 prepared a new doctrine for internal security management, which took into account the fanaticism of Pakistani jihadist groups. Known as the Counter-Terror Doctrine (CTD), it signified a distinct shift in official tolerance levels of political violence.[140]

Political Timidity Weakens Indian Counterterrorist Performance

As per the IB's proposals, terrorist groups henceforth would have to agree to suspend violent activities before negotiations could begin. The act of 'terrorism' itself would be designated a federal crime. This would allow the central law enforcement and intelligence agencies free rein to pursue terrorist suspects anywhere in India, without waiting for permission from the concerned state governments. Furthermore, the agency urged the central government to introduce new anti-terrorism legislation, in order to match the challenges of the worsening threat environment.[141] Wary of endorsing a tough counter-terrorism posture that could be criticised by civil libertarians, Prime Minister Manmohan Singh declined the IB's request.[142]

In the next four chapters, we shall see how political inconsistency and partisanship, as well as ground-level operational constraints, have prevented Indian decision makers from acting on ample intelligence warnings. Reluctance, as well as inability to sanction offensive action by the security forces, has thus allowed the knowledge gaps between strategic and tactical intelligence to flourish.

CHAPTER 3

A LACK OF POLITICAL CONSISTENCY

Despite being plagued by terrorism problems over the years, Indian policy makers have not adopted a consistently offensive counterterrorist posture. The policy shifts by different Indian governments in directing counterterrorist efforts are outlined in this chapter. To a large extent, these inconsistencies appear to have been prompted by partisan politics. Thus, even when intelligence agencies accurately predict the emergence of a long-term security threat, the political leadership can still fail to prevent its actualisation. To forestall an anticipated escalation or expansion of terrorist activity, governments need to allow security forces to fight for intelligence. That is something Indian policy makers are loath to do.

The 'Strategy of Pygmies'

The government's reluctance stems from a politically-motivated need to downplay the magnitude of a terrorist threat because it reflects adversely on their own popularity.[1] The highly divisive nature of Indian politics further compounds this problem. Ajit Doval, a former DIB who is widely regarded as the intelligence community's leading strategic thinker, describes them as:

> ... the politics of dividing the electorate – and society – on as many issues as possible until one's own tiny segment becomes the biggest. It is the strategy of pygmies. It has to be substituted by the strategy of consolidation and integration of as many segments and interest groups

> as possible till one acquires the critical mass that gives legitimacy to rule.[2]

Many Indian politicians (particularly at the state level) find this too cumbersome a business. Rather than address complex problems in the quality of governance, they prefer to accentuate existing inter-caste, inter-ethnic and inter-religious tensions with a view to creating captive vote banks. Where such tensions do not exist they are manufactured through radicalisation of local political discourse.[3] All three terrorist movements examined in this book were initially products of vote-bank politics. Once they had acquired a certain critical mass, it was easy for the Pakistani Inter Services Intelligence (ISI) to get involved. In each case, the groundwork for political subversion was done not by the disaffected groups or even the ISI, but by supposedly 'mainstream' political parties.

This chapter deals with three case studies. Let us first examine the nature of Indian counterterrorist policy vis-à-vis Sikh separatism. We find that, though the problem began in 1981, until 1992 the central government in New Delhi had no consistent approach to resolve it. Hard and soft policies of varying degrees were tried on an ad hoc basis, and it was only after they had failed that a more consistent offensive policy was adopted.

On the other hand, the case of Jammu and Kashmir appears to be exceptional. Indian counterterrorist policy here has been remarkably consistent since the outbreak of large-scale violence in 1990. This is due to the sheer obviousness of Pakistani support for terrorist groups, which has hardened Indian political resolve and helped focus counterterrorist efforts.[4] Consequently, Islamabad's shenanigans have got nowhere.

However, with regard to the third and most recent case study, Pan-Islamist jihadism, there has been no overarching policy that links counterterrorist efforts. These efforts have remained largely disjointed. From a comparison of these three case studies, it can be deduced that offensive action by security forces is critical to counterterrorism success, since it helps penetrate terrorist counterintelligence. Only when strategic intelligence is followed by offensive operations can 'actionable' information be obtained.

Case Study I: Emergence of Militancy in Punjab

The Khalistan movement that created havoc in Punjab between 1981 and 1993 is the first example of a politically-instigated militancy mutating into a national-security threat. Its origins lay in mid 1978, a period described by contemporary writers as the 'summer of discontent'.[5] The national Emergency had recently been lifted. For the first time in 30 years, the Congress (I) had been voted out of power in New Delhi. Almost coincidentally, political agitations and small-scale terrorist violence suddenly exploded across India.[6] One such incident in Punjab brought to prominence a charismatic village preacher called Jarnail Singh Bhindranwale. He was a Congress acolyte, whose subsequent meteoric rise in politics was fuelled by covert support from the party's leadership in Punjab.[7]

At that time, the ruling party in the state was the Akali Dal, which commanded support from 80 per cent of the Sikh electorate. The Akalis were also in a political alliance with the Congress (I)'s opponents – the new central government in Delhi. To eat into the Akali vote bank, the Congress (I) floated a politico–religious group called the Dal Khalsa.[8] Its unofficial patron was a Congressman named Zail Singh who later became the home minister and then the president of India.[9] With the tacit support of the party leadership, Bhindranwale was projected as more militant about protecting Sikh interests than even the Akali Dal. He launched tirades against corruption of the Sikh faith. When the Congress (I) returned to power in 1980, he built up his credentials as a local strongman, surrounded himself with armed bodyguards and even raised a private militia.[10]

Indira Gandhi's victory in the 1980 general elections caused dismay in the Pakistani military establishment. The latter regarded her as the prime mover behind the vivisection of Pakistan in 1971. Within a few months of her return to power, the ISI began to provide covert paramilitary training to Dal Khalsa cadres. The Pakistani agency also activated contacts with radical elements among the Sikh diaspora in Europe and North America.[11] These foreign-based Sikhs, together with their ISI handlers, were the original founding fathers of the Khalistan movement, and not Sikh leaders within Punjab itself. With Bhindranwale gradually militarising Punjabi politics however, there was a convergence of interests among the foreign and domestic forces of subversion. Now the stage for separatist rebellion was set.

In the first act of a macabre drama, assassinations of prominent Hindus took place. Intelligence officers posted in the state monitored the worsening communal situation and warned that it could lead to massive clashes.[12] Their assessments took note of the fact that there were roughly 500,000 legal and illegal firearms in Punjab, and that many ex-soldiers were attracted to Bhindranwale's ultra-rightist ideology.[13] Taking note of these warnings, the Home Ministry in New Delhi ordered surveillance of the World Sikh Convention, which was to be held in the city of Amritsar in July 1981. Its concern was fuelled by the fact that prominent Khalistani ideologues based in the UK and US were scheduled to attend.[14]

From this point onwards, one can detect a counter-current emerging in New Delhi's policy response to Sikh separatism. On the one hand, Mrs Gandhi declared that she would not permit secessionist ideology to gain momentum in a sensitive border state like Punjab.[15] On the other hand, directives from the Indian Home Ministry (now headed by none other than Zail Singh) to the Punjab government were ignored, allegedly at the intervention of Zail Singh loyalists in the state. No action was taken on IB advisories for the Punjab Police to arrest or put under surveillance suspected Khalistani activists. One of those earmarked for special attention was a Dal Khalsa activist named Gajinder Singh. Despite being on the watch list, he was able to hijack an Indian Airlines flight to Pakistan in September 1981.[16]

Between 1981 and 1984, terrorist violence in Punjab raged unimpeded owing to lack of policy directives to the security forces. While the Punjab Police's intelligence wing was well-informed about developments pertaining to separatist activity, they could do little more than watch from the sidelines.[17] To respond, they needed to dismantle Bhindranwale's network, which was slowly but surely starting to get enmeshed with that of the ISI. Permission to do this was denied. A key intelligence question facing the IB and R&AW therefore was: how deep was ISI involvement with his group?

Answering this was not easy. The ISI-run training camps for Khalistani terrorists were located across the border in Pakistan. ISI operatives were very careful about screening potential recruits, in order to weed out Indian agents. All that Indian agencies could do was monitor cross-border movements of Khalistani activists, and put them under close surveillance upon their return.[18] Not until the Pakistani agency escalated its support for Sikh separatist terrorism in 1983–84 (thus loosening its vetting procedures) was Indian intelligence able to penetrate the training camps. In the interim, it focused on monitoring Bhindranwale, who by now was ensconced in the Golden Temple – the holiest of Sikh shrines, located in the city of Amritsar.

Operation Bluestar and After

The first half of 1984 saw a spike in terrorist activity across Punjab. Over the previous three years, 101 people had died from terrorist attacks. Fatalities from January to May 1984 were in the vicinity of 300.[19] It was clear to IB analysts that the state was slipping into anarchy, and that a parallel government had been set up in the Golden Temple.[20] There were disturbing reports that ISI operatives had established a presence within the Temple, and were advising Bhindranwale on how to prepare for an insurrection.[21] Under these circumstances, the Indian Army was ordered to launch counterterrorist operations against Bhindranwale and his cohorts across Punjab. The main operation, which centred on the Golden Temple, was codenamed Bluestar. At the time, it was the 'biggest and most significant counter-terrorist action undertaken anywhere in the world'.[22] Up to 70,000 soldiers fanned out across Punjab within 24 hours. The massive deployment was only partly for action at the Golden Temple: most of the troops were used to prevent Hindu–Sikh communal violence.

Opinion has since remained divided as to whether Operation Bluestar was a 'success' or a 'failure'. While it neutralised Bhindranwale and his entire group, it also angered Sikhs both within and outside India. Resentment over the army's action led to Indira Gandhi's assassination in October 1984, as well as the assassination of a retired army chief in 1986. Since Mrs Gandhi's murder in turn led to a pogrom of Sikhs across northern India, which further alienated the community, there are grounds for arguing that the operation eventually proved counterproductive.[23] Yet, this is not the view of some intelligence analysts and senior government officials. They argue that the army's counterterrorist offensive halted Punjab's descent into complete lawlessness, and that with the elimination of Bhindranwale, the Khalistan movement lost its local infrastructure. Any terrorist violence that took place after June 1984 was lacking in overall strategic direction since there was no central leadership.[24]

What is certainly true is that figures for non-combatant casualties, which had skyrocketed during the first half of 1984, suddenly came down after the army offensive. The assault on the Temple allowed the police to build up intelligence dossiers on 1,100 Khalistani terrorists in Punjab, of whom 53 were killed and another 600 arrested by November 1984.[25] Also, it bought New Delhi more than a year's time to hammer out a compromise agreement with the Akali Dal, which was calculated to assuage Sikh sentiments. Under the July 1985 Punjab Accord (also called the Rajiv–Longowal Accord), elections were held to the state Assembly in September 1985; the Akalis won. By conceding power to a regionalist party, Prime Minister Rajiv Gandhi hoped to deny Sikh separatism a popular support base.

Second Escalation of Violence

The Punjab Accord hinged on a quid pro quo: while the Akali Dal government would mount an offensive against Sikh separatist groups, New Delhi would arbitrate in favour of Punjab in inter-state disputes. This basically meant that Punjab's long-standing grievances over water-sharing arrangements and land disputes with its neighbouring states were to be redressed by the central government. By doing so, New Delhi would strengthen the credibility of the Akali government among Sikh voters, and provide political space for a locally-led counterterrorist offensive.

Such designs could not be translated into reality for two reasons: the Akali Dal did not share New Delhi's belief that a 'hard' counterterrorist posture was necessary, and New Delhi itself reneged on the Accord. Rajiv Gandhi's Congress (I) party realised that ruling in favour of Punjab would lose it votes in Hindu-majority states. Making such concessions without any substantial counterterrorist successes to show for it would have been bad electoral strategy.[26] A stalemate ensued, with the central government and the state government each waiting for the other to fulfill its part of the bargain first.

Meanwhile, Khalistani groups adjusted to the new security situation that prevailed after Operation Bluestar. Despite losing their bases in Punjab, they could count on continued covert support from Pakistan, which henceforth acted as a safe haven. Moreover, their ranks were swelled by a number of rural Sikh youths fleeing from the Indian security forces. From 1986 onwards, violence levels in Punjab rose again, as the terrorists took advantage of the state government's reluctance to proactively hunt them down.

This reluctance stemmed primarily from the well-intentioned but mistaken beliefs of the Akali Dal leadership, particularly state chief minister Surjit Singh Barnala. Barnala viewed the Khalistan movement as entirely a product of the Congress (I)'s initial support for Bhindranwale. With Bhindranwale dead and a popularly elected government in power, it seemed reasonable to suppose that many Khalistani activists would abjure violence if allowed to repent.[27] Operating from this assumption, Barnala made efforts to reach out to the separatists by ordering the release of 2,000 suspected militants from police custody. Not only that, he also provided government jobs to a number of these individuals, including with the Punjab Police. His generosity proved misplaced, as the vast majority of the released extremists went straight back to supporting the separatist movement. Police intelligence officers had warned that this would happen, but were ignored.[28]

From 1985 onwards, right up to 1992, counterterrorist policy in Punjab flip-flopped between coercion and conciliation. Political leaders of different hues ruled in both New Delhi and the state, and there was no general agreement on how terrorism was to be combated. Rising terrorist violence eventually led to the dismissal of Barnala's government in May 1987, and direct federal rule was imposed from Delhi. Thereafter, the state governor of Punjab was responsible for implementing the central government's directives. Even this did not lead to an improvement in the security situation, owing to frequent personnel changes in the security bureaucracy.

Between 1983 and 1990, the Punjab civil administration saw eight governors, seven chief secretaries and six police chiefs assume office only to be removed shortly thereafter by New Delhi. One journalist lamented at the time that governance in Punjab had become 'a cruel game of musical chairs while the need of the hour is consistency'.[29] In the absence of clear-cut policy directives, security forces action against the Khalistanis became reactive and episodic, occurring mostly in response to terrorist incidents. Occasionally, offensive action would be undertaken to track down and neutralise a senior terrorist leader, but that was all. There was no comprehensive assault on the separatist movement.

Operation Black Thunder and a Fresh Offensive Against Terrorism

A partial respite came in mid 1988. For several months, intelligence reports had indicated that the Khalistanis were once again stockpiling weaponry in the Golden Temple. Their intention was apparently to provoke a security-forces assault. Mindful of the resentment that Operation Bluestar had caused among Sikhs, this time New Delhi made sure that intelligence preparation of the battlefield was total. Specialist assault troops were sent in to reconnoitre the Temple while wearing police uniforms.[30] IB operatives infiltrated Khalistani gangs active within the complex, providing detailed information as to their intentions. Other operatives were tasked to report on the mood among the rural Sikh population, so that New Delhi could predict the fall-out of any storming operation.[31]

Roughly four months of preparation and planning went into what became known as Operation Black Thunder. Over the course of a week in May 1988, soldiers of the National Security Guards (NSG, a Special Forces formation raised in 1985) cleared the Golden Temple. They suffered no fatalities. Terrorist gangs that had publicly vowed to fight until they attained collective martyrdom surrendered tamely instead. Following this success, the Punjab

Police launched an all-out attack on separatist gangs that were spread out across the state. Within months, violence against non-combatants declined noticeably.

The counterterrorist offensive of 1988 was driven significantly by intelligence reports. It had become clear to Indian policy makers that Pakistani aid to the Khalistan movement was substantial.[32] The scale of the ISI's training programme and the frequency with which terrorists crossed the Indo–Pakistani border demanded a systemic response. For the first time, serious efforts were made to fence the border and improve infrastructure for patrolling in forward areas.[33] Even this action was taken belatedly, in response to a series of terrorist bombings across northern India. The bombings had been predicted by intelligence agencies, but their warnings were not followed up. Alarmed by the operational reach of Khalistani groups, the central government finally approved offensive operations by the Punjab Police.[34]

Third and Final Escalation of Violence

By end-1989, the Khalistan movement was nearing collapse. A twist of political fate intervened to give it another two years' life. In general elections to the Indian Parliament, the Congress (I) suffered a surprise defeat and lost power to a loose alliance of opposition parties, led by VP Singh. The new National Front government, which took office in December 1989, immediately went about undoing all that had been achieved since 1988. Already, electoral considerations had led the Congress to slow down its counterterrorist offensive in Punjab.[35] The National Front went further, and made conciliatory gestures towards the terrorists.

It issued unwritten orders for the release of hardened terrorists and for the security forces to suspend offensive operations.[36] As part of an initiative to win hearts and minds, it distanced itself from the Punjab Police, which had acquired a reputation for brutality. Prime minister VP Singh believed that the Khalistanis were 'misguided youth' who needed to be given a chance to rejoin the national mainstream. In this, he exhibited the same view that had characterized the Akali government of Surjit Singh Barnala: that terrorism in Punjab had been kept alive solely by the Congress (I)'s policies. As long as the National Front discontinued these policies, violence levels would automatically subside.[37] Offensive operations against separatist groups were thus halted and the government repeatedly asserted that it was prepared to compromise with the separatists. Emboldened, the latter intensified their activities and the effects were immediately apparent. Violence levels doubled within just the first six weeks of the National Front government taking power.[38] For roughly another two years, VP Singh and his prime ministerial successor Chandra Shekhar searched in vain for a negotiated settlement to the Punjab problem.

The Final Crackdown

Finally, in late 1991, a consistent policy of offensive action was adopted. Yet another general election had returned the Congress (I) to power in New Delhi. Punjab was still under federal rule, and elections to the state Assembly were scheduled for February 1992. To protect political candidates as well as the electorate, a massive security blanket was imposed across the state. Acting in aid of civil authority, the Indian Army poured in troops under an operation codenamed Rakshak II. Due to the combined firepower and manpower deployed for protective security, the terrorists sensibly decided to lie low until the election was over.

They were in for a nasty shock: the Assembly elections were won by the Punjab unit of Congress (I). Ever since Indira Gandhi's assassination, this party had been irreconcilably hostile to the Sikh separatist movement.[39] Upon coming to power, its members adopted a no-concessions policy towards the Khalistanis at the level of both the central and state government. After February 1992, efforts to bring about a negotiated settlement were abandoned for good and the Punjab Police was ordered to relentlessly hunt down the terrorists. Over the next 18 months, the Khalistan movement suffered devastating losses under the weight a combined army–police offensive. Non-combatant fatalities fell precipitously as the terrorists were forced to concentrate on sheer physical survival. They never got a chance to regroup and rebuild their subversive networks within Punjab, with the result that peace finally returned to the state.

Right from the start of Khalistani terrorism in the early 1980s, the central government had vacillated between coercion and conciliation. In the process, it cancelled out the positive effects of both, while allowing the Khalistanis a breathing space to recover from previous setbacks. Only after partisan politics had played themselves out, and all options for a negotiated settlement had been tried and found wanting, did New Delhi opt to eradicate Sikh separatism by force. By that time (1991–92), the security situation in Punjab had deteriorated to the point where deployment of the military became essential. Policy makers realised that counterterrorism in the state needed to be unrelentingly offensive if it was to yield lasting results. Their

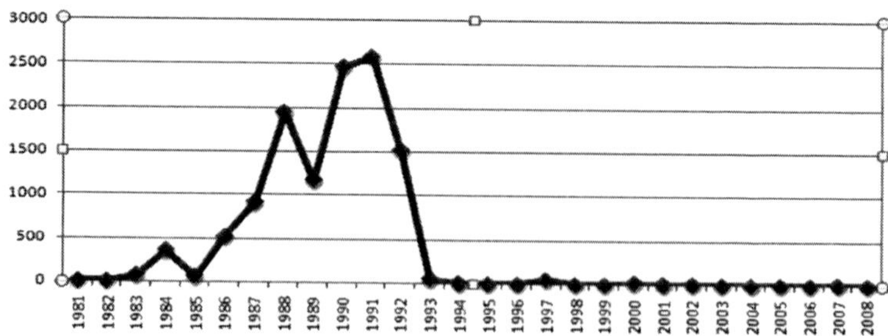

Graph 1 Yearly noncombatant fatalities in Punjab, 1981–2010

acknowledgement of this reality marked the first step towards defeating Sikh separatist terrorism.

Case Study II: Rebellion Breaks out in Jammu and Kashmir

The emergence of a separatist movement in Jammu and Kashmir had always been assessed as a possibility by Indian intelligence.[40] Since 1947, Pakistan had pursued an interventionist policy in the state. That year, Pakistan had fought its first war with India, and seized a third of the state's territory – subsequently known in India as Pakistan Occupied Kashmir. Having fought off two attempts by Pakistan to seize the remaining territory militarily, the Indian security establishment was alert to the risk of foreign subversion.[41]

What it was not prepared for was the possibility of subversion from within. From the mid 1970s, political parties in Kashmir had been resorting to an increasingly communal rhetoric in order to capture vote banks.[42] Their agendas inadvertently dovetailed with that of the ISI, which was seeking to Islamise the Kashmir Valley so as to create a sense of religious solidarity with Pakistan. The ISI hoped that, by replacing the liberal strand of Sufi Islam followed in Kashmir with fundamentalist Wahhabi ideology, it could prepare conditions for a popular revolt against New Delhi.[43]

This aim received a strong boost in 1987, when elections were held to the Jammu and Kashmir State Legislative Assembly. The ruling National Conference (NC) party rigged the polls in substantial measure. Ironically, it need not have bothered since it probably would still have won an overall majority.[44] However, the blatancy with which rigging was done alienated supporters of the opposition Muslim United Front (MUF) alliance. The MUF was a grouping of 13 parties, spearheaded by the Islamist Jamaat-e-Islami (JeI). Its activists convinced themselves that they had been cheated of an electoral victory.

Resentment over what the Islamists called a 'stolen election' contributed to the emergence of Kashmiri separatist terrorism. At a meeting in April 1987, detained MUF activists decided to embark on an armed struggle against the NC and its national-level partner, the Congress (I).[45] This in effect set the Islamists on a collision course not only with the state government in Srinagar, but also with the central government in New Delhi. In February 1988, eight MUF activists crossed the Line of Control (LoC) and entered Pakistan Occupied Kashmir to receive arms training from the Pakistani authorities.[46] They were the first of thousands to do so.

Although the IB was pre occupied with the worsening security situation in Punjab, it monitored the growing Islamisation of the Kashmir Valley.[47] The Jammu and Kashmir Police was constantly intercepting arms shipments being smuggled into India from Pakistan.[48] The sheer frequency of these interceptions was sufficient to warn of an impending revolt.[49] Moreover, between 1988 and 1990, intelligence operatives tracked the movements of Kashmiri youths who left their homes to cross the LoC for paramilitary training.[50] They also noticed the sudden emergence of new ISI training camps along the LoC, and accurately assessed that Pakistan was preparing to foment an insurrection in Jammu and Kashmir.[51]

The agency's reports on these developments were ignored both by the Home Ministry in Delhi and by the state government of Jammu and Kashmir. The former was focused on the Punjab situation and had no resources to spare for formulating a policy response.[52] The latter was unwilling to accept the scale of popular alienation that had been engendered by the rigged 1987 elections. Although intelligence reports from the state police supplemented the IB's warnings, these too were ignored.[53] The National Conference and the Congress (I) had been alliance partners in the Assembly elections, which gave both a vested interest in understating the problem.

Second Phase of the Rebellion

Beginning in 1988, there were sporadic acts of terrorism. These gave way to a massive upsurge of militancy in December 1989. That month, cadres of the Jammu and Kashmir Liberation Front (JKLF – at the time the biggest separatist organisation in the state) kidnapped the daughter of the then Indian

Home Minister, Mufti Mohammed Saeed. The newly-elected National Front government swiftly acceded to their demands and released five top terrorists in exchange for the hostage. Kashmiris jubilated, believing that New Delhi's humiliation would lead to an automatic collapse of Indian rule. Their illusions were sustained in part by Pakistani propaganda, which broadcast television footage of the collapse of Eastern European dictatorships. Kashmiris were urged to similarly rise and overthrow their 'oppressors'.[54]

While these events were unfolding, the state government led by chief minister Farooq Abdullah remained frozen in inaction. By now Abdullah had some idea of the extent of his unpopularity, and was reluctant to order a crack down on the separatists. Like Surjit Singh Barnala in Punjab, he was caught in a political trap, where taking offensive action against terrorism would make him look like New Delhi's puppet.[55] Eventually, his indecision led to the induction of a hawkish state governor, Jagmohan Malhotra, and the imposition of federal rule over Jammu and Kashmir on 19 January 1990.[56]

Malhotra ordered an immediate offensive against the terrorists. He subsequently claimed that this move had been motivated by an intelligence report. The report said that the JKLF was planning to declare independence from India on 26 January 1990. The date was significant, as 26 January is celebrated yearly as India's Republic Day. According to the information, the JKLF intended to invite foreign media representatives to its independence ceremony, where the formation of a new People's Republic of Independent Kashmir would be announced.[57]

Cross-Border Terrorism

Malhotra's crackdown had psychological significance. Raids on terrorist strongholds led to the arrest of 125 hardcore militants and the elimination of another 200. Although these neutralisations by themselves did not change the situation for the better, they slowed the pace of political transformation in the Kashmir Valley.[58] The demonstration of force had conveyed that New Delhi was not willing to let Jammu and Kashmir go without a fight. Lack of popular support for the government did not automatically mean that Indian forces would withdraw from the region. It just meant that they would have to go looking for intelligence, instead of waiting for the local populace to bring it to them. Faced with an intensive assault on their urban infrastructure, the terrorists retreated towards the relative safety of rural areas. This created a strategic stalemate.

Hitherto, popular support for separatism had been confined to the towns in the Kashmir Valley. The rural populace had remained aloof from radical politics. Owing to its indifference, terrorist groups began forcibly recruiting youths and extorting money from villagers. On the one hand, this was a positive development for the security forces, since the terrorists grew isolated from their indigenous support base. On the other hand, the poor quality of intelligence coverage in rural areas meant that mopping up operations could not be launched. Any further offensive action risked causing collateral damage to non-combatants, which would be counterproductive.[59] An impasse resulted, with the security forces being in firm possession of population centres while the separatists ran amuck in the countryside.

There was another complication: Pakistan's involvement in supporting terrorism in Kashmir was of a far greater magnitude than its covert interference in Punjab. For example, during 1989 it was estimated that the Pakistani agency had supplied roughly 500 Kalashnikov assault rifles to Khalistani groups. In contrast, during the nine months between January and September 1990, 600 such rifles were seized from captured or killed Kashmiri separatists. Security forces estimated that this figure accounted for only 10–20 per cent of the total terrorist arsenal in Jammu and Kashmir.[60]

Given the importance of Pakistan Occupied Kashmir as a staging area and a safe haven for Kashmiri separatist groups, counterterrorism became a matter of improving border security. Together with operations in the rural hinterland, anti-infiltration measures along the Line of Control became the crucial strategic ingredient for controlling violence levels. At such a stage, the Indian Army was called out to man border outposts along the LoC and interdict terrorist movements. From April 1990, it became the main counterterrorist force in Jammu and Kashmir, with the local police and the central government's myriad paramilitary forces fulfilling a distinctly subordinate role.

It was during this period that New Delhi defined its counterterrorist objective in Jammu and Kashmir: preservation of the territorial integrity of India through all means, including war. Intelligence reports of the time suggested that Islamabad was considering an escalation of its support for the separatist movement. There was speculation that the Pakistan army might launch an overt military incursion into the Indian-administered portion of the state.[61] On 10 April 1990, prime minister VP Singh shared his assessment of the Pakistani game plan with Indian parliamentarians. According to Singh, Islamabad hoped to continue supporting the rebellion without provoking an all-out war. Unless the situation on the ground was enormously favourable, Pakistani troops would not intervene militarily in support of the separatists. Singh sent a blunt message to his Pakistani counterpart, warning against any foolhardy adventurism: 'You won't get away with it. The cost will be heavy. And we have the capacity to inflict this cost.' He also stated that India was prepared to match Pakistani threats of nuclear escalation, if any were made.[62]

This uncharacteristically tough response set the tone for subsequent counterterrorist efforts in Kashmir. Although New Delhi's posture was strategically defensive, in that it only aimed to retain territory already under Indian control, it was prepared to be tactically offensive in the process. On the basis of interrogation reports as well as voluntary disclosures by Kashmiri terrorists, it is now known that Singh's interpretation of Pakistani strategy was accurate.[63] ISI handlers told their Kashmiri trainees that Pakistan would not come militarily to their aid unless local conditions were overwhelmingly favourable.[64] Since mid 1990 therefore, all that India has had to do is follow a counterterrorist policy that denied Islamabad this favourable mix of conditions.[65]

A War of Attrition

During the first half of the 1990s, New Delhi developed a four-pronged counterterrorist strategy for the Jammu and Kashmir situation. It would: 1) wage a war of attrition in rural parts of the state to wear down separatist groups, 2) interdict reinforcements as they tried to cross the LoC, 3) revitalise the local economy and 4) launch a diplomatic offensive to expose Pakistani support for terrorism.[66] The first two aspects of this strategy were military/security initiatives while the latter two were economic and diplomatic, respectively. Prime Minister Narasimha Rao's Congress (I) government, which was in power for a full five-year term between 1991 and 1996, crafted this approach. By the end of his tenure, Rao had set in place a counterterrorist policy that has largely been followed by subsequent central governments.

As a result of relentless attrition of indigenous separatist groups, by 1996 violence levels in the state had dropped steeply. That year, elections to the Indian parliament yielded a 40 per cent voter turnout in Jammu and Kashmir – twice the figure that intelligence agencies had predicted.[67] The voter turnout indicated that, except for certain pockets in the state, anti-Indian sentiment was waning. Emboldened by this development, the central government decided to allow Assembly elections. Jammu and Kashmir had been under federal rule for over six years; the restoration of popular governance in September 1996 went a long way towards reducing sympathy for the separatists.

Since 1993, the ISI had been alarmed at the attritional strategy pursued by New Delhi. It became clear to Pakistani decision makers that India had enough manpower reserves to bleed the indigenous Kashmiri separatists dry. All that Indian security forces had to do was rotate their personnel through the state with monotonous regularity while the original crop of separatist militants shrunk each year. To forestall this eventuality, the ISI began to push in foreign mercenaries from Pakistan and other Muslim countries under the guise of a pan-Islamic jihad.[68] They were helped in this endeavour by the rise of the Taliban in Afghanistan.

Indian intelligence had predicted such a move. As early as 1988, the R&AW had established that events in Kashmir were connected to the status of the Soviet–Afghan War.[69] Pakistan's support for the Afghan resistance fighters (or mujahiddin) had given Islamabad enormous influence over Afghan affairs, not to mention a vast pool of CIA-supplied light weaponry, which could be used against India. Once the Soviets withdrew from Afghanistan, the ISI had continued to expand its influence in the country. According to an R&AW assessment, up to 500 ISI personnel were operating in Afghanistan by 1992, gradually strengthening Islamabad's control over the anarchic country. Analysts warned that if this trend continued, there would be an influx of religious militants from Afghanistan into Kashmir, via Pakistan.[70]

This is exactly what happened. Although authoritative figures on infiltration rates are hard to come by, most commentators agree that the nature of terrorism in Kashmir began to change from 1995. While there was still a very large indigenous component to the separatist movement, a growing proportion of those infiltrating across the LoC were mercenaries of foreign origin. These individuals dominated violence in the state during the late 1990s, carrying out attacks far out of proportion to their numbers. From 1998, they massacred Hindus living in remote rural parts of Jammu and Kashmir.

Since the mercenaries were experienced fighters, with many having served in Afghanistan, they were adequately prepared for the privations of jihad in rural areas. Unlike their much softer Kashmiri counterparts, Pakistani and Afghan terrorists based themselves in high mountain ranges and thickly forested areas.[71] By living off the land, they minimised contact with the local population and thus reduced intelligence leaks. The central government, now led by the hard-line Bharatiya Janata Party (BJP), was hard pressed to develop a strategic response to the rapidly spreading terrorist activity across the state.

The 'Proactive Policy'

In May 1998, under the aegis of the then home minister Lal Krishna Advani, the BJP intensified the attritional campaign in Jammu and Kashmir. Only a broad outline of its 'Proactive Policy' will be considered here; a more detailed discussion will follow in subsequent chapters. Basically, the security forces were ordered to launch large-scale sweeps of the inaccessible upper heights of mountain ranges. The objective was to deny mercenaries safe havens within the state. A second option, of going in hot pursuit of the terrorists into Pakistan Occupied Kashmir, was also discussed. Both initiatives were difficult to implement: the first option because of scarce operational resources, the second was impeded by Pakistan's nuclear deterrent.

The Pakistani nuclear tests of May 1998 had led Islamabad to believe that it was now immune from any Indian military threat.[72] Thus emboldened, the Pakistan army launched an incursion into Indian-controlled territory. Over the winter of 1998–1999, Pakistani troops and mercenaries crossed the LoC into the Kargil sector of Jammu and Kashmir. They were detected only in May 1999, and repulsed after heavy fighting.

Even as the intruders were retreating, Indian intelligence agencies predicted an escalation of terrorist activity within the state.[73] Their forecasts were based on comparative analyses of infiltration figures: whereas in 1997 and 1998, 634 and 918 terrorists respectively entered the state from Pakistan Occupied Kashmir, the figure for a five-month period in mid-1999 was 1,119.[74] Communication intercepts also revealed that the ISI was instructing all terrorists in the state (roughly 2,000 in the Kashmir Valley and another 1000 in the Jammu region) to intensify their attacks. In addition to tracking troop movements and sabotaging vital infrastructure, the terrorists were told to hit 'soft' targets so as to tie down the security forces. Furthermore, estimates available with the Jammu and Kashmir Police suggested that another 3,000 terrorists were in Pakistan Occupied Kashmir, waiting to cross the Line of Control.[75]

Intelligence assessments in the post-Kargil period projected that foreign mercenaries would henceforth dominate violence in Jammu and Kashmir, marginalising the indigenous Kashmiri separatists.[76] Relations between indigenous terrorists and foreign ones had deteriorated sharply during the Crisis, when the former did not escalate their operations to aid Pakistani forces fighting in Kargil.[77] Sceptical of the performance of Kashmiri terrorist groups, the ISI began favouring mercenary organisations like the Lashkar-e-Toiba (LeT) and Harkat-ul-Mujahiddin (HuM). As a result of the ISI's discriminatory policy, a rift soon developed between the Hizb-ul Mujahiddin, the largest indigenous terrorist group, and the LeT and HuM.

At this juncture (late 1999–early 2000) Indian intelligence began to implement a third facet of Advani's Proactive Policy: splitting the indigenous terrorists from the foreign ones. First, a concerted offensive was launched against Kashmiri separatist groups, with the objective of imposing a sense of war-weariness upon their members. During the first half of 2000, 180 of the 321 terrorists killed in Jammu and Kashmir were local Kashmiris, with the majority being from the Hizb. So severe was security forces' pressure upon the group that senior Hizb members stopped claiming association with it so as to avoid being eliminated.[78] While this was going on, intelligence operatives moved in to sharpen ideological and personal differences within the indigenous separatist movement. They started by playing on the resentment, which many junior and intermediate-ranking Hizb cadres felt at the ISI's treatment of them.[79]

Subsequently, another point of convergence came about when a combined LeT–Hizb squad massacred 35 Sikhs in the village of Chittisinghpura in March 2000. Since US president Bill Clinton was on a scheduled visit to India at the time, intelligence analysts had predicted such an attack months in advance.[80] From past experience, they knew that the ISI was looking to attract international attention to the separatist movement through executing well-timed 'spectaculars'. However, they did not expect that the terrorists would target Sikhs, who had hitherto been left untouched by separatist violence in Kashmir. Although this incident was undoubtedly a failure of tactical intelligence, it still served a larger strategic purpose. Recriminations broke out among senior Hizb leaders over the wisdom of such attacks, which were tarnishing the group's image.[81] Intelligence officers built on this intra-organisational friction within the Hizb.

On 24 July 2000, the group's most senior commander in Jammu and Kashmir, Abdul Majid Dar, declared a three-month ceasefire with Indian security forces. Yusuf Shah, the Hizb's supremo who was based in Pakistan Occupied Kashmir, endorsed Dar's declaration. Within two weeks, Shah succumbed to pressure from the ISI and announced that he was terminating the ceasefire. Yet, significantly, the Hizb-ul Mujahiddin did not then go on to intensify its operations in the state as would logically have been expected. Behind-the-scenes negotiations continued between Indian Intelligence and senior Hizb leaders for a resumption of the ceasefire. While these talks were on, local-level commanders on both sides were issued orders not to provoke each other.[82]

To further widen the rift between indigenous separatists and foreign mercenaries, the central government announced a unilateral ceasefire of its own. Starting 19 November 2000, to mark the Muslim festive season of Ramzan, security forces commanders were instructed not to launch offensive operations in Jammu and Kashmir.[83] Initially intended to last just one month, the ceasefire was eventually extended over six months. During this period, security forces adopted a completely defensive posture, thus encouraging terrorist groups to grow bolder. The latter began to venture out of their rural strongholds and move into densely populated areas.[84]

By all accounts, this lack of offensive action led to an increase in terrorist attacks, as seen in the chart produced below:

ATTACKS DURING THE 2000–2001 RAMZAN CEASEFIRE

Category	Before Cease-Fire	During Cease-Fire
Violent incidents	1,120	1,530
Suicide attacks	4	17
Civilians killed	381	404
Security/troops killed	134	208
Political workers killed	11	36
Informers killed	62	156
Militants killed	950	506
Militants injured	186	295

Source: *India Today*[436]

A Partial Success

Since there was an increase in non-combatant fatalities, one could argue that the central government's ceasefire of 2000–2001 was a failure of strategic intelligence.[85] Yet, there is a strong counter-argument: certainly, the principal beneficiaries of the ongoing ceasefire were the terrorists, but upon its termination this dynamic was reversed. The split between the moderates and the hardliners in the Hizb-ul Mujahiddin widened as a result of the government's initiative. It culminated in an internecine war between the two factions. This would not have happened had the security forces resumed their offensive against indigenous separatist groups after the Hizb's abortive ceasefire of July 2000. In-fighting within the Hizb also divided the local support structure that foreign mercenaries had hitherto relied on. Groups like the LeT henceforth had to raise their own infrastructure to operate independently in the state.[86] While doing so, they provided the IB with an opportunity to infiltrate their ranks – a mistake which led to a number of terrorist networks being destroyed in 2003.[87]

While the 'Proactive Policy' failed to deliver upon its objective of preventing terrorist attacks, it did make progress towards another objective – weakening the nexus between foreign and indigenous terrorists in Jammu and Kashmir. The dividends of this effort started to manifest themselves during 2002. Faced with a hostile international mood post 9/11, Pakistani mercenaries in the state were unable to merge with local terrorist groups. Meanwhile, New Delhi's long-standing diplomatic offensive had forced Islamabad to disassociate itself from non-Kashmiri militants, or risk international censure. Under the ISI's instructions, mercenary groups suspended cross-border movements during May-June 2002, which was the best time of year to infiltrate across the LoC (due to the thawing of snow-covered passes).[88] They thus lost a window of opportunity to build up a massive operational presence in Jammu and Kashmir, and disrupt the Assembly elections which were due to be held the following September. New Delhi took advantage of the brief respite and, under international supervision, held a free and fair election that further delegitimised the separatist movement. Since then, violence in the state has declined steadily, and by 2008, yearly non-combatant fatalities had fallen to their lowest since 1988.

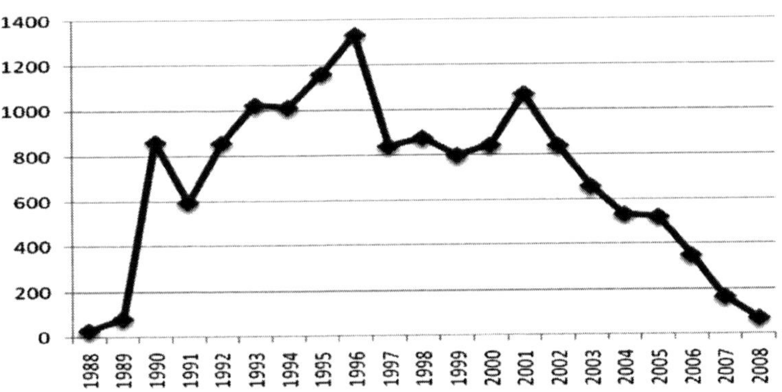

Graph 2 Yearly non-combatant fatalities in Jammu and Kashmir, 1988–2010

Indian counterterrorism in the state of Jammu and Kashmir was politicised to a far lesser extent than in Punjab. Barring the early years of the Kashmiri separatist rebellion (1987–1990), counterterrorist policy has been primarily guided by professional security considerations. Although this policy has not been as offensive as it might have been, there is still an underlying consistency in New Delhi's approach to Kashmiri separatism.

Since the early 1990s, successive central governments have sought to win over moderate factions of the separatist movement, while engaging hardliners in a war of attrition. Negotiations with Pakistan remain an anathema owing to the presence of several hundred Pakistani mercenaries in Kashmir. As long as India feels it is being blackmailed into talks by state-sponsored terrorism, the possibility of an amicable settlement with Islamabad remains non-existent. Meanwhile, the war of attrition continues, gradually turning in favour of the side possessing better resources ie. India.

Case Study III: Communalisation and Pan-Islamist Jihadism

On close study, one characteristic of Indian counterterrorist efforts against pan-Islamist jihadism becomes apparent – they are not guided by a policy framework. Unlike the fight against Sikh and Kashmiri separatism, counterterrorism in the Indian heartland has no overarching 'war aim'. In Punjab as well as Jammu and Kashmir, it was understood that the purpose of defeating terrorism was to preserve the territorial integrity of India. Since the strategic objectives of pan-Islamist groups are obscure, the political establishment and security forces do not have a clear perception of the threat.

Until the November 2008 Mumbai attacks, conventional wisdom in Delhi held that pan-Islamist groups attacking Indian citizens were not sponsored by the Pakistani state.[89] As late as two months before the attacks, intelligence officials told the author that Pakistan could not be blamed for all jihadist activity within India. They brushed aside reminders that the ISI had long aspired to expand its covert war beyond Kashmir and hit major Indian cities using local proxies. Instead, they harped on the then-fashionable argument that pan-Islamist jihadism had grown into a Frankenstein's Monster and so posed a common threat to both India and Pakistan. Only after the Mumbai attacks did these same officials conclude that jihadism directed at India was in fact still a state-sponsored threat.

Here, in this book, jihadism in India is viewed as mostly originating from Pakistani territory. The book conceptualises Pan-Islamist terrorism as a continuation of the ISI's Plan K2M, which was developed in 1991.[90] Rather than being a religious/ideological movement by non-state actors, such terrorism is at least partially calibrated by elements within the Pakistani security establishment.

Support for this view comes from the empirical fact that after the Mumbai attacks, there was a sudden drop in jihadist activity within India. The capture of one of the attackers, who was later confirmed to be a Pakistani national, exposed ongoing collusion between the Pakistani army and the ISI on the one hand, and the jihadist groups on the other. As a result of the international opprobrium thus generated, the ISI reduced its paramilitary operations against India for over a year. Only after foreign governments began to press for a resumption of Indo–Pakistani peace talks, did jihadist attacks slowly resume. The first such attack was a bombing in the south Indian city of Pune on 13 February 2010, which killed 17 people.

Furthermore, over the course of three decades, neither the R&AW nor the IB have found evidence of jihadist funding to the main schools of Islamic teaching in India.[91] Though foreign donations to these establishments have been under scrutiny since at least the early 1980s, it appears thus far that their sponsors are entirely above board. Unlike their Pakistani counterparts, most Indian *madrassas* (Islamic seminaries) thus far appear to serve as mainly centres of democratic mobilisation rather than as radical hubs.[92]

For instance, leaders of the orthodox Islamist Deobandi sect (one of the most influential in South Asia) continue to exercise their right of free speech responsibly, despite occasional provocations from ultra-right Hindu groups. While blaming the United States and Israel for the plight of Muslims globally, these leaders have never shown disloyalty to India.[93] Jihadist propaganda does not originate from them, but from a handful of ISI-funded *madrassas* that have come up in border areas adjoining Bangladesh and Nepal.[94]

The book's argument is also bolstered by the assessment of US-based scholar Mohammed Ayoob, who suggests that there are two strains of pan-Islamist jihadism in Pakistan.[95] One, dominated by Al Qaeda, is focused on attacking American interests. The other, nurtured by the ISI, operates primarily in Kashmir and the Indian heartland. Though there are strong ideological links between the two strains, the operational infrastructures that sustain their respective activities are distinct and separate. Global jihadism in Pakistan does not enjoy institutionalised state backing, but those groups that are focused on targeting India do.

Indian politicians are well aware that the ISI is the main sponsor of pan-Islamist jihadism in India. However, they choose to remain silent on the issue due to the fragile state of inter-communal relations between Hindus and Muslims. These tensions have been magnified by partisan politics, indulged by mainstream political parties.

For example, in 1986, the Congress (I) government of Rajiv Gandhi decided to throw open a controversial mosque in the central Indian town of Ayodhya to the Hindus. Its motive was to eat into the right-wing Bharatiya Janata Party's vote bank. The Ayodhya mosque was allegedly built during the fifteenth century over the ruins of a Hindu temple; since 1947, it had been a point of controversy with Hindu fundamentalists. This action of the Congress was countered by the BJP, who subsequently demanded that the mosque be demolished and replaced with a temple. Matters came to a head on 6 December 1992, when several thousand Hindu extremists converged on Ayodhya and tore down the mosque. Their action led to communal riots across India, and radicalised large pockets of the Muslim population.[96]

Plan K2M

The December 1992 riots gave the ISI an opportunity to revitalise its K2M (Khalistan, Kashmir and Muslim Militancy) operation. Just months previously, on 16 July 1992, the Pakistani agency had suffered a serious setback when IB operatives tracked down a senior Khalistani terrorist called Manjit Singh.[97] This man was responsible for coordinating shipments of arms and explosives to Khalistani cells in western India. For the ISI, he was a crucial link in the emerging nexus between Sikh and Kashmiri terrorist groups. Manjit Singh's interrogation led the police to large arms caches that had been stored in the state of Gujarat. The police also gained invaluable data on the ISI's plans to create a pan-Indian terrorist network. The targets of this network were strategic: they included a nuclear installation and economic assets such as oil refineries and the Madras Stock Exchange.[98] Although Indian intelligence had known of the existence of Plan K2M since at least May 1992, Manjit Singh provided specific details about it.[99]

A manhunt was launched to apprehend members of the K2M network. Interrogations of captured terrorists led to the arrest of a top ISI operative, Mohammed Sakib Abdul Nachan. Also arrested was Tahir Jamal, the secretary-general of the Student's Islamic Movement of India (SIMI). SIMI had been formed in April 1977, funded by generous donations received from Arab states like Libya and Saudi Arabia. These countries were initially hoping only to contain the influence of Hindu fundamentalist organisations, but during the late 1980s SIMI developed more aggressive aims of its own.[100] Many of its members were active in the numerous plots set up under Plan K2M, the most ambitious of which was a conspiracy to bomb the Bhabha Atomic Research Centre (BARC), located at Trombay in western India.[101]

On 20 January 1993, the R&AW disseminated a report about Pakistani threats to Indian internal security. The report stated that the ISI had rebuilt its subversive infrastructure within the country, and was still seeking to bomb the Bhabha atomic plant.[102] It also mentioned the ISI's motive: to engineer a major nuclear incident and thereby discredit the safety measures surrounding India's strategic nuclear arsenal. Should the resultant international outcry be powerful enough, Islamabad reasoned, New Delhi might be compelled to roll back or scale down its nuclear program. As a result of this warning, security was tightened at nuclear installations across India.[103] Yet, unknown to Indian Intelligence, the ISI had already switched to a back-up plan: attacking soft targets in India's financial capital, Mumbai.

During the first quarter of 1993, Indian intelligence was gripped by a sense of siege.[104] Priority was given to hardening critical national infrastructure against attack. Sometime in February, according to *India Today* magazine, the Director of the Intelligence Bureau sounded a comprehensive warning on the strategic threat posed by ISI-sponsored terrorism. His note to prime minister Narasimha Rao (correspondence no. 27/DIB/Desp93) asserted: 'India is on the threshold of Muslim militancy'.[105] It mentioned that moderate Indian Muslims were losing ground to religious fanatics, particularly from SIMI. The ISI was meanwhile keenly exploiting the sense of vulnerability among Indian Muslims. It had managed to set up networks of saboteurs across the country. The DIB's letter ended on an ominous note: India needed to diversify its suppliers of oil, so as to minimise its dependence on the Arab world. Goodwill from Islamic countries would be scarce in the years ahead.[106] As the jihadist threat was a long-term one, combating it would require a series of political initiatives. None were forthcoming.

On 12 March 1993, the ISI succeeded in executing eleven simultaneous bomb blasts in Mumbai. In a radical shift from past methods, it relied on hired gangsters and not on ideologically-motivated individuals to execute the attacks. The mafia syndicate that planted the bombs was headed by a Dubai-based smuggler called Dawood Ibrahim. Through his influence with corrupt Indian law enforcement officials and politicians, Ibrahim helped the ISI smuggle roughly seven tons of high explosive and 300 firearms into India.[107] Like other transnational crime organisations, his network had not been considered a national security threat. It had therefore, not been monitored by the IB and R&AW.[108]

Corruption and Conciliation Hamper Counterterrorism

Following the March 1993 blasts, a massive crackdown began on ISI-backed jihadist cells across India. Tactical-intelligence support for these operations came from police surveillance and prisoner interrogations. For instance, in late 1993, police in the south Indian city of Hyderabad detected the involvement of local Muslim gangsters in assassination plots against Hindu politicians. Follow-up on this lead helped dismantle a 32-man network across India, which was carrying out low-intensity terrorist bombings.[109]

An ad hoc effort was also mounted to improve coastal security and interdict any further ISI explosives shipments. Based on intelligence reports that the Kutch coast in Gujarat had become a hub for ISI operatives involved in supporting jihadist cells, the central government ordered intensified patrolling of the area. On 7 April 1993, a meeting of senior bureaucrats in Delhi adopted a three-tiered border security plan that called for greater coordination between local police forces, national intelligence agencies and the Armed Forces. Like all such initiatives however, its effectiveness was dependent upon state-level politicians not interfering in security efforts, and being willing to cease their patronage of smugglers.[110]

The problem with these initiatives was that they were short-term, tactical measures. There was no effort to evolve a long-term response to what was a long-term threat. Since 1993, the ISI has been using trans-border smugglers to push large consignments of military-grade explosive into India. New Delhi's response has been lackadaisical: it has not even enforced its own anti-smuggling laws. Using a network headed by Dawood Ibrahim's second-in-command Mushtaq Ali Memon (now based in Karachi, Pakistan), the ISI continued to pump approximately a ton of high explosives into India every year.[111]

The Pakistani agency's success in setting up sabotage and subversion networks in India is largely due to rampant corruption prevailing in government organisations. Border Security Force (BSF) and Customs officials stationed in forward areas are prepared to ignore smuggling for a price. Meanwhile, Hindu businessmen with access to explosive materials are happy to sell them to anyone.[112] The scale of such racketeering was exposed in a 2006 investigative story by *Outlook* magazine. Reporters travelled to remote towns along the Indo–Bangladesh border and found that military-grade explosives could be purchased for INR 80,000 per kilogram. Local BSF officials were bribed into inactivity whenever a consignment was smuggled in, and some were kept busy by prostitutes employed by the smugglers.[113]

As elsewhere, the Indo–Bangladesh smuggling networks were patronised by local politicians. This meant that gathering intelligence through offensive action was not possible.[114] All that national intelligence agencies could do in this situation was map out the patronage systems and identify which politician was supporting what gang.[115] Despite receiving numerous warnings that Bangladesh was becoming a safe haven and transit route for pan-Islamist jihadists operating from Pakistan, successive central governments failed to enhance border security. Policy recommendations were made in 2000 by a specialist task force on border management, calling for the issuance of identity cards to villagers and better coordination between security forces. These remained unimplemented.[116]

Policy Shifts of State (Provincial) Governments

With successive central governments failing to formulate a clear-cut policy to guide counterterrorist efforts, state governments have also got away with being inconsistent. Operations launched against jihadist terrorism are governed, not by situational requirements and intelligence assessments, but by political considerations. Policy shifts are almost customary with each change of government.

The 1998 Coimbatore Blasts

Such fluctuations led to counterterrorist failure on 14 February 1998, when bombings in the city of Coimbatore in Tamil Nadu state killed 60 people.[117] For years previously, the two most powerful parties in the state, the DMK and the AIADMK, had been on opposite sides of local Hindu–Muslim disputes. While the DMK was perceived to be sympathetic towards Muslims, the AIADMK was thought to favour Hindu nationalism.

Between 1991 and 1996, when the AIADMK was in power in Tamil Nadu, tough police action against jihadists and their supporters prevented terrorist violence. However, Hindu fundamentalist groups held rallies and organised meetings under the benign tolerance of the government. In the process, they aggravated the Muslim minority's sense of alienation and vulnerability. The police meanwhile went about methodically increasing their presence in Muslim-dominated neighbourhoods. Extra checkpoints were set up to interdict the movements of wanted criminals and subversive individuals, as well as of weaponry. Random searches of young Muslims created a strong sense of resentment. Cashing in on this, the DMK promised that it would remove police pickets from Muslim localities if voted to power.[118]

This came to pass in 1996. The DMK promptly fulfilled its promise to the Muslims. A militant organisation called the Al-Umma established its own (highly fundamentalist) code of governance in Muslim neighbourhoods.[119] This organisation held sway in Muslim localities until February 1998, when its cadres carried out the bombings mentioned above.[120] It later emerged that the Tamil Nadu Police intelligence had warned authorities in Coimbatore on 31 January 1998 of the prospect of terrorist attacks.[121] Home minister LK Advani was scheduled to visit the city in February and there were concerns about possible assassination attempts against him. On 12 February, a second note was dispatched to the Coimbatore administration, listing steps to be taken in preparation for the visit. Among its recommendations were pro-active measures such as raiding known jihadist hideouts and searching vehicles in sensitive areas. Neither of these missives had any effect in the prevailing political climate. Despite being forewarned, the local police could not take any action as it would have been inconvenient for the DMK government.[122]

Home-grown Jihadism

The 1998 Coimbatore bombings were locally planned, since the Al-Umma had only a loose ideological connection with the ISI and Pakistani jihadist groups.[123] At the same time, the bombings indicated that terrorism in the Indian heartland was gaining ground. What complicated any counterterrorism effort was the ill-defined nature of the threats. Though there appeared to be a causal link between communal violence and terrorist incidents, radicalisation by ISI-sponsored groups was also on the rise.[124] Under an operation codenamed 'Garland', the agency was attempting to forge a united front of rebellious organisations within India, who could then jointly resist the central government's authority.[125] As part of this effort, it had already recruited Abdul Karim alias 'Tunda', a resident of Uttar Pradesh state. Karim became the Lashkar-e-Toiba's chief of operations in India.[126]

Terrorism in the Indian heartland therefore originated from a combination of domestic politics and foreign (i.e. Pakistani) material support and ideological subversion. Proof of this comes from terrorist incidents that followed the Gujarat Hindu–Muslim riots of 2002. Much expert commentary suggests that SIMI activists were driven to form terrorist groups like the

'Indian Mujahiddin' in order to avenge the riots. This is not borne out by facts. As this chapter has pointed out, SIMI was integral to the execution of the K2M plan from its early stages. The organisation was banned on 27 September 2001, several months prior to the Gujarat riots, on the basis of police reports that its leaders were advocating jihad against India.[127] While the riots might have subsequently strengthened their convictions, they certainly were not the sole cause of jihadist terrorism in India.

Terrorist–Mafia Nexus

As is clear from above, jihadist terrorism is a multi-headed threat, with the ISI serving as a common body. Its components include Indian radicals, Pakistani mercenary groups and transnational crime syndicates. Even without the complicity of Indian Muslims, terrorist attacks can be carried out by Pakistani mercenaries and Indian mobsters. An example is the abortive nexus which was forged in 2002 between Pakistan-based groups and the UAE-based smuggler, Aftab Ansari.

According to the arrangement worked out between Ansari and the Pakistani jihadists, he would provide them shelter and logistics support in India. In exchange, they would put their battle skills to use in helping him dominate the Indian mafia.[128] The deal was discovered in January 2002 when Ansari's men carried out a drive-by shooting on the United States Information Service (USIS) office in Calcutta. This incident brought him to the attention of the Federal Bureau of Investigation. Already under pressure from Washington to clamp down on terrorist fund transfers after 9/11, the UAE authorities extradited Ansari to India.[129]

Indian Intelligence had been closely tracking Ansari's movements and intercepting his emails well before the USIS attack. When investigators learnt that \$100,000 of the total amount used to finance the 9/11 attacks might have originated from Calcutta, his involvement with jihadist groups came under scrutiny.[130] The city was Ansari's main base in India. Accordingly, IB operatives coordinated the operations of six state police forces to launch a Pan-Indian crackdown on the Ansari network. Partly because of this, the perpetrators of the USIS attack were swiftly identified and neutralised.[131]

Despite maintaining a high level of vigilance against jihadist terrorism, the intelligence community was not able to prevent an upsurge of terrorist attacks from 2005 onwards. Its failure in this regard did not stem from underestimation of the threat, but from policy makers' unwillingness to institute a systemic response to it. All that Indian counterterrorism presently relies on to fight pan-Islamist jihadism is the output from national-intelligence agencies. Covert intelligence gathering by local police stations is almost non-existent owing to a lack of resources. The only other alternative: overt intelligence gathering through offensive action, which is politically frowned upon.

It is little wonder then that Indian counterterrorism has fallen into a gap between rhetoric and reality: while politicians rhetorically promise to fight terrorism, in reality they do not or are unable to fulfill these promises.[132]

Summary: The Importance of Threat Recognition

In all the three cases discussed examined above, the ISI and communal tensions are the two common factors. While partisan politics fuelled the emergence of terrorist movements, the ISI sustained them and enhanced their lethality. Yet there was a difference in the effectiveness of counterterrorist measures between the case studies. It can be argued that the difference arose from a tendency to selectively politicise internal-security management and overlook the very real threat of Pakistani support for terrorism.

While combating Khalistani terrorism in Punjab, the central government was slow to formulate a systemic response to the ISI factor. Steps to enhance border security were adopted belatedly, and only in response to large-scale escalation of violence. Not until 1992 did policy shifts cease, with the election of a state government committed to wiping out the Sikh separatist movement. However slow this development was, it still played a crucial role in imparting to the security forces a sense of strategic purpose and gave counterterrorist policy a degree of consistency which had previously been missing.

Counterterrorism in Jammu and Kashmir showed greater consistency and clarity of purpose – the highest among all the three case studies. Although between 1987 and 1990 there was initial confusion about how to stem the progressive deterioration of the security situation, this gave way to a more focused effort by 1990. Part of the reason for this was the swiftness with which New Delhi identified the main driver of militancy – Pakistan – and took measures to contain its influence over the separatist movement. Since the ISI's sponsorship of terrorism was much more blatant than elsewhere, it was also combated more vigorously. With external factors like terrain and nuclear deterrence narrowing its strategic options, the Indian policy making establishment did not politicise counterterrorism to the degree seen in Punjab.[133]

In the case of pan-Islamist jihadism, there appears to be no consistency in counterterrorist efforts. Firstly, there is no agreement on the nature of the threat. Until the 2008 Mumbai attacks, it was seen as an amorphous non-state challenge which could generally be ignored. Since the attacks, Indian politicians have been high on rhetoric but low on action. The Prime Minister in particular, remains unwilling to adopt a confrontational policy towards Pakistan. Many of his advisors are unconvinced about the wisdom of such restraint, arguing that it will only embolden the jihadists and their patrons in the ISI. Owing to continuing differences of opinion at the top-most level of the government, no policy response has yet been formulated to the pan-Islamist threat.

CHAPTER 4

A LACK OF POLITICAL CONSENSUS

Besides political consistency, counterterrorist efforts need political consensus and a unanimous approach to be effective. In a democracy, such efforts can be seriously hampered by non-cooperation from provincial and foreign governments. In the case of Indian counterterrorism initiatives, the threat perception itself differs at the sub-national as well as the international level. This has unfortunately left Indian counterterrorism bereft of offensive power.

In deference to sensitivities over human rights, New Delhi has limited the quantum of force employed against terrorist groups. The result is tangible: counterterrorist operations lack the strategic punch which could uproot the support networks of terrorist groups and deter individuals from joining them. Instead of fearing government power and authority, violent extremists become emboldened to launch more audacious attacks in the knowledge that counter-action will be diffused. By criticising the security forces for alleged human-rights violations through sponsored propaganda groups, they further slow down the pace of offensive operations.

Transnational terrorist networks exploit differing threat perceptions to their advantage. By basing themselves in one region, setting up support structures in another, and carrying out attacks in a third region, these terrorist groups seek to evade pursuit.[1] Overcoming this tactic requires cooperation from both foreign governments and regional-level politicians within India. As we shall see from all the three case studies examined in this book, counterterrorist efforts have suffered from a lack of such cooperation. There is no agreement on the nature and severity of terrorist threats, let alone the means of combating them.

Obtaining political consensus in domestic and international policy making circles is a slow process.[2] In the case of counterterrorism efforts in Punjab, it took 12 years to get local politicians and foreign governments to support the counterterrorist drive. Finally, it was not the central government's persuasive powers that won the day. Rather, the terrorists themselves alienated local and international opinion from their cause. However, in Jammu and Kashmir, an ambiguous international stance on the legitimacy of Pakistani support for terrorism prolonged the conflict. Only after 9/11 did foreign governments pressure Pakistan to tone down its involvement in the state. This produced a partial de-escalation of violence. The fight against pan-Islamist jihadism, however, has foundered on the basis of domestic concerns over minority rights. Furthermore, a nexus between political parties, crime syndicates and terrorist groups allows all three to prosper. In this situation, a domestic consensus on counterterrorism is virtually impossible.

Case Study I: Disagreement Between Akali Dal and New Delhi

The military assault on the Golden Temple in June 1984 is regarded as a watershed event in the history of the Khalistan movement. As violence in Punjab escalated dramatically during the preceding months, Prime Minister Indira Gandhi became convinced of the need to build a consensus across political divisions. The approach was two-pronged: while her son Rajiv handled talks with Akali Dal leaders in the state, the R&AW secretly negotiated with Khalistani activists based abroad.[3]

According to one news report, the decision to storm the Golden Temple was finalised after a meeting between Akali leaders and Mrs Gandhi's senior advisors on 25 May 1984. The R&AW hosted the meeting at a safe house in Delhi.[4] Indira Gandhi meanwhile extensively briefed parliamentary opposition leaders about her intentions. She wanted to win the covert support of the Akali Dal and isolate Bhindranwale politically before the actual assault was launched. Her efforts paid off: the opposition unanimously supported the army's intervention in Punjab, in a display of political unity that had not been seen since the 1971 Indo–Pakistani War.[5]

However, the rushed manner in which Operation Bluestar was executed proved problematic, as the political consensus forged at the top-most level could not be conveyed downwards. Second and third-rung Akali leaders were unaware of the convergence of views between the government and their own seniors in the party. Consequently, none responded positively to overtures by intelligence officers, who attempted to dissuade them from launching agitations against the government. Furthermore, the top leadership of the Akali Dal had been taken into protective custody during the assault and so was incommunicado and/or discredited with the Sikh masses.[6]

The net result of Bluestar was that many if not most Sikhs were left bewildered, angry and humiliated by what they saw as a disproportionate use of force in a holy place. Their alienation provided fertile ground for the Akali victory in the 1985 state Assembly elections. It also introduced a complication: the Akali Dal's approach towards Khalistani terrorism needed to be markedly different from that of the Congress. Eager to build credibility with the Sikh electorate, the party announced that it would 'tackle the terrorists with love'.[7]

In effect, what this outlandish statement meant was that offensive counterterrorist operations were to be halted. As already mentioned in Chapter 3, the 'softly-softly' approach was driven by a genuine belief that harsh governmental action had aggravated the problem. A change of style was necessary in order to soothe the hurt sentiments of the Sikh community. As part of this change, the Akali government in Punjab began to oppose New Delhi's efforts to implement a systemic policy response to the terrorist threat. Coming at a time when evidence of Pakistani covert interference in the state was accumulating, the Akali stance was unhelpful, to say the least.

For instance, the state government was slow to approve a proposal for establishing border outposts manned by the federally controlled Central Bureau of Investigation (CBI). Indian security officials had hoped that this measure would increase the output from interrogation of Khalistani terrorists caught infiltrating Indian borders from Pakistan.[8] Another step that the central government proposed in mid 1986 was to create a 'security belt' along the 2,500 kilometre Indo–Pakistani border. (It needs to be mentioned at that time, the border was demarcated only by short pillars lying in the midst of wheat and sugarcane fields. Khalistani terrorists could literally walk across, while the Indian security forces were legally constrained from pursuing them into Pakistan.)

Akali politicians strongly opposed the 'belt plan', for understandable reasons. Agricultural cultivation in Punjab's border areas continued right up to the zero line (the actual border). Creating a security belt would have involved either resettling large numbers of Punjabi farmers or depriving them of their livelihood.[9] The move would have been politically unpopular and would have lent ammunition to the Akali government's many critics. Lastly, there were concerns that the proposed cordon sanitaire would dilute the authority of the state government. Many saw it as an attempt by Prime Minister Rajiv Gandhi to impose a de facto state of emergency in the border areas, without calling it such.[10]

For the reasons cited above, the Akali Dal resisted the central government's initiatives. Consequently, the security situation in Punjab drifted from bad to worse. Eventually, the central government tired of the Akalis' timidity, and in May 1987 assumed direct responsibility for governing Punjab. With this development, work began in earnest on securing the Indo–Pakistani border. First, identity checks were carried out in all villages lying within five kilometres of the border. After conducting a house-to-house census, the security forces issued identity cards to everyone above 13 years of age. Even short-term visitors, such as migrant workers returning home, had to seek the authorities' permission to move about in the border areas.[11]

Drift in Counterterrorist Policy

Hitherto, the terrorists had been comfortable in the knowledge that the Akali Dal's politics would protect them from a police crackdown. Dismissal of the Akali government in May 1987 meant that they were compelled to seek hideouts in other states.[12] A more aggressive operational posture on the part of the police also improved tactical intelligence, as was evident in the following example. On 1 November 1987, six unidentified terrorists entered a village and shot dead eight inhabitants, besides wounding another eight. Within 30 hours, security forces tracked down the killers and shot four of them dead. One of these was a particularly notorious gunman responsible for several past killings.[13]

Such incidents led the terrorists to intensify their attacks on unprotected targets. Although any extortions or kidnappings for ransom that were carried out by them were ostensibly for the Khalistani cause, these soon assumed a momentum of their own. Abduction, rape and murder of women became frequent. Despite all this, certain Akali politicians attributed the rise in terrorist violence to deniable ie. 'dirty tricks' operations carried out by the security forces.[14] They could afford to condone or overlook the separatists' actions since they no longer held responsibility for governance.

In 1988, the 59th Amendment to the Indian Constitution was introduced. It gave the central government direct and indefinite control over Punjab. This did not endear the central government to local politicians. Without their support it was virtually impossible for counterterrorist efforts to produce lasting results. Both the Akali and some state-level Congress (I) leaders in Punjab were opposed to the expansion of police powers, fearing that these would be abused. Their opposition caused the PM to flip-flop on his Punjab policy. On the one hand, he still attempted to explore avenues for a political solution. On the other, he insisted that substantive concessions were impossible.[15]

This period (1987–1991) was characterised by a drift in counterterrorist policy. However, one marginal party took the initiative to build up a popular consensus against Khalistani terrorism. These were the Naxalites, an ultra-leftist party. They viewed the communalisation of Punjab as advocated by the Khalistanis to be a bigger threat than the Indian government.[16] Accordingly, they fought Sikh separatism on two levels: through mass-mobilisation programmes and through serving as police informers. In the border districts, they played a key role in fostering Hindu–Sikh amity. One village in Amritsar district even became known as '*commredan da pind*' (village of comrades) after local Naxalites took it upon themselves to defend Hindus from terrorist attacks.[17]

Notwithstanding such isolated cases, political views on the severity of the Khalistani threat and the means to combat it remained divergent. Sympathetic elements within the political class of Punjab helped terrorist groups weather substantial losses. Information was occasionally leaked to terrorists about the movements of senior police officers, which allowed the former to mount assassination attempts.[18] Any officer who was actively involved in counterterrorist operations became the target of threats made over the post and telephone. One favourite tactic used by the terrorists was to threaten legal action over false allegations of human-rights violations. Through sympathetic human-rights lobbies and political activists, Khalistani groups would disseminate rumours about massacres of innocents by the police.[19] Their objective in doing so was to break the momentum of counterterrorist efforts.

The terrorists were emboldened by the concern which foreign governments (especially those of the UK, US and Canada) showed on the issue of human rights. Delegations from these countries visited Punjab to ascertain if claims of 'state terror' made by Khalistani spokesmen were true.[20] Such claims extended up to accusing New Delhi of having initiated an anti-Sikh genocide. Initially, the Indian government was on the back foot as it sought to refute these accusations. However, over time it managed to rebuild its credibility with Washington, London and Ottawa and enlist their support for its fight against Sikh separatist terrorism.[21]

A Consensus Slowly Emerges

As Khalistani groups intensified their activities within Punjab, some of their actions damaged their image overseas. The first of these was the assassination of Indira Gandhi in October 1984. Although the US Defense Intelligence Agency (DIA) had assisted the ISI in training Sikh separatists during the early 1980s, such collaboration ended after Mrs Gandhi's assassination.[22] Moreover, British Prime Minister Margaret Thatcher ordered her intelligence agencies to extend full counterterrorist cooperation to the R&AW and IB. Her decision was motivated by disgust at the manner in which some British Sikhs openly celebrated the assassination of Mrs Gandhi, who had been a longtime friend of hers.[23]

The bombing of Air India Flight 185 from Vancouver to Mumbai in June 1985 was also counterproductive to the Khalistani cause. By attacking a civilian aircraft and killing 325 passengers, a majority of whom held Canadian passports, Sikh separatists lost a great deal of international sympathy that they had received following Operation Bluestar. The event led to greater information sharing between the Canadian and Indian governments.[24] All this while, the United States government had been unwilling to share information on Khalistani terrorist groups, for fear of implicating its long-time ally, Pakistan. Now it too cracked down on Sikh extremists within its borders. Pressure was brought to bear upon prominent Khalistani fundraisers to desist from supporting terrorism abroad. Aggressive surveillance by the Federal Bureau of Investigation (FBI) underscored the message.[25]

Within Punjab, the terrorists slowly but surely built up a consensus against themselves by their lack of discipline and indiscriminate targeting strategy. At the urging of the ISI, Khalistani groups eliminated any Sikh politician who was less than unequivocal in his support of Sikh separatism.[26] This meant that virtually the entire political class of Punjab was on the separatists' hit-list.[27] As this became increasingly evident, the IB was able to open covert channels of communication with all political parties in the state and weave them into an informal anti-separatist coalition.[28]

ISI's Crucial Blunder

It took two years for this coalition to deliver a decisive blow to the Khalistan movement. The catalyst was supplied by the ISI, which was directing the terrorists' stance on the electoral process within Punjab. At the behest of the Pakistani agency, terrorist groups grew more strident in their opposition to the holding of Assembly elections. A clear pattern thus emerged that enabled

Indian agencies to predict with considerable certainty that if elections were announced, the separatists would declare a boycott.[29]

Based on this pattern, New Delhi crafted a political strategy. It announced that elections would be held to the Punjab Assembly in February 1992, and then carefully watched the Khalistanis' response. Here, the latter committed a strategic blunder. Upon orders from the ISI, they not only rejected the call to elections, but also attempted to intimidate all factions of the Akali Dal party into observing a boycott. Electronic surveillance of the Akali leadership confirmed that they were being threatened into keeping away from the electoral process.[30] What this meant was that the next largest party in the state – the Congress (I) – would have a free run at the polls. Since the Congress was also in power in New Delhi and was bitterly opposed to the Khalistanis, a perfect mix of conditions was created to forge a counterterrorist consensus.

With a state government in Punjab that was committed to wiping out Sikh separatism, New Delhi was finally able to crackdown on the Khalistan movement. An Akali politician later commented that boycotting the February 1992 election was the best decision his party could have made, under the circumstances. It allowed the Congress to come into power with a comfortable majority and set about crushing the separatist terrorists.[31] Though this was what the Akalis had themselves come to wish for, having been targeted by the latter for years, they felt compelled for purely ideological reasons to take a soft stance against terrorism. By allowing the Congress (I) to romp to power in 1992, the ISI had inadvertently killed off the Khalistan movement. One can speculate that the most likely reason for the Pakistani agency's mistake was that it was too heavily focused on promoting terrorism in Kashmir, and had become distracted from the Punjab situation.[32]

Case Study II: The Kashmir Issue and International Opinion

The attitude of foreign governments has significantly influenced counterterrorist operations in Jammu and Kashmir. While there is a consensus within the Indian political elite about keeping the state within the Indian Union, support for this position is not forthcoming from the international community.[33] The Muslim-dominated Valley of Kashmir, if not the entire state (which constitutes the Valley, along with the Hindu-dominated Jammu region and the Buddhist-dominated Ladakh region), is viewed as disputed territory. This stance has empowered Pakistan to disregard any need for plausible deniability in its support for Kashmiri separatist groups. In effect, since 1990, India and Pakistan have been fighting an undeclared war in Jammu and Kashmir.[34]

New Delhi's strategy has been consistent. It treats Kashmiri separatism as a purely domestic matter, and rejects the notion of Islamabad having any *locus standi* in it. Indian political discourse is prepared to recognise the legitimacy of Kashmiri grievances. It is even willing to compromise with indigenous terrorist groups.[35] There is no such flexibility on the issue of Pakistan's right to sponsor terrorist activity on what India regards as its sovereign territory. This obviously precludes the option of recognising Islamabad as a negotiating partner. Under international pressure however, Indian policy makers have been forced to do just that.

For instance, New Delhi reluctantly began talks with Islamabad in late 1993, in order to get the Pakistanis to drop a UN Resolution on Kashmir that they had planned to table in the General Assembly.[36] Pressure to negotiate with Pakistan was also exerted by Washington. These talks led nowhere, as India was still smarting from the ISI's role in the March 1993 Mumbai blasts and was in no mood to compromise. Yet, the mere fact that it had been compelled to reverse a decades-old policy of refusing to negotiate on Kashmir was a strategic victory for Pakistan.[37] When violence erupted in the Kashmir Valley in 1990, Islamabad had used it as an excuse to seek international endorsement of its support for separatist groups. It launched a propaganda campaign accusing India of massive human-rights violations, thereby seeking to justify its involvement on humanitarian grounds. Thanks to the complementary efforts of groups like Amnesty International, Pakistani propaganda yielded results.[38]

Matters came to a head at Geneva in March 1994, when Pakistan sought revenge for India's efforts to get it labelled a terrorist state after the 1993 Mumbai blasts.[39] It proposed a resolution at the UN High Commissioner for Human Rights conference to have India censured for its counterterrorist practices in Kashmir. Hectic lobbying by Indian diplomats prevented the Pakistani resolution from acquiring any support, whereupon it was ignominiously withdrawn.[40] The episode was assessed, correctly, as more an instance of diplomatic over-reach by Islamabad than a vote of support for New Delhi. A clear warning had still been conveyed that India's human rights record in Kashmir was under close scrutiny, and it would do well to improve on this. Although foreign governments had not been impressed with the manifestly exaggerated charges levelled by Pakistani diplomats at Geneva, their inaction could not be taken for granted.[41]

Henceforth, New Delhi focused on diluting international sympathy for the Kashmiri separatist movement. It did this by revitalising the democratic process in Jammu and Kashmir, as well as disciplining its security forces to better cope with the psychological demands of counterterrorist operations. As in Punjab, the Indian government adopted an 'open door' policy towards foreign delegations, allowing them to visit Kashmir and interact with separatist ideologues. This gesture went a long way towards blunting the offensive thrust of Pakistani propaganda.[42] Reports from their emissaries convinced Western governments that the conflict in Kashmir was not just about human-rights violations. Pakistan's role in supporting terrorist groups also came under critical scrutiny. Gradually, a view began to emerge that the Indians were dealing with a difficult situation as best as they could.[43]

International opinion eventually stabilised at an equilibrium position: it allowed Pakistan to continue sponsoring terrorism, and India to continue combating such terrorism. At no point did foreign governments consider Pakistani involvement in Jammu and Kashmir a violation of Indian sovereignty, which befitted an aggressive response. Thus, New Delhi could not launch a synchronised, high-visibility counterterrorist offensive as it had in Punjab during 1992–93. Instead of cracking down suddenly on separatist groups, the Indian government was forced to adopt a strategy of slowly wearing them down through attrition. Its progress in this direction forced the ISI to induct Pakistani and Afghan mercenaries into the conflict, as mentioned in previous chapters.

1998 Indian Nuclear Tests and the Aftermath

Following the Assembly elections in September 1996, violence levels in Jammu and Kashmir dwindled perceptibly. International attention too shifted away from the conflict. Indian security forces worked unobtrusively to restore a sense of normalcy in urban areas. Their operations drove terrorist groups into the higher mountainous ranges of the state. Penetration by the IB also decimated some of these groups, particularly the Harkat-ul Mujahiddin.[44] All this changed with the Indian nuclear tests of 11 May 1998, and the announcement a week later that henceforth, New Delhi would proactively combat terrorism in Jammu and Kashmir.

Pakistan used the international anger that followed the nuclear tests to ratchet up violence in the state.[45] It hoped that this would refocus attention on the separatist movement. Terrorist gangs massacred Hindus in isolated rural settlements, triggering off an exodus towards urban areas. Under pressure to implement a firm response, Home Minister Lal Krishna Advani announced his Proactive Policy. Its basic tenets were to:

1. Assign the lead role for counterterrorism to the Jammu and Kashmir state government, headed since September 1996 by National Conference leader Farooq Abdullah
2. Widen the incipient differences between indigenous separatist groups and foreign mercenaries, since the latter commanded very little support among the Kashmiris
3. Launch special operations into terrorist strongholds within the state and establish the writ of the government over rural areas, and
4. Hasten developmental activity and thus create positive incentives for Kashmiris to disassociate themselves from separatist groups.[46]

The main problem with the Proactive Policy was that it could not address the pressing need for a massive infusion of additional security forces into Jammu and Kashmir. All that it did was provide existing forces with a more benign political climate to carry out their functions. Thus, the difficulties faced by security personnel on the ground did not change.

The hostile international reaction generated by the nuclear tests meant that India could not pump in more troops to Jammu and Kashmir. Such a move would have provoked US diplomatic intervention in the conflict, which was exactly what Pakistan wanted.[47] Indian embassies were already working hard to quell international criticism of India; it was important not to hinder their efforts. Against this backdrop, the Proactive Policy was actually a *reactive* measure intended to contain an anticipated escalation of terrorist violence.[48]

Kargil and Agra: Pakistan Begins to Over-reach itself

The escalation was not long in coming. However, it did not take the form of terrorist activity. Instead, the Pakistan army intruded into Indian territory and precipitated the Kargil crisis. When the intruders were eventually repulsed in July 1999, the ISI ordered terrorist groups in Jammu and Kashmir to intensify their operations. From 1999 to 2001, non-combatant fatalities from terrorist violence rose steadily, despite the best efforts of Indian security forces. During this period, the international community remained indifferent to Indian accusations against Pakistan. While the US and UK governments were quick to counsel restraint upon New Delhi whenever

Pakistani troops launched attacks across the Line of Control, they failed to condemn these attacks.[49]

It was in this climate of international hostility that in May 2001, Indian Prime Minister Vajpayee invited Pakistani President Musharraf to negotiate on Kashmir. Like the 1993 talks, the gesture may well have been intended purely as a public-relations exercise.[50] During the talks, Advani made an effort to impress upon the Pakistani leader the depth of public concern that was felt in India over cross-border terrorism. Musharraf treated Advani's comments as political rhetoric. He perceived the Indian Home Minister as an uncompromising hawk and Prime Minister Vajpayee as a dove who could be flattered, browbeaten and otherwise manipulated. Musharraf's negotiating strategy was to exploit differences between the two and wrest concessions on Kashmir.

Here, Musharraf came up against a wall. The two Indian leaders differed only in terms of personal style, but their ideological positions were similar. Moreover, the R&AW had briefed them about the Pakistanis' perception of a divided Indian establishment, and so neutralised Musharraf's preferred strategy.[51] The negotiations broke down acrimoniously. Upon his return to Pakistan, Musharraf ordered terrorist groups to resume their activities in Kashmir.[52] (Previously, they had been told to lie low so as to avoid jeopardising the prospects for a negotiated settlement). Indian intelligence had anticipated such a reaction, and counter-measures were put in place to deal with the escalation of violence.

Security-forces commanders along the Line of Control received orders to closely monitor movements for up to 10 kilometres inside Pakistan Occupied Kashmir. They were provided with imagery obtained from aerial and satellite surveillance to help in this task. In addition, battlefield surveillance radars were set up and hand-held thermal imagers distributed to forward positions to help monitor infiltration attempts in real-time.[53] Just two months after the failure of negotiations, the 9/11 attacks happened, forcing Pakistan to modify (though not fundamentally alter) its foreign policy. No longer could its military afford to brazenly support cross-border terrorism, particularly when the Indians were urging the United States to take action against Pakistani jihadist groups.

Operation Parakram: 2001–2002 Military Standoff

On 13 December 2001, five Pakistani gunmen attacked the Indian Parliament. Soon after, New Delhi mobilised its Armed Forces and deployed them along the border in preparation for an invasion of Pakistan. Codenamed Operation Parakram, this deployment is widely perceived to have been a failure since it did not deter Pakistan from continuing to support terrorist activity against India.[54] What it did however was force the international community to finally take sides and serve notice to Islamabad that its covert operations needed to remain below the threshold of plausible deniability. A highly provocative attack on India, such as that launched on 13 December, would only prove counter-productive for Pakistan itself.

Under pressure from Washington, Musharraf announced a host of counterterrorism measures on 12 January 2002. Among these was a ban on the two Pakistani jihadist groups thought responsible for the Indian Parliament attack – the Lashkar-e-Toiba and the Jaish-e-Mohammad (JeM). Shortly thereafter, Indian intelligence intercepted a Pakistani message to these groups that completely negated all that he promised. The message reassured LeT and JeM that the President's speech was only eyewash intended to placate the US government. Pakistan would not abandon the jihadists or curtail their activities.[55]

This information, as well as content analysis of intercepted ISI communications, convinced New Delhi that Islamabad was staging an elaborate farce. While Pakistani diplomats reassured foreign governments that the country was fully committed to fighting terrorism, on the ground Pakistani soldiers continued to advise terrorist groups on operational matters. Partly as a result of their counsel, from 2002 jihadist groups in Jammu and Kashmir switched to using satellite phones to guard against interception by Indian communications intelligence (COMINT).[56]

New Delhi did not know how to respond to Islamabad's duplicity. Ironically, as in Punjab, the solution was supplied by the ISI. On 14 May 2002, a three-man LeT squad believed to be acting on ISI instructions barged into an Indian Army camp in Jammu.[57] Heading for the family quarters, the terrorists gunned down 30 people (mostly the wives and children of soldiers) before being cornered and killed. Tensions rose again, with the Indian Army preparing to launch reprisals along the Line of Control. Once again, the United States pressured Islamabad to stop aiding cross-border terrorism and indicated that this time failure to comply would not be tolerated. With great reluctance, the ISI ordered Pakistani terrorist groups operating in Jammu and Kashmir to cease activity for a few weeks, until international pressure had subsided. As a demonstration of its seriousness, it reduced radio communications with these groups.[58]

COMINT analysis by Indian agencies later confirmed that there had been a 40 per cent drop in cross-border radio traffic from Pakistan Occupied Kashmir to Jammu and Kashmir. Reports from both human and technical sources suggested that the ISI would observe a 'lay off period' for about six weeks, and infiltration levels would come down substantially.[59] In any case, the massed deployment of Indian troops along the LoC had made cross-border movement highly risky.[60] Previously groups of 15 terrorists used to cross over. With intensified Indian patrolling, it became suicidal for more than five terrorists to infiltrate at a time.[61] Around this period, New Delhi began to use Operation Parakram as a massive security screen behind which it could hold Assembly elections in Jammu and Kashmir. The elections were due in any case, but there was a high probability that, given a choice, Islamabad would mobilise its terrorist surrogates to disrupt them. By first holding the election, and only then withdrawing its troops from the border, India managed to ensure an orderly transfer of power in the state.

	1999	2000	2001	2002
May	250	320	179	165
Jun	520	250	313	99
Jul	205	394	354	38*

* Data for July 2002 is up to the 14th of the month.

Estimated terrorist infiltration into Jammu and Kashmir during the period May-July, which is the 'best' season for border crossings due to the thawing of snow-covered valleys near the Line of Control. The relatively low figure for May 2001 was due to a brief ceasefire between Indian and Pakistani forces.[62]

The September 2002 Assembly elections were a significant milestone in the political history of Jammu and Kashmir. Not only were they free and fair, but they also led to the installation of a soft-line government headed by the National Conference's main rival, the People's Democratic Party (PDP). Indigenous separatist groups like the Hizb-ul Mujahiddin had played a crucial role in the PDP's victory, by targeting activists of the National Conference during the polling process. When the PDP came to power, it reciprocated by adopting a soft-line (a so-called 'healing touch') approach to counterterrorism.[63] The new policy of conciliation won international sympathy for India, since New Delhi was no longer seen as a cynical manipulator of Kashmiri politics.

After 2002, Pakistan had to face up to the reality that its interference in Kashmir could not escalate to pre 9/11 levels. This realisation led Islamabad to announce on 23 November 2003 that it would observe a ceasefire along the Line of Control. Henceforth, Pakistani troops would not provide covering fire to terrorists infiltrating into Jammu and Kashmir.[64] Islamabad's gesture significantly enhanced the effectiveness of counter-infiltration operations by the Indian security forces. The latter immediately speeded up construction of a security fence along the LoC, which had been ongoing since 2001. The idea was to impede cross-border movement, as had been done in Punjab, and thereby hasten the pace of attrition against terrorist groups. As we shall see in the next chapter, the anti-infiltration fence became a crucial asset in the war against terrorism within Kashmir.

Case Study III: Counterterrorism against Jihadist Threats Gets Politicised

Unlike the previous two case studies, the jihadist threat to India has been allowed to proliferate because of an enduring lack of both political consistency and consensus. Not even the beginnings of a long-term or 'strategic' response to pan-Islamist militancy can be detected in India. With politicians showing no understanding as to the permanence of the threat, it is unsurprising that they cannot agree on how to combat it. Ironically, such procrastination continues even as developed countries such as the UK and the US, with far less experience of counterterrorism, have excelled at homeland security.

The ISI's Plan K2M had aimed to exploit a crucial weakness in the Indian internal-security system: its inability to overcome divergent political agendas and forge an integrated counterterrorist response. Basically, the fractious politics of India's Third-World-style democracy have eroded the ability of security forces to combat a cross-jurisdictional threat.[65] Moreover, pan-Islamist terrorism has drawn sustenance from the communal hostility between Hindus and Muslims. With Indian politicians themselves perpetuating this hostility, it would be no exaggeration to say that they and the jihadists complement each other's activities.

As proof of this assertion, one need only turn to the Ayodhya Mosque demolition in 1992. There existed at the time, a fundamental split in threat perceptions between the central government and the state government of Uttar Pradesh. Congress (I) headed the former, while the state was headed by the BJP, which sat in the opposition in Parliament. Both parties were to blame for stoking communal tensions, but it was inaction by the state government that eventually permitted Hindu extremists to destroy the mosque. Despite receiving IB warnings that the large numbers of Hindu extremists gathering at Ayodhya were about to turn violent, local officials did not seek help from Delhi.[66] They merely watched as the mosque was torn down, brick by brick.

At any rate, counterterrorist discourse in India has been communalised since 1992, with the BJP accusing Congress of mollycoddling Islamist extremism and itself being accused of terrorising religious minorities. The counterterrorist policies of the two largest political parties are thus driven more by transient electoral considerations than any long-term, apolitical ones. Consequently, internal security has suffered. State governments too have focused on preserving their vote banks rather than combating security threats. In this situation, jihadist groups have exploited the lack of consensus within the Indian political establishment to their own benefit.

For instance, although the state government of West Bengal is aware of jihadist infiltration from Bangladesh, it chooses not to act. The IB and Military Intelligence have frequently warned that illegal Bangladeshi migrants are a potential national-security threat.[67] Yet, no counter-action has been taken as the migrants are constantly absorbed into local electorates by politicians eager to corner their votes. Thus enfranchised, the migrants obtain immunity from deportation. The task of counterterrorism gets hampered, with lack of political approval preventing the police from taking offensive action.[68]

Jihadists from Pakistan and Bangladesh have slipped in along with the migrants. For the present, they are lying low in order to avoid inviting a crackdown. In the meanwhile, West Bengal has become a recruitment base and a launching pad for terrorist operations elsewhere in India.[69] On the rare occasions that police track down potential jihadists, they face an uphill task proving to the courts that these individuals are not Indian nationals, but have actually arrived from across the border. This problem persists because political parties are reluctant to acknowledge it for fear that doing so would cut into their share of the Muslim vote bank.[70]

A Triple Alliance: Politicians, Gangsters and Terrorists

It is also believed that some Indian politicians have links with criminal syndicates that are in turn, linked with terrorist groups.[71] Through this network, the latter are able to buy protection for their cadres. The best example of this is the mafia gang headed by Dawood Ibrahim.[72] Since 1993, it has been the main link between the ISI and pan-Islamist jihadist groups. Though Ibrahim fled to Pakistan after his involvement in the 1993 Mumbai Blasts was exposed, his network in India has survived.[73] Substantial payments to influential patrons have ensured this. While the IB and R&AW have been regularly monitoring these connections, they remain powerless to act.[74] As professional intelligence agencies, they lack arrest powers while the state police forces who have these powers, are prevailed upon not to use them.

Minority Appeasement: An Asset or Hindrance to Counterterrorism?

It is extremely difficult to gauge objectively whether protecting the Muslim minority in India from counterterrorist action is beneficial in the long-term. Certainly, Indian Muslims have shown exemplary loyalty to the country, and have as much right to be protected from police excesses as the majority Hindu community. Only a minuscule number have been receptive to radical propaganda peddled by Pakistan-based jihadist groups like Lashkar-e-Toiba. However, pro-minority politicians have also gone to outrageous extents to constrain the security forces from taking action against the support networks of jihadism. Without such action, strategic intelligence cannot be developed into tactical intelligence since overt-intelligence gathering is rendered impossible.

A good example of this dynamic in play is the 25 August 2007 synchronised bombing of soft targets in the south Indian city of Hyderabad.[75] Just days before, the IB had warned the city police of a terrorist threat.[76] Its note specified that local jihadist cells were awaiting the arrival of senior cadres from Bangladesh before carrying out attacks. As the Hyderabad Police was pre-occupied with monitoring opposition politicians prior to an upcoming election, they ignored the lead.[77] Subsequently, they justified this inaction by arguing that the IB's report was not 'actionable'. While this was true, it was also the case that the police did not make any effort to develop on it independently.

Their lack of action was partly due to interference from local politicians. Those parts of Hyderabad where jihadists were known to operate were strongholds of the Majlis-e-Ittehadul Muslimeen (MIM), an ally of the ruling Congress (I) party. Any police action against Muslims would inevitably generate political pressure to go slow. Moreover, although nobody can suggest that the MIM had any links with jihadist terrorism, both it and the Congress had previously reaped electoral benefits from Hindu–Muslim polarisation in the city.[78] As protectors of minority rights, they felt obligated to constrain the security forces unless the latter could obtain highly specific information about terrorist plots.[79]

This question of 'minority appeasement' is a controversial one. Objectively it appears as though an unapologetic policy of repression might produce good results, albeit at a high cost to both human rights and the government's image.[80] Under an ultra-hardline BJP government, the state of Gujarat not only carried out a pogrom against Muslims in 2002, but also subsequently instilled such fear among the community that there were few takers for retaliatory action. Groups like the LeT found that Gujarati Muslims were terrified of being targeted again, and so did not respond to its recruitment efforts. Meanwhile, local bureaucrats and police officials harassed Muslims to the point of desperation, and were able to create informer networks by selectively easing pressure on those who cooperated.[81] The result: Gujarat remained free from terrorist attacks after 2002, but the state government was reviled for its brutal counterterrorist measures.

Few can support the Gujarat model, particularly since it seems to negate the very ideals of Indian secularism. Discrimination and stigmatisation of Indian Muslims contravenes every notion of civilised political behaviour and is rightly condemned by a large majority of Indians. At the same time, some politicians have done immense damage to Indian internal security under the pretext of safeguarding secular values. Pro-minority parties have made criticism of security forces a virtual industry, thus inadvertently creating safe zones for jihadist groups to operate. One example is the Samajwadi Party, which commands a large following in the state of Uttar Pradesh.[82] Since the early 1990s, the IB had been warning that ISI-backed jihadist cells were keen to carry out attacks in the state. Uttar Pradesh is the most populous province in India, and thus is politically very important.[83] Any crisis that destabilised the political system here would automatically have a pan-Indian impact, as had been proved in the past by the Ayodhya Mosque demolition.

Even so, on certain occasions when the Samajwadi Party formed the state government of Uttar Pradesh, offensive action against jihadist networks was frowned upon.[84] One incident in late 1994 brings out the party's conciliatory position towards religious minorities in stark terms. Acting on an IB report, police officials in the city of Lucknow raided an Islamic theological centre. Their objective was to capture a Kashmiri terrorist who, interrogation reports had indicated, was staying on the campus.[85] Seven students were arrested and released after their antecedents were verified. Eager to avoid offending the Muslim community, state government officials promptly awarded massive financial compensation to the Islamic centre and those who had been arrested. This was not enough for local politicians: they went further and ordered harsh punishments for the policemen who had acted on the IB's information. Unsurprisingly, the message that went out to other police personnel was that it did not pay to work in counterterrorism.[86]

Foreign Cooperation through Intelligence Liaison

Unlike with counterterrorism in Jammu and Kashmir, India has so far had limited cause to complain about foreign governments' attitudes to jihadist attacks on the Indian heartland. (Pakistan is of course, the exception). Growing concerns in the UK and US about Islamist extremism during the late 1990s led to the emergence of information-sharing arrangements with New Delhi.[87] The UK government banned Lashkar-e-Toiba and Jaish-e-Mohammad in 2000, and the US followed suit the following year.[88] The R&AW had in any case established a counterterrorist liaison system with the intelligence services of Egypt and Algeria during 1992–93.[89] Thus, by the turn of the millennium, there was a relatively strong international consensus on the need to combat pan-Islamist jihadism in South Asia.

This occasionally led to preventive successes. For instance, in 2000 the FBI provided initial information about an Al Qaeda threat to the US embassy in Delhi, which was further developed by the IB. Cooperation between the two agencies allowed the Delhi Police to disrupt a conspiracy to car-bomb the embassy.[90] Similarly, in September 2008, US agencies warned the R&AW that terrorists would attempt to land along the Mumbai coast and attack luxury hotels.[91] This input could not be developed further, and so was by itself not sufficient to thwart the attack, which took place on 26 November. Even so, the fact that it was shared and that the US subsequently endorsed India's stand that Pakistani jihadists were responsible, suggests that foreign cooperation is considerable.

Indian officials suspect that the FBI withheld more detailed information about the Mumbai conspiracy from them in order to protect American agents operating in Pakistan.[92] There have also been hints that US counterterrorism officials remain disinterested in breaking up jihadist networks focused on India, unless these networks are also seen as threatening the West.[93] If valid, such complaints only bear out the old adage that 'there might be friendly nations, but no friendly intelligence services'.[94] India has few grounds for complaint if Washington cooperates only partially in counterterrorism, since the US intelligence community does not exist to safeguard Indian interests. Instead, New Delhi should focus on a more proximate problem: the lack of a domestic counterterrorist consensus within India.

Lack of Domestic Consensus: Power Struggle between Central and State Governments

Under India's federal constitution, the maintenance of law and order is a state-government responsibility. Hitherto, terrorism has been classified as a law-and-order problem and not as a national-security threat.[95] This means that the central government cannot assume the lead role in combating it. Without dismissing the elected state government of a terrorism-affected area (as was done in Punjab, as well as Jammu and Kashmir), New Delhi cannot directly supervise counterterrorist efforts. Its role is thus confined to providing advice and financial and informational assistance.[96] As long as terrorist violence was confined to a single state, this constitutional restriction did not pose serious problems to Indian counterterrorism. With the emergence of nation-wide terrorist networks in the 1990s, things changed for the worse.

Dissatisfaction with this disjointed approach led the central government in 2001 to introduce a common anti-terrorist law. Called the Prevention of Terrorism Act (POTA), it was the only such legislation in India. Between 2001 and 2004, POTA was subjected to misuse by local politicians in states that faced no real terrorist threat. Political dissidents and minority groups were harassed.[97] The parliamentary opposition, then headed by Congress (I), promised to repeal the Act if elected to power. When they won the 2004 general elections, they did just that. Thereafter, India lacked a clear-cut law under which terrorist supporters could be prosecuted and the subversive infrastructure of terrorist groups dismantled. The repeal of POTA immensely complicated the task of Indian security forces. Wiretap evidence was deemed inadmissible in court. Confessions made by suspected terrorists to police officers could be retracted. Many terrorists were thus able to walk free because the authorities had no legal means to keep them in custody.[98]

Other measures to tighten surveillance over the Indian population in general, and Muslims in particular, were thwarted on the flimsiest of excuses. Spirited opposition from civil rights groups forced the BJP and later, the Congress (I) governments in New Delhi to go slow on issuing national identity cards to all Indians. A proposal to create a pan-Indian database of citizens' personal details had been made by the Home Ministry in 1999.[99] Only in 2009 did its implementation commence. Similarly, in 2002, the central government sought the cooperation of state governments in regulating the activities of *madrassas*. It recommended that all Islamic seminaries be registered with local authorities, and have their curriculum subjected to governmental scrutiny. However, political parties were worried that such a move would lose them Muslim votes. They promptly scotched the plan.[100]

Summary: Relationship Between Political Consensus and Offensive Counterterrorist Action

In summation, it can be said that without political consensus on the need for offensive security-forces action, terrorist activities cannot be thwarted. Indian intelligence agencies did reasonably well in tracking macro-level trends within the terrorist movements studied. Their strategic intelligence was however insufficient to prevent terrorist groups from escalating attacks. Only when regional politicians and foreign governments endorsed the counterterrorist policy adopted by New Delhi did violence cease in Punjab and fall considerably in Kashmir. Since no such domestic support has been forthcoming on the jihadist threat, the quantum of force employed against it has been minimal.

The problem in Punjab was prolonged over twelve years mainly because political consistency and consensus did not co-exist. Starting in 1981 there were phases when a strong political consensus was wasted, because the central government had no counterterrorist policy. An example is Operation Bluestar in June 1984. Despite having widespread political backing, the central government could not develop a long-term policy response to Pakistani sponsorship of terrorism, and focused only on clearing the Golden Temple of terrorists. At other times, political consistency was not met by a consensus on the part of state-level politicians. Only in 1992 did both consistency and consensus come together in one final burst of security forces action, which resolved the problem within 18 months.[101]

In the case of Kashmir, Pakistan's heavy involvement in sponsoring terrorism, and the willingness of foreign governments to ignore this, has constrained the Indian response. Since international opinion does not favour a military solution to the problem, New Delhi has to periodically go through the motions of negotiating with Islamabad. All the while however it remains committed to finding a solution within the framework of the Indian Constitution. Put simply, the Kashmiri terrorists are expected to renounce separatism and break their links with Pakistan if they are to be recognised as a legitimate negotiating partner. For Pakistan itself, New Delhi has nothing to offer but endless attrition of mercenary groups (i.e., groups that are composed of non-Kashmiri militants).

It was only after 2001, when international pressure forced Pakistan to stop overtly assisting cross-border infiltration across the Line of Control, that Indian security forces were able to bring down violence levels in Jammu and Kashmir. Previously, information sharing between the R&AW and Western intelligence agencies had proved counterproductive, since this information was inevitably passed on to the ISI. (This incidentally constituted a violation of the 'Third Party rule' – a norm according to which intelligence shared bilaterally cannot be passed on to a third party without the originator's consent.) Usually, the data shared by R&AW related to radio frequencies used by the terrorists, infiltration routes through which they would enter Indian territory, and training camps in Pakistan Occupied Kashmir. Alerted to the coverage that Indian intelligence had of its activities, the ISI would promptly change the radio frequencies, relocate terrorist camps and establish new infiltration routes.[102]

With regard to counterterrorist efforts against pan-Islamist jihadism, the Indian political elite can only blame themselves. True, Pakistan's support of groups such as Lashkar-e-Toiba has strengthened the latter's operational capacities to the point where they can launch attacks outside of Kashmir, deep into the Indian heartland. However, such support did not materialise overnight. It was the product of years of close collaboration between the ISI and pan-Islamist terrorists. Indian policy makers failed to prepare for this nexus coming to fruition, especially as violence in Jammu and Kashmir dwindled after 2002. Analysts had predicted at the time that henceforth the Indian heartland would be the jihadists' favoured battleground, as operating in Kashmir was becoming too difficult.[103] Such warnings went unheeded by a political class preoccupied with inter-party bickering.

According to some Indian officials, the expansion of jihadist networks across India has been a direct consequence of coalition politics. Until 1996, the country was governed by a one-party central government – led by the Congress (I). Even if opposition parties were in power in some states the overall balance of power was firmly weighted in favour of New Delhi. The latter could thus enforce its writ upon the state governments if it chose to do so. This began to change from the mid 1990s onward as a period of political instability set in. Two weak coalition governments were formed in New Delhi and toppled by defections, and state governments began to exercise greater autonomy in decision-making. Or rather, they began to exercise the prerogative of *not* making any decisions when these might lose them local votes.[104] As a result, despite having completely stamped out terrorism in Punjab and controlled it in Jammu and Kashmir, the Indian security forces have been unable to contain the spread of jihadist violence throughout India.

CHAPTER 5

A LACK OF OPERATIONAL CAPACITY

The reasons for Indian counterterrorist failures are many and varied. Lack of political consensus, inconsistency in basic approaches, as well as power struggles between the centre and the state governments are of course, major factors that have been plaguing efforts to combat terrorism. However, another significant factor is operational weakness, which is not only a setback in progressive efforts but also imposes a negative cascading effect. In particular, the inability of local police forces to independently follow up on intelligence warnings is partly responsible for Indian counterterrorist failures.

Such inability derives from the poor operational capacity of the police, which encompasses lack of manpower, weaponry, training, communications and transportation facilities. Consequently, the police 'lean' heavily on national intelligence agencies for tactical informational support.[1] Given that even these agencies have finite resources, a situation develops where neither national nor local intelligence producers can keep track of an unfolding terrorist threat. In such situations, the only option is to arrest the growth of the threat by calling out the army and buying time for intelligence capabilities to expand sufficiently.

During this phase of military deployment, the operational capacity of the local police needs to be expanded, since the beat constable is the first responder to a terrorist incident. For a counterterrorist campaign to succeed in eradicating terrorist groups, it must be spearheaded by policemen recruited from within the terrorists' own community.[2] Such individuals possess a degree of public legitimacy which is not available to security forces personnel recruited from outside the community. Informers are also less likely to feel like traitors to their terrorist comrades if they report to handlers with whom they share an ethnic or religious affinity.[3] Furthermore, if offensive action is necessary for intelligence to be generated, it is better that those arresting and interrogating suspects should be local policemen. That way, public anger at the government is more muted than if a military-led crackdown were launched.

Even so, the deployment of army personnel in counterterrorist duties has many advantages. First, it increases the 'actionability' of intelligence reports, since more security forces personnel are available to follow up on minor leads provided by national agencies.[4] Secondly, it gives the police a distinct tactical advantage vis-à-vis the terrorists, by allowing the former to call upon army patrols for fire support. Thirdly, it imposes a check on police corruption, which would otherwise be rampant if local officials choose to misuse their authority and harass the populace.[5] Lastly, it reduces the quantum of terrorist activity at any given point of time by forcing the terrorists to lie low. Intelligence assets thus gain time to track down high-value targets in the terrorist movement, such as key ideologues or operational planners.[6]

We have seen how two terrorist movements – Sikh and Kashmiri separatism – were confined to distinct geographic areas that could be flooded with troops. While the Indian Army kept violence levels under control, the state police forces of Punjab and Jammu and Kashmir were strengthened so that they could assume the lead role in counterterrorism. In the case of Punjab, the police did eventually become the key component in the counterterrorist effort; in Jammu and Kashmir, the army remained the dominant force owing to the active support that Pakistan provided the terrorists. However, the army has no role whatsoever to play in combating pan-Islamist jihadism in the Indian heartland. This gives the jihadists extensive operational space to move within, and allows them to evade police pursuit.

Case Study I: Operation Bluestar and its Aftermath

One of the most frequently asked questions about the Khalistani terrorist problem is whether the army's assault on the Golden Temple in June 1984 was avoidable. Critics of Operation Bluestar insist that the Punjab Police should have been assigned the job, with the army in a supportive role. They point to Operation Black Thunder, a much better planned assault that the police carried out jointly with central paramilitary forces in May 1988. Such views do not take into account the lack of police preparedness in 1984 to deal with the military hardware available to Khalistani groups.

During 1983, intelligence reports warned that the armaments being stockpiled by terrorists in the Golden Temple were sufficient to resist a battalion-level assault.[7] These were made all the more formidable by Pakistan-manufactured infantry weapons sourced from trans-border smugglers. By mid 1984, the terrorists' weaponry was superior to even that of the Central Reserve Police Force (CRPF – a federal paramilitary force).[8] The Punjab Police, who had no experience of urban warfare, had very little chance of success. Furthermore, there were reports that the terrorists were planning to orchestrate mass agitations across Punjab if the Temple was besieged.[9] A swift, surgical assault seemed the only option, for which the army was best suited.

Offensive action was necessary for another reason: knowledge gaps had begun to appear in the IB's coverage of the terrorist movement.[10] Since 1983, the agency had had just one Deputy Director heading a desk that dealt collectively with Pakistan, the Gulf countries and the rest of the Islamic world. Also, one of the two posts of Joint Director responsible for counterintelligence had been lying vacant for six months, even as violence in Punjab escalated massively.[11] The agency was over-stretched since its mandate included responsibility for combating terrorism all over India. During February 1984, it had to monitor escalating militancy in six states simultaneously. Consequently, the IB was relegated to being a mere spectator of the deteriorating situation in Punjab.[12]

Once Operation Bluestar restored a semblance of normalcy to the state, the central government gained a breathing space. It went about strengthening its intelligence network in Punjab. A new post of Joint Director was created at the IB's office in Chandigarh. Police officers from other states were transferred to Punjab to help in processing intelligence. The latter move was necessitated by the fact that the local police were suspected of sympathising with the terrorists.[13] Consequently, there was reluctance to trust them with intelligence work. The withdrawal of the army from counterterrorist duties however, soon made it imperative that policing capabilities be strengthened. Contemporary estimates held that the force's operational capacity needed to be increased four-fold to cope with the additional counterterrorist duties.[14]

Overseas, the IB and R&AW expanded their presence in Indian diplomatic missions. Cities that were hubs of expatriate Khalistani activism such as Toronto, Vancouver, Washington, New York, London, Paris and Bonn became key intelligence stations. Intelligence officers posted under diplomatic cover monitored Khalistani fund-raising efforts and the separatists' close inter-actions with Pakistani diplomats.[15] Until mid 1985, their work dominated the agencies' output on Khalistani terrorism, with the emphasis being on strategic intelligence. Only after an exhaustive database had been compiled on the separatist movement's foreign and domestic linkages did the agencies begin to focus on tactical intelligence. In this however they were handicapped by the fact that many of the terrorists who became active after 1984 had no prior police record.[16] To use a term popular with British Intelligence, they were 'clean skins' and their activities were inherently difficult to predict.[17]

Strengthening of Police Intelligence

The collapse of the 1985 Punjab Accord led to a rise in terrorist violence. Finding itself short of policy options, the central government began strengthening the operational capacity of the Punjab Police. Since suspicions still lingered as to the loyalties of the constabulary, upgradation of police weaponry – the single most important issue – proceeded very slowly. The state police chief told a reporter in 1986 that his force lacked resources to do anything more than merely contain terrorist activity at existing levels. The police had to make do with the support of one company of federal paramilitary troops to cover every 15–20 villages. Moreover, such 'saturation' deployment could only be mounted in the two highly disturbed districts of Amritsar and Gurdaspur. The rest of the state had a much lighter security cover.[18]

Frustrated by the inability of national agencies to produce 'actionable' intelligence, some police officers established their own agent networks. For instance, in Amritsar district in mid 1986, petty criminals were recruited to infiltrate terrorists' support networks. Their task was to get into close proximity with senior Khalistani leaders who were known to frequent the Golden Temple in the guise of religious devotees. Once they had identified these individuals, the agents would point them out to plainclothes policemen who would arrest them. This tactic proved quite successful, and was soon replicated across the state. Thus, the 'cat' system was born.[19] Paid informers were called 'cats', since it was their job to locate 'mice' (codeword for terrorists).

Emergence of 'Cat' System

Cats were intended mostly for shallow-penetration missions. In its early stages, the system was quite rudimentary: policemen would stop passenger buses, order the occupants out, and march them past hooded informers who would point out Khalistani activists. The terrorists soon got around this tactic by frequently switching buses and travelling on foot in the vicinity of police checkpoints.[20] Thereafter, the police used 'cats' as instruments of local surveillance, whose job was to identify terrorist supporters and sympathisers in rural areas. Whenever a group of terrorists entered a village, the police would know within a matter of hours who among the inhabitants had hosted them. Sustained official harassment of anyone fingered by the 'cats' as a Khalistani sympathiser gradually forced villagers to refuse shelter to the terrorists.[21]

Even as the 'cat' system was being established, the Punjab Police received a massive infusion of funds from New Delhi. With a 1986 budget of INR 1 billion (a 500 per cent increase from the 1983 police budget), the police were able to recruit a substantial number of 'cats'.[22] Three types of motives drove these informers: fear, greed and revenge. Some were captured terrorists who were press-ganged into working for the police in exchange for leniency. Others were mercenaries prepared to take enormous risks by gathering intelligence due to the large financial rewards on offer. These rewards could go up to INR 1 million.[23] The third group consisted of those who had lost close relatives to terrorist violence: they were motivated by a deep personal hatred of the Khalistanis. Generally, the best information came from the second and third type of informers.[24]

Subsequently, 'cats' provided the informational base for leadership decapitation efforts by the Punjab Police. They were encouraged to take extraordinary risks by virtue of the bounties placed on the heads of prominent terrorists. Once a high-value target had been neutralised by security forces, the resultant payout would be shared between the policemen and the informer who had provided the crucial tip-off. A number of senior Khalistani leaders were eliminated after their close associates betrayed them in return for money. By 1987, even the terrorists were acknowledging that the police had succeeded in infiltrating their ranks and that this had led to heavy losses. In response, they decided to assassinate anyone suspected of being an informer, together with his or her family.[25]

'Cats' remained the primary source through which 'actionable' information was acquired, but there were rare instances when the IB produced coups of its own.[26] One example was the agency's entrapment of a notorious terrorist named Talwinder Singh Parmar, who was a Canadian national. Parmar had masterminded the 1985 Air India bombing which killed 325 people, and was known to be in close contact with the Pakistani ISI. As a high-priority intelligence target, he was monitored by Canadian Intelligence whilst living in Vancouver and by the R&AW in Pakistan.[27] Sometime in the latter half of 1992, he entered India through the port of Chennai (then called Madras) and was lured by the IB to Punjab, to a trap set in the small town of Phillaur. His death was announced in October 1992 and marked one of the biggest successes in the fight against Khalistani terrorism.[28]

However, not all intelligence breakthroughs came from secret sources. Some issues still needed to be cracked open with offensive operations, like nuts with a nutcracker. For instance, despite their relatively good knowledge of terrorist activity during 1986–87, the Punjab Police underestimated the extent of ISI involvement in the conflict. Only after interrogating Khalistani leaders captured during Operation Black Thunder in May 1988 did the police understand the depth of Pakistani interference. Interrogation reports revealed that many individuals who were previously thought to be terrorist masterminds were actually only mouthpieces for communiqués prepared by ISI officials. Operational plans were not drawn up in the Golden Temple, as was previously thought, but across the border in ISI safe houses.[29] This newly acquired knowledge spurred the central government into allowing the police to assume a more offensive counterterrorist posture. Police operational capacity was also expanded to deal with what had become a proxy war.

Shoring up Operational Capacity

Even as the Punjab Police was adapting itself to the task of combating terrorism on a war footing, a new police chief was appointed. KPS Gill proceeded to address long-standing deficiencies in the operational capacity of the force. One of his earliest initiatives was to introduce a strict regime of record-keeping, to keep track of trends and patterns in terrorist activity. He also started the practice of publishing Monthly Terrorism Reviews containing the latest strategic intelligence data.[30] The reviews were distributed to all senior police officers, so as to improve situational awareness on the Khalistani threat.

To increase the offensive power of the Punjab Police, Gill introduced a radical change in manpower usage. Hitherto, 40–50 per cent of total police strength had been assigned to static guard duties, in order to create an illusion of security amongst the public. Policemen were engaged in innumerable checkpoints and barricades across the state. Gill dispensed with static defences, and ordered that the additional manpower thus made available be used for offensive action. At a stroke, the operational strength of the Punjab Police went up from 50 per cent to 85 per cent of total force strength.[31] Special 15-man teams were constituted to go after the most prominent terrorists, whose number usually ranged between 30 and 40 at any given point of time.[32] Databanks were created in each police district to map out their movements and identify their associates.

After the ISI pumped in massive quantities of Kalashnikov assault rifles from May 1987, police weaponry also had to be upgraded. At Gill's insistence, Light Machine Guns (LMGs) were distributed to a number of police stations in areas that were the worst affected by terrorist violence.[33] He lobbied the Indian Home Ministry to provide Self-Loading Rifles (SLRs) to the Punjab Police, thus replacing the unreliable bolt-action rifles then in use. Initially, the Ministry tried to economise, releasing only limited quantities of SLRs. Gill fought a bureaucratic battle for the force and eventually managed to achieve a comprehensive modernisation. He pointed out that it was unrealistic to expect the Khalistanis to only attack those policemen who carried SLRs, and chivalrously refrain from attacking others equipped with bolt-action weapons.[34]

Other upgrades in operational capacity also had an impact. The strength of the Punjab Police was increased from 35,000 to 60,000, of whom 65 per cent were Sikhs. Housing was constructed for the families of police personnel inside protected enclaves, where they would be safe from the threat of terrorist attack. This allowed policemen to pursue terrorists without having to worry about reprisals against their kin. The size of the police vehicle fleet was tripled, and a sum of INR 140 million was allocated for the purchase of communications equipment.[35] Lastly, the Border Security Force (BSF – a federal paramilitary force tasked with frontier security) began fencing the Indo–Pakistani border. Its purpose was to block off the terrorists from their patrons in Pakistan. Completed in phases, the fence eventually extended along the length of the 540-kilometre long border that Punjab shared with Pakistan. Deprived of their safe haven, the Khalistani terrorists became vulnerable to relentless pursuit and attrition by the Punjab Police.[36] Owing to these measures, the number of non-combatant fatalities from terrorist attacks dropped sharply from 1,266 in the first half of 1988 to 688 in the second half.[37] Fearing for their survival, some terrorist leaders made surreptitious overtures to the police, offering to surrender in exchange for leniency.

Operation Rakshak I

The abrupt policy shift brought about by the National Front government in New Delhi in December 1989 undid all that had been achieved by Gill. Convinced that the government lacked the will to stamp out terrorism, Khalistani groups proliferated across the Punjabi countryside. After 1989, a change in the nature and scale of terrorist violence was discernible. The total number of terrorists swelled from roughly 1,200 to 5,000 within a matter of months. Most of the new entrants to the Khalistan movement were petty hoodlums who acted out of purely criminal motives. Their targets encompassed anyone wealthy, irrespective of whether they were Hindu or Sikh. In a bid to pillage and extort money out of the largest possible number of victims, terrorist groups expanded out of their traditional stronghold – the border district of Amritsar – to other parts of Punjab. Whereas until 1989 70 per cent of all terrorist attacks had taken place in Amritsar district, now the focus of violence shifted to the state's interior, particularly the city of Ludhiana.[38]

It was in this situation that, in November 1990, the Indian Army conducted Operation Rakshak I. The Operation aimed to bring down violence in the border districts and close down infiltration routes from Pakistan. It was partially successful: while violence levels fell substantially along the border, this decline was more than offset by a spurt in terrorist activity elsewhere in Punjab. The criminalised nature of terrorism had allowed Khalistani groups to remain operationally viable by recruiting unemployed youths. The year 1991 emerged as the worst for terrorism in Punjab: 5,265 people were killed in total, including 2,591 noncombatants. Spiraling violence eventually forced the central government, now led by prime minister Narasimha Rao, to deploy the army throughout the entire state in November 1991. This maneuver was known as Operation Rakshak II, and was the single biggest cause of the defeat of Sikh separatist terrorism.

Operation Rakshak II

Rakshak II featured a prodigious amount of manpower, which firmly tipped the strategic balance against the Khalistanis.[39] Over 200,000 security forces personnel were pitted against some 4,000 terrorists. These forces were subdivided as follows: 53,000 Punjab Police, more than 70,000 BSF and CRPF troops, 28,000 Home Guards, 10,000 Special Police Officers (SPOs) and 115,000 army personnel.[40] The last element was crucial, since the army moved into Punjab with a speed that stunned the terrorists and left them with no time to recover. Within two weeks of the operation commencing in mid November, nearly 140 army battalions fanned out across Punjab. Their presence had an immediate effect: in Amritsar district, non-combatant deaths for November 1991 totaled 10, as opposed to 32 a month earlier. Meanwhile, the police killed 30 terrorists in November, up from 24 in October. Overall, the total number of noncombatant deaths in Punjab for November 1991 was 168, a marked decline from the 297 killed in October.[41]

Under a plan that had been prepared in advance, the army placed three battalions for every 100 square kilometres of the countryside. Taken together with the dispersal of troops into section-sized patrols, this meant that the army could respond to an incident anywhere in the state within 30 minutes.[42] Tactical radio networks were interlinked with those of the Punjab Police, allowing the latter to call for support from the army whenever required.[43] Joint army–police raids on terrorist hideouts forced the Khalistanis to concentrate on survival and led to a sharp decline in their attacks on non-combatants. The situation began improving rapidly, as the following figures demonstrate:

Deaths from Khalistani terrorism in the Border Range of the Punjab Police, the worst-affected region of the state

Year	Non-combatant Fatalities	Police Fatalities	Terrorist Fatalities
1988	1066	71	198
1989	552	152	313
1990	1038	310	891
1991	731	192	1181
1992	383	98	1061
1993	–	4	210

Source: Amritsar police statistics, reproduced in *Frontline*[44]

During Rakshak II, intelligence served as a complement to offensive action, not a substitute or a pre requisite for it. Between November 1991 and February 1992, aggressive patrolling by infantrymen kept the terrorists' heads down. The army sent out 10,961 patrols, laid 4,754 ambushes and searched 394 villages. The bulk of this activity was not guided by any specific information, other than background data on where the terrorists operated and which routes they frequented. Eventually, 34 Khalistanis were killed and 1,600 arrested.[45] Once the public gained confidence in the government's determination to wipe out terrorism, 'actionable' information began flowing to the police from casual informants. (The latter were distinct from the 'cats', who were paid informers working full-time for the Punjab Police). Much of this information came through anonymous calls from newly constructed public phone booths in rural areas. Often, the caller's motive was to settle scores with a terrorist who had extorted money or raped one of his female relatives.[46] So sudden and voluminous was the flow of local intelligence in 1992–93 that KPS Gill later spoke of a 'pressure cooker effect'. He noted that information on terrorist groups starting pouring in from members of the public only once the need for it had begun to wane.[47] This last point demonstrates the galvanising effect that sustained offensive action had on tactical intelligence. It also suggests that complete dependence on such intelligence prior to taking offensive action is a recipe for perpetual paralysis.

Once operational capacity had been expanded to cope with the demands of the situation, Indian security forces in Punjab grew less dependent on intelligence support from national agencies. They could meet their own informational requirements through prisoner interrogations, as well as informer networks run directly by police personnel. On balance, operational capacity demonstrated a direct relationship with 'actionable' information – the more there was of one, the more there was of the other.

Case Study II: The Indian Army in Jammu and Kashmir

The same can be said of counterterrorism in Jammu and Kashmir. Security operations in the state are dominated by the Indian Army, which has played a decisive role in lowering violence levels. When first called out to undertake counterterrorist operations in April 1990, the army faced a massive intelligence deficit.[48] Not only was the IB unable to meet its informational requirements, but even the state police had no real-time data on the terrorists.[49] Police intelligence had dried up after a dozen officials were assassinated in 1989 and three others were killed within a span of 12 days in January 1990. The separatists had focused on crippling the Criminal Investigation Department (CID), which maintained records of terrorist activity. Fearing for their lives, many police informers put out advertisements in local newspapers, disavowing their links with the force.[50]

Sealing the Border

Aware that Pakistani support was crucial to the continuance of terrorism, the army's first task was to secure the Line of Control that divided Jammu and Kashmir from Pakistan Occupied Kashmir. A five kilometre wide *cordon sanitaire* was created along the length of the LoC. Indian border guards were issued shoot-to-kill orders. A dusk-to-dawn curfew was imposed on villages in the border areas, and the army carried out a census of the inhabitants. All locals were issued with photo-identity cards that they had to produce when asked, so as to distinguish them from infiltrators. Though these measures caused resentment among the villagers, who felt humiliated and inconvenienced by the movement controls, the security forces accepted that as an unavoidable evil.[51]

Military Intelligence identified 72 infiltration routes used by Kashmiri terrorists along the LoC. The army had only enough manpower to plug 50 of these. Even so, its presence in the border areas made crossings particularly hazardous, and Pakistan was compelled to increase the quantum of its support to the separatists. Between November 1990 and June 1991, the army arrested 1,400 terrorists who were attempting to infiltrate into Kashmir and killed 442 others. During this period, it suffered total losses of just 36 men.[52] Pakistan's response to these developments was to provide covering fire during infiltration attempts. Such attempts eventually spread over the entire length of the LoC. Roughly 5,000 terrorists entered Jammu and Kashmir in the summer of 1991.[53]

Army Begins to Increase Operational Capacity

The sheer scale of the terrorist threat necessitated a long-term response. Increasing the army's operational capacity for low-intensity conflicts was one of the first steps. Starting in July 1990, the army raised a specialized counterterrorist force to operate exclusively in Jammu and Kashmir. Called the Rashtriya Rifles (RR), it became instrumental in bleeding dry the separatist movement in a long-drawn war of attrition. By 2005, its total strength had gone up to 60 battalions. The creation of the RR enabled the army's regular infantry battalions to return to training for conventional warfare. They had not been able to do this since 1987, when the army had been deployed to Sri Lanka.[54] Over the course of a decade, the RR neutralised 7,000 terrorists, seized 6,000 weapons and won 2,000 awards. It established a kill ratio of 4.48 terrorists for every soldier lost, which was far better than the BSF (1.98: 1) and the CRPF (0.38: 1) during the same time.[55]

To overcome the antagonism aroused during cordon and search operations amongst the Kashmiri populace, the army initiated a civic action programme – Operation Goodwill. Battalion commanders were ordered to assist Kashmiri locals as far as they could. For instance, the army built schools, dispensaries and water channels for villages. This overtly friendly approach paid dividends, since it induced several terrorists to defect. They in turn, were persuaded into acting as spotters. Faces concealed, they would sit in vehicles during raids and identify their former colleagues as they were filed past. Whenever a spotter expressed guilt about his 'betrayal', his handlers explained that by helping the security forces, he was saving the lives of countless innocents who would otherwise have been killed by terrorists.[56]

Revamping the State Police

As in Punjab, there were strong suspicions that members of the Jammu and Kashmir Police sympathised with the terrorists. So pervasive were these views that no order was put into writing and sensitive messages could not be sent via the police radio network.[57] The fact that the police had been the first agency to warn about the growing alienation of Kashmiri Muslims during the 1980s was forgotten. Also overlooked were deficiencies in the force's operational capabilities, which came to the fore between 1990 and 1996, when violence escalated. These deficiencies included a shortage of personnel trained in high-intensity urban combat, and a weak intelligence network, relative to the need of the times.[58] Police presence on the streets was minimal, such that whenever the government lifted the daily curfew between 1800 and 2200 hours, the terrorists promptly imposed a 'curfew' of their own. Despite significant hardships and food shortages, no one among the non-combatant population dared defy the terrorists' curfew. The streets of large towns thus remained eerily deserted round the clock.[59]

Building up operational capacity in the Jammu and Kashmir Police was a gradual process. A modest start was made in June 1994, when a 12-man Special Operations Group (SOG) was set up in the state capital, Srinagar. Using former and current members of terrorist groups as informers, SOG personnel tracked down and eliminated senior terrorist leaders.[60] As their 'kills' piled up, the size of the unit increased until, by 2003, it compresed 1,500 personnel. SOG troopers were not specially trained in covert tradecraft but were regular policemen who were rotated for counterterrorist duties. During their operational tours, they acquired invaluable combat experience, which moulded them into highly effective team leaders when later dispatched to lead other policemen. They also learnt to work closely with the army and the BSF, overcoming these organisations' initial mistrust by their impressive operational results.

When Gurbachan Jagat, a veteran of counterterrorism in Punjab, took over as Jammu and Kashmir Police chief in February 1997, there was a marked improvement in the force's functioning. The SOG, already at the forefront of operations, was shaped into a sophisticated terrorist-hunting unit. By mid

March, it had decimated the top leadership of several terrorist groups, such as Hizb-ul Mujahiddin and Harkat-ul Mujahiddin. So relentless was the police onslaught that eight senior terrorists were shot dead in the course of a single day.[61] The first quarter of 1997 saw twice as many terrorists being killed or arrested as during the latter half of 1996. In response, terrorists began systematically targeting the police in a manner not seen since 1990.[62]

The methods used by Jagat to revitalise the force were identical to those previously employed by Gill in Punjab. Attention was paid to policemen's welfare and financial incentives were instituted to motivate field-level personnel to take risks in pursuing terrorists. Service in the SOG became a route to faster promotions. Commando teams were also set up to carry out raids in high-altitude areas that had previously been left to the army.[63] Policemen were inserted deep into forested areas, where they operated independently for up to 30 days. After gaining the trust of local villagers, they would gather information on terrorist movements and hideouts. Policemen handled the task of assaulting the hideouts, with the Indian Army only being called in to render fire support.[64] By 1998, one third of all weapon recoveries in the state were accounted for by the Jammu and Kashmir Police. This was all the more remarkable given that the police constituted less than one tenth of total security forces deployed.[65] The SOG deserved the bulk of the credit: by 2003, its personnel had neutralised more terrorists than the army, regular police, BSF and CRPF put together.[66]

Over the course of 15 years (1993–2008), the Jammu and Kashmir Police grew from 34,000 personnel to 70,000 (not counting auxiliaries).[67] Its comparative advantage in gathering local intelligence (relative to the army and central paramilitary forces) brought about a change in the nature of terrorist attacks. Unable to bear the losses that intelligence-led police raids were inflicting on them, terrorist groups switched from ambushes to using remotely triggered explosive devices.[68] They also made attempts to subvert the loyalties of policemen, which were occasionally successful. In one instance, a former government official was assassinated in September 2002 after policemen provided real-time information on his movements to the terrorists.[69] Generally however, the state police proved difficult to subvert since many of its members were not ethnic Kashmiri Muslims, who formed the bulk of the separatist movement. Instead, they were Gujjar Muslims recruited from areas adjoining the Line of Control.[70] The Gujjars had a history of troubled relations with Pakistan and so were not inclined to view it as an ally vis-à-vis India. Nor did they care much for the Kashmiri Muslims, who reciprocated their hostility.

In this situation, the Gujjars in the Jammu and Kashmir Police served as a bulwark against separatist terrorism. Their local knowledge also proved invaluable to other security forces, which were composed overwhelmingly of Hindu personnel recruited from the Indian heartland. It would be fair to say that, owing to the state police, the finite operational resources of the army, the BSF and the CRPF were put to optimum cost-effective use.

Onset of Communal Massacres in Jammu

Since the early 1990s, the Pakistani ISI is thought to have kept Jammu and Kashmir destabilised by instigating massacres of Hindus by terrorist gangs. If this perception is correct, the Pakistani agency was not surprising anyone. R&AW analysts had predicted exactly such a move: after being stalemated in the Kashmir Valley, the ISI would attempt to radicalise Muslims in the Jammu region.[71] Unlike the Valley, Jammu had a sizeable Hindu population and the risk of communal clashes was ever present. Separatist sentiment did not run as strongly among the Muslims in Jammu as it did in Kashmir, but a prolonged bout of Hindu–Muslim hostility could change that. The state police was aware of the ISI's intentions, but was unable to take any pre-emptive measures. Manpower levels and policing infrastructure (i.e. weaponry, transportation and communication facilities) were woefully inadequate for the purpose.[72] As a result, good strategic intelligence did not lead to good tactical intelligence. When a spate of bombings in Jammu killed 13 persons and injured six times as many in late 1992, the authorities were caught on the back foot.[73]

Terrorist Bases in Doda District

During 1993, terrorist groups began to establish bases in Jammu. They focused in particular on the vast and remote district of Doda. Spanning over 11,691 square kilometres and with a population of just 525,000, Doda offered an ideal terrain for guerrilla warfare. Less than a sixth of its 651 villages could be approached by road.[74] Furthermore, the hilly nature of the terrain allowed terrorist groups to observe security forces advancing towards their hideouts and escape. Given this situation, the spread of terrorism from the Valley into Doda could not be prevented because the security forces were spread too thinly across rough terrain. Six BSF battalions and one army battalion were left to monitor the entire district, at altitudes that varied from 8,000 to 14,000 feet. As a result of the inadequate manpower deployment, terrorist strength in Doda went up from 800 in 1993 to 2,000 a year later.

Some foreign mercenaries were even emboldened to set up training camps in densely forested areas, where they indoctrinated and armed local Kashmiri recruits. Between 1991 and 1994, 30 terrorists were killed in the district, while 50 security forces personnel were slain – a stark indicator of how great was the terrorists' tactical-level advantage.[75] Reversing this situation would require a massive increase in operational capacity, featuring more policemen and more soldiers.

It was only in 1994 that Indian counterterrorist efforts in Doda turned serious. An 8,000-man detachment of the Rashtriya Rifles (RR), dubbed the Delta Force, was deployed in August. It promptly mounted offensive operations, aiming to dominate the terrain and heights previously held by the terrorists. Attacks were mounted on the latter's hilltop hideouts at night, during which advancing columns of troops could not be seen by the adversary. High-altitude posts were set up to provide a base for reacting swiftly to local intelligence. Lastly, two large-scale operations in February 1995 destroyed terrorist training camps that had been set up in the hills. Senior terrorist leaders in the district were either killed or compelled to leave for safer areas. Despite these successes, the security forces still faced an intractable problem: poor intelligence coverage in rural areas.[76] Although the number of soldiers deployed in Doda had gone up, the strength of the district police had remained the same. Already over-stretched by operational responsibilities, the force was in no position to take on the additional load of unravelling the terrorists' support infrastructure.

This weakness became a serious issue in 1998, as the ISI allegedly directed foreign mercenaries in Doda to carry out massacres of Hindu villagers. For the past four years, national intelligence agencies had been carefully monitoring the changing profile of the terrorist movement in Jammu and Kashmir. From being an indigenous revolt against Indian rule, it had mutated over the years into a slugging match between Pakistani mercenaries and the Indian Army. In 1994, the IB and Military Intelligence noted the first major influx of non-Kashmiri terrorists into the state.[77] Since then, estimates of terrorist infiltration across the LoC suggested that up to 70 per cent of the infiltrators were Pakistani nationals. The significance of this development was readily apparent, since during the early 1990s, only 15–20 per cent of the terrorists in the state were foreigners.[78] Intelligence analysts accordingly warned in 1995 that Pakistan was pushing mercenaries into Jammu and Kashmir with a view to escalating violence and disrupting New Delhi's conflict resolution efforts.[79]

The mercenaries' attacks on Hindus in Doda, though predicted, could not be prevented owing to a lack of security forces. To get around the shortage in manpower, the state police drew up a plan to create an operations grid in Rajouri and Punch. These two districts abutted the LoC and provided ingress for terrorists into Doda. The proposal called for 7,300 policemen to be deployed in 240 posts across the region, but only 900 were available. For the rest, as one BSF officer admitted, security became a matter of firefighting: 'The entire game is played on maps. All we do after each massacre is look at the map and decide from where to pull out troops'.[80]

Building Operational Capacity After Kargil

At the time the Kargil crisis erupted in May 1999, there were 58 army battalions in the whole of Jammu and Kashmir engaged in counterterrorist duties within a 27-square grid. ('Gridding' is a system in counterterrorist operations, where an area is sub-divided into squares of equal size. Each square has a moderately-sized force deployed within it, for managing security.) The Pakistani-military incursion into Kargil forced New Delhi to redeploy these battalions for war-fighting.[81] This left counterterrorist efforts severely disrupted. Many of the redeployed battalions came from the Kupwara district in northern Kashmir, through which most of the infiltration routes into the Valley passed. Their withdrawal offered the terrorists and their Pakistani mentors a window of opportunity, which was fully exploited. Taking advantage of the poor security forces presence, an estimated 1,550 terrorists crossed the LoC into Indian territory. The majority of these were foreign mercenaries.[82]

Over the following months, COMINT analysis revealed that the ISI was intent on using these foreign mercenaries to avenge Pakistan's humiliating defeat in the Kargil war. The Pakistan army's 1st and 10th Corps had begun training terrorists in monthly batches of 500 for commando-style operations. Expecting Pakistani border posts to actively assist the infiltrators by providing covering fire, the Indian Army prepared accordingly. Its strategy called for immediate pursuit of infiltrators in case they managed to cross the LoC and reach the interior of the state. For this purpose, aircraft were requisitioned for likely use in Doda. The Rashtriya Rifles also raised specialised strike forces. A separate Force Headquarters (equivalent to a division-level command) was set up for the RR in northern Kashmir. It was called Kilo Force. Another headquarters was created in Punch and Rajouri districts in the Jammu region, and was known as Romeo Force.[83] This meant that as the RR entered the bloodiest phase of the conflict (2000–2001), it had four division-sized formations to contain violence. (Victor Force had already been created during the 1990s to combat terrorism in the Kashmir Valley, and Delta Force was in existence to control Doda).

Co-opting the Local Population

Post Kargil, there were enough indications that an intensification of terrorist activity was imminent. To prepare for this, the Jammu and Kashmir Police strengthened the capacities of isolated villages to resist terrorist attacks. It requisitioned 10,000 rifles and 1,500 wireless sets to establish a number of Village Defence Committees (VDCs) in the Jammu region.[84] First created on an experimental basis in 1993, the VDCs were not a popular feature of the counterterrorist effort as they were Hindu-dominated. Claims had been made that they were little more than vigilante organisations operating with state patronage, which targeted innocent Muslims. Although it is certainly true that Muslim participation in the VDC initiative was low, the worsening threat scenario in 1999 left the government with no option but to arm the people of remote rural settlements. There simply were not enough troops and policemen to protect them from terrorist attacks.

By end 1999, the number of VDCs had quadrupled from 400 to 1,600, with a total membership of 15,000 armed cadres. These groups not only deterred the terrorists from attacking villagers but also denied them easy movement to and from their mountain hideouts.[85] They functioned as a cheap and reliable resource for intelligence-gathering. Listening in on hand-held radio sets, VDC members monitored terrorist communications and often acquired information that enabled them to mount ambushes. In one instance, villagers overheard a Pakistani terrorist leader ordering his men to attack a wedding reception. They decided to carry on with the festivities regardless, while preparing a special reception for the attackers. What followed was a ten-hour gun battle during which the local VDC was reinforced by those of neighbouring villages. After a gruesome mauling, the Pakistani mercenaries decided to cut their losses and retreat.[86]

Another source of local intelligence was the Special Police Officer (SPO) scheme. Security forces in the Jammu region trained village women in the use of firearms and tasked them to gather information on terrorists. Disguised as cowherds, these SPOs tracked the cross-country movements of terrorist gangs and occasionally ambushed them. Together, the VDCs and SPOs helped double the security forces' kill rate in Jammu.[87]

Fencing the LoC

It was evident that the above measures could only contain the anticipated escalation of violence, not prevent or reverse it. In order to inflict a long-term or 'strategic' blow upon the terrorist movement, the Indian security forces needed to seal off the LoC and stop cross-border infiltration. Given that the terrorists depended upon their sanctuaries in Pakistan Occupied Kashmir for rest and recuperation, depriving them of the same would greatly erode their effectiveness. An attempt to erect a security fence along the LoC had been made in 1995 (as was done in Punjab during the late 1980s). It was aborted after Pakistani troops fired upon the civilian labourers contracted for the job. Rather than escalate tensions, New Delhi opted to suspend the project despite being conscious of the negative repercussions of doing so.[88] During 2001, officials from the Home Ministry and army once again raised the proposition of fencing the LoC. Their argument was buffered by the increased assertiveness shown by terrorist groups during the six month-long Ramzan ceasefire. However, opponents of the plan claimed that it would further worsen relations with Pakistan.[89]

It took the terrorist attack on the Indian Parliament (13 December 2001), and the ten-month military standoff between India and Pakistan to discredit the doves' argument. Relations with Pakistan became a lesser issue vis-à-vis securing Jammu and Kashmir from foreign mercenaries. Even so, fencing the border was a formidable enterprise. In 1990, the army had estimated that establishing a picket for every 100 metres along the Line of Control would require 50,000 men. Added to this number would be logistics and reserve troops, who would have to fight off any attempt by the Pakistani military to break through the Indian front. Put together therefore, the option of manning the entire length of the LoC was deemed prohibitively expensive. Instead, the army had opted to hold the LoC with a deployment of medium intensity. A frontage of between 10 and 15 km was manned by a battalion, which dominated the high ground so as to enhance the defensibility of its positions. The problem with this arrangement was that it could not prevent terrorists from infiltrating into the state along low-lying and broken terrain.[90] Estimates prepared in 1999 revealed that, counting ravines and riverbeds, there were roughly 400 possible infiltration routes that lay open to use by terrorists.[91]

Creating a fence that could comprehensively block off terrorist infiltration along the LoC was thus a significant achievement, albeit a very expensive one. Each kilometre of the 12-foot high and 12-foot deep fence required 260 aggregate tons of steel wiring, sand, iron and cement.[92] This load had to be transported over rough terrain where even foot patrolling was difficult for the infantry during normal times. Per kilometre, the cost of construction varied between INR 2.5 and 3 million, depending on the terrain. Work proceeded slowly owing to regular bombardments by Pakistani artillery, which in turn prompted Indian gunners to retaliate. Occasionally, heavy firing from across the LoC forced Indian sappers to work at night under heavy guard. Upon construction, each section of the fence was electrified and tracker dogs pressed into service to aid quick-reaction teams to hunt down the infiltrators.[93] Together with battlefield intelligence gained through offensive operations elsewhere in the state, these measures reduced the number of terrorists in Jammu and Kashmir, from 3,000 in 2002 to about 575 in 2010.[94] The result was a steady fall in non-combatant fatalities, which has since continued.

Operational capacity was hugely enhanced by the completion of the LoC fence. Together with an assertive state police and a sizeable military force dedicated specifically to counterterrorism duties, it played a crucial role in lowering violence levels in Kashmir. Like the border fence in Punjab, it magnified the effect of India's attritional strategy. Terrorist groups (both indigenous and foreign) were thus forced to conserve their resources, or risk being worn down. There was however, also a negative effect: with the drop in terrorist quantity came a rise in terrorist quality.

Previously, mercenaries deployed by the ISI in Kashmir had been a mix of hardcore Pakistani Islamists and poorly motivated peasants, criminals and drug addicts. The latter three groups constituted the bulk of the mercenary threat at one point (1999–2002) since, being easily replaceable, they were pushed en masse into Indian territory by Pakistani authorities. As cross-border infiltration became more difficult thereafter, the ISI stopped relying on such poor quality material and instead began sending only highly trained and motivated jihadists, knowing that they stood a better chance of surviving a border crossing. It also gave them specific instructions to prepare sections of the Kashmiri population for violent protests, through infiltrating the front organisations of local separatist groups. With the limits of its force-dependent strategy having been exposed by effective Indian counter-operations, Pakistan switched to a strategy of political subversion. The impact of this will be discussed in Chapter 7.

Case Study III: Growth of Jihadist Networks in India

There is no escaping the fact that the pan-Islamist threat facing India has its roots in Pakistani territory. One of the ISI's goals is to weaken the Indian economy and towards this, it has sought to radicalise Indian Muslims. Though the K2M Plan was scotched in 1992–93, ISI support to terrorism in Indian metropolises continued unabated. Until 2002, jihadist activities in the Indian heartland were dominated by Kashmiri splinter groups and gangsters like Dawood Ibrahim.[95] In that year, there was a pogrom against Muslims in the state of Gujarat. This generated a huge wave of resentment. It also benefited the ISI–jihadist combine, providing them with a steady stream of recruits from other states in the Indian Union. With this, the ISI's offensive capability shot up. LeT emerged as Islamabad's preferred weapon for attacking the Indian heartland, and it began recruiting members of the Indian Muslim diaspora from 2003.[96] Much of this recruitment was done from amongst Indian migrant workers in the Persian Gulf; an alternative to recruiting from Kashmir.

Hitherto, numerous jihadist plots had been compromised by Kashmiri informers working for Indian Intelligence. Following the construction of the LoC fence, tactical intelligence against terrorist groups had produced some spectacular operational successes. During analysis of the informational yield from these engagements, IB officials were able to glean details of jihadist networks in the heartland as well.[97]

However, not all of this information could be developed to an actionable standard, as it was dependent upon the capacity of local police forces for follow-up. In densely policed states like Delhi, tactical intelligence identified 30 ISI cells that were dedicated to supporting jihadist activity. Similar results could not be generated in states like Uttar Pradesh, Bihar and West Bengal, even though these states were known to be hotbeds of pan-Islamist subversion.[98] This was because they had understaffed, poorly equipped police forces. Since the IB depended on state police Special Branches for much of its raw data, wherever police capabilities were weak the agency faced difficulties in tracking terrorist activity.[99] Unfortunately, unlike in Jammu and Kashmir and in Punjab, 'actionable intelligence' in the heartland could not be developed by deploying the army for counterterrorism.[100] Intelligence gathering therefore, remained under the purview of local police stations (which are known throughout India as *thanas*).

Manpower Deficit Hampers Intelligence Production

Aware that the IB was handicapped by poor coverage of rural areas, the ISI-jihadist combine built up a subversive infrastructure in small towns across India.[101] By 2005, strategic intelligence revealed that approximately 1,280 of the country's 60,000 *madrassas* (Islamic seminaries) had become centres of pan-Islamist subversion. Many of these were in states that were heavily affected by non-Islamist militancy, such as Bihar, Andhra Pradesh and Assam.[102] The first two faced a large-scale threat from Maoist insurgency, and their police forces were too pre-occupied with combating it to pay any attention to jihadism. Likewise, Assam was wracked by ethno–nationalist terrorism and was already subject to massive infiltration of illegal Muslim migrants from Bangladesh. In this situation, jihadist recruiters found safe havens to operate within Indian borders.

As the jihadist threat is still developing, the IB's capability to monitor it is not being commensurately enhanced. In 2008, the agency's total strength was 25,000 personnel, of whom a third were administrative and support staff. Only 13,500 of its employees were actually engaged in intelligence production, and just 3,500 of these dealt with collection activities.[103] The strength of the IB's counterterrorism division was somewhere between 300 and 400 personnel.[104] It faced the onerous task of monitoring 175 terrorist groups in a country of 1.2 billion people.[105] Plans prepared in 2001 to recruit 3,000 additional operatives had been very slow to take effect: by 2008, only 1,400 new posts had been created.[106] Furthermore, the entire operations directorate of the IB had just two Deputy Directors, and was handicapped by shortages of both technical and linguistic expertise.[107]

Likewise, state police forces were also poorly off in terms of manpower. Most suffered from deficiencies that averaged around 16.6 per cent of their total sanctioned strength.[108] Even if these shortages were ignored, India was still left with an abysmally low police-to-population ratio of 1:728.[109] This was way below the prescribed United Nations standard of having one policeman for every 450 citizens. Only one police station (or *thana*) existed for every 87,000 people, and half of these stations were manned by less than 30 personnel. Furthermore, only 1–1.5 per cent of total police manpower was assigned to intelligence duties.[110] For a long time, government expenditure on upgrading police capabilities was categorised as 'non-productive' since it did not directly lead to economic development. Starved of funds, most state police forces spent 90 per cent of their budgets on paying employees' salaries.[111]

These factors compelled local police forces to depend heavily on the IB for tactical intelligence. After bomb blasts killed 52 people in Mumbai on 25 August 2003, city police officials admitted that their own informer network was under-resourced and poorly motivated. Furthermore, it was oriented towards monitoring the activities of local mafias, rather than jihadist groups. As the jihadist threat was a recent one, it was nearly impossible to identify potential terrorists since they did not have police records. Moreover, lack of financial incentives to engage in intelligence work had dissuaded policemen from opting for the local Special Branch.[112]

Mumbai 2006 – Intelligence Efforts Overwhelmed by Scale of Terrorist Activity

For three years after the August 2003 blasts, Mumbai was spared any further acts of jihadist terrorism. During the first half of 2006, the state police forces of Maharashtra (the state of which Mumbai is the capital) and Gujarat thwarted at least six terrorist plots.[113] An IB tip-off led the Maharashtra Police to intercept a massive consignment of arms and explosives that was being smuggled into India by Lashkar-e-Toiba.[114] While examining the haul, intelligence officials realised that they were confronted with a 'swarming' offensive. The sheer frequency of jihadist conspiracies against the Indian heartland aimed to stretch intelligence and law enforcement agencies to breaking point. It was virtually certain that, if current trends continued, one of these conspiracies would succeed.

Accordingly, in May–June 2006 the IB warned the Mumbai Police that a LeT attack on the city was likely. Probable targets included the local railway network, with support being provided by activists of the now-illegal Students' Islamic Movement of India (SIMI). The police were asked to submit an 'action taken' report on the IB's information.[115] Barely two weeks later, on 11 July 2006, seven bombs ripped through commuter trains on the Mumbai suburban-railway system. In the following weeks, it emerged that little had been done after the warnings were received to harden targets or otherwise deny the terrorists an opportunity to strike. No public awareness campaign was mounted to encourage greater vigilance on the part of commuters, nor had the railway authorities been alerted.[116] A proposal to install closed-circuit television cameras in railway stations had been languishing in official cupboards for three years.[117] Sketchy eyewitness accounts meant that the police were unable to identify and apprehend the bomb planters (who escaped to Pakistan). Meanwhile, poor preparedness on the part of emergency response teams left the victims to fend for themselves. Eventually, the death toll from the attacks reached 200.

Mumbai 2008 – Consequence of Resource Constraints

In November 2008, ten Pakistani terrorists sailed into Mumbai in a fishing boat and attacked four locations in the city. Two of these were luxury hotels, one a train station, and the last a Jewish cultural centre. The resultant shoot-out with Indian security forces lasted 60 hours, and left 186 persons dead. This incident exposed glaring deficiencies in India's coastal security. However, two years previously a former IB officer had listed these deficiencies in stark terms:

> Besides over a dozen major ports, the western coast has nearly 150 minor ports, over 200 landing sites and over 500 shallow landing creeks. The police and Customs presence in the major ports aside, there is skeletal or no Customs or police presence in minor ports and nothing at all in the landing sites and shallow creeks. The police departments have a few slow moving dhows and negligible fast boats without GPS technology. Pakistan and other jihadist forces can land any amount of arms and explosives through the vast unmanned western coastal area. India has no blueprint to combat this menace.[118]

From the above extract, it is apparent that knowledge of the threat of maritime terrorism was not lacking. What was inadequate was the capability of Indian security forces to guard against it. Fifteen years previously, the central government had tried to create a coastal security system, but the initiative had failed due to insufficient finances. For instance, New Delhi was supposed to release INR 5.5 billion for procurements but by end 2008, only INR 130 million had been sanctioned.[119] When the November 2008 Mumbai attack took place, there were just five boats available for patrolling Maharashtra's 760-kilometre coastline, of which two were non-operational. The Indian Home Ministry itself had only made very modest plans for maritime surveillance. According to its Annual Report for 2007–2008, funds had been allocated for '73 coastal police stations which (were to) be equipped with 204 boats, 153 jeeps and 312 motor cycles'.[120] This was the extent of the security infrastructure intended to police a coastline that stretched 7,516 kilometres from Pakistan to Bangladesh.

In December 2006, the Mumbai Police had received an intelligence report that Pakistani terrorists could enter the city masquerading as fishermen. The police responded by ordering intensified surveillance of fishing vessels.[121] As time passed, the warning faded away from the force's institutional memory. Once again, the onus of providing specific information on terrorist plots fell on the IB and the R&AW. In March 2007, a lucky break allowed the IB to penetrate a Lashkar-e-Toiba network that was sending eight Pakistanis to Mumbai on a suicidal mission. In a joint operation with the Mumbai Police, the agency intercepted and neutralised the terrorists.[122] However, such coups were rare and the November 2008 assault succeeded because neither the IB nor the R&AW knew when the next group of terrorists would reach Mumbai. All they had was a series of COMINT reports, indicating that the LeT's intention to attack Mumbai was unchanged. These reports were shared as a matter of routine with the Joint Intelligence Committee and the Armed Forces, where they were deemed 'unactionable'.[123]

After the attacks had taken place, it was estimated that a sum of INR 10 billion needed to be immediately pumped into police intelligence networks to prevent similar incidents.[124] This figure was INR 1 billion higher than what had been projected just two years earlier, when terrorists bombed suburban trains in Mumbai in July 2006.[125] According to Ajai Sahni, a leading expert on terrorism studies, it would take a minimum of five years to reorient intelligence production so as to generate actionable intelligence.[126]

Sahni argues that:

> The principal deficiency is not the inability to communicate and act on some abundant flow of intelligence, or to coordinate between various agencies, but rather the acute paucity of actionable intelligence, and severe deficits in the capacities for generating such intelligence, and for preventive action.[127]

Inadequacy of Border-Security Systems

Evidence that resource constraints have hampered counterterrorism is not confined to terrorist attacks on Mumbai. Across the country, security forces have failed to prevent Pakistani jihadists from infiltrating via Nepal and Bangladesh. Though Indian intelligence has known since 1990 that the ISI is operating in both countries through religious charities, no follow up action has been taken.[128]

For instance, the state of Uttar Pradesh has been extremely slow to tighten surveillance along the Indo–Nepal border, due to shortage of funds. Orders restricting the entry of foreign nationals into India have been disregarded since local police *thanas* lack the means to enforce them.[129] During 2000, Uttar Pradesh had just 400 border guards spread across 22 checkpoints, to track terrorist activities along an 821 kilometre-long international boundary.[130] This pathetic surveillance system, combined with an extremely poor police-to-population ratio of 1:1000, allowed jihadist groups to thrive in the state. A 2006 intelligence assessment revealed that 34 districts (out of a total of 70) were affected by pan-Islamist militancy.[131]

The following year, a United Nations report severely indicted India's counterterrorism apparatus, voicing special concern over border policing. It pointed out that only 33 out of 76 checkpoints were equipped with computers, and these were strewn along a land border that stretched up to 15,100 kilometres. In this situation, the report stated, it was doubtful whether India could effectively fight terrorism.[132]

Summary: Intelligence Performance and Operational Capacity

Intelligence production in India is severely hampered by resource constraints. The effect of cash crunches is felt right from national-level agencies to local police *thanas*. One such effect is the shortage of linguists to translate the vast number of communications intercepts that come in daily. Only a fraction of these get transcribed and conveyed to desk officers handling counterterrorism or Pakistan.[133] At the other end of the spectrum, the ability of local police forces to operate independently from the IB and R&AW also needs to be strengthened. Only once this is done can counterterrorist efforts be successful, as was demonstrated in the case of Punjab.

Armed with an enormous budget of INR 2.6 billion, the Punjab Police in 1992 created what one journalist described as the 'best intelligence apparatus in the country'.[134] A surveillance grid was established across the state, with local police stations being given the authority and infrastructure to meet their own intelligence requirements. Dossiers were compiled on all *amritdhari* (baptised) Sikhs, who were automatically considered suspect, as they tended to be more orthodox than other Sikhs.[135] Furthermore, increments to offensive capabilities such as weaponry and transportation increased the intelligence yield of operations. They allowed the police to capture ever-larger numbers of terrorists. Thereafter, interrogation of the latter provided additional details on the strategy of Khalistani groups.

In the case of Jammu and Kashmir, the Indian Army, which was the lead agency in counterterrorism, had to create its own intelligence network amidst considerable hostility from the Kashmiri population.[136] It developed its own methodology: upon being deployed for internal security duties, each battalion carried out a survey of political opinions in its area of operations (AO). Locals were classified into 'pro', 'anti' and 'neutral' groups and attempts were made to win them over through civic action. Where popular resentment against the government ran high, the emphasis was on damage control.[137] Army units deployed in such areas avoided interfering with the daily activities of the local population and focused on surgical pursuit of terrorists. Towards this, they relied primarily on intelligence obtained by aggressive patrolling and paid informers and much less so on community liaison.[138] The latter task was left to the Jammu and Kashmir Police, which built informer networks through its premier counterterrorist unit, the Special Operations Group.

Unlike in Punjab and Kashmir, unorthodox methods of enhancing operational capacity have not been tried in the fight against Pan-Islamist jihadism. There are no equivalents of the 'cats' or the Village Defence Committees in the Indian heartland. Instead, there has been a progressive deterioration of even the rudimentary surveillance systems established during the colonial era. Until 1947, it was obligatory for community leaders to keep the local *thana* informed of all developments in their area, irrespective of how innocuous these were. Failure to report to the *thana* on a weekly basis would result in police harassment.[139] When India became independent, this system was allowed to atrophy on the grounds that it was too repressive. Indian policy makers believed, naively, that democracy would act as a palliative to all societal grievances and obviate the need for a large police force or widespread surveillance network. Although sporadic efforts have since been made to enlist community support in counterterrorist efforts, these have not yet been institutionalised.[140] Neither has the Indian Army been used to buy time for the police to expand their operational capabilities.

The three case studies examined above suggest that operational capacity is crucial to counterterrorist success. It allows intelligence consumers to develop on initially vague threat assessments and convert them into 'actionable' products. Only in rare cases, will national-intelligence agencies come into possession of highly specific information that enables a tactical counteraction to be launched.[141] Most of the time, details of either the target chosen by the terrorists, or the attack time and technique, will remain unknown. A resource-starved police would not be able to follow up on the information provided by national agencies. Yet, a large, well-financed and well-led police force can take the lead in converting strategic intelligence into tactical intelligence. Although the deployment of soldiers for counterterrorist duties substantially increases operational capacity, it is the local police who eventually gather the most intelligence.

CHAPTER 6

A LACK OF OPERATIONAL COORDINATION

Lack of political consistency and political consensus combined with weak operational capacity are three of the constraints that have contributed to perpetuating the discontinuity between strategic and tactical intelligence. The fourth, final and most frequently cited weakness is poor operational coordination among intelligence agencies as well as security forces. However, lack of operational coordination is not a stand-alone factor. Rather it is a culmination of all the other weaknesses.

Former R&AW Additional Secretary B Raman has described poor coordination as the 'bane' of Indian Intelligence, especially in trans-border operations.[1] His views are echoed by another officer of the same agency:

> On the border, several intelligence networks operate. The BSF has its own intelligence, so does the army, the air force and the police force in the region. So the small-time operatives who criss-cross the border to get information soon get wise to this. They get a single report, photocopy it and pass it on to all intelligence agencies. Rather like a freelance journalist. The fact that there are many copies of the report is then seen as corroborating evidence, the Government is informed, there is panic and sometimes even troop deployments are ordered. And all because there just isn't enough cooperation between sister intelligence agencies.[2]

While a lot might be said for getting intelligence managers to sit together and share information, such arguments miss the point. It is not just within the intelligence community that coordination lapses lead to counterterrorist failures, but also at the interface between intelligence consumers themselves. Inter-services rivalry between the local police and central security forces such as the army, BSF and CRPF detract from the efficacy of counterterrorist efforts. Caught up in their own turf wars, they lose sight of the bigger picture. The result is a differential between the threat awareness levels of national intelligence agencies and local security forces.

Examples of this disconnect abound, with local security forces demonstrating a very poor knowledge of pan-Indian terrorist networks. One instance in June 1982 involved a terrorist group called the People's Liberation Army. The PLA was an indigenous group based in the north-eastern state of Manipur. The IB had warned the Delhi Police that PLA activists were planning an expeditionary bombing campaign in the city. Assuming that the agency actually meant the Palestinian Liberation Organization (PLO), the Delhi Special Branch focused its surveillance on Arabs. Not until three bombs were discovered planted in a crowded marketplace, with the PLA issuing a statement of responsibility, did the police realise their mistake.[3] In another case, Military Intelligence officers in the north-east surprised their IB counterparts one day by proudly announcing that they had captured a senior activist of the Salvation Army.[4] Their embarrassment on learning that the Salvation Army was an internationally recognised charity engaged in humanitarian work can only be imagined.

On several occasions, communications security in terrorism-affected regions has been compromised because of poor radio discipline on the part of local police forces. While the original sender encrypts a message, policemen relay it in 'plain' language. With both 'code dress' and 'plain dress' messages available to them, terrorists and their patrons in the ISI obtain the key to deciphering Indian codes.[5]

From the information gathered for this book, it does not appear that 'information-sharing' per se is a problem. Lack of coordination encompasses a much broader range of maladies than just a failure to pool together relevant bits of data and compile a threat assessment. It is not as though all the information necessary to thwart a terrorist offensive/attack is 'in the system', waiting to be analysed.[6] Rather, additional details always have to be actively sought by intelligence consumers and producers, with both adopting their own unique methods of acquiring information. At the root of counterterrorist failures is therefore, the misfit between the core competency of national intelligence agencies (strategic intelligence) and the requirement of security forces on the ground (tactical intelligence).

Case Study I: Operation Coordination Against Khalistani Terrorism

Coordination within Punjab first began to experience problems in 1982. That year, the R&AW began collecting intelligence on Khalistani groups within the state. Hitherto, this task had been under the purview of the IB. Since the Sikh separatist movement was covertly supported by the ISI, the R&AW had an argument for becoming involved.[7] At the same time, its interference ensured that lines of accountability became blurred. The situation got even more complicated in February 1984, when Military Intelligence (MI) was ordered to monitor the situation in Punjab, as a preparatory measure for possible military action.[8]

After Operation Bluestar, the Indian Army criticised the IB for underestimating the terrorists' motivation to hold out in the Golden Temple.[9] This criticism is not entirely justified for the following reason: the army itself had a professional intelligence cadre, which could have gathered this information. Organised into company-sized detachments called Intelligence and Field Security Units (I&FSUs), MI operatives were accustomed to covertly gathering information in high-risk areas.[10] During the 1980s, I&FSUs produced high-level information obtained from within the Pakistani armed forces. Their personnel, being soldiers, were prepared to take greater risks than civilian intelligence operatives while acquiring intelligence.[11] Consequently, it makes little sense to blame the IB for underestimating the terrorists' motivation, when even the army failed to gather any information on the matter.

However, there is a case to be made that there was no information-sharing between the army and the Punjab Police. This was probably due to the abruptness with which the army was asked to intervene in Punjab. The police felt humiliated by the army's complete takeover of the state in June 1984. Information that could have been of use to the battalions tasked with rounding up Khalistani activists was withheld. For instance, the army did not know of a small exit near the Golden Temple, through which several hundred terrorists escaped during the night of 5–6 June 1984. While policemen stationed in the area had knowledge of the escape route, they did not volunteer it to the soldiers.[12]

Immediately after the operation at the Golden Temple, the IB's first priority was to collate all available data on known Khalistani terrorists, to prevent further lapses. Analysts built up an exhaustive databank on the identities of terrorists, their biographies, and known associates. On the basis of this information, security forces were able to arrest 100 hardcore Khalistanis during a four-month period in 1985. Furthermore, 150 of the roughly 400 terrorists who had escaped from the Golden Temple during Operation Bluestar were tracked down and either arrested or placed under surveillance.[13] Close monitoring of these individuals' movements and correspondence helped the IB piece together details of the Pakistani proxy-war plan in Punjab.[14]

Shortcomings of the Punjab Police

During all this, the Punjab Police remained a secondary actor, unable to deal with terrorism owing to its unfamiliarity with the problem. An internal report submitted to the Punjab Governor in 1984 claimed that police intelligence had failed because of a lack of systematic data collation and local follow-up. It recommended that one common intelligence staff should handle information pertaining to crime trends, political violence and Pakistani espionage. Since all these threats were inter-linked, dividing them up between departments would only fragment the intelligence picture and hamper the development of 'actionable' intelligence. The report's recommendations could not be immediately implemented owing to a lack of suitably qualified and reliable police officers to handle intelligence operations. As late as 1986, the Punjab Police depended heavily on the IB for tactical intelligence.[15] Since the national agency was focused on strategic assessment, this meant that counterterrorist operations fell into a gap between consumer expectations and producer priorities.

The Punjab Police tried to remedy their own shortcomings, but their efforts were handicapped by the indifference of other states. For instance, it was well known that Khalistani terrorists were infiltrating into Punjab from Pakistan via the neighbouring state of Rajasthan. The Rajasthan Police admitted as much. However, the state government refused to acknowledge that Khalistani terrorists were using its territory.[16] Likewise, other states did not respond positively to appeals by the Punjab Police to depute competent officials for counterterrorism. The prevailing logic was: Khalistani terrorism is exclusively Punjab's problem; there is no imperative on us to help in combating it. Consequently, the Punjab Police Criminal Investigation Department, once among the most efficient state intelligence units in India, was left to its own devices.[17]

Without an intelligence-gathering capability, the police could not launch counterterrorist operations. Their inactivity fuelled suspicions on the part of the central government's security forces that Punjab Policemen harboured sympathies for the Khalistanis. Relations grew particularly tense between the local police and the Central Reserve Police Force (CRPF). Since the Punjab Police was Sikh-dominated while the CRPF consisted overwhelmingly of Hindus, hostility between the two had latently communal overtones. In mid 1986, the two forces exchanged shots on the streets of Amritsar city. After this incident, senior officials drew up a long-term plan to prevent any further deterioration of inter-service relations. It was agreed that counterterrorist operations would be conducted under the leadership of the Punjab Police, and state police officers would coordinate the activities of CRPF detachments. Overall command over the 60,000-strong central security forces in the state was entrusted to the Punjab Police chief.[18]

Operational Coordination Improves Under Punjab Police

The appointment of KPS Gill as Punjab Police chief in April 1988 led to a marked improvement in coordination. Immediate orders were issued that intelligence reports should be distributed to all security forces commanders. Joint interrogation teams consisting of the Punjab Police and CRPF personnel were instituted to minimise dependence on cumbersome liaison channels.[19] Henceforth, the informational yield from captured terrorists would be disseminated swiftly at the local level, without having to go up to the IB for distribution. This reduced the national agency's workload and enhanced the 'actionability' of information. In 1989, a coordination committee of senior officials, chaired by Gill, was formed. It gave counterterrorist operations a sense of direction.[20]

Operation Black Thunder

With the IB gradually being freed of responsibility for tactical intelligence, its limited resources could focus on more strategic tasks. One of these was Operation Black Thunder, launched in May 1988. Although the operation's objective was identical to that of Bluestar – to clear the Golden Temple of terrorists – this time the lines of responsibility were much better understood. The army carried out a pre-assault reconnaissance of the Temple. Operational planners viewed video footage of the interiors, shot during Operation Bluestar.[21] Simultaneously, the IB's best operations expert infiltrated the terrorists' decision-making loop. He provided invaluable information on their morale and plans, and also of the severity with which they had desecrated the Temple's interior. It was from his reports that the central government crafted its military and propaganda strategy during Operation Black Thunder.[22]

Propaganda experts saw a golden opportunity to discredit the Khalistanis amongst ordinary Sikhs. Based on their advice, television channels were allowed into the Temple immediately after the assault. They captured footage of women who had been used as sex slaves by the Khalistanis, mass graves of terror victims, and the utter disrespect that the terrorists had shown to Sikh religious practices.[23] Operation Black Thunder marked a turning point, as it delegitimised the separatists at the very time the police was gearing up to hunt them down. Not only did the terrorists lose the Golden Temple as a sanctuary, subsequently they were deprived of safe houses across the state. Wherever they went, they were seen not as political revolutionaries but as bandits, thugs and rapists. As an exercise in counter-subversion, Black Thunder was highly successful.

As the Khalistan movement degenerated into a massive gang war in 1989–90, counterterrorist coordination suffered. Hitherto, the vast bulk of terrorist activity had been confined to the border districts of Amritsar and Gurdaspur. Now it expanded across the state. This meant that every police station had to adapt to counterterrorism on an impromptu basis.[24] Far larger numbers of central security forces were needed than previously. Eventually, only the massive deployment of the Indian Army in Operation Rakshak II was enough to arrest the growth of terrorist activity.

Coordination during 1992–93

KPS Gill has termed the counterterrorist offensive of 1992 as an experiment in 'cooperative command'.[25] It combined the strengths of the police with those of the army. Police stations supplied local intelligence on terrorist movements, while the army provided the manpower and firepower needed to interdict these. Unlike in Operation Bluestar, the police was clearly understood to have the leadership role in counterterrorism. Army officers in fact went out of their way to tell Sikh community leaders that they would not gather intelligence on the terrorists. Counterterrorism, they emphasised, was a police responsibility and their task was only to assist the Punjab Police as and when required.[26] As a propaganda line, this approach was quite successful even if it did not reflect the whole truth. The reality was that the army and the police worked very closely in defeating the Khalistani threat, as the Punjab Police's official records show:

> The basics of the strategy were to have day-to-day working liaison at the corps level through officers of the rank of IGP [Inspector-General

> of Police] and at the level of the lower formations at the rank of DIsG [Deputy Inspectors-General] and SPs [Superintendents]. Operational perceptions and intelligence were shared on regular basis. SP-rank officers were attached to the brigades for day-to-day liaison. A company of the PMFs [paramilitary forces] was attached with each of the brigades for joint operations. A reserve of the Punjab Policemen was made available to each battalion for local-level coordination and operations. These were extremely useful arrangements as the professionalism of the army was harmoniously blended with the local knowledge and tactical supremacy of the *thana*-level police. With these arrangements, the army was able to assist the local police in various conventional and unconventional roles under full legal cover [sic].[27]

Information-sharing was carried out through the simple device of having army officers attached to police control rooms. These officers were authorised to monitor incoming information and pass it on in real-time to the concerned battalion.[28] Although there were occasional glitches in liaison arrangements, these were unavoidable because of tight operational security. For instance, one episode in 1992 saw the Punjab Police using a captured terrorist to send disinformation back to his handlers in Pakistan. What the police did not know was that the IB was monitoring these messages and, thinking them genuine, feeding them back to the police as COMINT reports. This went on for a while before someone noticed the pattern.[29]

Another example of how coordination was not entirely satisfactory during 1992 is that of the elimination of Khalistani leader Gurbachan Singh Manochahal. His group, the Bhindranwale Tiger Force of Khalistan, was responsible for a large number of killings in Punjab. This made him a priority target for police intelligence. Yet, even as members of the security forces were hunting him down, Manochahal met secretly with IB officers to discuss a possible solution to terrorism.[30] In effect, he was an intelligence target as well as an intelligence asset. A combined army-police team eventually killed Manochahal in February 1993. His death took place amidst the general collapse of the Khalistan movement.

Operational Coordination Outside Punjab

Owing to the Sikhs' genius for entrepreneurship, members of the community were scattered all over India, living well-integrated lives with citizens of other faiths. Had these individuals become active supporters of the

Khalistan movement, they would have constituted a security nightmare for the central government. The fact that they remained law-abiding citizens was more a matter of luck for the Indian government, than of skill in counterterrorist coordination. The only significant spillover of terrorism occurred in the hilly *terai* region of Uttar Pradesh, which had a large population of Sikh farmers.

Terrorism spread from Punjab to Uttar Pradesh in 1988–89. The expansion was reflexive, carried out in response to the pressure created by security forces activity within Punjab. It was not part of a larger strategic design to carry the war the inside the enemy's heartland, as the 1991 K2M Plan was. A secondary reason was the considerable resentment that impoverished Hindus of the *terai* felt towards the relatively wealthy Sikh settlers. Thus, there was already ground for inter-communal tension. Lastly, harassment of Sikhs by the Uttar Pradesh Police exacerbated the situation. All this made an expansion of Khalistani-style terrorism into Uttar Pradesh feasible.[31]

The IB had warned the Uttar Pradesh government of this well in advance. In 1986 the government ordered a census of the 650,000 Sikhs living in the *terai*. The region was densely forested, with just 42 police circles to cover 600 square kilometres. This provided favourable conditions for guerrilla warfare.[32] Intelligence analysts warned that it would make an excellent alternative base for the Sikh separatists, should police pressure in Punjab force them out of that state. Reports also came in that Sikh settlers in the *terai* were smuggling arms from Nepal, and stockpiling these in their farmhouses. While the IB surmised that such behaviour was due primarily to the Sikhs' own insecurity, the state government took no chances and increased surveillance.[33]

Consequently, when the Khalistanis first began to move into the *terai* region in large numbers during 1989, the Uttar Pradesh government was alert to the threat they posed. On 12 June the previous year, an intelligence operative had been killed at a *gurudwara* (Sikh prayer house) in a small *terai* town. Police records showed that cases of weapon-snatching and banditry had been steadily rising since 1987, when pressure had first built up on the Punjab terrorists. Attempts had also been made to derail trains. Thus, while the Uttar Pradesh Police lacked the means to track terrorists' movements in real-time, strategic intelligence had provided ample evidence of their intentions to expand into the *terai*. Responding to these warnings, in April 1989 the police set up a coordination committee with their counterparts in the states of Haryana and Delhi. Surveillance was intensified at public-transport hubs and twelve additional checkpoints were set up along the border with Nepal, to interdict terrorists trying to flee India.[34]

A unique innovation was the creation of specialised snatch teams within the Punjab Police, which were authorised to arrest suspected Khalistanis anywhere in the country. According to a former IB officer, 'Punjab police teams used to be sent to other states to apprehend wanted terrorists. These teams, known in police circles as "missile" squads, were given almost unfettered freedom to move anywhere and often transgressed the legal requirement of taking the local police into confidence'.[35] Their targets were prominent Khalistani leaders who sought to escape police activity in Punjab by relocating to less volatile regions. Local police forces were unhappy at having their turf invaded by the Punjab Police but could do little, since the central government endorsed the 'missile' squads. Uttar Pradesh, Maharashtra and Bengal were just some of the states where these squads operated. To hasten information-sharing on the whereabouts of wanted terrorists, Punjab Police officers were also embedded with the forces of other states.[36]

Inadequate Police Resources and Security Awareness Hamper Operational Coordination

These measures helped in containing the spread of terrorism outside Punjab. Police officials were able to make the best use of scarce resources because intelligence agencies predicted major decisions made by the terrorists. For instance, after the Uttar Pradesh Police in a staged gun battle killed 10 Sikh pilgrims in July 1991, the IB warned the state government to expect retaliation. This came on 17 October, when two bombings in the town of Rudrapur killed 60 people. The incident marked the beginning of a fresh offensive in Uttar Pradesh by Khalistani terrorists, which the government knew was imminent but lacked the resources to prevent. After November 1991, as terrorists poured into the *terai* from Punjab to escape Operation Rakshak II, the police struggled to contain violence levels. So meagre were their resources that the senior police officer in charge of counterterrorist operations had to function without an office, accommodation, transportation or telephone.[37] It is hard to imagine a more Third-Worldly approach to combating terrorism and yet the police managed to contain the spillover of violence from Punjab.

Elsewhere in India, responses to the Khalistani threat were generally hampered by an initial lack of security awareness. Though information was shared between the police forces of North Indian states, this did not always lead to counterterrorist success because terrorism was an entirely new kind of threat for these forces.[38] Getting the rank-and-file to view it as a serious issue was difficult. The most prominent example was that of the Delhi Police. During the early 1980s, counterterrorist failures in the national capital saw politicians being gunned down along with their police bodyguards. Usually, prior warnings were received from intelligence agencies but were ignored.[39]

Only in 1986 did the force start to gear up for the counterterrorism mission. A 'Special Cell', manned by eight inspectors and 12 sub-inspectors, was created to keep watch on suspected terrorists and their associates.[40] Its mandate included surveillance of both Khalistani activists as well as members of radical Hindu groups. The latter were deemed to be as serious a security threat as the terrorists, since they were intent on targeting law-abiding Sikhs in retaliation for Khalistani atrocities. To boost its covert intelligence-gathering capability, the Cell raised a group of 200 civilian watchers. These individuals monitored suspected extremists within their localities.[41] Even so, most information on the terrorists arrived through battlefield intelligence. Offensive action remained the key to breaking the code of secrecy surrounding terrorist gangs. It even thwarted major terrorist plots that intelligence agencies were completely unaware of.

For instance, in mid 1992 the Mumbai Police arrested four Khalistani terrorists after overwhelming them in a shoot-out. During interrogation, it emerged that they had been sent to Maharashtra to abduct the Indian Prime Minister's granddaughter, who was residing in the state.[42] Another example of counterterrorist success being achieved through local police initiative occurred in Delhi in January 1997. Alerted by an IB warning that Pakistan-based Khalistani splinter groups were planning bomb attacks in India, the Delhi Police tightened vigilance. Acting on a casual tip off, they raided a house where suspicious activities had been reported. It transpired that the police had inadvertently stumbled upon an ISI-backed bomb conspiracy.[43]

From these examples it appears that it was the degree of consumer sensitisation to the terrorist threat that made all the difference between counterterrorist success and failure. Overall, it is fortunate that the Khalistani terrorists did not venture too far outside Punjab in pursuit of their objectives. It is very likely the Indian security forces would not have been able to comprehensively defeat the movement if it had been more diffused.

Case Study II: Efforts at Coordination in Jammu and Kashmir

In Jammu and Kashmir, operational coordination was much more difficult to achieve than in Punjab. Counterterrorist efforts were split between the four security forces: the Indian Army, the Border Security Force (BSF), the Central Reserve Police Force (CRPF) and the state police. The army's dominance caused considerable resentment among the other forces. The overbearing manner of army officers at both junior and senior levels made their civilian counterparts chafe under what became known as 'cantonment raj'.[44]

The history of inter-services squabbling goes back to 1990. At that time, the sheer scale of separatist violence had paralysed the state police. There were even suspicions that policemen sympathised with the terrorists. In this situation, the BSF and CRPF were rushed into the state, pell-mell. The Jammu and Kashmir Police virtually revolted, protesting against the humiliating treatment meted out to its personnel by the outsiders. For instance, despite showing their service identity cards, state policemen were still stopped at random and searched by paramilitary troopers.[45]

Meanwhile, the conduct of the central paramilitary forces was hardly exemplary. BSF and CRPF troopers acquired a reputation for being ill disciplined, and prone to panicking under heavy fire. On a number of occasions, Kashmiri villagers and townspeople levelled credible accusations of human-rights violations at them. These violations usually occurred in the aftermath of successful terrorist attacks that left the troopers scared and yet thirsting for revenge.[46] Pakistani propagandists made great play of such atrocities, albeit preferring to attribute them to the Indian Army. In fact, the army was the only force whose personnel conducted themselves with integrity and courage during these years. It was for this reason that it came to dominate the counterterrorist effort.[47]

Coordination improved to some extent when a former R&AW chief, Girish Chandra Saxena, was appointed governor of Jammu and Kashmir in May 1990. As an intelligence veteran, Saxena understood the importance of information-sharing and strove to get the senior commanders of different forces to work together. For this, they first had to recognise each other's limitations and tailor their own expectations of tactical intelligence. The BSF for instance only had expertise in running human intelligence networks in areas adjoining the Line of Control. It had no sources in the interior of the state. Likewise, the army had targeted its entire intelligence-gathering effort towards monitoring military activity in Pakistan Occupied Kashmir. The state police CID was ineffective, owing to both terrorist penetration of its ranks as well as poor leadership. IB operatives were too busy rebuilding their agent networks in the Kashmir Valley and studying the still-unfolding strategic context to meet the security forces' demand for tactical intelligence. In this situation, the Saxena administration opted to give local commanders responsibility for meeting their own intelligence requirements.[48]

They resorted to similar techniques as had been used in Punjab: driving 'turned' terrorists around in unmarked cars and using them as spotters. A number of raids on urban-terrorist hideouts took place on the basis of local intelligence developed from such methods.[49] The Saxena administration scored major operational successes as a result of the enhanced tactical-intelligence effort. This in turn complemented the IB's strategic intelligence. Within months, nearly two-thirds of the leadership of the Jammu and Kashmir Liberation Front (JKLF – the biggest separatist group) had been arrested. The catches included the JKLF's self-styled commander-in-chief Yasin Malik, and his deputy. These developments led an intelligence officer to confidently assert that the JKLF was a 'spent force' in the state. By late 1990, the Kashmiri terrorists had started to become heavily dependent on Pakistani patronage in order to survive. Governor Saxena publicly claimed that the separatist movement could be destroyed in three months, but only if cross-border infiltration ceased.[50]

The Counter-Militant Experiment

It was around this time that the IB noticed a schism developing within the ranks of the Kashmiri separatists. Instead of being a unitary entity, the JKLF was divided between pro-independence and pro-Pakistan factions.[51] The ISI too noticed this schizophrenia in the group. Fearful that the pro-independence faction would carry popular opinion with it, Pakistani operatives set about undermining all separatist leaders who did not advocate accession to Pakistan.[52] Towards this, they created the Hizb-ul Mujahiddin. The Hizb was explicitly Islamist in nature; its goal was to attain the merger of Jammu and Kashmir with Pakistan. The ISI bankrolled the Hizb, while gradually shutting off supplies of funds and military hardware to the now greatly weakened JKLF.[53]

These machinations of the Pakistani agency did not endear it to the Kashmiris. Several separatist leaders questioned Islamabad's motives. Their ISI handlers told them that an independent Kashmir would threaten the identity of Pakistan as a multi-ethnic nation united only by Islam. Accession of Kashmir to Pakistan was therefore, the only option acceptable to Islamabad. These disclosures generated a backlash among prominent terrorist leaders.[54] Several of them gave up the armed struggle altogether, rather than serve as cannon-fodder for Pakistani agendas. Their disillusionment led to the emergence of an ideological counter-current to separatism, which became colloquially known as 'counter-militancy'. In 1994, the IB scored a significant coup when it made contact with one such former terrorist, named Mohammad Yusuf Parrey, and recruited him. Parrey soon became known to the Indian press by his *nom de guerre*, Kuka Parrey. He was to spearhead the Indian counter-subversive effort in Jammu and Kashmir.

Under an agreement worked out with Indian Intelligence, Parrey built up a sizeable militia that combined former terrorists and victims of terrorist attacks. Its single-point objective was to hunt down members of pro-Pakistani terrorist groups. In this, it enjoyed a surprisingly high amount of popular support.[55] Between 1990 and 1994, terrorists from the Hizb-ul Mujahiddin and other pro-Pakistani groups had alienated large sections of the rural Kashmiri population. Forced recruitment of children as combatants, extortion, rape and murder had not won these groups any friends among Kashmiri villagers.[56] Parrey built on this sense of anger by generously dispensing funds for developmental projects.[57] Several of his militiamen were driven by personal hatred for the pro-Pakistani groups. One admitted to the press that his family had initially sheltered the separatists, but changed sides when they raped his sister and shot his mother. Another wanted to kill as many Hizb activists as he could, since his mother had been roasted alive in a haystack by a Hizb leader.[58]

It was these acts of purely criminal violence by pro-Pakistani groups which allowed the counter-militants to become operationally viable. Besides Kuka Parrey, the IB covertly assisted at least seven other counter-militant leaders. These men made it a point to highlight the atrocities committed by the separatists, and projected themselves as true freedom-fighters since they sought to liberate Kashmiris from Pakistan-sponsored violence. The extent of their popular support was acknowledged even by well-known separatist ideologues. One of these, Azam Inquilabi, attributed the rise of counter-militancy to Newton's Third Law of Motion, arguing that atrocities committed by the separatists had generated an equal and opposite reaction.[59]

Since the counter-militants had better knowledge of the terrorists' support infrastructure than even the Jammu and Kashmir Police, they made excellent local-intelligence assets.[60] Paradoxically, it was the sheer usefulness of these groups that eventually killed the entire experiment. Although the concept had originally been engineered by the IB, responsibility for its day-to-day management soon passed to local security forces commanders. These officers began to compete with each other to gain control over the most effective groups.[61] Owing to its clout within the state's counterterrorist hierarchy, the army acquired exclusive access to Kuka Parrey's militia.

This upset the BSF. Several militiamen complained of being beaten by BSF troopers, who told them to stop reporting to the army. Relentless poaching of intelligence assets thus converted counter-militancy into the epicentre of a turf war among the security forces themselves.[62]

In 1995–96, there was a massive expansion in the number of counter-militants. Different security forces sponsored their own militias. However, lack of funds to pay for them led many local commanders to look the other way when these militias started to carry out petty crimes. Besides killing pro-Pakistani terrorists, they also extorted money from individuals who were only marginally involved in the separatist movement. Over time, they became increasingly mercenary in their actions. Public support for counter-militancy waned, with Kuka Parrey and his ilk being perceived with as much antipathy as pro-Pakistani terrorist groups. The ISI was quick to take advantage of this: upon its instructions, the Hizb-ul Mujahiddin launched a propaganda war vilifying the counter-militants.[63] In this situation, the army tried to hand back control of its militias to the Intelligence Bureau. However, the IB was well aware of the average Kashmiri's dislike for the counter-militants and refused to take charge. Its argument was that the army and other security forces had created a Frankenstein's Monster, and they alone should be saddled with responsibility for taming it.[64]

Thus was lost a historic opportunity to build up an anti-Pakistan constituency in the Kashmir Valley. Orphaned by the IB, and targeted by rival commanders in the army, BSF and state police respectively, the counter-militants became a spent force after 1996. They had played a crucial role in bringing down violence levels, thus allowing New Delhi to hold elections to the Jammu and Kashmir Assembly in September 1996.[65] However, once popular governance had been restored to the state, Kashmiri politicians saw the counter-militants as a threat to their own political supremacy. Kuka Parrey for one, had made no secret of his desire to enter mainstream politics and had even floated a party to run in the elections. As a way of clipping his wings, the elected state government starved his group of funds and allowed the police to harass its members. Parrey continued to operate as a counter-militant leader, but he never regained the prominence which he enjoyed during the mid 1990s. In 2003, he was shot dead by a Hizb-ul Mujahiddin assassin squad.

The Unified Command – A Forum for Operational Coordination

In May 1993, the Indian Home Ministry established a Unified Command in Jammu and Kashmir. Although intended to introduce unity of purpose into counterterrorist efforts, it was bedevilled by lack of political guidance. Beyond the broad principles of breaking the separatist movement through attrition, guarding the LoC, winning over Kashmiris through civic action and exposing Pakistani interference, India had no time-bound counter-terrorist strategy. Ever since 1990, opinions had been divided on the advisability of negotiating with the separatists to bring about a compromise settlement. Dissension over this issue had been rife in the Home Ministry itself.[66] Caught up in tussles between various power factions, security forces in Jammu and Kashmir were left with no intermediate-term blueprint for action. As long as major policy decisions were not required, this did not matter and the war of attrition went on relentlessly in India's favour. It did, however, mean that they had to pay close attention to intelligence assessments of the ISI's proxy war strategy.

Responsiveness to strategic intelligence prevented further radicalisation of the Kashmiri Muslim population. Intelligence agencies had learned previously that the ISI planned to maximise its covert destabilisation of the Kashmir Valley by 1994. Owing to the intensity of New Delhi's response to separatist violence after 1989, these plans had been disrupted. Try as it might, the ISI was unable to escalate violence in the Kashmir Valley, due to the strong security-forces presence there. The Pakistani agency therefore, cast around for a means to relieve the pressure on the separatists. It found the answer by inciting communal violence in Doda district, which lies in the Jammu region. This was a second front, intended to divert Indian security forces from the Valley.[67]

Armed with foreknowledge of ISI plans, the security forces responded by doing just the opposite of what the Pakistanis wanted. Post March 1994, they *intensified* offensive operations against separatist groups in the Valley, thereby forcing large numbers of foreign mercenaries to shift into the Doda wilderness. The hurried nature of the terrorists' relocation meant that they were unable to carry out any preparatory subversion of the local Muslim population. Consequently, the latter were not willing to shelter the terrorists or participate in their operations. Indian Intelligence ascertained that the ISI was disappointed by the lukewarm response of the Muslims in Doda. While terrorist incidents in the district averaged 20 per month in mid 1994, the ISI had expected a higher rate of activity.[68]

Once the Kashmir Valley had been made relatively secure, security forces turned up the heat on terrorist gangs in Doda itself. Intelligence analysts predicted that the ISI would attempt to isolate the Valley from outside reinforcement by interdicting vehicular movement.[69] To pre-empt this, vital transportation links that ran through Doda such as the Jammu and Kashmir Highway and the strategically-positioned Banihal Tunnel were secured. Local intelligence was gathered on arms caches that the terrorists were building up in the Pir Panjal mountains, which separated Doda from the Valley. Thereafter, hunter–killer missions were launched to track down terrorist groups. Caught off-guard by the security-forces reaction, some terrorist gangs were further compelled to move out of Doda itself and into the neighbouring state of Himachal Pradesh (south of Jammu and Kashmir). In response, the police forces of Jammu and Kashmir, Punjab and Himachal Pradesh set up an intelligence-sharing mechanism to prevent a militant spillover across Northern India.[70]

When the terrorists began to carry out attacks outside Kashmir, local police forces were well prepared to react. On 3 August 1998, 35 people were massacred by foreign mercenaries in the remote Chamba region of Himachal Pradesh. The Indian Home Minister later admitted that intelligence reports had predicted an attack in the region, but these were not by themselves sufficient to prevent it. What was needed for that was manpower, which the security forces in Doda and Chamba did not have. Even so, the government's response was prompt and efficacious. 20,000 people were evacuated from Chamba – a fifth of the region's total population – in order to starve the terrorists of food and information. The alien nature of the terrorists meant that local support for them was extremely low anyway. Thus, the Himachal Pradesh Police was able to swiftly identify and arrest those locals who had sheltered the terrorists and spotted targets for them. Furthermore, 150 Village Defence Committees of between eight and ten members were raised within a matter of months, to deter the mercenaries from attempting an encore.[71]

Inter-Service Relations

Coordination problems in Jammu and Kashmir derive from the fact that there is no clear-cut leader of the counterterrorist effort. Between 1990 and 1996, the Indian Army was given operational control over all security forces in the state, but even this was not complete. Terrorists captured by the army, the BSF or the CRPF still needed to be sent to the state police's Joint Interrogation Centre, which processed all battlefield intelligence.[72] The BSF also gathered its own intelligence through a specialist wing known as the 'G' Branch. The CRPF did not have an intelligence capability, and consequently depended on the other forces for information. Though these forces occasionally shared information at the tactical level, their effectiveness was limited by a lack of high-level coordination.[73]

After a popularly-elected government came to power in 1996, chairmanship of the Unified Command was vested in the state chief minister. One of his first initiatives was to set up a Unified Headquarters under the leadership of the Jammu and Kashmir Police. The idea fell through because the Indian Army was not prepared to take orders from policemen.[74] Yet, both these forces needed to work together, owing to the limitations of each. Certain areas of the state were simply too inaccessible for the police to maintain a regular presence, and had to be handled by the army. Policemen lacked both the physical and mental toughness to operate in these areas, which were heavily forested and/or situated at great heights.[75] Their strength lay in the towns, where local intelligence from informers was easier to pick up. Unlike in Punjab, where the army only needed to be called out during times of grave crisis, in Jammu and Kashmir the poor quality of infrastructure meant that their deployment had to be continuous. Thus, there were two leading counterterrorist organisations operating in the state. The army operated largely in rural areas while the police were concentrated in the towns. Each had a strong claim to overall leadership of the campaign.

Coordination of their activities was carried out by the state chief minister. Any force movements in the counterterrorist grid required his approval.[76] Under his supervision, Unified Headquarters were set up in the towns of Srinagar (in the Kashmir Valley) and Jammu (in the Jammu region). Each Headquarters had an Operations Group and an Intelligence Group. This arrangement was replicated by the central government in 1998, when the Indian Home Ministry set up its own Operations and Intelligence Groups to monitor the counterterrorist effort.[77]

By forging arrangements for coordination at both the state level as well as the national level, New Delhi introduced some measure of unity into counterterrorist efforts. These paid off after 2003, when the Indian government began to withdraw moderately-sized detachments of the BSF from the Kashmir Valley. Ordinarily, such a move would have led to a marked escalation in terrorist violence. This did not happen because over the previous years, the Jammu and Kashmir Police had acquired considerable expertise in tactical intelligence from the BSF 'G' Branch. Officers of the two forces even jointly ran informers on a number of occasions. This meant that BSF assets could be handed over to new handlers in the police without much difficulty. Thus, the pace of counterterrorist operations did not slow down.[78]

Operational coordination in Kashmir, while not refined to the same degree as in Punjab, has tended to improve over the years from the situation that prevailed in the 1990s. The decline in terrorist activity post 2002 brought down the threshold of counter-violence that New Delhi had to engage in. Consequently, the Jammu and Kashmir Police was able to assume greater prominence in the counterterrorist effort, despite being the least militarised security force in the state. Even so, the police still do not have a clear-cut leadership role and the potential for inter-services competition, though diminished, still lingers.

Case Study III: Complete Lack of Coordination in the Indian Heartland

During the colonial era, the IB was intended to coordinate the intelligence activities of provincial police forces. It was not in and of itself a front line source of intelligence.[79] Rather, the power hierarchy of the colonial government was weighted heavily in the agency's favour. It was the key coordinator of internal-security management, and its advice was not to be ignored.[80] This arrangement persisted for a few years after Indian independence, when the IB was an intelligence monolith, with both foreign and domestic concerns. The creation of R&AW in 1968 marked the beginning of dilution of the IB's authority. A second development that worked to the IB's detriment was the hostility with which Prime Minister Indira Gandhi came to view it, after her defeat in the 1977 elections. Upon returning to power in 1980, she made the founder-chief of R&AW her intelligence advisor. R&AW itself was given the added responsibility of intelligence collection within India. With its greater budget it was able to poach agents who had been recruited and handled by the IB.[81]

Matters took a turn for the worse after Mrs Gandhi's assassination, when the central government decided to create the Special Protection Group (SPG). The SPG was an elite organisation intended exclusively to handle physical security arrangements for the Prime Minister. Its creation undermined the prestige of the IB, which had hitherto been the nodal agency for Prime Ministerial security. Under the old system, the IB wielded supreme authority vis-à-vis the state police forces by virtue of its importance to the PM. Now, the SPG became the new Praetorian Guard and the IB was demoted to a fact-finding role.[82] Instead of wielding authority over state police Special Branches, it was regarded as at par with them. The agency could no longer exercise informal control over counterterrorism arrangements in the states, particularly since law and order was a state-government responsibility. This meant that with the rise of pan-Islamist terrorism in India there was no all-India coordination of the counterterrorist response.

After 1993 Mumbai Bombings: Information Sharing Improves but Operational Coordination Lags

Following the 1993 Mumbai bombings, information sharing between the IB and the state police forces improved. Indian security forces hunted down ISI operatives in India and their jihadist confederates.[83] From February 1994, the IB made a concerted effort to raise awareness levels among state police forces about ISI subversion. Instructions were issued for strengthening police-intelligence networks. Strategic assessments were disseminated about Pakistani intentions to trigger communal violence. Tactical intelligence was streamlined through ad hoc information-sharing arrangements at the level of states, administrative divisions and districts. There were periodic reviews of the action taken by the state governments.[84] As a result of these measures, even states with poorly motivated and under-equipped police forces began to yield useful battlefield intelligence. For instance, through prisoner interrogations the IB learnt of an ISI plan to bomb Hindu shrines in pilgrimage towns across Uttar Pradesh. The attacks had been planned for December 1994, to coincide with the second anniversary of the Ayodhya Mosque's demolition.[85]

Due to the ferocity of the Indian counterterrorist offensive, the ISI remained quiescent for three years. It could afford to, having already raised a special group of Kashmiri terrorists for long-range strikes across India. The group's name was Ikhwan-ul Muslimeen (IuM), and it was formed on 28 April 1991. Most of its members were former cadres of the Jammu and Kashmir Students' Liberation Front (JKSLF) – a radical youth wing of the JKLF. They believed, like the ISI, that the only way to force India to surrender Kashmir was to damage the Indian economy.[86] For this purpose, they advocated attacks against soft targets in the Indian heartland. The IuM's first major action was on 21 May 1996.[87] A car bomb in a crowded market place in Delhi killed 25 people. A day later, another bomb in the nearby state of Rajasthan killed 14 people. The central government subsequently admitted that intelligence agencies had predicted the attacks, but that there was not enough information to prevent them.[88]

As the police investigations in Delhi and Rajasthan unfolded, it became clear that the real problem was not lack of intelligence warning, but lack of consumer responsiveness. Over the past five months, the Jammu and Kashmir Police's Special Operations Group had made life unbearable for terrorists in Kashmir. Its personnel had killed more than 60 top-ranking terrorist leaders during this period.[89] Moreover, increased police aggressiveness had led to a five-fold increase in voluntary surrenders.[90] Given these conditions, the IB anticipated that fringe groups within the Kashmiri-separatist movement would carry out terrorist attacks elsewhere in India.

However, alertness levels had varied between police forces, and this led to the counterterrorist failures of May 1996. The Delhi Police in particular, had been quite cavalier about terrorist threats to the capital. While investigating an earlier bomb attack, it had made some minor arrests and then went on to claim before the media that it had wiped out an entire bomb-making network. The deception became apparent after the market bombing, which was conducted by some terrorists closely associated with those already in custody.[91] Considering that the Delhi Police is the only police force in India directly controlled by the central government (and not by state-level politicians), its lack of professionalism was surprising.[92]

Though the nation-wide reach of the jihadist threat placed heavy responsibility on the IB, the agency still had limited power and resources. It faced an uphill task in convincing state police forces of the need to proactively gather intelligence on jihadist groups. Given the differing agendas and priorities of various state governments, there was no over-arching framework within which counterterrorist operations could be mounted. South Indian states in particular, were inclined to view pan-Islamist militancy and ISI subversion as distant problems that did not directly concern them.[93] Even among North Indian states, there was a tendency to place responsibility for tactical intelligence upon the IB and the R&AW. This became apparent in 2000–2001, as Pakistani jihadists began to carry out *fedayeen* (suicide squad) attacks in Delhi.

Pan-Islamist Groups Intensify Operations Against the Indian Heartland

The first *fedayeen* attack in the Indian heartland was conducted by Lashkar-e-Toiba terrorists on 24 December 2000. Their target was the Red Fort in Delhi – a symbol of India's military might. Two gunmen infiltrated the compound and sprayed fire indiscriminately with assault rifles before fleeing. Security forces at the scene were slow to react. It fell to the IB to track down the terrorists and their local accomplices. The Delhi Police, acting upon information provided by the agency, arrested a LeT 'sleeper' agent who had been infiltrated into the capital months before.[94] His interrogation established that jihadist groups were preparing to wage a long-drawn war in the Indian heartland, and that an infrastructure for more *fedayeen* strikes was being created.[95]

Disrupting the jihadist offensive proved difficult, due to lack of cooperation from political leaders. No amount of information sharing could overcome the handicaps caused by their poor responsiveness to intelligence warnings. The most prominent such failure was the 13 December 2001 *fedayeen* attack on the Indian Parliament. Although intelligence agencies knew that the building was at risk from a suicide assault, their options for taking preventive action were limited. Members of the Indian political class were exempt from the indignity of being stopped and searched by security forces, and took offence at the mere suggestion. This meant that access control to the Parliament complex could not be enforced, as doing so would inconvenience politicians.[96] Intelligence agencies thus came under pressure to track down the suicide squad before it struck. Together with the Jammu and Kashmir Police, they passed on all available information to the Delhi Police. Before this information could be developed into 'actionable' intelligence, the terrorists struck.[97]

Political Apathy for Intelligence Reforms

Even before the attack on Parliament, it had become clear to Indian policy makers that the intelligence apparatus was afflicted by serious problems. Following the 1999 Kargil crisis, the then-ruling BJP government in New Delhi ordered a comprehensive review of the intelligence community. A task force of six experts, led by former R&AW chief Girish Saxena, was put together to study the existing system and recommend reforms. Its report, submitted in February 2000, is still classified. However, enough leaks have since appeared in the print media as to give a general overview of its contents. Basically, the Saxena Task Force Report called upon Indian agencies to take 'an honest and in-depth stock of their present intelligence effort and capabilities to meet challenges and problems'.[98] Changes in recruitment policy and personnel management were recommended, along with equipment upgrades and greater accountability.

The relevant aftermath is the slew of changes which were made to tasking and coordination mechanisms. These can be divided into two categories: apex-level changes and organisational changes. The former involved the creation of an Intelligence Coordination Group (ICG) in 2001, intended to:

1. supervise the allocation of resources to intelligence agencies
2. set annual priorities for intelligence collection
3. conduct annual reviews of intelligence performance
4. examine forecasts and estimates produced by these agencies.[99]

Establishing the ICG became necessary because the Joint Intelligence Committee had been disbanded in 1998. Since the JIC had met only once during the previous 12 months, its abolition was a logical step.[100] However, after an initial spurt of enthusiasm, the ICG went down the same route. As per the intentions of its creators, the Group would have over-riding responsibility for strategic intelligence. All intelligence agencies were to hold monthly meetings with the National Security Advisor, and their inputs would be consolidated into a single strategic assessment.[101] Yet, with the change of government in New Delhi in 2004, the ICG lapsed into quiescence and started to meet much less frequently than was originally envisaged. The result: intelligence tasking ceased to be centrally coordinated and quality review of intelligence inputs stopped.[102]

Even more unfortunate was the fate of the organisational changes recommended by the Saxena Report. As the jihadist threat to India grew perceptibly after 2001, the IB was designated the nodal agency for counterterrorism and counterintelligence. Its authority over the state police forces, considerably weakened over the past several years, was to be revitalised. To accomplish this, the government set up a Multi Agency Centre (MAC) within the IB to consolidate all terrorism-related information into a common national database. The MAC, located in Delhi, was to be assisted by five Subsidiary MACs in Srinagar, Mumbai, Hyderabad, Calcutta and Guwahati. Their task was to synergise the counterterrorist efforts of state and central law enforcement agencies.[103] Another two entities set up on the recommendations of the Saxena Report were Inter-state Intelligence Support Teams and Joint Task Forces on Intelligence (JTFIs). The former were intended to strengthen the operational capacity of state police forces by providing them with modern surveillance technology and counterterrorist training. The JTFIs were to have offices in each state capital, for the purpose of rapidly disseminating IB data to local police forces.

All three of these initiatives were frustrated by financial constraints, despite the best efforts of intelligence agencies to lobby for them. State governments refused to pay for the maintenance of the Intelligence Support Teams and JTFIs, leaving them with no infrastructure for training or for communicating with Delhi. Back in the national capital, the Finance Ministry refused to sanction a paltry INR 30 million per year to pay for the salaries of the MAC's projected 140 personnel.[104] As a result, the MAC functioned on a skeleton staff of 50 personnel, who did not even have a mainframe computer for data storage.[105] The restrictions placed on them began to tell from 2005 onwards, as pan-Islamist jihadists began an urban bombing campaign across India. Their first target, ironically, was the seat of the central government and its intelligence apparatus: Delhi.

On 29 October 2005, two bombs exploded in marketplaces across the national capital. The attacks had been specifically timed to coincide with the Hindu festival of Diwali, since the markets would be crowded with shoppers. During previous years, the IB had routinely issued Unofficial Orders (UOs) warning the Delhi Police of terrorist plans to strike during Diwali. This year, the same UO was sent but it was not acted upon. Established practice held that receipt of a UO prior to important festivals or national holidays would automatically lead to police raids on suspected terrorist harbourers. Even if the conspirators themselves were not caught through such activity, they would be forced to concentrate on evading capture and so missed the time window to carry out a sensational strike. With the removal of a key officer who had broken up numerous terrorist cells in the past, the Delhi Police Special Cell failed to carry out its customary offensive against the LeT. As a result, the October 2005 bombers were able to plan and prepare for their mission in relative peace.[106]

It emerged during the post-blasts investigation that the alleged mastermind behind them had been under IB surveillance for the past six months. A Kashmiri from Srinagar, his involvement was established after analysis of telephone records. The suspect had been in contact with senior Lashkar-e-Toiba activists in Pakistan, and R&AW intercepts of terrorist phone conversations contained references to his name. Based on this evidence, IB operatives snatched the suspect on 10 November 2005 in Srinagar, and handed him over to the Delhi Police. The Jammu and Kashmir Police were kept completely unaware about the agency's moves, so as to avoid any leaks.[107]

With security considerations requiring that relations between intelligence producers and consumers be compartmentalised, it is hardly surprising that the MAC remained only partially operational. Reportedly, even the IB was uncomfortable about sharing information with other agencies through the MAC. At an early meeting of the Intelligence Coordination

Group, officials from the IB and R&AW insisted they would only share information on a case-by-case basis and opposed the creation of a centralised counterterrorism databank.[108]

Turf warfare has claimed other casualties. An example is the National Technical Research Organization (NTRO – the Indian equivalent of the US National Security Agency). Set up in accordance with the recommendations of the Saxena Report, the NTRO was supposed to have sole possession of technical-collection assets. Determined resistance from the R&AW and the IB killed this proposal. The new agency was denied control over R&AW's aerial-intelligence wing, the Aviation Research Centre. More importantly, in late 2005, the IB disputed NTRO's claim to managing a new technical-collection system that would intercept terrorist communications. The IB argued, not necessarily wrongly, that as the lead agency for counterterrorism, electronic surveillance of terrorists fell within its purview. Owing to the disagreement, the proposed system could not be made operational.[109]

While such examples prove that the Indian intelligence community is indeed bedevilled by organisational rivalries, they do not suggest that the solution lies in structural reforms. After all, such rivalries often have their origins in earlier attempts at reform, which only multiplied the number of agencies and made coordination that much more difficult.

Summary: Information Sharing Becomes Crucial only when Security Forces Fail to Coordinate Operations

Former DIB Ajit Doval has provided an acute insight into the problems affecting counterterrorist coordination in India:

> Lack of coordination is often blamed for many intelligence failures. However, intelligence being a sensitive and multilayered activity with diverse consumer requirements, perfect coordination conceptually is neither attainable nor desirable. What needs to be attempted is system-calibrated convergence at different levels on need-to-know basis. Convergence is an inbuilt automated mechanism, as part of the process itself, while coordination is an outside effort to combine two or more vectors through institutional or individual effort. Instead of convergence, we inadvertently encouraged divergence through steps like splitting the Intelligence Bureau into IB and RAW, allowing mushrooming of intelligence outfits with nebulous objectives and ill-defined accountability.[110]

The implications of the above quotation need to be carefully pondered. It supports the view that lack of operational coordination is merely a spin-off of a deeper malaise: lack of political will and operational capacity. Only when resources and political resolve are scarce do policy makers attempt to economise and start relying entirely on intelligence to combat terrorism. Such situations generate intense pressure to make sure that all available information is conveyed to the right decision-maker at the right time. Information simply cannot be sent to the wrong person or otherwise be 'lost in transmission'.

Coordination problems occur at both the tactical and strategic levels, but while the former are inescapable irritants, the latter can be resolved by constant political guidance. Given the inherent competitiveness between security forces commanders on the ground, it takes a time-bound, multi-force operation to create effective coordination between them. During the 1992–93 offensive in Punjab, the police was 'sharing intelligence and analysis of emerging situations at operational levels of the field officers covering the army formations, CPOs [central police organisations], DGsP [Director-Generals of Police] of major states and Government levels at the Centre and in the State'.[111] The system-calibrated convergence referred to by Ajit Doval was achieved because a comprehensive assault on Khalistani groups was underway. It did not matter who neutralised a particular terrorist, so long as it was understood that only the Punjab Police would claim the credit.

Such understanding has been muted in Jammu and Kashmir and is completely missing in the fight against pan-Islamist jihadism. Even when the Jammu and Kashmir Police started to assume a more offensive posture vis-à-vis terrorist groups in the late 1990s, coordination remained poor because of ego clashes with the army. It was only as terrorist violence declined following the construction of the LoC fence in 2003–04 that the police was able to assume a leading role in counterterrorism. Until then, it still remained subordinate to the Indian Army in operational terms.

In the fight against jihadism, it has been lack of high-level coordination which has hampered counterterrorist efforts the most. Under the BJP government, there were five terrorist attacks in the Indian heartland between 2001 and 2004. After the BJP lost power to the Congress (I) in May 2004, there were 18 terrorist attacks in the following four years. Moreover, investigators did not succeed in apprehending many individuals implicated in terrorist attacks after 2004.[112] Some of these jihadists escaped to Pakistan, where they found sanctuary. Had initiatives like the MAC and JTFIs been made fully operational, it is highly unlikely that terrorists would have managed to enter and leave India at will. Their ability to do so can be explained by the concept of 'flash-to-bang time', which was first developed in the United Kingdom to illustrate the analytic difficulties associated with counterterrorism intelligence.

British counterterrorism officials had observed during 2005–07 that the average time required to plan, prepare for and implement a jihadist plot was reducing. They found that on a number of instances, such as the 'airliner plot' of August 2006, intelligence agencies only discovered the existence of terrorist conspiracies shortly before they were about to be enacted. Given that the window of opportunity needed to disrupt terrorist attacks seemed to be narrowing, counterterrorism analysts conceptualised the problem in terms of reduced 'flash-to-bang times'.

As 'Flash-to-Bang Time' Reduces, So Does Possibility of Preventing Terrorist Attacks

Basically, flash-to-bang time is the interval between the first indication of an impending event, and the event itself. For instance, a thunderclap is preceded by a lightning strike, and then a few seconds later, by the actual sound of thunder. The few seconds' time difference in this case is the flash-to-bang time.[113]

When intelligence consumers fail to follow-up on strategic warnings of terrorist threats, the interval between 'flash' and 'bang' gets compressed. Due to lack of police action, terrorist groups acquire a breathing space to set up support networks for their attack cells. Planning and preparation of terrorist strikes becomes easier, since the logistics requirements for these can be swiftly met. Eventually, a situation emerges where the first tactical-level indicator of a terrorist strike comes too late for the security forces to take preventive action.

India has now reached that situation vis-à-vis jihadist terrorism. By under-reacting to Pakistan's sponsorship of pan-Islamist groups since 1993, policy makers have allowed the ISI to build up a subversive network within India. Growing awareness of the threat was not matched by overt offensive action against it, for fear of losing minority votes. Eventually, the scale of the domestic jihadist threat grew to the point where it defied the intelligence agencies' ability to handle it alone. An elaborate network of safe houses and covert transportation channels allowed top jihadist leaders, many of whom were known to the Indian intelligence agencies, to continue planning attacks and yet evade capture.

With groups like the Student's Islamic Movement of India (SIMI) now combining forces with Pakistani jihadists, the interval between the first warning of a terrorist strike, and the strike itself, has reduced.[114] Intelligence agencies are constantly racing against the clock to disrupt plots that are planned outside Indian territory but require very little lead time to be implemented. Now that they have an in-country infrastructure to support their operations, the ISI and the Lashkar-e-Toiba have narrowed the window of opportunity available to Indian Intelligence to disrupt their plans. Wiping out their network and annihilating the terrorists would require a mindset change, on the same scale as that which gripped the US after 9/11.

CHAPTER 7

REFLECTIONS AND CONCLUSIONS

Indian counterterrorist experience against Sikh and Kashmiri separatism as well as pan-Islamist jihadism suggests that most 'intelligence failures' are actually 'action failures'. Let us revert to the narrow definition of 'intelligence failure', as coined by the American neoconservative scholars Abram Shulsky and Gary Schmitt, rather than the open-ended sense in which the term is used in media commentary.

To recap the definition:

> An intelligence failure is essentially a misunderstanding of the situation that leads a government (or its military forces) to take actions that are inappropriate and counterproductive to its own interests. Whether it is subjectively surprised by what happens is less important than the fact that the government or the military is doing or continues to do the wrong thing.[1]

Therefore, an intelligence failure occurs when a government misreads the strategic context in which it finds itself, and takes actions which later prove to be counterproductive. Merely being caught unawares by a development does not imply that the government's intelligence agencies have failed. By definition, every adverse incident, whether it is a terrorist bombing or a surprise military attack is a failure of tactical intelligence. It is logical to assume that if precise foreknowledge about the incident had been available, timely action could have been taken to avert it. Yet, if the government's response is measured and appropriate, such tactical intelligence failures can be still subsumed into larger strategic intelligence successes.[2]

Two ready examples of this dynamic are the 1962 Cuban Missiles crisis and the 1999 Kargil crisis. In both cases, strategic intelligence had led to the prior conclusion that it would be counterproductive to the enemy's own interests if they initiated offensive action. The CIA assessed, correctly, that the Soviet Union only stood to lose face if it smuggled missiles into Cuba and was then compelled to withdraw them.[3] Likewise, in 1999, R&AW analysts thought it would be irrational for Pakistan to attack India at a time when it was incapable of withstanding a retaliatory assault.[4] Both agencies failed to predict the specific course of action chosen by the adversary, but ended up having their overall assessments vindicated by events. Seen from this perspective, the real intelligence failures appear to have been on the Soviet and Pakistani sides. After all, both Moscow and Islamabad came out of the respective crises humiliated, having initiated action whose results were beneficial to the adversary (in these examples, the United States and India).

Like the noise-to-signals ratio argument developed by Roberta Wohlstetter, this book relies on hindsight to support its analysis.[5] (In a landmark study of the 1941 Japanese attack at Pearl Harbour, Wohlstetter had argued that warning signs of an attack come piecemeal to intelligence analysts, embedded amidst a great deal of irrelevant data. The warnings are 'signals' which are drowned out by confusing background 'noise' as intelligence analysts attempt to predict an enemy's next move. Only once the attack has already occurred does it become clear to the analysts just which pieces of available information could have helped in predicting it).

This book takes a similar retrospectively-oriented view of Indian strategic intelligence. It argues that at no point did intelligence agencies fail in predicting major shifts in terrorist strategy, whether of an escalatory or expansive nature. Where they proved inadequate was in developing such warnings to an 'actionable' standard. The IB and the R&AW could not satisfy local intelligence requirements so as to prevent the anticipated terrorist activity. All that these agencies could do was to provide policy makers with insights as to the 'big picture', and so steer counterterrorist efforts away from serious mistakes.

It appears that, given this limitation, the agencies served the cause of Indian counterterrorism reasonably well. Barring one exception (the 2006 offer to create a joint counterterrorism mechanism with Pakistan – which we shall discuss later), New Delhi has not blundered while combating Pakistan-sponsored terrorism. Indian policy makers did not react inappropriately to escalations or expansions of terrorist violence. Instead, they failed to react vigorously enough. True to the pattern manifested in democracies elsewhere, Indian counterterrorism has unfolded along the lines of 'disjointed incrementalism'.[6] Put simply, this means that counterterrorist efforts have remained ad hoc and insufficiently robust to reverse the tide of terrorist violence. At most, they have only succeeded in mitigating its effects. Preventing the occurrence of such violence in the first place, through intelligence-led intervention, has not been feasible.

Punjab: Total Counterterrorism Success

There were three counterterrorist failures in Punjab, which were reflected in terms of heightened yearly non-combatant fatality rates. The first occurred between 1981 and 1984. Beginning gradually, it saw 13 non-combatants being killed annually in both 1981 and 1982. This figure went up to 75 in 1983, as communal massacres began to be carried out by Khalistani groups. However, the six months prior to Operation Bluestar (June 1984) were by far the worst, leaving 298 people dead.[7] To arrest this trend, the Indian Army was ordered to storm the terrorists' headquarters in the Golden Temple. Its offensive action led to an immediate improvement in the security situation, and casualties dropped to around 60 in the latter half of 1984. The following year saw an even greater improvement, with the number of non-combatant deaths dropping to 63 in total (see Appendix 1 for the full Table of yearly noncombatant fatality rates).

During this period (1984–85), the central government in New Delhi developed a clear-cut, uncompromising policy towards Sikh separatism. By deploying the army in a counterterrorist role, it succeeded in restoring order within a state that was hurtling towards anarchy. Gaps in intelligence were filled up by offensive operations that hunted down terrorist cadres and extracted a rich trove of information from their interrogations. Detailed profiles were built up on individual terrorist leaders and their groups, and the divide between strategic and tactical intelligence was reduced. This promising trend was reversed in 1986, when the newly elected state government of Surjit Singh Barnala opted to pursue a conciliatory policy towards the terrorists.

Between 1986 and 1988, terrorist violence once again rose, with 3379 non-combatant deaths over the three-year period. The most dramatic escalation took place in 1987–88, *after* the Barnala government had been dismissed and direct rule imposed by New Delhi. Whereas 910 people were killed in 1987, the corresponding figure for 1988 was 1,949. The sudden increase in fatalities occurred as a result of the terrorists' improved weaponry: from May 1987 onwards, Pakistan provided the Khalistanis with large quantities of Kalashnikov assault rifles. Initially, the Punjab Police were mesmerised by the lethality of the new weapon, especially since many of the force's rank-and-file had never seen it before. So intense was their fear that gossip within the force soon credited the AK-47 with a near-mythological capacity for destruction.[8]

Only after KPS Gill took charge of the Punjab Police, and emphasised an offensive-operational posture, was counterterrorist operational capacity increased. Upgrades were effected in police weaponry, manpower, communications and transport infrastructure. Coordination was improved with the BSF and CRPF battalions operating in the state, and a comprehensive assault was mounted on the Khalistani groups. At considerable cost to themselves, the security forces succeeded in bringing down the non-combatant fatality rate. The death toll for 1989 was 1,168; Gill has since maintained that another six months of offensive action would have wiped out the Khalistan movement.[9]

However, even as operational capacity and coordination increased, political consistency proved fleeting. After coming to power in December 1989, the central government of prime minister VP Singh reversed the policy adopted by his predecessor, Rajiv Gandhi. Instead of continuing with the campaign against Khalistani terrorism, Singh adopted a conciliatory approach, thereby providing the terrorists with a breathing space. The first quarter of 1990 saw a 40 per cent surge in terrorist violence as the police were forced to suspend offensive operations.[10] Unlike the previous two counterterrorist failures, this last escalation of Khalistani terrorism (1990–91) was primarily caused by the government's own policy.

It is therefore tempting to label this period as an 'intelligence failure'. Before making such a generalisation however, one needs to examine the long-term impact of the 'healing hearts' approach pursued by prime minister VP Singh. In the short run, it led to a massive increase in non-combatant fatality rates, and so was unquestionably a *counterterrorist* failure. Yet, over a period of time, this same failure helped forge a political consensus both domestically and internationally on the need to crush Sikh separatism. By allowing the Khalistanis to run wild and kill without limitation, the government actually hastened the process of de-legitimising separatist violence.[11] After 1989, Sikh separatism came to be perceived as a movement dominated by hooligans with no religious or political ideals. Increasing incidents of rape, extortion, kidnapping and mass murder lost bona fide separatist ideologues any popular sympathy that they might have once had.[12] Gradually, the political road was cleared for the counterterrorist offensive of 1992–93, which ultimately wiped out Sikh separatism.

The 'Decompression' Effect

The events of 1990–91 were an extreme manifestation of the 'theory of decompression', which is propounded by some Indian security officials.[13] Put simply, this theory holds that the quickest and most effective way for the government to 'win hearts and minds' is to allow terrorists to run riot, thereby alienating their own supporters. That way, the government and its security forces can argue to domestic and international audiences that they are only restoring order, rather than suppressing a popular revolt. The theory is derived from a belief that reducing a rebellion's popular support base accomplishes more in the long term than neutralising individual activists, no matter how violent their operations.[14]

By following such a policy, Indian strategists adhere to the maxims prescribed by British counterinsurgency experts such as Robert Thompson. According to the latter, counter-subversion must always take precedence over efforts to control political violence.[15] Especially in situations where operational resources are limited, greater emphasis must be given to developing a long-term perspective rather than focusing on short-term concerns. Although this view of internal-security management has notable and highly eminent detractors, who argue that it provides a convenient excuse for counterterrorist failure, the fact remains that it does form part of the analytical framework of Indian decision-making.

Seen from this perspective, VP Singh's soft counterterrorist policy does not qualify as an intelligence failure in a strategic sense. At most, it created a situation where security forces were unable to prevent an escalation of terrorist activity, owing to political constraints. Once these constraints were removed and operational capacities upgraded to meet the new demands of the situation, an all-out assault could be launched on the Khalistanis. Thus, when the Punjab unit of the Congress (I) won the 1992 state Assembly elections, it confidently asserted that no concessions towards the terrorists were necessary.[16] All that was offered to the Khalistani activists was the option of surrendering and being granted amnesty, or being wiped out. Faced with such political resolve, and crippled by aggressive security forces operations, the terrorist groups simply folded up.

Operation Rakshak II and the subsequent multi-force campaign of 1992–93 represented the only time in India's fight against Pakistan-backed terrorism when all the four constraints were simultaneously removed. The intensity and scale of this synchronised assault on the Khalistan movement defied the terrorists' ability to adapt to it. Although scattered gangs did begin to operate in other Indian states to take pressure off their comrades in Punjab, their actions had no strategic impact. The *raison d'être* for Sikh separatism had always been the territorially-defined conflict in Punjab. Once the security situation in that state improved, Khalistani activities elsewhere in the Indian hinterland automatically subsided.

It might be useful at this point to quote a report by the Punjab Police's Intelligence Wing, describing the situation in 1993:

> Disintegration of militant outfits in Punjab and the powerful onslaught of the security forces led to several things. Recruitment came to a near-end. Their courier system was disrupted. Willing harbourers were not available and old harbourers became panicky. There was shortage of funds with them due to firm control over robberies, extortions and kidnappings for ransom. Terrorist leaders suffered from mutual distrust due to the betrayal by several insiders [sic]. The Punjab in every respect became a dangerous place to operate.[17]

So dangerous in fact did Punjab become, that 15 terrorists were being killed for every non-combatant or police fatality.[18] During 1992, the security forces adopted a strategy of leadership decapitation. After identifying the leader of a particular terrorist group, they would focus on tracking him down and eliminating him. The idea was to exert a demonstrative effect over the separatist movement, and strike fear amongst the ranks of the less motivated terrorists.[19] There was an immediate payoff: terrorist violence declined and members of the population were emboldened to volunteer additional information. This, in turn, was used to finish off the lower-rung Khalistanis.

Armed with the mandate and resources needed to combat terrorist groups, the Punjab Police did not have to depend on national agencies for tactical intelligence. Although the R&AW provided considerable support to the police during 1992, its role in counterterrorism remained a secondary one. Disillusioned supporters of the separatist movement supplied information to the agency, which in turn fed the data into liaison channels for routine dissemination.[20] The deployment of the Indian Army was far more critical to the eventual success of the counterterrorism campaign. KPS Gill later admitted that the army was instrumental in turning the situation around during 1992–93.[21] Had its soldiers not operated alongside the police, it is unlikely that the Khalistan movement would have been so comprehensively defeated.

Secure in the knowledge that the newly-elected state government backed his aggressive approach, Gill crafted a long-term counterterrorist strategy. Since intelligence reports were warning that the ISI had instructed Khalistani terrorists to engage in spectacular assaults, security at vital installations was enhanced. A five-year plan for counterterrorist operations from 1992 to 1997 was drawn up.[22] It involved increasing police manpower and raising Special Weapons and Tactics (SWAT) battalions within the force. The Punjab Police had already experimented with commando-type units since the late 1980s and found them to be excellent for surgical interventions. Well-trained and highly-motivated, these units were quick to follow up on intelligence reports and engage with the terrorists wherever they were spotted. Eventually, nearly one-sixth of the 60,000-strong Punjab Police force was trained and equipped for special operations.[23]

Confronted with a determined foe, the ISI was unable to gain the operational depth in Punjab that was necessary to continue supporting the Khalistan movement. Its agent network in the state was smashed by joint police–IB operations. During the mid 1990s, Pakistani operatives made efforts to facilitate sensational acts of terrorism by Sikh separatists. Only two of these succeeded. One, in 1995, resulted in the assassination of the Punjab chief minister. Although Indian Intelligence was aware at the time of ISI plots to assassinate senior officials, complacency on the part of the security forces led to its reports being ignored.[24]

The other devastating terrorist attack occurred in 1997, when 38 people were killed in a train bombing. Significantly, the involved terrorist group did not claim responsibility for the attack, aware that it would only arouse public anger against itself.[25] Even so, the Punjab Police possessed a sufficiently robust local-intelligence network to track down the perpetrators and bring them to justice. Currently, the police and IB are keeping a close watch on former Khalistani terrorists and politico-religious leaders in Punjab.[26] Their concern stems from awareness that the ISI is using such elements to revive Sikh separatism. In June 2007, timely IB detection thwarted an attempt by the Pakistani agency to instigate sectarian violence among the Sikhs.[27] It is likely that similar attempts will continue to be made. At the time of writing however, they appear unlikely to meet with even a modicum of success.

Jammu and Kashmir: Partial Counterterrorist Success

Like Punjab, the conflict in Jammu and Kashmir saw three major escalations in terrorist activity. Throughout the period under study (1988–2010), Indian intelligence agencies were focused on long-term analysis. Their strategic assessments became all the more crucial given the limited policy options facing New Delhi. While Pakistan provided massive amounts of military, financial and diplomatic support to the separatist groups, India could not retaliate militarily. Pakistan's nuclear arsenal ruled out raids on terrorist training camps located across the Line of Control in Pakistan Occupied Kashmir. Any battlefield intelligence that was gathered by security forces therefore had to be acquired within Indian-administered territory itself.

In this situation, the best that the Indian government could do was monitor infiltration levels across the LoC, and strive to lower these through better border security. Meanwhile, a long-drawn-out war of attrition was being conducted in the interiors of Jammu and Kashmir state so as to wear down the rebels. Launching a comprehensive crackdown on the lines of Punjab was not an option, due to lack of international support. In effect, ever since large-scale violence erupted in the state, Indian counterterrorist policy has remained consistent but has not received the support of international consensus. Foreign governments have viewed Kashmir as disputed territory, and not as an integral part of India like Punjab. They are thus pointedly ambivalent about the right of Pakistan to covertly support Kashmiri separatism.[28] Over time, this has extended even to ignoring the involvement of non-Kashmiri terrorists in the conflict.

Lack of international support for Indian counterterrorist efforts has played a disproportionately large role in causing counterterrorist failures.[29] It has reduced the extent to which India can militarise counterterrorism – although militarisation is necessary for a lasting counterterrorist success. When violence originally escalated between 1988 and 1990, the state police was unprepared to deal with it. The decimation of the IB's agent network required security forces to initiate offensive operations and gather their own intelligence. Shortfalls in operational capacity were only made good during 1990, when the Indian Army, BSF and CRPF were deployed on counterterrorist duties. As a result of their intervention in support of the local law enforcement apparatus, non-combatant fatalities fell from 862 in 1990 to 594 in 1991 (see Appendix 2 for the full Table of yearly non-combatant fatality rates).

Over the following years, the ISI and Kashmiri separatists jointly adapted to the new challenges posed by Indian troop deployments in Jammu and

Kashmir. Terrorist training was imparted on a near-industrial basis in camps within Pakistan Occupied Kashmir, and infiltration rates across the LoC rose steadily. This escalation could not be controlled despite close scrutiny by Indian intelligence agencies because of the risk of attracting international censure. Pakistani diplomats were making strenuous efforts to depict the conflict in Kashmir as a case for humanitarian intervention. India was being roundly criticised in international human rights forums for using heavy-handed tactics to suppress a popular uprising. Any escalation of counter-terrorist activity from the Indian side, beyond the bare minimum needed to govern the state, would have been counterproductive.

This dynamic was broken in 1996–97, after the Indian government held elections to the Jammu and Kashmir Assembly. With a popularly-elected government installed in Srinagar, India could claim that its counterterrorist campaign enjoyed local support. Furthermore, the strengthening of the state police's operational infrastructure improved tactical intelligence, since the police had greater local knowledge than other security forces. Problems persisted in operational coordination however, with the responsibilities of different security forces overlapping. Institutional egos hampered the emergence of an integrated force for counterterrorist efforts, since the Indian Army was unwilling to take orders from any other force.

Even so, it was not poor operational coordination but lack of political consensus at the international level that facilitated the next escalation of terrorist violence. Sensing that India was diplomatically isolated after its May 1998 nuclear tests, Pakistan intensified its involvement in Jammu and Kashmir. First, the Pakistan army launched an ill-fated adventure in the Kargil region of the state and, when this backfired, it shifted focus back to the Kashmir Valley. In any case, after 1995, a large number of Pakistani mercenaries had been operating in the Valley, marginalising the indigenous Kashmiri militants. Post 1999, the ISI used foreign terrorists to raise violence levels in Kashmir.

Interestingly, Indian security forces did quite well in containing the post-Kargil escalation. Barring the Ramzan ceasefire, which lasted between November 2000 and May 2001, terrorist groups were relentlessly battered by aggressive security operations. Although 2001 saw the highest number of fatalities of any year in the conflict, this was largely because of terrorist deaths. In terms of non-combatant fatalities, 2001 was the third most violent year in Jammu and Kashmir, with 1,067 deaths as opposed to 1,161 in 1995 and 1,333 in 1996. Moreover, security forces fatalities were far lower than those of the terrorists', and in fact *declined* even when the latter were

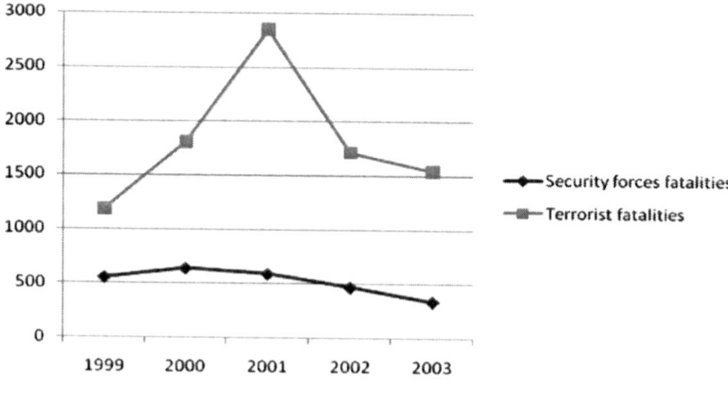

Graph 3 The kill rate after Kargil

still rising. This indicates that the most severe years of the Kashmir conflict (2000–2001) were years that the Indian security forces were well prepared for.

It is at this point that one can detect the 'theory of decompression' being applied in Kashmir. Most commentators have argued that the Ramzan ceasefire was a policy blunder. It led to increased non-combatant fatalities, fewer terrorist deaths, and a disruption of the police intelligence network.[30] While this was true, the ceasefire also had one long-term positive result: it exacerbated simmering tensions within the terrorist movement. Already, Kashmiri separatists were split into two camps – those who wanted independence from India and those who wanted merger with Pakistan. The former camp was dominated by the Jammu and Kashmir Liberation Front, which had declared a ceasefire with the Indian government in 1994. The latter camp was dominated by the Hizb-ul Mujahiddin, which had become the largest terrorist group in the state.

By extending a ceasefire offer to the Hizb, New Delhi managed to further split the terrorist movement along ethnic differences. Intelligence agencies knew by 2000 that the Hizb, which was dominated by ethnic Kashmiris, was bitterly resentful of the ISI's treatment of its cadres. Convinced that Pakistani and Afghan mercenaries were more trustworthy, the Pakistani agency had accorded them special treatment. While a Hizb fighter received a monthly stipend of between INR 3,000 and 10,000, remuneration for foreign terrorists was between INR 10,000 and 15,000. Furthermore, foreign terrorists were paid lump sums of INR 200,000–250,000 upon completion of their two-year contracts in Jammu and Kashmir. Kashmiri terrorists received no such payment, and were instead expected to continue fighting Indian security forces forever.[31]

After 2001, the Hizb gradually became defunct as a terrorist group.[32] Its cadres divided into moderates and hardliners, and were soon at war with each other. ISI efforts to forge a measure of unity failed. The Pakistani agency thereafter had to rely on mercenary-dominated groups like the Lashkar-e-Toiba, Harkat-ul Mujahiddin and Jaish-e-Mohammad. These organisations were overwhelmingly Pakistani in their composition. Their enhanced profile in Jammu and Kashmir soon proved counterproductive for Islamabad. India finally was able to claim that it was not fighting a people's revolt in Kashmir, but a proxy war waged by Pakistan itself.[33] Once 9/11 drove home the threat of pan-Islamist terrorism to countries like the US, India's stance on the Kashmir issue received more international sympathy.

Groups such as LeT, HuM and JeM thus became liabilities for the ISI. Try as it might, the Pakistani government failed to convince US policy makers that these groups were indigenous to Jammu and Kashmir.[34] Although Washington did not immediately put pressure on Islamabad to clamp down on terrorist infiltration across the LoC, a noticeable mood shift had taken place internationally. After the invasion of Afghanistan, the US could not escape accusations of 'double standards' if it denied India's right to active self-defence. Taking advantage of this, New Delhi resorted to coercive diplomacy, threatening to go to war if Pakistan did not reduce cross-border infiltration. It was helped in the process by the ISI's own mistakes: the Pakistani agency instigated two highly provocative attacks by jihadist terrorists on India. The first was the December 2001 attack on the Indian Parliament and the second was the May 2002 attack on Indian military families in Jammu.

With the Indian Army poised to invade Pakistan Occupied Kashmir and its own conduct under intense international scrutiny, Islamabad was forced onto the defensive. It could not complain to the US about Indian sabre-rattling, as would have been the case prior to 9/11. By deploying its military in forward positions, the Indian government also achieved a similar force saturation effect as was obtained during Operation Rakshak II in Punjab. Cross-border movements became virtually impossible along the LoC, and infiltration levels began to drop. Despite trying hard, terrorist groups were unable to disrupt the September 2002 Jammu and Kashmir Assembly elections, which were widely recognized as free and fair. The ten-month military standoff along the Indo–Pakistani border in 2001–02 therefore served a strategic purpose.

Between 2002 and 2010, terrorist violence declined steadily in Jammu and Kashmir. Prodded by the US, from November 2003 Pakistan stopped using artillery fire to cover terrorist infiltration across the Line of Control. Its (reluctant) restraint allowed the Indian Army to aggressively hunt down terrorists in the border areas, and the number of 'kills' surged.[35] A year later, an anti-infiltration fence had also been constructed along the LoC. Its completion reduced the battle between terrorism and counterterrorism to a game of numbers. With fewer terrorists entering the state, larger numbers of troops were left free to hunt down those terrorists already in-country. By 2004, tactical intelligence had improved to the point where security forces could concentrate on leadership decapitation, as had been done in Punjab. Over the course of five years (2003–08), 179 'commanders' of the Hizb-ul Mujahiddin were killed, while the Lashkar-e-Toiba and Jaish-e-Mohammad lost 126 and 64 senior leaders respectively.[36] The sheer rate of attrition of these groups made many junior terrorists reluctant to assume leadership roles for fear of being eliminated.

Despite the overall improvement in counterterrorist performance since 2002, there remains a strong risk of violence levels rising at some point in the future. Few policy makers in New Delhi or Islamabad have forgotten that recent Indian counterterrorist successes are mostly due to the ceasefire along the LoC.[37] If Pakistani troops were to once again provide artillery support to terrorist infiltrators, attacks on non-combatants in Jammu and Kashmir would certainly grow more frequent. Owing to this, Indian Intelligence is currently tracking terrorist activity in Pakistan Occupied Kashmir, with a view to ascertaining if the ceasefire is likely to be abrogated.[38] Indian policy makers meanwhile remain reluctant to launch an all-out attack on the remaining terrorist cadres in Jammu and Kashmir for fear of exhausting international support.

At present, it appears that international opinion is attempting to rein in Indian counterterrorist efforts without actually restricting them. Mopping up operations in Jammu and Kashmir have been hindered by lack of adequate security forces. Flushing out the last vestiges of terrorist groups requires deploying additional troops in uninhabited areas of the state.[39] Currently, these areas have no security forces presence and have become sanctuaries for terrorists seeking to escape the security dragnet in populated areas. An additional complication has been posed by Pakistan's constant demand, made since 2004, that India withdraw its army from counterterrorist duties in the Kashmir Valley. Although there is some international pressure on New Delhi to reciprocate Islamabad's 'good behaviour' since 2003, Indian analysts are opposed to demilitarisation. Their arguments are based on both moral and practical grounds.

KPS Gill for instance has scoffed at the logic 'that if a mass murderer agrees – even temporarily – to stop murdering our people, we owe him something by way of reward'.[40] Another writer had pointed out that the districts from which Pakistan has specifically asked for the Indian Army to be withdrawn lie adjacent to the Line of Control. Demilitarisation in these areas would immediately open up infiltration routes for terrorists from Pakistan Occupied Kashmir, which have been sealed since 2002.[41] Expecting that at some point, India will have to lower the pace of its security operations, the ISI has concentrated on building up a highly skilled core of terrorists within Jammu and Kashmir. Indian security forces have noted that those terrorists still active in the state are much better trained and equipped than their predecessors. While in the early 1990s, the 'kill ratio' was approximately seven terrorists for every security forces fatality, this fell to less than 3:1 in 2007.[42] Considering that violence continues (albeit at a much lower level than at any time previously), Indian counterterrorism in Jammu and Kashmir has only been partially successful.

Counterterrorist Efforts against Pan-Islamist Jihadism: A Failure

The fight against jihadist groups in the Indian hinterland is perhaps the most crucial one, which seems to be at risk of producing a classic intelligence failure. Failure to act on intelligence warnings is not as dangerous as misreading the strategic context which has given rise to pan-Islamist terrorism. With successive Indian governments unable to formulate an offensive response to the jihadist threat, attacks on non-combatants have grown more frequent and widespread.[43] Such leadership paralysis has increased the burden on intelligence agencies to prevent every single attack while the political executive sleeps.

From the evidence marshalled in this book, it would appear that Indian counterterrorist efforts against jihadism are crippled by all four constraints: lack of political consistency and consensus, as well as a lack of operational capacity and coordination. Current counterterrorist efforts are purely ad hoc, aimed at firefighting rather than getting ahead of events. The inadequacy of this approach is apparent in the growing frequency of jihadist attacks in recent years. All told, between December 2001 and December 2008 there were 23 notable incidents of pan-Islamist terrorism in India. Not all of these were successful. If, for the sake of simplicity, the definition of a 'successful' terrorist attack is restricted to one in which 10 or more non-combatants were killed, then there were 15 successful attacks between 2001 and 2008. 12 of these took place after the Congress (I) came to power in New Delhi, in mid 2004 (see Appendix 3 for the list of attacks).

Prior to 2001, there had been just three major jihadist attacks on India. The first of these was the synchronised bombing of Mumbai on 12 March 1993 by a transnational crime syndicate led by Dawood Ibrahim. The gangsters who carried out the bombings had been trained in explosives handling by ISI operatives in Pakistan. Another significant attack was the 21 May 1996 market bombing in Delhi. Once again, police investigators found that the bombers were in close contact with the ISI. Finally, a series of bomb blasts in the town of Coimbatore, in Tamil Nadu state, killed 60 persons on 14 February 1998. This attack too was tenuously linked to Pakistan although the actual bombers were Indian nationals.

It should be evident from the list above that between 1993 and 2008, pan-Islamist groups succeeded in subverting a growing number of Indian Muslims. This is not to deny that the vast majority of India's Muslim population remained law-abiding and patriotic. In May 2008 the Dar-ul Uloom *madrassa* in Uttar Pradesh, the most powerful Islamic seminary in South Asia, issued a *fatwa* (religious edict) against jihadist groups.[44] Following the November 2008 terrorist attack in Mumbai, which killed 166 non-combatants, the seminary's leadership called upon Indian Muslims to oppose religious fanaticism. As a community, the Muslims of India have shown exemplary moderation and rejected the nihilistic world-view of Arab jihadist groups like Al Qaeda and its Pakistani affiliates.

Yet, the fact cannot be denied that Pakistan-based terrorist groups have managed to create pockets of sympathy in Indian society. By failing to prevent this, Indian policy makers can be accused of having neglected to act on strategic intelligence. Ever since the discovery of the K2M Plan in 1992, Indian intelligence has warned of the ISI's intent to radicalise Indian Muslims through pan-Islamist ideology. Initially, Pakistani subversive efforts were easily detected and neutralised, owing to lack of sympathy from the Muslim community. Given the country-wide reach of ISI networks within India, the leadership role in disrupting jihadist conspiracies was handled by the IB. Local police forces were constrained by jurisdictional boundaries and could not pursue terrorists across the length and breadth of the country. Until the Gujarat riots of 2002, in which Hindu extremists killed several hundred Muslims, the scale of the jihadist threat was matched by the IB's ability to contain it. Post 2002 however, the threat grew at a faster rate than the agency's coverage of it.

Although its primary function is strategic intelligence, the IB has an excellent record in providing tactical support to state police forces – within reasonable limits. Between 1998 and 2003, it neutralised 250 ISI-backed jihadist cells across India, *excluding* Jammu and Kashmir and the north-eastern states.[45] This neutralisation rate of approximately one terrorist cell per week has been maintained even after the current spate of jihadist violence erupted in 2005.[46] Where problems have arisen is not so much in the IB's response to pan-Islamist terrorism, but in that of the political leadership. Put simply, there has been no policy response to ample warnings from the intelligence community since 2002 that Pakistan planned to target the Indian heartland.[47] That is, unless depending even more heavily on the IB to disrupt terrorist networks may be called a 'response'.

Since Indian policy makers do not even recognise Pakistan's intention to sponsor jihadist activity in India, there is no consensus on how to react. Besides vague promises to 'improve' intelligence acquisition, political parties have remained silent on precisely how jihadism in the heartland is to be countered. This should not be surprising, given the idiosyncratic policy pursued by New Delhi towards Islamabad – the main sponsor of pan-Islamist groups in South Asia.

Even since its creation in 1947, Pakistan has viewed Hindu-dominated India as an existentialist threat that could only be contained if Balkanised. This view was formalised as the Qurban Ali Doctrine, after the Pakistani intelligence officer who first articulated it.[48] It was the driving force behind the ISI support to separatist groups in the Indian north-eastern region during the 1950s, and has since been manifested in Punjab and Jammu and Kashmir. While Pakistan has consistently availed itself of opportunities to damage India, India has chosen to fight defensively in the vain hope that Pakistan would eventually relent.

Eager not to lose the moral high ground, Indian policy makers have rejected repeated calls from intelligence professionals to mount a retaliatory proxy war.[49] Consequently, India's counterterrorist policy in the urban heartland is heavily dependent on intelligence to warn where, when and how the jihadists will next strike. In the absence of any increments to police intelligence networks, either in terms of manpower or finances, this means that the IB's workload has steadily increased. Not only is it now required to predict major changes in terrorist strategy, but it is also expected to prevent specific attacks. State police forces meanwhile plead helplessness in following up on IB warnings due to lack of resources.

The result is a situation where Indian intelligence has degenerated into a glorified neighbourhood-watch service. Over-emphasis on tactical intelligence for immediate consumption by security forces has led to inadequate focus on strategic intelligence.[50] Producer–consumer responsibilities now overlap to an extent where both national agencies and local police forces can plausibly accuse each other of failing to generate 'actionable' information. Just who should assume the leadership role in tactical intelligence is a question that nobody wants to answer, as it would affix accountability for counterterrorist failures. Consequently, there is no clear-cut handover point in counterterrorist intelligence from the IB to the state police intelligence branches.

Bent on serving their own partisan interests, politicians compound the confusion. An example is the war of words which broke out between the chief minister of Uttar Pradesh state, Mayawati, and the central government in November 2007. Mayawati accused the IB of having failed in its duty, because it had not warned her that terrorists were planning to bomb court premises in Uttar Pradesh. Her charge completely ignored the federal/provincial division of powers and responsibilities as enshrined in the Indian Constitution. Moreover, the Uttar Pradesh Police had enough information in its own intelligence files to indicate a likelihood of jihadist attacks on the judicial system.[51] The problem was, neither it nor the IB could develop this information to an actionable degree, since both lacked the requisite sources.

Since the current phase of jihadist terrorism began (with the Delhi bombings of October 2005), counterterrorist failures have demonstrated a common pattern. Prior to an attack the IB usually issues a general warning about terrorist threats to a particular city and the likely targets. However, follow-up on such warnings is left in limbo, with state police forces waiting for the national agency to provide additional information. On occasions when the jihadist plotters happen to be careless about their communications security, electronic intercepts help in acquiring the necessary details.[52] Most of the time however, good terrorist counterintelligence leads to preventive failures, and the police have to rely on post-incident investigation to identify the perpetrators.

Despite being warned that ISI-backed jihadist networks are spreading their tentacles across India, policy makers have taken no action. Worse, they have actually increased the threshold of tolerance for Pakistani sponsorship of terrorism. In what was the first and only real 'intelligence failure' of Indian internal-security management, on 16 September 2006 Prime Minister Manmohan Singh publicly declared that India and Pakistan were both victims of terrorism. He also agreed, allegedly upon the intercession of the US, to establish a joint counterterrorism mechanism with Pakistan. By doing so, he fell into a trap set by the ISI to deflect Indian accusations that it was sponsoring terrorist groups.[53] Former government officials in India immediately criticised the PM's move, correctly predicting that in future Islamabad would simply demand that New Delhi furnish substantive 'proof' against Pakistan-based jihadist groups. By studying the evidence collected by Indian agencies, the ISI could refine its covert operations in India and so ensure that the jihadists' actions remained deniable.[54] To invite Pakistan to jointly conduct counterterrorism investigations with India was like asking a suspected murderer to participate in post-mortems of his victims.

One explanation for how the Prime Minister was drawn into this policy blunder might be forthcoming from the lessons of the 1962 Sino–Indian War. While analysing what went wrong, the then DIB, Bhola Nath Mullik, made a crucial observation. He argued that the problem with intelligence in 1962 was that there was too much of it for consumers to absorb and assimilate effectively. Instead of a shortage of information, it was the alacrity with which newly-acquired information was dispatched to the end-users that paralysed Indian decision-making.[55] The Indian Army and Ministry of External Affairs became desensitised to intelligence reporting, which was drip-fed to them, and so did not prepare contingency plans to meet a Chinese offensive. Rather, they remained static and allowed a mountain of alarming situational reports to accumulate under them.[56]

A similar state of events might be playing out in the producer–consumer relationship in Indian counterterrorism intelligence. Having constantly been warned about the threat of pan-Islamist terrorism, policy makers and security forces commanders alike have come to depend on intelligence agencies to combat it.[57] Rather than accept that intelligence is a supportive function, they see its role as transformative. Consequently, there is no effort to draw up a consistent counterterrorist policy, develop a bipartisan consensus, upgrade operational capacity or enhance coordination. Offensive action cannot be mounted against terrorist support structures due to lack of political will and operational resources. With the initiative ceded to the jihadists, it falls upon the IB and the R&AW to prevent the actualisation of terrorist plots. As a result, these agencies have begun to lose sight of the bigger picture – which was originally their area of expertise.

Counterterrorist efforts against pan-Islamist jihadism continue to be dogged by each of the four constraints. Policy makers have yet to recognise that continued Pakistani protection of groups such as the Lashkar-e-Toiba amounts to an act of war. Instead, they allow cultural and trade exchanges with Pakistan to continue unabated, providing the ISI with additional routes to infiltrate sleeper cells into India. ISI officials posted under diplomatic cover in New Delhi are allowed to meet with Kashmiri separatist leaders, while R&AW personnel in Islamabad are hounded brutally.[58] (The All Party Hurriyat Conference, an above-ground coordination forum for terrorist groups in Jammu and Kashmir, is believed by Indian security sources to be totally ISI-controlled. Its members allegedly receive instructions and funds from Pakistani 'diplomats' in Delhi, which are then passed on to terrorist leaders. These individuals also frequent the international conference circuit, providing a local façade to the Pakistani proxy war. It is testimony to the tolerance of the Indian state that it allows them free movement, unlike the ISI, which is widely suspected to have assassinated any Hurriyat activist who was prepared to consider reconciliation with New Delhi. An example: Abdul Ghani Lone, shot dead by suspected ISI-backed terrorists on 21 May 2002.)[59]

Neither can state governments rise above partisan politics and agree on either anti-terrorist legislation or on proposals to set up a federal agency for counterterrorism. Following the November 2008 terrorist attacks in Mumbai, a National Investigation Agency (NIA) was established to handle terrorist crimes on an all-India basis.[60] Opposition from regional political parties forced the central government to water down its plans for the organisation.[61] Instead of having both arrest powers and an intelligence function, the NIA was only given the former. For its raw data, it is dependent on the existing intelligence apparatus.[62]

This apparatus has proven itself woefully under-resourced for the task of combating techno-savvy, networked opponents. On the one hand, state police forces lack the personnel, equipment and training required for intelligence gathering. On the other hand, the IB lacks even a basic coverage of rural areas. Consequently, these areas have become staging points for jihadist attacks on Indian cities. While the terrorists are improving their coordination and creating task-specific cells and networks across India, there is no matching unity of effort between state police forces. Coordination of counterterrorism remains an IB responsibility, when it should be devolved to the level of district police officers.[63] Owing to the absence of a time-bound, integrated force approach to counterterrorism, information sharing at the tactical level remains poor. Unless a conscious effort is made to upgrade counterterrorist efforts in the Indian heartland to a wartime footing, it is unlikely that future attacks can be prevented.

In Summation: The Organisational Failure School is Right, but the Response Failure School is Even More Right

This book demonstrates that the overwhelming majority of Indian counterterrorist failures do not qualify as 'intelligence failures'. Their origins do not lie in faulty strategic assessments, but rather in the inability or unwillingness of consumers to follow up on these assessments. 'Action failures' is therefore a better term to describe them. Academic and journalistic criticism of the national-intelligence agencies' method of working is only relevant in so far as it deals with resource limitations. Beyond that, it is unclear how further efforts at intelligence reform, be they the introduction of legislative oversight, formal coordination mechanisms or open-market recruitment, would make any difference to counterterrorist performance.[64]

The school of thought that blames organisational failure is accurate when it identifies poor information sharing and neglect of strategic analysis as problems in counterterrorism intelligence, but it is off the mark as to the cause of these problems. Instead of being caused by improper organisational management, they are caused by the unwillingness of intelligence consumers to take independent follow-up action. Like the colonial Intelligence Bureau, Indian intelligence agencies are currently being forced by overwhelming consumer demand to prioritise tactical intelligence. Due to their finite resources, they have little capacity left over to assess underlying strategic trends, as well as undertake covert operations to weaken terrorist counterintelligence.

The school of thought that pinpoints response failure would regard such a situation as representing a failure to act on strategic intelligence, which has turned a full circle to damage the intelligence process itself. Thus, the arguments of the organisational failure school can be merged with those of the response failure school, without either losing their validity.

Where the two schools remain at loggerheads is on the issue of allocating responsibility for tactical intelligence. A possible solution has been indicated by the intelligence fusion school – tactical intelligence can be made a police responsibility, with the intelligence agencies only playing a secondary role. The task of data fusion could be devolved down to the police, leaving intelligence agencies free to focus on strategic analysis. Since the police are the end-users of tactical intelligence, it makes sense to create fusion centres at their level, rather than at the national level. Instead of just one large clearing house for information, there could be a countrywide network of fusion centres, sharing information with each other directly.

Creating such a network is however, only part of the solution. It is equally important to provide security forces with the political mandate and operational resources to aggressively seek out intelligence. The experience of Indian counterterrorism in Punjab is highly suggestive in this regard. Instead of adopting a threat-reactive posture and waiting for a conspiracy to develop before neutralising it, relentless attrition of terrorist groups is the best way to defeat them.[65] For this to happen, decision-makers have to first shift from a defensive mindset into an offensive one. Such a mindset needs to be capable of unshakable resolve, and to accept that 'actionable' intelligence is not the job of intelligence agencies alone.[66]

Prospects for Indian Intelligence and the Fight Against Pakistan-Sponsored Terrorism

Since 2008, the terrorist threat to India has not subsided in any meaningful way, but has only been relatively dormant. Contrary to the hopes of Indian government officials, neither Pakistani officials nor their terrorist allies appear to be impressed by empty threats of retaliation. As of early 2011, the ISI had assessed that international opinion was once again growing indifferent to its continued involvement with terrorism. With Pakistan remaining a sanctuary and planning base for jihadist groups worldwide, Western governments were terrified of losing Pakistani cooperation in their own individual 'wars' on terror. However, so long as this terror was not directed at them, they were prepared view it as a purely bilateral issue between India and Pakistan, and implicitly equate the two countries in moral terms.

As early as 2009, it became clear that to keep Islamabad appeased, some Western policy makers were prepared to sacrifice Indian interests. Barely two months after the 2008 Mumbai attacks, the then British foreign secretary David Miliband made an appallingly insensitive statement. He told an audience in Mumbai that the attacks were a byproduct of the Kashmir issue.[67] The Indian equivalent of such a *faux pas* would have been for a cabinet-rank minister to tell a British audience that the 2005 London bombings resulted from Whitehall's tolerance for radical Islam during the 1990s. (The British government had previously allowed Islamist militants to remain in the UK as long as they did not harm British interests. This secret deal was known as the 'Covenant of Security', and inadvertently facilitated the spread of jihadist ideology among British Muslims).[68] Miliband's misplaced remark implied that India, a victim of terrorism, bore responsibility for its own misfortune, thereby overlooking Pakistan's suspected involvement.

The Miliband fiasco of January 2009 was an early indication that Western governments found Pakistani counterterrorist cooperation altogether too indispensable to risk it for India's good. Instead, over the next year, diplomatic pressure was quietly exerted upon India to hold talks with Pakistan. Dialogue between the two countries had been suspended, as evidence from the Mumbai attacks investigation strongly suggested official ISI involvement. Not only did foreign governments airbrush this evidence, they also began marginalising Indian strategic interests in Afghanistan.[69] Thus, in deference to Pakistani demands, India was pointedly excluded from a January 2010 conference held in Istanbul on the Afghanistan situation.

Meanwhile, ever alert to changing international moods, from February 2010 the ISI began using LeT cadres to kill Indian aid workers and government personnel in Afghanistan. That month, nine Indians were killed in Kabul hotels in a *fedayeen* assault eerily similar to Mumbai. Yet, the attack drew a nonchalant response from American decision-makers.[70] This contrasted sharply with the forceful stance taken by US intelligence agencies in July 2008, when they had openly accused the ISI of targeting Indian diplomats in Kabul. What then changed between July 2008 and February 2010?

The short answer is: international security priorities. From 2008, US counterterrorist policy became markedly unilateral and minimalist, focused only on protecting the US homeland from jihadists while simultaneously negotiating a withdrawal from Afghanistan. Islamabad was quick to recognise its own importance in the attainment of these objectives. It thus lobbied Washington to force India into holding peace talks, knowing that this would require New Delhi to overlook ISI involvement in the Mumbai attacks. Such lobbying continued even after the arrest of a Pakistani–American LeT operative in late 2009 confirmed that the attacks had been masterminded by officials within the ISI.[71]

The LeT operative, named David Headley, revealed to US interrogators that at least five serving ISI officers were (and probably still are) based in Karachi, planning further terrorist attacks on India in cooperation with the LeT.[72] Their so-called 'Karachi Project' represented a joint venture between the Pakistani state and jihadist groups, intended to destabilise India through strategic terrorism.[73] These officers were secure in the belief that sponsorship of terrorism was a risk-free enterprise, both to them personally as well as Pakistan in general. Events have so far proved them right – instead of hitting back covertly with lethal force, New Delhi has yielded to international pressure and persisted in seeking talks with Islamabad.

Although the Singh government can be faulted for being overly soft on Pakistan, no other Indian government had really taken a firm stance against cross-border terrorism. The collective failure of Indian political leaders to designate Pakistan as a long-term adversary, whose covert operations need to be reciprocated, has left Indian citizens vulnerable to further terrorist attacks. Taking advantage of this leadership vacuum, the ISI has developed a propaganda strategy to widen rifts in the Indian policy-making establishment and generate paralysis. The origin of this strategy dates back to 2006.

Shortly after Manmohan Singh made his September 2006 blunder by describing India and Pakistan as common victims of terrorism, the ISI developed a plan to exploit the propaganda potential thus created. In December 2006, it circulated instructions to Pakistani diplomatic missions, including the one in New Delhi, asking them to identify journalists who could be cultivated to project a view sympathetic to Pakistan in the local press. The idea was to use the Indian government's own conciliatory statements against it, by implying that henceforth, New Delhi was being inconsistent whenever it accused Pakistan of sponsoring terrorism.

The ISI seems to have worked according to a Leninist model of cultivating 'useful idiots', ie., dupes who could be used to sow discord in the local polity and mask preparations for further attacks. Indian peace activists, as well as selected Western journalists and scholars, were thus employed as pawns in a point-scoring game whose sole purpose was to project New Delhi as unreasonable. Since Mumbai 2008, Pakistani covert warfare against India has thus de-emphasised violent attacks on civilian targets and taken the form of 'agitational terrorism'.[74]

The switch in methods was well-timed: with its involvement in the Mumbai attacks exposed as a result of evidence gathered by Indian and Western intelligence agencies, Pakistan shifted to a campaign of political subversion. Through 2009, it repeatedly violated the ceasefire along the Line of Control using small arms fire, thereby allowing jihadists to infiltrate into Jammu and Kashmir. In keeping with the trend of recent years, these jihadists were highly trained and well-disciplined. Their task however, was not to kill non-combatants but to infiltrate the indigenous Kashmiri separatist movement and prepare it for an *intifada*-type uprising. This was then to be used to emphasise the 'local' roots of the rebellion to foreign governments.

Thus, infiltration attempts into Kashmir increased 45 per cent in 2009 as compared to 2008. The actual number of terrorists entering Indian territory went up by 100 per cent – an indication that weaknesses along the LoC fence had been identified and were being exploited.[75] Logically, this influx of terrorists should have led to an increase in violence, particularly since the Indian government had withdrawn 35,000 soldiers from the state under international pressure.[76] However, instead of attacking civilians, the terrorists infiltrated anti-government political groups and worked them into a frenzied rage. An epidemic of stone-throwing followed. During June and July 2010, 1,266 security forces personnel were injured in 872 violent incidents. Seen from the Indian perspective, the security forces' response was commendably restrained and thus managed to contain the disturbances. Only 60 protestors were killed during this period; an extremely low figure considering the casualties that security forces had suffered.[77] Compared to what might follow in the years ahead however, such agitational terrorism might be just a 'pleasant' interlude.

Meanwhile, Western governments seem increasingly indifferent to Indian concerns about Pakistan-sponsored terrorism, having calculated that they can count on Islamabad to firewall its proxy war against India and prevent a spill-over of jihadist violence against Western targets. Notwithstanding expressions of sympathy for India, these governments are ensuring that they do not make any gesture of support that would annoy Pakistan. Thus, the entire basis of Indian counterterrorist policy might now need to be re-examined.

Hitherto, Indian diplomacy has focused on raising awareness of Pakistani support to jihadist groups, in the hope of rallying the international community against Islamabad. This strategy might however have backfired, as it has made neutral governments even more reluctant to antagonise a nuclear-armed rogue state that could turn its proxy warriors onto them. It seems likely that rather than ignorance of Pakistani involvement with terrorism, the key problem for India is that foreign governments are all too aware of it.

India needs therefore to reduce its dependence on international opinion as a counterterrorist instrument. It needs instead to take a unilateral two-pronged approach against pan-Islamist jihadism. On the one hand, it has to fully implement the domestic security reforms that were supposed to follow the 'lessons' of Mumbai 2008. At present, the changes being made to counterterrorism structures range from cosmetic to substantive. For instance, a new post of Internal Security Advisor has been created in the Home Ministry. This is being filled by a senior intelligence officer.[78] Intelligence fusion centres are being set up at the state level, in the form of 30 Subsidiary Multi-Agency Centres. A national grid (NATGRID) of 21 computerised databases is being established to facilitate the collation, storage and dissemination of strategic intelligence.[79]

However, considering the difficulties that have accompanied implementation of similar 'reforms' in the past, there is cause for scepticism. Resource constraints also remain a serious challenge, and many state governments remain complacent about jihadist threats, notwithstanding periodic entreaties from New Delhi for increased vigilance. Despite the best efforts of intelligence chiefs and security managers at the national level therefore, there are limits to what can realistically be expected from domestic organisational reforms.

The second and more productive approach could be to take the counterterrorist offensive inside Pakistan itself. This would be a daring move, requiring considerable political courage to initially be implemented. Once started however, it has the potential to exert a strong deterrent effect upon the ISI and Pakistani jihadists. The latter manifestly believe that they have the full measure of Indian decision-making. If this complacency could be shattered through a campaign of covert neutralisation, along the lines normally associated with Israeli Intelligence, the terrorists' strategic calculus would be severely disrupted.

Support for this view comes from K Shankaran Nair, a highly respected R&AW veteran who headed the agency during the late 1970s. Two weeks after the November 2008 Mumbai attacks, the author asked Mr. Nair how India should respond to the provocation. Offering to speak on the record, Mr. Nair said: 'If what Pakistan does within our borders exceeds our capacity to control it, then we must take the fight to their doorstep. There is no question'. Hoping for favourable international intervention would be foolish and counterproductive. Strikes against terrorist masterminds, including 'rogue' or 'freelance' ISI officials, would thus be an integral component of an ideal Indian counterterrorist policy.

As former Director IB Ajit Doval notes:

> Pakistan has made 'covert offensive' against India a part of its state policy, to bleed its more powerful adversary. It estimates that its nuclearisation has raised India's tolerance threshold infinitely high, giving it space to operate with impunity and indefinitely. India cannot afford to indefinitely play the game in defensive mode, which is like playing soccer with a single goalpost in which you only receive the hits. By mathematical logic, the defending team can never win. Developing credible covert capacity, whose use can be controlled and calibrated, will be an effective deterrent against Pakistan.[80]

Indian policy makers need to critically evaluate whether in fact, a 'strong and stable Pakistan is in India's interests'. The eminent scholar Ajai Sahni has observed that, other than India, no country in history has been so gullible as to believe that its interests would be served by a strong and stable enemy.[81] To hit jihadists and their handlers on home turf, what is first required is a security policy that avoids conflating Indian interests with those of sympathetic powers that have different interests. Thus, the current policy of mortgaging Indian counterterrorist efforts to Western strategic agendas might have to be jettisoned.

In the final analysis, it is unreasonable of New Delhi to expect foreign governments to protect its citizens, when its own political resolve and operational capability are repeatedly found wanting. Similarly, it is also unreasonable of foreign governments to press for Indo–Pakistani dialogue, when India is under continuing threat of terrorist attack and Pakistan seeks to use this situation to strengthen its bargaining position. While warm relations with Washington and London should be maintained as a matter of course, India can simultaneously explore options for disciplining the Pakistani establishment through covert action.

The adoption of an offensive counterterrorist policy would require massively upgrading Indian intelligence capabilities and orienting them for offensive use. It would also involve crafting a diplomatic strategy that portrays Pakistan as a weak state unable to control radical elements within its borders. For purely tactical purposes, India can partially endorse the official line by Islamabad that cross-border terrorist attacks are the work of non-state actors. New Delhi can then use the diplomatic space thus created to liquidate Pakistani terrorists, while insisting that it does not seek to target or otherwise undermine the Pakistani state. Symbolic peace talks can also be held with Islamabad for the sake of retaining international goodwill. Although the ISI and LeT can be expected to hit back, at least they would no longer enjoy impunity while doing so. Eventually, given the sheer asymmetry of power between India and Pakistan, the former is bound to win a covert war. For this to happen however, it has to cease relying on defensive counterterrorist policies and shift to a posture of active defence.

APPENDIX 1: YEARLY FATALITIES IN PUNJAB

Year	Noncombatants	Security Forces	Terrorists	Total
1981	13	2	14	29
1982	13	2	7	22
1983	75	20	13	108
1984	359	20	77	456
1985	63	8	2	73
1986	520	38	78	636
1987	910	95	328	1333
1988	1949	110	373	2432
1989	1168	201	703	2072
1990	2467	476	1320	4263
1991	2591	497	2177	5265
1992	1518	252	2113	3883
1993	48	25	798	871
1994	2	0	76	78
1995	0	0	11	11
1996	0	0	3	3
1997	56	2	1	59
1998	0	0	0	0
1999	0	0	0	0
2000	18	0	0	18
2001	1	0	0	1
2002	5	0	0	5
2003	0	0	0	0
2004	0	0	0	0
2005	0	0	0	0
2006	0	0	0	0
2007	7	0	0	7
2008	0	0	0	0
2009	0	0	0	0
2010	0	2	2	4

Source: www.satp.org

APPENDIX 2: YEARLY FATALITIES IN JAMMU AND KASHMIR

Year	Civilians	Security Forces	Terrorists	Total
1988	29	1	1	31
1989	79	13	0	92
1990	862	132	183	1177
1991	594	185	614	1393
1992	859	177	873	1909
1993	1023	216	1328	2567
1994	1012	236	1651	2899
1995	1161	297	1338	2796
1996	1333	376	1194	2903
1997	840	355	1177	2372
1998	877	339	1045	2261
1999	799	555	1184	2538
2000	842	638	1808	3288
2001	1067	590	2850	4507
2002	839	469	1714	3022
2003	658	338	1546	2542
2004	534	325	951	1810
2005	521	218	1000	1739
2006	349	168	599	1116
2007	164	121	492	777
2008	69	90	382	541
2009	55	78	242	375
2010	36	69	270	375

Source: www.satp.org

APPENDIX 3: MAJOR ATTACKS BY PAN-ISLAMIST JIHADISTS IN INDIA (2002–2008)

Serial No.	Date of Attack	Place	Method	Non-combatant Fatalities	Terrorist group responsible
1.	24 September 2002	Gandhinagar, in the state of Gujarat	Suicidal assault by two gunmen	32	Lashkar-e-Toiba
2.	13 March 2003	Mumbai, capital of the state of Maharashtra	Train bombing	10	Jaish-e-Mohammad, in collaboration with the Student's Islamic Movement of India (SIMI)
3.	25 August 2003	Mumbai	Two bomb attacks	52	Lashkar-e-Toiba, in collaboration with SIMI
4.	29 October 2005	Delhi	Three bomb attacks	62	No conclusive identification of group responsible
5.	7 March 2006	Varanasi, in the state of Uttar Pradesh	Three bomb attacks	21	No conclusive identification
6.	11 July 2006	Mumbai	Seven bomb attacks on local trains	200	Lashkar-e-Toiba, in collaboration with SIMI

Continued

Continued

Serial No.	Date of Attack	Place	Method	Noncombatant Fatalities	Terrorist group responsible
7.	8 September 2006	Malegaon, in the state of Maharastra	Three bomb attacks	40	Lashkar-e-Toiba, in collaboration with SIMI
8.	19 February 2007	Diwana, in the state of Haryana	Fire-bombing of a train	66	No conclusive identification
9.	18 May 2007	Hyderabad, capital of the state of Andhra Pradesh	Bomb attack	11	No conclusive identification
10.	25 August 2007	Hyderabad	Two bomb attacks	44	No conclusive identification
11.	23 November 2007	Varanasi, Faizabad and Lucknow. All three are cities in Uttar Pradesh	Bomb attacks in court premises	15	Attacks claimed by a hitherto unknown group calling itself the Indian Mujahiddin. Suspected to be a front for joint operations between the Pakistani Lashkar-e-Toiba, the Bangladeshi Harkat-ul Jihad Islami and SIMI
12.	13 May 2008	Jaipur, capital of the state of Rajasthan	Eight bomb attacks	80	Indian Mujahiddin
13.	26 July 2008	Ahmedabad, capital of the state of Gujarat	Seventeen bomb attacks	53	Indian Mujahiddin
14.	13 September 2008	Delhi	Five bomb attacks	24	Indian Mujahiddin
15.	26–29 November 2008	Mumbai	Suicidal assault by ten gunmen	166	Lashkar-e-Toiba

Source: www.satp.org

SOURCES

Interviews (in chronological order)

Note: Some of the interviewees served in the Intelligence Bureau for a relatively short period of time, before going on to serve with great distinction elsewhere. Their ranks, as cited, reflect only the time period when they served in the IB, and not their final designation, unless the latter is also of relevance to this book. Also, some of the interviewees (both intelligence and non-intelligence personnel) have expressed a desire to remain anonymous. So they shall.

Former Indian Home Secretary CG Somaiah, Bangalore, 12 August 2004 and 19 July 2008.

Former R&AW Additional Secretary B Raman, Chennai, 28 December 2004.

Former Director General of Punjab Police, KPS Gill, New Delhi, 3 January 2005 and 20 June 2007.

Former IB Additional Director – B1, New Delhi, 5 January 2005 and 8 September 2008. Also, telephonic interview, 19 March 2005.

Telephonic interview of former IB Additional Director Kalyan Rudra, 6 January 2005.

Former Delhi Police Joint Commissioner Maxwell Pereira, New Delhi, 13 January 2006, 22 July 2006 and 8 September 2008.

Political journalist Harinder Baweja, New Delhi, 22 July 2006 and 29 March 2008.

Former Director, Intelligence Bureau – A1, New Delhi, 19 June 2007, 6 September 2008 and 27 December 2008.

Defence analyst Dr. Manoj Joshi, New Delhi, 26 March 2008.

Former IB Agent – H, New Delhi, 28 March 2008.

Major General (Retired) Afsir Karim, New Delhi, 2 July 2008.

Former IB Special Director DC Nath, New Delhi, 3 July 2008 and 4 July 2008.

Former Director General, Border Security Force, EN Rammohan, New Delhi, 3 July 2008.

Former Secretary (Research) – A2, New Delhi, 4 July 2008.

Defence analyst Air Commodore (Retired) Jasjit Singh, New Delhi, 4 July 2008.

Lieutenant General (Retired) VK Nayyar, New Delhi, 5 July 2008.

Former R&AW Special Secretary R Swaminathan, Chennai, 15 July 2008.

Former R&AW Special Secretary – B2, Bangalore, 19 July 2008.

Former R&AW Special Secretary S Gopal, Bangalore, 20 July 2008.

Telephonic interview of former IB Assistant Director RN Kulkarni, 21 July 2008.

Former Secretary (Research) – A3, London, 25 July 2008.

Former Secretary (Research) N Narasimhan, Bangalore, 27 August 2008.

Inspector General of Karnataka Police Sanjay Vir Singh, Bangalore, 28 August 2008.

Defence analyst Dr. Bidanda Chengappa, Bangalore, 29 August 2008.

Defence analyst Dr. Bhashyam Kasturi, New Delhi, 1 September 2008.

Former IB officer and Director General, Border Security Force, Prakash Singh, New Delhi, 1 September 2008.

Former Indian Army Brigadier involved in counterterrorism operations – G, New Delhi, 2 September 2008.

Pakistan Studies expert Sushant Sareen, New Delhi, 3 September 2008.

Terrorism Studies expert Dr. Ajai Sahni, New Delhi, 3 September 2008.

Former R&AW Special Secretary Kalyan Mitra, New Delhi, 4 September 2008 and 7 September 2008.

Former Secretary (Research) Vikram Sood, 4 September 2008.

Former R&AW Joint Secretary VK Singh, 4 September 2008.

Former IB Joint Director Maloy Dhar, 6 September 2008.

Defence analyst and former Joint Intelligence Committee Chairman K Subrahmanyam, New Delhi, 7 September 2008.

Former Chief of the Army Staff, General (Retired) Ved Malik, New Delhi, 9 September 2008.

Former IB Assistant Director Dr. KS Subramanian, New Delhi, 9 September 2008.

Security affairs analyst Praveen Swami, New Delhi, 10 September 2008.

Former senior officer of the Directorate of Revenue Intelligence (DRI) – R, Bangalore, 15 September 2008.

Former Secretary (Research) PK Hormese Tharakan, Bangalore, 20 September 2008.

Former IB Deputy Director and Director, Central Bureau of Investigation, RK Raghavan, London, 29 September 2008 and 8 October 2008.

Former Director IB and Joint Intelligence Committee Chairman DC Pathak, New Delhi, 27 December 2008.

Former Secretary (Research), Amarjit Singh Dulat, 28 December 2008.

Former Indian Army Brigadier involved in military intelligence and counterterrorism operations – V, New Delhi, 3 January 2011.

Lectures and Speeches

David Hadley, Director of Group Strategic Analysis, at the Royal United Services Institute (RUSI), London, 10 November 2006.

Dennis O'Connor, Her Majesty's Inspector of Constabulary, at RUSI on 14 February 2007.

Frank Gregory, University of Southampton, at RUSI on 15 February 2007.

Chris Bryne, SO15 Counter Terrorism Command, Metropolitan Police at RUSI on 6 March 2007.

Niki Tompkinson, Director, Transport Security and Contingencies Directorate, Department for Transport, at RUSI on 29 May 2007.

Former Pakistani Information Minister Mushahid Hussain, at the Royal Society for Arts, London, 27 June 2008.

Lieutenant General (Retired) Vinayak Patankar, at the Observer Research Foundation (ORF), New Delhi, 5 September 2008.

Official Documents Cited in the Text

Bureau of Police Research and Development Report entitled 'Data on Police Organization as on 01/01/07'.

The Jain Commission Report on the Assassination of Rajiv Gandhi, accessed online via www.india-today.com, on 15 June 2008.

The Shah Commission Report: Circumstances Leading to Declaration of Emergency (New Delhi: Delhi Press, 1978).

K Subrahmanyam, KK Hazari, BG Verghese and Satish Chandra, *From Surprise to Reckoning: The Kargil Review Committee Report* (New Delhi: Sage, 2000).

'Government of Bengal, Political Department, Political Branch, No. 1065 PSD', Indian Political Intelligence Collection, India Office Records, File No. L/P&J/12/398, Document No. P&J(S) 907 1934.

'Minute from Military Secretary W Johnston – Terrorism in Bengal, Conference at Government House, etc.', IPI Collection, IOR, File No. L/P&J/12/398, Document No. P&J(S) 907/34.

'Superior staff in the Intelligence Bureau', IPI Collection, IOR, File No. J&P(S) 243 1924, Document No. L/P&J/12/181.

Official 1962 War History, prepared by the Indian Defence Ministry and accessed online at http://www.bharat-rakshak.com/ARMY/History/1962War/PDF/1962Chapter10.pdf, on 31 March 2009.

Official 1965 War History, prepared by the Indian Defence Ministry and accessed online at http://www.bharat-rakshak.com/ARMY/History/1965War/PDF/1965Chapter09.pdf, on 31 March 2009.

Official 1971 War History, prepared by the Indian Defence Ministry and accessed online at http://www.bharat-rakshak.com/ARMY/History/1971War/PDF/1971Chapter19.pdf, on 31 March 2009.

Reforming the National Security System – Recommendations of the Group of Ministers, Chapter V, accessed online at http://mod.nic.in/newadditions/chapter-v.pdf, on 2 April 2009.

Review of Terrorist Activities in Punjab for the month of May 1991, compiled by the Office of the Additional Director-General of Police Intelligence, Punjab.

Review of Terrorist Activities in Punjab for the month of January 1994, compiled by the Office of the Additional Director-General of Police Intelligence, Punjab.

Review of Terrorist Activities in Punjab for the month of March 1995, compiled by the Office of the Additional Director-General of Police Intelligence, Punjab.

Review of Terrorist Activities in Punjab for the month of May 1995, compiled by the Office of the Additional Director-General of Police Intelligence, Punjab.

Review of Terrorist Activities in Punjab for the year 1993, compiled by the Office of the Additional Director-General of Police Intelligence, Punjab.

Review of Terrorist Activities in Punjab for the year 1994, compiled by the Office of the Additional Director-General of Police Intelligence, Punjab.

Review of Terrorist Activities in Punjab for the year 1997, compiled by the Office of the Additional Director-General of Police Intelligence, Punjab.

A Status Paper on Punjab Terrorism, dated 3 July 1998 and compiled by the Office of the Additional Director General of Police Intelligence, Punjab.

White Paper on the Punjab Agitation, released by the Government of India on 10 July 1984.

Ministry of Home Affairs Annual Report 1990–1991.

Ministry of Home Affairs Annual Report 1999–2000.

Ministry of Home Affairs Annual Report 2000–2001.

Ministry of Home Affairs Annual Report 2002–2003.

Ministry of Home Affairs Annual Report 2003–2004.

Ministry of Home Affairs Annual Report 2007–2008.

The National Investigation Agency Bill 2008, accessed online at www.prsindia.org/docs/bills/1229428259/1229428259_The_National_Investigation_Agency_Bill__2008.pdf, on 12 April 2009.

National Commission on Terrorist Attacks Upon the United States, accessed online via http://www.9–11commission.gov/report/index.htm, on 12 April 2009.

Official Documents Consulted

'Appreciation of the terrorist situation in Bengal, prepared by the Deputy Inspector-General of Police, Intelligence Branch, CID, for the Conference that is to be held in July 1934', IP Collection, IOR, File No. L/P&J/12/398, Document No. P&J(S) 776 1934.

'D-O. No. 520-C., dated Chittagong, 30 May 1934, from EN Blandy, Commissioner, Chittagong Division to the the Chief Secretary of Bengal', IPI Collection, IOR, File No. L/P&J/12/399 [No document number].

'Extract from Weekly Report of the Director, Intelligence Bureau of the Home Department, Government of India, dated Simla, 17 April 1930', IPI Collection, IOR, File No. L/P&J/12/389, Document No. P&J(S) 961 1930.

'Extract from Weekly Report of the Director, Intelligence Bureau, Home Department, dated Simla, 22 September 1932', IPI Collection, IOR, File No. L/P&J/12/391, Document No. P&J(S) 1127 1932.

'Extract from Weekly Report of the Director, Intelligence Bureau, Home Department, dated New Delhi, 26 January 1933', IPI Collection, IOR, File No. L/P&J/12/392, Document No. P&J(S) 191 1933.

'Extract from Weekly Report of the Director, Intelligence Bureau, Home Department, dated New Delhi, 30 November 1933', IPI Collection, IOR, File No. L/P&J/12/392, Document No. P&J(S) 1316 1933.

'Minute' on Anglo-French Counterterrorism Cooperation in Bengal, IPI Collection, IOR, File No. L/P&J/12/6, Document No. P&J(S) 394/33.

'No. 10/R.A/33–1, Intelligence Bureau, (Home Department), Government of India, Simla, dated 4 May 1933', IPI Collection, IOR, File No. L/P&J/12/466, Document No. P&J(S) 591 1933.

'Report on the Work of the Central and District Intelligence Branches for the three years 1930, 1931 and 1932', IPI Collection, IOR, File No. L/P&J/12/466, Document No. 591 1933.

Ministry of Home Affairs Annual Report 1991–1992.

Ministry of Home Affairs Annual Report 1992–1993.

Review of Terrorist Activities in Punjab for the month of January 1991, compiled by the Office of the Additional Director-General of Police Intelligence, Punjab.

Review of Terrorist Activities in Punjab for the month of February 1991, compiled by the Office of the Additional Director-General of Police Intelligence, Punjab.

Review of Terrorist Activities in Punjab for the month of March 1991, compiled by the Office of the Additional Director-General of Police Intelligence, Punjab.

Review of Terrorist Activities in Punjab for the month of April 1991, compiled by the Office of the Additional Director-General of Police Intelligence, Punjab.

Review of Terrorist Activities in Punjab for the month of June 1991, compiled by the Office of the Additional Director-General of Police Intelligence, Punjab.

Review of Terrorist Activities in Punjab for the month of July 1991, compiled by the Office of the Additional Director-General of Police Intelligence, Punjab.

Review of Terrorist Activities in Punjab for the month of August 1991, compiled by the Office of the Additional Director-General of Police Intelligence, Punjab.

Review of Terrorist Activities in Punjab for the month of September 1991, compiled by the Office of the Additional Director-General of Police Intelligence, Punjab.

Review of Terrorist Activities in Punjab for the month of October 1991, compiled by the Office of the Additional Director-General of Police Intelligence, Punjab.

Review of Terrorist Activities in Punjab for the month of November 1991, compiled by the Office of the Additional Director-General of Police Intelligence, Punjab.

Review of Terrorist Activities in Punjab for the month of March 1994, compiled by the Office of the Additional Director-General of Police Intelligence, Punjab.

Review of Terrorist Activities in Punjab for the month of April 1994, compiled by the Office of the Additional Director-General of Police Intelligence, Punjab.

Review of Terrorist Activities in Punjab for the month of July 1994, compiled by the Office of the Additional Director-General of Police Intelligence, Punjab.

Review of Terrorist Activities in Punjab for the month of August 1994, compiled by the Office of the Additional Director-General of Police Intelligence, Punjab.

Review of Terrorist Activities in Punjab for the month of September 1994, compiled by the Office of the Additional Director-General of Police Intelligence, Punjab.

Review of Terrorist Activities in Punjab for the month of October 1994, compiled by the Office of the Additional Director-General of Police Intelligence, Punjab.

Review of Terrorist Activities in Punjab for the month of November 1994, compiled by the Office of the Additional Director-General of Police Intelligence, Punjab.

Review of Terrorist Activities in Punjab for the month of February 1995, compiled by the Office of the Additional Director-General of Police Intelligence, Punjab.

Review of Terrorist Activities in Punjab for the month of April 1995, compiled by the Office of the Additional Director-General of Police Intelligence, Punjab.

Review of Terrorist Activities in Punjab for the month of January 2001, compiled by the Office of the Additional Director-General of Police Intelligence, Punjab.

Review of Terrorist Activities in Punjab for the month of May 2001, compiled by the Office of the Additional Director-General of Police Intelligence, Punjab.

Review of Terrorist Activities in Punjab for the year 1999, compiled by the Office of the Additional Director-General of Police Intelligence, Punjab.

Statement of Mr Farooq Khan, Senior Superintendent of Police, Anantnag District, Jammu & Kashmir, before the Commission on the Chittisinghpura Massacre, dated 8 August 2000.

The 9/11 Investigations: Staff Reports of the 9/11 Commission, edited by Steven Strasser (New York: PublicAffairs, 2004).

Intelligence and Security Committee Report into the London Terrorist Attacks on 7 July 2005.

Books, Articles and Monographs Cited in the Text

Vishal Agraharkar, 'Political Incentives and Hindu-Muslim Violence: A Study of Hyderabad, India', Bachelor of Arts dissertation, submitted to Williams College, Williamstown, Massachusetts, in May 2005.

MJ Akbar, *Nehru: The Making of India* (London: Penguin, 1988).

Keith Alexander, 'Transforming Army Intelligence While at War', *Army*, October 2004.

Vinod Anand, 'An Integrated and Joint Approach Towards Defence Intelligence, *Strategic Analysis*, Vol.. 24, No.8 (2000).

NC Asthana and Anjali Nirmal, *Terrorism, Insurgencies and Counterinsurgency Operations* (Jaipur: Pointer, 2001).

Desmond Ball, 'Signals Intelligence in India', *Intelligence and National Security*, Vol. 10, No.3 (1995).

Bradley WC Bamford. 'The Role and Effectiveness of Intelligence in Northern Ireland', *Intelligence and National Security*, Vol. 20, No.4 (2005).

YM Bammi, *War Against Insurgency and Terrorism in Kashmir* (Dehra Dun: Natraj Publishers, 2007).

Steven Banovac, Peter Dillon, Matthew Hennessy, Ronald Idoko, Christine Patterson, Augustine Paul, Ian Sonneborn, Christina Steve and Kate Stubbe, *Anatomy of a Terrorist Attack: Terror at Beslan* (Pittsburgh, Matthew B Ridgeway Center for International Secuirty Studies, 2007).

CA Bayley, *Empire and Information: Intelligence Gathering and Social Communication in India, 1780–1870* (Cambridge: Cambridge University Press, 1996).

Navnita Chadha Behera, *State, Identity and Violence: Jammu, Kashmir and Ladakh* (New Delhi: Manohar, 2000).

Richard Betts, 'Surprise Despite Warning: Why Sudden Attacks Succeed', *Political Science Quarterly*, Vol. 95, No.4 (1981).

Richard Betts, 'Intelligence Warning: Old Problems, New Agendas', *Parameters*, Spring 1998.

GS Bhargava, *The Battle of NEFA: The Undeclared War* (New Delhi: Allied Publishers, 1964).

Subir Bhaumik, 'Insurgencies in India's Northeast: Conflict, Co-Option and Change', accessed online at www.eastwestcenter.org/fileadmin/stored/pdfs/EWCWwp010.pdf, on 31 March 2009.

Crispin Black, *7–7: The London Bombs – What Went Wrong?* (London: Gibson Square, 2005).

KS Brar, *Operation Blue Star: The True Story* (New Delhi: UBSPD, 1993).

David Brooks, 'The Elephantiasis of Reason', *Atlantic Monthly*, January-February 2003.

James Burch, 'A Domestic Intelligence Agency for the United States? : A Comparative Analysis of Domestic Intelligence Agencies and Their Implication for Homeland Security', *Homeland Security Affairs*, Vol. 3, No. 2 (2007).

Daniel L Byman, 'Friends Like These: Counterinsurgency and the War on Terrorism', *International Security*, Vol. 31, No. 2 (Fall 2006).

Bhumitra Chakma, *Pakistan's Nuclear Weapons* (London: Routledge, 2009).

David Charters, 'British intelligence in the Palestine campaign, 1945–47', *Intelligence and National Security*, Vol.6, No. 1 (1991).

RS Chowdhary, *A Short History of the Intelligence Corps* (Pune: Military Intelligence Training School, 1985).

Carl von Clausewitz, *On War*, (London: Everyman's Library, 1993).

Hillel Cohen and Ron Dudai, 'Human Rights Dilemmas in Using Informers to Combat Terrorism: The Israeli-Palestinian Case', *Terrorism and Political Violence*, Vol. 17, No. 1 & 2 (2005).

Charles Cogan, 'Hunters not Gatherers: Intelligence in the Twenty-First Century', *Intelligence and National Security*, Vol. 19, No. 2 (2004).

Stephen Cohen, *India: Emerging Power* (New Delhi: Oxford University Press, 2002).

Ronald Crelinsten, 'Analysing Terrorism and Counter-terrorism: A Communication Model', *Terrorism and Political Violence*, Vol. 14, No. 2 (2002).

Ronald Crelinsten, *Counterterrorism* (Cambridge: Polity, 2009).

Martha Crenshaw, 'Terrorism, Strategies and Grand Strategies', in Audrey Kurth Cronin and James M Ludes, eds., *Attacking Terrorism: Elements of a Grand Strategy* (Washington D.C: Georgetown University Press, 2004).

Pushpita Das, 'National Investigation Agency: A Good Start but not a Panacea', *IDSA Strategic Comments*, 12 January 2009.

Mike Dennis, *The Stasi: Myth and Reality* (London: Pearson Education Limited, 2003).

Kevin Michael Derksen, 'Commentary: The Logistics of Actionable Intelligence Leading to 9/11', *Studies in Conflict & Terrorism*, Vol. 28, No. 3 (2005).

Maloy Krishna Dhar, *Open Secrets: India's Intelligence Unveiled* (New Delhi: Manas, 2005).

Maloy Krishna Dhar, *Fulcrum of Evil: ISI-CIA-Al Qaeda Nexus* (New Delhi: Manas, 2006).

Kirpal Dhillon, *Police and Politics in India* (New Delhi: Manohar, 2005).

John Diamond, *The CIA and the Culture of Failure: US Intelligence from the End of the Cold War to the Invasion of Iraq* (Stanford, California: Stanford University Press, 2008).

Everett Carl Dolman, 'Military Intelligence and the Problem of Legitimacy: Opening the Model', *Small Wars and Insurgencies*, Vol. 11, No. 1 (2000).

Ajit Doval, 'Terrorism: The Response Strategy for India', *Eternal India*, Vol. 1, No. 4 (2009).

Ajit Doval, 'Need for a National Response on Security', *Eternal India*, Vol. 2, No. 9 (2010).

John Dziak, 'The Study of the Soviet Intelligence and Security System', in Roy Godson ed., *Comparing Foreign Intelligence* (London: Pergamon-Brassey's, 1988).

Richard Falkenrath, 'The 9/11 Commission Report: A Review Essay', *International Security*, Vol. 29, No. 3 (2005).

Ahmad Faruqui, *Rethinking the National Security of Pakistan: The Price of Strategic Myopia* (Burlington, VT., Ashgate, 2003).

Michael Freeman, *Freedom or Security: The Consequences of Democratic States Using Emergency Power to Fight Terror* (London: Praeger, 2003).

George Friedman, *America's Secret War: Inside the Hidden Worldwide Struggle between the United States and its Enemies* (London: Little, Brown, 2004).

David Galula, *Counter-insurgency Warfare: Theory and Practice* (London: Pall Mall, 1964).

Boaz Ganor, *The Counter-terrorism Puzzle: A Guide for Decision Makers* (London: Transaction Publishers, 2005).

Raymond L Garthoff, 'US intelligence in the Cuban missile crisis', *Intelligence and National Security*, Vol. 13, No. 3 (1998).

Shlomo Gazit, 'Estimates and Fortune-Telling in Intelligence Work', *International Security*, Volume 4, Number 4 (1980).

Shlomo Gazit and Michael Handel, 'Insurgency, Terrorism and Intelligence', in Roy Godson ed., *Intelligence Requirements for the 1980s: Counterintelligence* (Washington D.C: National Security Strategy Information Centre Inc, 1980).

Samarjit Ghosh, 'Mumbai Terror Attacks: An Analysis', *Institute of Peace and Conflict Studies Special Report, February 2009.*

KPS Gill, 'Endgame in Punjab: 1988–1993', *Faultlines: Writings on Conflict and Resolution*, Vol. 1 (1999).

KPS Gill, 'Technology, Terror and a Thoughtless State', *Faultlines: Writings on Conflict and Resolution*, Vol. 3 (1999).

Melvin Goodman, '9/11: The Failure of Strategic Intelligence', *Intelligence and National Security*, Vol. 18, No. 4 (2003).

Namrata Goswami, 'India's counter-insurgency experience: the "trust and nurture" strategy', *Small Wars & Insurgencies*, Vol. 20, No. 1 (2009).

Lester W Grau, 'Something Old, Something New: Guerrillas, Terrorists, and Intelligence Analysis', *Military Review*, July -August 2004.

Colin Gray, *Modern Strategy* (Oxford: Oxford University Press, 1999).

Frank Gregory, 'An assessment of the contribution of intelligence-led counter-terrorism to UK homeland security post-9/11 within the 'contest' strategy', in

Paul Wilkinson ed., *Homeland Security in the UK: Future preparedness for terrorist attack since 9/11* (London: Routledge, 2007).

Shaun Gregory, 'The ISI and the War on Terrorism', *Pakistan Security Research Unit (PSRU) Brief No. 28* (2008).

Percival Griffiths, *To Guard My People: The History of the Indian Police* (London: Ernst Benn Limited, 1971).

Wajahat Habibullah, 'The Political Economy of the Kashmir Conflict: Opportunities for Economic Peacebuilding and for U.S Policy', *United States Institute of Peace Special Report 121* (2004).

Husain Haqqani, *Pakistan: Between Mosque and Military* (Washington D.C, Carnegie Endowment for International Peace, 2005).

John Hollister Headley, 'Learning from Intelligence failures', *International Journal of Intelligence and CounterIntelligence*, Vol. 18, No. 3 (2005).

Michael Herman, *Intelligence Power in Peace and War* (Cambridge: Cambridge University Press, 1996).

Michael Herman, 'Counter-Terrorism, Information Technology and Intelligence Change', *Intelligence and National Security*, Vol. 18, No. 4 (2003).

Philip Heymann, *Terrorism and America: A Commonsense Strategy for a Democratic Society* (London: MIT Press, 1998).

Alistair Horne, *A Savage War of Peace: Algeria 1954–1962* (London: Macmillan, 1977).

Zahid Hussain, *Frontline Pakistan: The Path to Catastrophe and the Killing of Benazir Bhutto* (London, I.B Tauris, 2008).

Vijendra Singh Jafa, 'Ten O' clock to bed: Insouciance in the face of Terror', *Faultlines: Writings in Conflict and Resolution*, Vol. 5 (2000).

NS Jamwal, 'Counter Terrorism Strategy', *Strategic Analysis*, Vol. 27, No. 1 (2003).

Peter Janke, *Terrorism and Democracy: Some Contemporary Cases* (London: Macmillan, 1992).

Loch K Johnson, 'Sketches for a theory of strategic intelligence', in Peter Gill, Stephen Marrin and Mark Phythian eds., *Intelligence Theory: Key Questions and Debates* (Abingdon, Oxon: Routledge, 2009).

Calvert Jones, 'Intelligence Reform: The logic of information sharing', *Intelligence and National Security*, Vol. 22, No. 3 (2007).

Seth Jones, 'Fighting Networked Terrorist Groups: Lessons from Israel', *Studies in Conflict and Terrorism*, Vol. 30, No. 4 (2007).

Mallika Joseph, 'Counter Terror Operations: Limitations to Security Forces', *Institute of Peace and Conflict Studies (IPCS) Research Paper 1.*

Manoj Joshi, *The Lost Rebellion: Kashmir in the Nineties* (New Delhi: Penguin, 1999).

Manoj Joshi, *Combating Terrorism in Punjab: Indian Democracy in Crisis* (London: Research Institute for the Study of Conflict and Terrorism, 1993).

David Kahn, 'A Historical Theory of Intelligence', *Intelligence and National Security*, Vol. 16, No. 3 (2001).

AS Kalkat, 'Aspects of Internal Security', *Eternal India*, Vol. 2, No. 8 (2010).

Afsir Karim, *Counter-terrorism: The Pakistan Factor* (New Delhi: Lancer, 1991).

Bhashyam Kasturi, *Intelligence Services: Organization, Analysis and Function* (New Delhi: Lancer, 1994).

Bhashyam Kasturi and Pankaj Mehra, 'Geo-Politics of South Asian Covert Action: India's Experience and Need for Action Against Pakistan', *Indian Defence Review*, Vol.16, No. 2 (2001).

Bhashyam Kasturi, 'The Present State of the Naxalite Movement', *AAKROSH: Asian Journal on Terrorism and Internal Conflicts*, Vol. 10, No. 4 (2007).

Bhashyam Kasturi, 'Unified Command HQ in Counter Insurgency and Role of Intelligence in J&K', *India Defence Review*, Vol. 16, No. 1 (2001).

John Keegan, *Intelligence in War: Knowledge of the Enemy from Napoleon to Al Qaeda* (London: Hutchinson, 2003).

AA Khan, *Surrender* (Mumbai: Yogi Impressions, 2004).

Rashid Ahmad Khan and Muhammad Saleem, *RAW: Global and Regional Ambitions* (Islamabad: Islamabad Policy Research Institute, 2005).

Ashish Khetan, 'Karachi to Mumbai: Terror, Step by Step' in Harinder Baweja ed., *26/11: Mumbai Attacked* (New Delhi: Roli, 2009).

Frank Kitson, *Bunch of Five* (London: Faber and Faber, 1977).

Frank Kitson, *Low Intensity Operations: Subversion, Insurgency and Peacekeeping* (London: Faber and Faber, 1991).

Amos Kovacs, 'Using Intelligence', *Intelligence and National Security*, Vol. 12, No. 4 (1997).

Amos Kovacs, 'The Nonuse of Intelligence', *International Journal of Intelligence and CounterIntelligence*, Vol. 10, No. 4 (1998).

RN Kulkarni, *Sin of National Conscience* (Mysore: Kritagnya, 2004).

Suneel Kumar, 'Sikh Ethnic Uprising in India and Involvement of Foreign Powers', *Faultlines: Writings in Conflict and Resolution*, Vol. XVIII (2007).

Y Lakshmi, *Trends in India's Defence Expenditure* (New Delhi: ABC Publishing House, 1988).

Walter Laqueur, *The New Terrorism: Fanaticism and the Arms of Mass Destruction* (London: Phoenix Press, 1999).

William Latimer, *What Can the United States learn from India to Counter Terrorism?*, Master's Thesis submitted to U.S Naval Postgraduate School, Monterey, California in March 2004.

Bernard-Henri Levy, *Who Killed Daniel Pearl?* (London: Duckworth, 2003).

Prem Mahadevan, 'Counterterrorism in the Indian Punjab: Assessing the "Cat" System', *Faultlines: Writings on Conflict and Resolution*, Vol. 18 (2007).

Prem Mahadevan, 'The Gill Doctrine: A Model for 21 Century Counterterrorism?', *Faultlines: Writings on Conflict and Resolution*, Vol. 19 (2008).

Prem Mahadevan, 'The November 2008 Fidayeen Attack in Mumbai: Origins and Implications', *RIEAS Research Paper Number 127* (2009).

Inder Malhotra, *Indira Gandhi: A Personal and Political Biography* (Boston: Northeastern University Press, 1989).

Jagmohan Malhotra, *My Frozen Turbulence in Kashmir* (New Delhi: Allied Publishers, 1991).

Ved Malik, 'India's Politico-Military Establishment and Decision-Making', *Centre for Policy Research Occasional Paper, February 2004.*

Ved Malik, *Kargil: From Surprise to Victory* (New Delhi: Harper Collins, 2006).

Francis Marlo, 'WMD Terrorism and US Intelligence Collection', *Terrorism and Political Violence*, Vol. 11, No. 3 (1999).

Stephen Marrin, 'Preventing Intelligence Failures by Learning from the Past', *International Journal of Intelligence and CounterIntelligence*, Vol. 17, No. 4 (2004).

Stephen Marrin, 'Intelligence analysis and decision-making', in Peter Gill, Stephen Marrin and Mark Phythian eds., *Intelligence Theory: Key Questions and Debates* (Abingdon, Oxon: Routledge, 2009).

Ved Marwah, *Uncivil Wars: Pathology of Terrorism in India* (New Delhi: HarperCollins, 1997).

Thomas Mathew, 'India's Confrontation with Terror: Need for Bold Initiatives', *IDSA Policy Brief, 25th February 2009.*

JE Menon and NM Komerath, 'The Hizbul Mujahideen Ceasefire: Who Aborted It?', *Bharat-Rakshak Monitor*, Vol. 3, No. 2 (2000).

Gil Merom, 'The 1962 Cuban intelligence estimate: A methodological perspective', *Intelligence and National Security*, Vol. 14, No. 3 (1999).

Stephen Metz, 'Insurgency and Counterinsurgency in Iraq', *The Washington Quarterly*, Vol. 27, No.1 (2003).

BN Mullik, *My Years With Nehru: The Chinese Betrayal* (New Delhi: Allied Publishers, 1971).

BN Mullik, *My Years With Nehru: Kashmir* (New Delhi: Allied Publishers, 1971).

Pervez Musharraf, *In the Line of Fire: A Memoir* (London: Simon & Schuster, 2006).

VS Naipaul, *India: A Million Mutinies Now* (London: Minerva, 1991).

VN Narayanan, *Tryst with Terror: Punjab's Turbulent Decade* (Delhi: Ajanta, 1996).

K Sankaran Nair, *Inside IB and RAW: The Rolling Stone that Gathered Moss* (New Delhi: Manas, 2008).

DC Nath, *Intelligence Imperatives for India* (New Delhi: India First Foundation).

Kuldip Nayar and Khushwant Singh, *Tragedy of Punjab: Operation Blue Star and After* (New Delhi: Vision Books, 1984).

Peter Neumann and MLR Smith, 'Strategic Terrorism: The Framework and its Fallacies', *Journal of Strategic Studies*, Vol. 28, No. 4 (2005).

James M Olson, 'The Ten Commandments of Counterintelligence', *Studies in Intelligence*, Vol. 45, No. 5 (2001).

David Omand, 'Countering International Terrorism: The Use of Strategy', *Survival*, Vol. 47, No. 4 (2005).

David Omand, 'Reflections on Secret Intelligence', in Peter Hennessy ed., *The New Protective State: Government, Intelligence and Terrorism* (London: Continuum, 2007).

Bard O'Neill, *Insurgency and Terrorism: From Revolution to Apocalypse* (Dulles, Virginia: Potomac, 2005).

Ranjit K Pachnanda, *Terrorism and Response to Terrorist Threat* (New Delhi: UBSPD, 2002).

DK Palit, *War in the High Himalaya: The Indian Army in Crisis, 1962* (London: Lancer International, 1991).

G Parthasarathy, 'Pakistan and Challenges to National Security', in PC Dogra ed., *Changing Perspective on National Security* (New Delhi: Lancer's, 2004).

DC Pathak, *Intelligence: A Security Weapon* (New Delhi: Manas, 2003).

DC Pathak, 'Internal Security and Foreign Policy', *Eternal India*, Vol. 2, No. 4 (2010).

Ralph Peters, 'Our Strategic Intelligence Problem', *Military Review*, July-August 2006.

Giadomenico Picco, 'The Challenges of Strategic Terrorism', *Terrorism and Political Violence*, Vol. 17, No. 1 (2005).

Paul Pillar, 'Intelligence' in Audrey Kurth Cronin and James M. Ludes, eds., *Attacking Terrorism: Elements of a Grand Strategy* (Washington D.C: Georgetown University Press, 2004).

Paul Pillar, 'Good literature and bad history: The 9/11 commission's tale of strategic intelligence', *Intelligence and National Security*, Vol. 21, No. 6 (2006).

Paul Pillar, 'Adapting intelligence to changing issues', in Loch Johnson ed., *Handbook of Intelligence Studies* (London: Routledge, 2007).

Harish K Puri, Paramjit Singh Judge and Jagrup Singh Sekhon, *Terrorism in Punjab: Understanding Grassroots Reality* (New Delhi: Har-Anand, 1999).

Rajesh Rajagopalan, 'Restoring Normalcy: The Evolution of the Indian Army's Counterinsurgency Doctrine', *Small Wars and Insurgencies*, Vol. 11, No. 1 (2000).

B Raman, *Intelligence: Past, Present and Future* (New Delhi, Lancer, 2002)

B Raman, 'India's National Security Management & Cross-Border Terrorism', in Lakshami Krishnamurti, R Swaminathan and Gert W Kueck eds.,

Responding to Terrorism: Dilemmas of Democratic and Developing Societies (Madras: Bookventure, 2003).

B Raman, 'Dimensions of Intelligence Operations', *USI Journal*, April–June 2004.

B Raman, *The Kaoboys of R&AW: Down Memory Lane* (New Delhi, Lancer, 2007).

M Maroof Raza, *Low Intensity Conflicts: The New Dimension to India's Military Commitments* (Meerut, UP: Kartikeya, 1995).

William Reno, 'Shadow States and the Political Economy of Civil Wars', in Mats Berdal and David Malone eds., *Greed and Grievance: Economic Agendas in Civil Wars* (Boulder, Colorado: Lynne Rienner Publishers, 2000).

Julio Ribeiro, *Bullet for Bullet: My Life as a Police Officer* (New Delhi: Penguin, 1998).

Manila Rohatgi, *Spy System in Ancient India: From the Vedic Period to the Gupta Period* (Delhi: Kalpa Publications, 2007).

Herbert Romerstein, 'Soviet Intelligence in the United States', in Roy Godson ed., *Intelligence Requirements for the 1980s: Counterintelligence* (Washington D.C, National Security Information Centre Inc., 1980).

Joshua Rovner and Austin Long, Amy Zegart, 'Correspondence': How Intelligent is Intelligence Reform', *International Security*, Vol. 30, No. 4 (2006).

Kalyan Rudra, *Rise and Fall of Punjab Terrorism 1978–1993* (New Delhi: Bright Law House, 2005).

Richard Russell, *Sharpening Strategic Intelligence: Why the CIA Gets It Wrong and What Needs to be Done to Get It Right* (Cambridge: Cambridge University Press, 2007).

Ajai Sahni, `Counter-Terrorism and The Flailing State', *Eternal India*, Vol. 1, No. 5 (2009).

Sunil Sainis, 'Intelligence Reforms', *Bharat Rakshak Monitor*, Vol. 3, No. 4 (2001).

Sunil Sainis, 'Rameshwar Nath Kao (1918–2002)', *Bharat-Rakshak Monitor*, Vol. 4, No. 5 (2002).

NS Saksena, *Law and Order in India* (New Delhi: Abhinav Publications, 1987).

AR Saluja, 'Reorganizing Indian Intelligence Organization', *Indian Defence Review*, Vol. 13, No. 3 (1998).

Len Scott And Peter Jackson, 'The Study of Intelligence in Theory and Practice', *Intelligence and National Security*, Vol. 19, No. 2 (2004).

Len Scott, 'Sources and Methods in the Study of Intelligence: A British View', *Intelligence and National Security*, Vol. 22, No. 2 (2007).

LP Sen, *Slender was the Thread: Kashmir Confrontation 1947–48* (New Delhi: Orient Longmans, 1969).

M Shamsur Rabb Khan, 'Poor policing and weak intelligence gathering', *Institute of Peace and Conflict Studies*, 10 October 2007.

LN Sharma and Umesh Kumar, 'A Need for Cogent Counter-Terror Doctrine', *Eternal India*, Vol. 1, No. 11 (2009).

VN Sharma, 'Whither India?', in PC Dogra ed., *Changing Perspective on National Security* (New Delhi: Lancer's, 2004).

Chandra Shekhar, 'India's Security Environment: An Indian View', *Studies in Conflict and Terrorism*, Vol. 15, No. 4 (1992).

Anil Shorey, 'Proliferation of Internal Security and Allied Agencies in India', *Strategic Analysis*, Vol. 12, No. 4 (1989).

Abram N Shulsky and Gary J Schmitt, *Silent Warfare: Understanding the World of Intelligence* (Dulles, Virginia: Brassey's, 2002).

Jennifer Sims, 'Intelligence to counter terror: The importance of all-source fusion', *Intelligence and National Security*, Vol. 22, No. 1 (2007).

RK Jasbir Singh, *Indian Defence Yearbook 2000* (Dehra Dun: Natraj, 2000).

Sarab Jit Singh, *Operation Black Thunder: An Eyewitness Account of Terrorism in Punjab* (New Delhi: Sage, 2002).

Ujjwal Kumar Singh, *The State, Democracy and Anti-Terror Laws in India* (London: Sage, 2007).

Prakash Singh, *Kohima to Kashmir: on the Terrorist Trail* (New Delhi: Rupa, 2001).

Tavleen Singh, *Kashmir: A Tragedy of Errors* (New Delhi: Penguin, 1996).

Satyindra Singh, 'The Kargil Review Committee Report: Much to Learn and Implement', *Indian Defence Review*, Vol. 15, No. 1 (2000).

VK Singh, *India's External Intelligence: Secrets of Research and Analysis Wing (RAW)* (New Delhi: Manas, 2007).

SK Sinha, 'Jammu and Kashmir: Past, Present and Future', *USI Journal*, April-June 2005.

Stephen Sloan, 'Meeting the Terrorist Threat: The Localization of Counter Terrorism Intelligence', *Police Practice and Research*, Vol. 3, No. 4 (2002).

Ashish Sonal, *Terrorism and Insurgency in India: A Study of the Human Element* (New Delhi: Lancer, 1994).

VK Sood and Pravin Sawhney, *Operation Parakram: The War Unfinished* (New Delhi: Sage, 2003).

John D Stempel, 'Error, Folly, and Policy Intelligence', *International Journal of Intelligence and CounterIntelligence*, Vol. 12, No. 3 (1999).

Brian Stewart, 'Winning in Malaya: An Intelligence Success Story', *Intelligence and National Security*, Vol. 14, No. 4 (1999).

K Subrahmanyam and Arthur Monteiro, *Shedding Shibboleths: India's Evolving Strategic Outlook* (Delhi: Wordsmiths, 2005).

KS Subramanian, *Political Violence and the Police in India* (New Delhi: Sage, 2007).

LN Subramanian, 'CI operations in Jammu & Kashmir', *Bharat-Rakshak Monitor*, Vol. 3, No. 2 (2001).

Aisha Sultanat, 'Madrassas in India', *Institute of Peace and Conflict Studies Issue Brief, 14 November 2003.*

Praveen Swami, *India, Pakistan and the Secret Jihad: The covert war in Kashmir 1947–2004* (New York: Routledge, 2007).

George K. Tanham, *Indian Strategic Thought: An Interpretive Essay* (Santa Monica, CA., RAND, 1992).

Ashley J. Tellis, 'Pakistan's Record on Terrorism: Conflicted Goals, Compromised Performance', *The Washington Quarterly*, Vol. XXXI/2 (2008).

Pradeep Thakur, *Militant Monologues: Echoes From the Kashmir Valley* (New Delhi: Parity Publishers, 2003).

Robert Thompson, *Defeating Communist Insurgency: Experiences from Malaya and Vietnam* (London: Chatto and Windus, 1966).

Robert Tomes, 'Schlock and Blah: Counter-insurgency Realities in a Rapid Dominance Era', *Small Wars and Insurgencies*, Vol. 16, No. 1 (2005).

George O'Toole, 'Kahn's Law: A Universal Principle of Intelligence?', *International Journal of Intelligence and Counterintelligence*, Vol. 4, No. 1 (1990).

Charles Townsend, *Terrorism: A Very Short Introduction* (Oxford: Oxford University Press, 2002).

Gregory Treverton, Seth Jones, Steven Boraz and Phillip Lipscy, *Toward a Theory of Intelligence: Workshop Report* (Santa Monica, CA: RAND, 2006).

Thomas Troy, 'The "Correct" Definition of Intelligence', *International Journal of Intelligence and Counterintelligence*, Vol. 5, No. 4 (1992).

Michael Turner, *Why Secret Intelligence Fails* (Washington D.C: Potomac, 2006).

Virender Uberoy, *Combating Terrorism* (New Delhi: Intellectual Book Corner, 1992).

Bruce Vaughn, 'The Use and Abuse of Intelligence Services in India', *Intelligence and National Security*, Vol. 8, No. 1 (1993).

BG Verghese, 'A Jammu and Kashmir Primer: From Myth to Reality', Centre *for Policy Research Occasional Paper, June 2006.*

Yaacov YI Vertzberger, *Misperceptions in Foreign Policymaking: The Sino-Indian Conflict, 1959–1962* (Boulder, Colorado: Westview, 1984).

NN Vohra, 'Integrated Management of National Security', in PC Dogra ed., *Changing Perspective on National Security* (New Delhi: Lancer's, 2004).

NN Vohra, 'National Governance and Internal Security', *Journal of Defence Studies*, Vol. 1, No. 2 (2008).

K Warikoo, 'Islamist Mercenaries and Terrorism in Kashmir', *Himalayan and Central Asian Studies*, Vol. 2, No. 2 (1998).

Michael Warner, 'Intelligence as risk shifting', in Peter Gill, Stephen Marrin and Mark Phythian eds., *Intelligence Theory: Key Questions and Debates* (Abingdon, Oxon: Routledge, 2009).

Sean P. Winchell, 'Pakistan's ISI: The Invisible Government', *International Journal of Intelligence and CounterIntelligence*, Vol. XVI/3 (2003).

Robert G Wirsing, *India, Pakistan and the Kashmir Dispute: On Regional Conflict and its Resolution* (Basingstoke, Hampshire: Macmillan, 1994).

Roberta Wolhstetter (1962), *Pearl: Harbour: Warning and Decision* (Stanford, California: Stanford University Press).

Amy Zegart, *Spying Blind: The CIA, the FBI and the Origins of 9/11* (Princeton: Princeton University Press, 2007).

Books and Journals Consulted

Paul Aussaresses, *The Battle of the Casbah: Terrorism and Counter-terrorism in Algeria, 1955–1957* (New York: Enigma, 2002).

Sashanka S Banerjee, *A Long Journey Together: India, Pakistan and Bangladesh* (London: Booksurge, 2008).

Richard Betts, 'Fixing Intelligence', *Foreign Affairs*, January-February 2002, reproduced in The War on Terror (*Foreign Affairs* editor's choice), (New York: Foreign Affairs, 2002).

Crispin Black, *7–7: The London Bombs – What Went Wrong?* (London: Gibson Square, 2005).

Jonah Blank, 'Kashmir: All Tactics, No Strategy', in Sumit Ganguly ed., *The Kashmir Question: Retrospect and Prospect* (London: Frank Cass, 2003).

Sudhir S Bloeria, *Pakistan's Insurgency Versus India's Security: Tackling Militancy in Kashmir* (New Delhi: Manas, 2000).

Jason Burke, *Al Qaeda: The True Story of Radical Islam* (London: Penguin, 2004).

Fernando Celaya, 'To what extent was Western intelligence at fault in failing to identify the nature of the terrorist threat before 9/11 and its aftermath?', *Athena Intelligence Journal*, Vol. 4, No. 1 (2009).

Bidanda M Chengappa, 'Pakistan's Secret Power: The Inter Services Intelligence', *Indian Defence Review*, Vol. 15, No. 1 (2000).

Brian Cloughley, *War, Coups and Terror: Pakistan's Army in Years of Turmoil* (Barnsby, South Yorkshire: Pen and Sword Military, 2008).

Martin van Creveld, 'On Counterinsurgency', in Rohan Gunaratna ed., *Combating Terrorism* (Singapore: Marshall Cavendish, 2005).

Mike Dash, *Thug: The True Story of India's Murderous Cult* (London: Granta, 2005).

Kirpal Dhillon, *Identity and Survival: Sikh Militancy in India 1978–1993* (New Delhi: Penguin, 2006).

Edna Fernandes, *Holy Warriors: A Journey into the Heart of Indian Fundamentalism* (London: Portobello Books, 2007).

Sumit Ganguly, *The Crisis in Kashmir: Portents of war, hopes of peace* (Cambridge: Cambridge University Press, 1997).

Dennis M Gormley, 'The Limits of Intelligence: Iraq's Lessons', *Survival*, Vol. 46, No. 3 (2004).

Rohan Gunaratna, 'Military and Non-military Strategies for Combating Terrorism', in Rohan Gunaratna ed., *Combating Terrorism* (Singapore: Marshall Cavendish, 2005).

Wajahat Habibullah, *My Kashmir: Conflict and the Prospects of Enduring Peace* (Washington: United States Institute of Peace, 2008).

Douglas Hart and Steven Simon, 'Thinking Straight and Talking Straight: Problems of Intelligence Analysis', *Survival*, Vol. 48, No. 1 (2006).

Steve Hewitt, *The British War on Terror: Terrorism and Counter-terrorism on the Home Front Since 9/11* (London: Continuum, 2008).

Peter Hopkirk, *The Great Game: On Secret Service in High Asia* (Oxford: Oxford University Press, 1991).

Robert Johnson, *Spying for Empire: The Great Game in Central and South Asia, 1757–1947* (London: Greenhill, 2006).

Verghese Koithara, *Crafting Peace in Kashmir: Through a Realist Lens* (New Delhi: Sage, 2004).

Suneel Kumar, 'Sikh Ethnic Uprising in India and Involvement of Foreign Powers', *Faultlines: Writings in Conflict and Resolution*, Vol. 18 (2007).

Suneel Kumar, 'Linkages between the Ethnic Diaspora and the Sikh Ethno-National Movement in India', *Faultlines: Writings in Conflict and Resolution*, Vol. 19 (2008).

Neil C Livingstone, 'Proactive Responses to Terrorism: Reprisals, Preemption and Retribution', in Neil C Livingstone and Terrell E Arnold eds., *Fighting Back: Winning the War against Terrorism* (Lexington, Mass: Lexington Books, 1986).

Geeta Madhavan, 'Cross-Border Terrorism', in Lakshmi Krishnamurti, R Swaminathan, Gert Kueck eds., *Responding to Terrorism: Dilemmas of Democratic and Developing Societies* (Madras: Bookventure, 2003).

Iffat Malik, *Kashmir: Ethnic Conflict, International Dispute* (Oxford: Oxford University Press, 2003).

Thomas Marks, 'Jammu & Kashmir: State Response to Insurgency – The Case of Jammu', *Faultlines: Writings in Conflict and Resolution*, Vol. 16 (2005).

Amitabh Mattoo, 'India's "Potential" Endgame in Kashmir', in Sumit Ganguly ed., *The Kashmir Question: Retrospect and Prospect* (London: Frank Cass, 2003).

Mohammad-Mahmoud Ould Mohamedou, *Understanding Al Qaeda: The Transformation of War* (London: Pluto Press, 2007).

Timothy Naftali, *Blindspot: The Secret History of American Counterterorrism* (New York: Basic Books, 2005).

John Newsinger, *British Counterinsurgency: From Palestine to Northern Ireland* (New York: Palgrave, 2002).

Peter Oborne, *The Use and Abuse of Terror: The construction of a false narrative on the domestic terror threat* (London: Centre for Policy Studies, 2006).

Alison Pargeter, *The New Frontiers of Jihad: Radical Islam in Europe* (London: I.B Tauris, 2008).

VG Patankar, 'Insurgency, proxy war, and terrorism in Kashmir', in Sumit Ganguly and David P Fidler eds., *India and Counterinsurgency: Lessons Learned* (London: Routledge, 2009).

Melanie Phillips, *Londonistan: How Britain is Creating a Terror State Within* (London: Gibson Square, 2006).

Richard Popplewell, *Intelligence and Imperial Defence: British Intelligence and the Defence of the Indian Empire* (London: Frank Cass, 1995).

Shinder Purewal, *Sikh Ethnonationalism and the Political Economy of Punjab* (New Delhi: Oxford University Press, 2000).

Humra Quraishi, *Kashmir: The Untold Story* (New Delhi: Penguin, 2004).

Asoka Raina, *Inside RAW: The Story of India's Secret Service* (New Delhi: Vikas, 1980).

K Santhanam, Sreedhar, Sudhir Saxena and Manish, *Jihadis in Jammu and Kashmir: A Portrait Gallery* (New Delhi: Sage, 2003).

Pravin Sawhney, *The Defence Makeover: 10 Myths that Shape India's Image* (New Delhi: Sage, 2002).

Victoria Schoefield, *Kashmir in Conflict: India, Pakistan and the Unending War* (London: I.B Tauris, 2003).

T Khurshchev Singh, 'Terror Trends: Mega Cities, Maximum Impact' *Strategic Analysis*, Vol. 30, No. 3 (2006).

L Randeep Singh, 'New Dimensions of Terrorism', *Strategic Analysis*, Vol. 13, No. 4 (1990).

Praveen Swami, 'Terrorism in Jammu and Kashmir in Theory and Practice', in Sumit Ganguly ed., *The Kashmir Question: Retrospect and Prospect* (London: Frank Cass, 2003).

Strobe Talbott, *Engaging India: Diplomacy, Democracy and the Bomb* (Washington D.C: Brookings Institution Press, 2004).

Mary Ann Weaver, 'Blowback', *Atlantic Monthly*, May 1996.

South Asia Intelligence Review (SAIR), accessed via www.satp.org

Asutosha Acharya, `Afghanistan-India-Pakistan: Troubled Triad', 29 March 2010, Vol. 8, No. 38.

Sandipani Dash, 'Trouble-makers Abound, but Fail', 14 January 2008, Vol. 6, No. 27.

KPS Gill, 'Diplomatic tourism: Powell in South Asia... Again', 29 July 2002, Vol. 1, No. 2.

KPS Gill, 'Gujarat: New Theatre of Islamist Terror', 30 September 2002, Vol. 1, No. 11.

Ajaat Jamwal, 'From Terrorism to "Agitational Terrorism" in Kashmir, 8 March 2010, Vol. 8, No. 35.

Kanchan Lakshman, 'J&K: No Respite from the Jehadis', 25 November 2002, Vol. 1, No. 19.

Kanchan Lakshman, 'J&K: A Violent Peace', 10 January 2005, Vol. 3, No. 26.

Kanchan Lakshman, 'J&K: Troop Withdrawal – Musharraf's Bid to Re-open Terror Routes', 10 October 2005, Vol. 4, No. 13.

Kanchan Lakshman, 'Pakistan: The ISI Exposed', 2 October 2006, Vol. 5, No. 12.

Kanchan Lakshman, 'Jammu and Kashmir: Respite from a Proxy War', 4 February 2008, Vol. 6, No. 30.

Kanchan Lakshman, 'The Expanding Jihad', 18 February 2008, Vol. 6, No. 32.

Kanchan Lakshman, 'J&K: Financing the Terror', 23 June 2008, Vol. 6, No. 50.

Ashok K Mehta, 'J&K: The Election Body-count Begins', 16 September 2002, Vol. 1, No. 9.

G Parthasarathy, 'A Prime Minister Surrenders', 25 September 2005, Vol. 5, No. 11.

Bibhu Prasad Routray, 'SIMI: Steady Subversion', 10 July 2006, Vol. 4, No. 52.

Ajai Sahni, 'The Arc of Terror Crystallizes Again', 12 August 2002, Vol. 1, No. 4.

Ajai Sahni, 'A Tide of Terror', 1 September 2003, Vol. 2, No. 7.

Ajai Sahni, 'No Surprises in Bangalore', 2 January 2006, Vol. 4, No. 25.

Ajai Sahni, 'Punjab: Terror in the Wings', 25 June 2007, Vol.5, No. 50.

Ajai Sahni, 'Augmenting Threat, Sclerotic Responses', 26 November 2007, Vol. 6, No. 20.

Ajai Sahni, 'Jaipur: Get to the basics', 19 May 2008, Vol. 6, No. 45.

Ajai Sahni, 'J&K: Idiot Philosophies', 25 August 2008, Vol. 7, No. 7.

Ajai Sahni, 'Strategic Vastu Shashtra', 22 December 2008, Vol. 7, No. 24.

Ajit Kumar Singh, 'J&K: Surging Shadows', 19 April 2010, Vol. 8, No. 41.

Ajit Kumar Singh, 'Kashmir: Orchestrated Rage', 23 August 2010, Vol. 9, No. 7.

Ajit Kumar Singh, 'LeT: Spreading Menace', 5 July 2010, Vol. 8, No. 52.

Ajit Kumar Singh, 'Uttar Pradesh: Looming Threat of Subversion', 8 January 2007, Vol. 5, No. 26.

Praveen Swami, 'J&K: The Taliban Take on Rajouri', 6 January 2003, Vol. 1, No. 25.

Praveen Swami, 'J&K: Operation Sarp Vinash – The Army Strikes Hard', 2 June 2003, Vol.1, No. 46.

Praveen Swami, 'J&K: Haze Shrouds the Hizb-ul-Mujahiddin', 19 January 2004, Vol. 2, No. 27.

Praveen Swami, 'J&K: An Abortive Revival', 3 October 2005, Vol. 4, No. 12.

Praveen Swami, 'J&K: Experiments with Terror', 3 July 2006, Vol. 4, No. 51.

Praveen Swami, 'Fresh Fears in Kashmir', 2 July 2007, Vol. 5, No. 51.

Praveen Swami 'Kashmir's Waning Jihad', 7 April 2008, Vol. 6, No. 39.

Praveen Swami, 'J&K's Party of Exiles, *SAIR*, 9 June 2008, Vol. 6, No. 48.

Praveen Swami, 'Mumbai: The Road to Maximum Terror', 15 December 2008, Vol. 7, No. 23.

Articles from South Asia Analysis Group (a website run by former R&AW officers)

B Raman, 'Psychological Warfare (Psywar) in the New Millenium', *South Asia Analysis Group*, 27 February 1999, accessed online at http://www.southasiaanalysis.org/papers/paper39.html, on 2 April 2009.

B Raman, 'The ISI Bogey: Really?', *South Asia Analysis Group*, 13 February 2000, accessed online at http://southasiaanalysis.org/notes/note69.html, on 12 April 2009.

B Raman, 'Pakistani sponsorship of terrorism', *South Asia Analysis Group*, 25 February 2000, accessed online at http://www.southasiaanalysis.org/papers2/paper106.html, on 3 April 2009.

B Raman, 'Intelligence and Counter-terrorism', *South Asia Analysis Group*, 21 April 2004, accessed online at http://www.southasiaanalysis.org/papers10/paper983.html, on 14 March 2008.

B Raman, 'Intelligence: As flawed as ever', *South Asia Analysis Group*, 20 July 2004, accessed online at http://www.southasiaanalysis.org/papers11/paper1060.html, on 2 April 2009.

B Raman, 'Terrorism: India should watch out', *South Asia Analysis Group*, 27 January 2005, accessed online at http://www.southasiaanalysis.org/papers13/paper1233.html, on 10 June 2009.

B Raman, 'Gen. Malik on Gen. Malik', *South Asia Analysis Group*, 5 May 2006, accessed online at http://www.southasiaanalysis.org/papers18/paper1788.html, on 14 March 2008.

B Raman, 'After Mumbai: Points For Action – International Terrorism Monitor–Paper No. 474', *South Asia Analysis Group*, 1 December 2008, accessed online at http://www.southasiaanalysis.org/papers30/paper2949.html, on 31 March 2009.

B Raman, 'Headley's Case: Indian Distrust of FBI Will Increase – International Terrorism Monitor – Paper No. 685', *South Asia Analysis Group*, 18 October 2010, accessed online at http://southasiaanalysis.org/papers42/paper4102.html, on 18 October 2010.

Other Websites

Online news service Rediff – www.rediff.com

Indian Parliament – www.parliamentofindia.nic.in

NOTES

Introduction

1. Marlo, Francis, 'WMD terrorism and US intelligence collection', *Terrorism and Political Violence*, Vol. XI/3, (1999), p. 53.
2. Charters, David, 'British intelligence in the Palestine campaign, 1945–47', *Intelligence and National Security*, Vol. VI/1, (1991), pp. 124–125.
3. Banovac, Steven; Dillon, Peter; Hennessy, Matthew; Idoko, Ronald; Patterson, Christine; Paul, Augustine; Sonneborn, Ian; Steve, Christina; Stubbe, Kate; *Anatomy of a Terrorist Attack: Terror at Beslan* (Pittsburgh, Matthew B. Ridgeway Center for International Security Studies, 2007), pp. 19–21.
4. Peters, Ralph, 'Our strategic intelligence problem', *Military Review*, July–August 2006, pp. 112–114.
5. Warner, Michael, 'Intelligence as risk shifting', in Peter Gill, Stephen Marrin and Mark Phythian eds., *Intelligence Theory: Key Questions and Debates* (Abingdon, Oxon: Routledge, 2009), p. 18.
6. Troy, Thomas, 'The "correct" definition of intelligence', *International Journal of Intelligence and CounterIntelligence*, Vol. V/4, (1992), pp. 433, 443, 449.
7. Ibid, pp. 446–449.
8. Ganor, Boaz, *The Counter-terrorism Puzzle: A Guide for Decision Makers* (London: Transaction Publishers, 2005), p. 48.
9. Russell, Richard, *Sharpening Strategic Intelligence: Why the CIA gets it wrong and what needs to be done to get it right* (Cambridge: Cambridge University Press, 2007), pp. 4–7.
10. Omand, David, 'Reflections on secret intelligence', in Peter Hennessy ed., *The New Protective State: Government, Intelligence and Terrorism* (London: Continuum, 2007), p. 105.
11. Herman, Michael, *Intelligence Power in Peace and War* (Cambridge: Cambridge University Press, 1996), p. 20. Herman points out that the 'key to British action against IRA terrorism has always been the efficiency of the Royal

Ulster Constabulary Special Branch (RUC(SB)), yet it has never been part of the formal national intelligence overviews and budgeting; the same applies to the Metropolitan Police Special Branch, also heavily involved in anti-terrorist action'. Ibid, p. 33.

12. 'Let Sgt. Friday fight terror', op-ed by Brian Michael Jenkins and Jack Weiss, accessed online at http://www.rand.org/commentary/092505LAT.html, on 13 March 2008. Also Sloan, Stephen, 'Meeting the terrorist threat: the localization of counter terrorism intelligence', *Police Practice and Research*, Vol. III/4, (2002), pp. 339–340 and 'Fight terrorism with intelligence, not might', op-ed by Sara Daly, accessed online at http://www.rand.org/commentary/122603CSM.html, on 12 March 2008.
13. Crelinsten, Ronald, 'Analyzing terrorism and counter-terrorism: a communication model', *Terrorism and Political Violence*, Vol. XIV/2, (2002), pp. 77–86.
14. O'Neill, Bard, *Insurgency and Terrorism: From Revolution to Apocalypse* (Dulles, Virginia: Potomac, 2005), p. 33.
15. Peter Neumann and M.L.R. Smith refer to this dynamic as the 'escalatory trap'. Neumann and Smith, 'Strategic terrorism: the framework and its fallacies', *Journal of Strategic Studies*, Vol. XXVIII/4, (2005), pp. 588–590.
16. During 1970–1980, the term 'counterterrorism' was occasionally used to signify governments' recourse to terroristic methods against violent dissidents. Without trying to put too fine a point on it, the use of force against terrorists aims to create a deterrent effect that will prevent further acts of aggression against noncombatants. To that extent, counterterrorism is indeed about mirroring the terrorists' own use of violence. Townsend, Charles, *Terrorism: A Very Short Introduction* (Oxford: Oxford University Press, 2002), pp. 114–115.
17. It should be evident to readers by now that the author strongly favours the war model of counterterrorism over the criminal-justice model. Such a bias might derive from the case studies – as will be elaborated upon later, the scale of the terrorist threat facing India is colossal. The author believes that the war model is best suited to combat this threat.
18. Quoted in Gray, Colin, *Modern Strategy* (Oxford: Oxford University Press, 1999), p. 286.
19. 'General Discussion' paper by Herbert Romerstein, entitled 'Soviet intelligence in the United States', in Roy Godson, ed., *Intelligence Requirements for the 1980s: Counterintelligence* (Washington D.C: National Security Information Centre Inc., 1980), pp. 209–210.
20. This book assumes that counterterrorism in democratic countries shares a common objective: the protection of the lives of innocents while they go about their daily business. See for instance, how the United Kingdom has

defined its long-term counterterrorist goals. Omand, David, 'Countering international terrorism: the use of strategy', *Survival*, Vol. XLVII/4, (2005), pp. 112–113.

21. Virender Uberoy, an Indian soldier-scholar, argues that counterterrorism consists of four phases: *discerning* the existence of a terrorist movement, *containing* its expansion, *isolating* it from supporters, and finally, *eliminating* it completely. With the discernment phase principally consisting of data collation, containment becomes the first proactive component of counterterrorism. It involves preventing the terrorist movement from acquiring supporters outside its existing area of influence. Inability to contain the geographic spread of terrorist incidents is thus a warning sign that counterterrorist responses are flawed. Uberoy, *Combating Terrorism* (New Delhi: Intellectual Book Corner, 1992), pp. 106–109.
22. Shulsky, Abram N., and Schmitt, Gary J., *Silent Warfare: Understanding the World of Intelligence* (Dulles, Virginia: Brassey's, 2002), p. 63.
23. An example of the hostility that can result between consumers and producers over differing perceptions of what constitutes 'intelligence failure' is provided by the 1999 Indo–Pakistani Kargil crisis. India's then Army chief, General V.P Malik, deemed the episode a failure of Indian intelligence. Former intelligence officer B. Raman however, hit back by asserting that the army had expected too much from the intelligence community. B. Raman, 'Gen. Malik on Gen. Malik', *South Asia Analysis Group*, 5 May 2006, accessed online at http://www.southasiaanalysis.org/papers18/paper1788.html, on 14 March 2008.
24. The existence of an intelligence gap between predicting a terrorist attack, and preventing it, has been alluded to by B. Raman. See 'Intelligence and counterterrorism', *South Asia Analysis Group*, 21 April 2004, accessed online at http://www.southasiaanalysis.org/papers10/paper983.html, and 'A case of intelligence failure?', *Frontline*, 12–25 October 2002, accessed online at http://www.flonnet.com/fl1921/stories/20021025007301400.htm, on 14 March 2008.
25. In 1965, the American scholar and intelligence analyst Sherman Kent outlined a three-dimensional definition of the term 'intelligence', as commonly used in the context of international relations. According to him, intelligence could be 'a kind of knowledge', 'the type of organization which produces the knowledge' and 'the activity pursued by the intelligence organization'. Michael Herman argues that the viability of the first and third dimensions of Kent's definition hinges upon the second. The core distinguishing characteristic of intelligence is thus the organization which produces it. Intelligence when considered as knowledge is merely the product brought out by the organization, and intelligence activity is its modus operandi for acquiring such knowledge. Herman, *Intelligence Power*, pp. 1–2.

26. Stewart, Brian, 'Winning in Malaya: An intelligence success story', *Intelligence and National Security*, Vol. XIV/4, (1999), pp. 267–284.
27. Galula, David, *Counter-Insurgency Warfare: Theory and Practice* (London: Pall Mall, 1964), pp. 117–120.
28. The Israeli General Security Service (the *Shabak*) has based its HUMINT recruitment efforts around the leverage provided by Israeli control over civilian movements in the Occupied Territories. Cohen, Hillel, and Dudai, Ron, 'Human rights dilemmas in using informers to combat terrorism: the Israeli-Palestinian case', *Terrorism and Political Violence*, Vol. XVII/1 & 2, (2005), pp. 232–234.
29. Gazit, Shlomo, and Handel, Michael: 'Insurgency, terrorism and intelligence', in Roy Godson ed., *Intelligence Requirements for the 1980s: Counterintelligence* (Washington D.C: National Security Strategy Information Centre Inc, 1980), p. 145.
30. Herman, *Intelligence Power*, pp. 79–80.
31. This view is derived in part from Keith Alexander, who served as Director of the United States National Security Agency (NSA). Alexander writes that military intelligence is subject to a paradox: 'the soldier out front has the best tactical view of the battlefield, but the poorest access to the specialized information available to national-level analysts. On the other hand, the national-level analyst has the best specialized information about enemy activities, but the poorest view of the tactical battlefield'. It is the author's view that a similar mismatch of core competencies and expectations exists in the case of counterterrorism intelligence. Alexander, Keith, 'Transforming army intelligence while at war', *Army*, October 2004, accessed online at http://findarticles.com/p/articles/mi_qa3723/is_200410/ai_n9446314/pg_1, on 14 March 2008.
32. Kovacs, Amos, 'Using intelligence', *Intelligence and National Security*, Vol. XII/4, (1997), p. 162.
33. All terrorist movements are vulnerable to attrition, which is defined as the rate at which terrorist cadres are arrested or killed, relative to the rate at which new cadres can be recruited and trained. If terrorists are neutralised at a faster rate than they can be replaced, a terrorist movement will simply wither away. See Heymann, Philip, *Terrorism and America: A Commonsense Strategy for a Democratic Society* (London: MIT Press, 1998), p. 106. Also, Freeman, Michael, *Freedom or Security: The Consequences of Democratic States Using Emergency Power to Fight Terror* (London: Praeger, 2003), pp. 30–34.
34. Jamwal, N.S., 'Counter terrorism strategy', *Strategic Analysis*, Vol. XXVII/1, (2003), pp. 19–20. Accessed online at http://www.idsa.in/publications/strategic-analysis/2003/jan/Jamwal.pdf, on 13 March 2008. In Indian

scholarly and bureaucratic lexicon, the preferred euphemism for 'offensive' strategy is 'pro-active' strategy.

35. Joseph, Mallika, 'Counter terror operations: limitations to security forces', *Institute of Peace and Conflict Studies (IPCS) Research Paper 1*, p. 9, accessed online at http://www.ipcs.org/IRP01.pdf, on 12 March 2008.
36. Kasturi, Bhashyam, 'The present state of the Naxalite movement', *AAKROSH: Asian Journal on Terrorism and Internal Conflicts*, Vol. X/4, (2007), pp. 69–70.
37. Shorey, Anil, 'Proliferation of internal security and allied agencies in India', *Strategic Analysis*, Vol. XII/4, (1989), pp. 457, 465–467.
38. The view that tactical intelligence is a primarily a local function and not a national-level one, is shared by a number of writers on terrorism. For instance, see Jones, Seth, 'Fighting networked terrorist groups: Lessons from Israel', *Studies in Conflict and Terrorism*, Vol. 30/4, (2007), p. 236. Also, Raza, M. Maroof, *Low Intensity Conflicts: The new dimension to India's military commitments* (Meerut, UP: Kartikeya, 1995), pp. 11–12.
39. Anand, Vinod, 'An integrated and joint approach towards defence intelligence, *Strategic Analysis*, Vol. XXIV/8, (2000), pp. 408–409.
40. Ball, Desmond, 'Signals intelligence in India', *Intelligence and National Security*, Vol. X/3, (1995), p. 402 and Kasturi, Bhashyam, *Intelligence Services: Organization, Analysis and Function* (New Delhi: Lancer, 1994), p. 80.
41. Vaughn, Bruce, 'The use and abuse of intelligence services in India', *Intelligence and National Security*, Vol. VIII/1, (1993), pp. 18–19. Manoj Joshi, quoted in Raza, *Low Intensity Conflicts*, pp. 69–70.
42. Subrahmanyam, K.; Hazari, K.K;Verghese, B.G; and Chandra, Satish; *From Surprise to Reckoning: The Kargil Review Committee Report* (New Delhi: Sage, 2000), pp. 237–238. Also Kasturi, *Intelligence Services*, pp. 56, 81.
43. This point is derived in part from Ajit Doval, 'Needed: war on error', op-ed in *The Indian Express*, accessed online at http://www.indianexpress.com/story/213413.html, on 14 March 2008. Also, Marrin, Stephen, 'Intelligence analysis and decision-making', in Peter Gill, Stephen Marrin and Mark Phythian eds., *Intelligence theory: Key Questions and Debates* (Abingdon, Oxon: Routledge, 2009), p. 139.
44. 'Intelligence Bureau among the top five in the world', *Times of India*, 3 August 2007, accessed online at http://timesofindia.indiatimes.com/Intelligence_Bureau_among_the_top_five_in_the_world/articleshow/2253440.cms, on 13 March 2008.
45. Sanghvi, Vir, 'It's reveille in Kargil', accessed online at http://www.rediff.com/news/1999/aug/09vir.htm, on 13 March 2008.
46. 'India vs. Pakistan', *Time* magazine, accessed online at http://www.time.com/time/printout/0,8816,501020506–234000,00.html, on 14 March

2008. Pakistani scholars tend to hugely exaggerate the R&AW's effectiveness, arguing that 'RAW has grown into such a fearsome and bloodthirsty monster that it constitutes a grave threat to the security of its neighbouring countries'. (Presumably this means India's neighbouring countries, unless the Pakistanis consider R&AW as a separate state of its own). Such discourse is peppered with allegations that remain unsupported by empirical evidence and couched in tones so visceral as to degenerate into crude attempts at propaganda. A representative example, in which the above quote appears, is Khan, Rashid Ahmad, and Saleem, Muhammad, *RAW: Global and Regional Ambitions* (Islamabad: Islamabad Policy Research Institute, 2005), p. 78. It would bode well for India if the quality of Pakistani scholarship remained stuck at this level of sophistication.

47. 'Eurasia' encompasses the territory covered by the Commonwealth of Independent States (CIS). This region, together with Europe and North and South America, lost a total of 3280 lives to terrorism between January 2004 and March 2007. See website of the US National Counterterrorism Center's Worldwide Incidents Tracking System, http://wits.nctc.gov/, accessed on 13 December 2007. Also see 'India loses maximum lives to terror except Iraq', *Times of India*, 27 August 2007, accessed online at http://timesofindia.indiatimes.com/Indias_terror_death_toll_second_only_to_Iraq/rssarticleshow/2312796.cms on 13 December 2007.
48. Separatist rebellions in India's north-eastern states have been ongoing since the 1950s. However, given their limited intensity and discriminating nature of violence, a case can be made that these movements do not constitute 'terrorism' as the term is generally understood. Deliberate and persistent attacks on non-combatants in urban localities were only started by militants in Punjab in 1981.
49. Since 2001, American academia has grown alert to the possibility of deriving lessons from India's counterterrorist experience. This is because both countries are threatened by religiously-motivated, transnational terrorist movements, and yet both share a deep commitment to democratic values. Latimer, William, *What Can the United States Learn from India to Counter Terrorism?*, Master's thesis submitted to U.S Naval Postgraduate School, Monterey, California in March 2004, pp. 2–3, 7.
50. It needs to be mentioned that the overall counterterrorist offensive did not actually have a codename. However, it began in November 1991, when the Indian Army launched Operation Rakshak II in order to drive down terrorist violence prior to an upcoming election.
51. 'Intelligence failure', op-ed by K.P.S Gill, *Outlook*, 26 November 2007, accessed online via www.outlookindia.com, on 14 March 2008.

52. Zegart, Amy, *Spying blind: The CIA, the FBI and the Origins of 9/11* (Princeton: Princeton University Press, 2007), pp. 3–4.
53. Falkenrath, Richard, 'The 9/11 Commission Report: a review essay', *International Security*, Vol. XXIX/3, (2005), p. 189.
54. *National Commission on Terrorist Attacks upon the United States* (hereafter referred to as the *9/11 Commission Report*), pp. 409–412, accessed online via http://www.9–11commission.gov/report/index.htm, on 12 April 2009.
55. Goodman, Melvin, '9/11: The failure of strategic intelligence', *Intelligence and National Security*, Vol. XVIII/4, (2003), p. 67.
56. Zegart, *Spying Blind*, pp. 91–92.
57. Diamond, John, *The CIA and the Culture of Failure: U.S Intelligence from the end of the cold war to the invasion of Iraq* (Stanford, California: Stanford University Press, 2008), pp. 370–372.
58. Jones, Calvert, 'Intelligence reform: the logic of information sharing', *Intelligence and National Security*, Vol. XXII/3, (2007), p. 391.
59. Friedman, George, *America's Secret War: Inside the Hidden Worldwide Struggle between the United States and its Enemies* (London: Little, Brown, 2004), p. 62.
60. Betts, Richard, 'Surprise despite warning: why sudden attacks succeed', *Political Science Quarterly*, Vol. XCV/4, (1981), p. 551.
61. Ibid, p. 561.
62. 'The big difference between intelligence and evidence', op-ed by Bruce Berkowitz, accessed online at http://www.rand.org/commentary/020203WP.html, on 17 March 2008.
63. Pillar, Paul, 'Good literature and bad history: the 9/11 Commission's tale of strategic intelligence', *Intelligence and National Security*, Vol. XXI/6, (2006), p. 1030.
64. Pillar, Paul, 'Adapting intelligence to changing issues', in Loch Johnson ed., *Handbook of Intelligence Studies* (London: Routledge, 2007), pp. 159–160.
65. Quoted in Nath, D.C., *Intelligence Imperatives for India* (New Delhi: India First Foundation), p. 237.
66. Kovacs, Amos, 'The non-use of intelligence', *International Journal of Intelligence and CounterIntelligence*, Vol. X/4, (1998), p. 383.
67. Headley, John Hollister, 'Learning from intelligence failures', *International Journal of Intelligence and CounterIntelligence*, Vol. XVIII/3, (2005), p. 446 and Peters, 'Our strategic intelligence problem', p. 114.
68. Herman, Michael, 'Counter – terrorism, information technology and intelligence change', *Intelligence and National Security*, Vol. XVIII/4 (2003), p. 42.
69. Cogan, Charles, 'Hunters not gatherers: intelligence in the twenty-first century', *Intelligence and National Security*, Vol. XIX/2, (2004), p. 317.
70. Ibid, pp. 316–319.

71. Sims, Jennifer, 'Intelligence to counter terror: The importance of all-source fusion', *Intelligence and National Security*, Vol. XXII/1, (2007), pp. 44, 49.
72. Gregory, Frank, 'An assessment of the contribution of intelligence-led counter-terrorism to UK homeland security post-9/11 within the "contest" strategy', in Paul Wilkinson ed., *Homeland Security in the UK: Future Preparedness for Terrorist Attack since 9/11* (London: Routledge, 2007), p. 190.
73. Ibid, pp. 196–197.
74. Claims of 'intelligence failure' have of late increasingly been met by counter accusations of action failure on the part of local police forces. The result: public cynicism over the performance of the intelligence apparatus as a whole, without any distinction made between tactical and strategic intelligence. Op-ed by V. Balachandran in the *Asian Age*, accessed online at http://www.asianage.com/archive/htmlfiles//OP-ED/Federal%20police%20force%20needed%20to%20tackle%20terror.html, on 14 March 2008.
75. For an overview of such arguments, see Dhillon, Kirpal, *Police and Politics in India* (New Delhi: Manohar, 2005), pp. 286–299.
76. Subrahmanyam et al, *From Surprise to Reckoning*, pp. 237–238.
77. Burch, James, 'A domestic intelligence agency for the United States? : a comparative analysis of domestic intelligence agencies and their implication for homeland security', *Homeland Security Affairs*, Vol. III/2, (2007), accessed online at http://www.hsaj.org/pages/volume3/issue2/pdfs/3.2.2.pdf, on 17 March 2008.

1 Strategic Intelligence in India

1. Betts, Richard, 'Intelligence warning: old problems, new agendas', *Parameters*, Spring 1998, pp. 26–35, accessed online at http://carlisle-www.army.mil/usawc/Parameters/98spring/betts.htm, on 24 May 2007. Also Scott, Len and Jackson, Peter, 'The study of intelligence in theory and practice', *Intelligence and National Security*, Vol. XIX/2 (2004), pp.139–169, 153.
2. O'Toole, George, 'Kahn's Law: a universal principle of intelligence?' *International Journal of Intelligence and CounterIntelligence*, Vol. IV/1, (1990), pp. 39–41.
3. Tanham, George K., *Indian Strategic Thought: An Interpretive Essay* (Santa Monica, CA., RAND, 1992), pp. 52–54.
4. Lakshmi,Y., *'Trends in India's Defence Expenditure'* (New Delhi: ABC Publishing House, 1988), pp. 22–24.
5. Interview of former Secretary (Research), A2, New Delhi, 3 July 2008.
6. Bayley, C.A., *'Empire and Information: Intelligence Gathering and Social Communication in India', 1780–1870* (Cambridge: Cambridge University Press, 1996), pp. 332–333.

7. Mullik, B.N., *'My Years with Nehru: The Chinese Betrayal'* (New Delhi: Allied Publishers, 1971), pp. 178–180.
8. Vertzberger, Yaacov ,Y.I., *Misperceptions in Foreign Policy Making: The Sino-Indian Conflict, 1959–1962* (Boulder, Colorado: Westview, 1984), p. 79.
9. Mullik, B.N., 'My *Years with Nehru: Kashmir'* (New Delhi: Allied Publishers, 1971), p. 181.
10. For a quick overview of how non-aggressive Indian foreign policy is, and how costly this pacifism has been, see Ved Malik, 'India's politico-military establishment and decision-making', *Centre for Policy Research Occasional Paper, February 2004*, accessed online at http://cprindia.org/papersupload/1215246610-Malik_Military.pdf, on 2 April 2009.
11. Some Pakistani analysts flatter themselves with the belief that India is committed to conquering Pakistan and absorbing it into a greater India. Such views command little credibility with either international scholars, or even with better-informed Pakistani ones. Faruqui, Ahmad, *Rethinking the National Security of Pakistan: The Price of Strategic Myopia* (Burlington,V.T., Ashgate, 2003), pp. 43–44.
12. Contrary to popular belief, Pakistan did not choose to acquire nuclear weapons in response to India's nuclear test of 1974. Rather, the decision to build a nuclear deterrent was taken in 1972, as a means of ensuring that the country would never again lose a war with India. Parthasarathy, G., 'Pakistan and challenges to national security', in P.C Dogra., ed., *Changing Perspective on National Security* (New Delhi: Lancer's, 2004), p. 69. Also see Chakma, Bhumitra, *Pakistan's Nuclear Weapons* (London: Routledge, 2009), pp. 20–21.
13. Shekhar, Chandra, 'India's security environment: An Indian view', *Studies in Conflict and Terrorism*, Vol. XV/4 (1992), p. 311.
14. 'Shadow-boxing on the border', *Frontline*, 7–20 February 1987, pp. 11–12.
15. IB officers trace their organisation's genealogy to the Thugee and Dakaiti department, set up in 1835, by the East India Company. The department was highly successful in eradicating the practice of Thugee (ritual strangulation) from India. Its personnel used link analysis to identify and apprehend members of the Thugee sect, who in exchange for leniency, then informed about their accomplices. This process continued until, within few years, the sect had been completely wiped out. Thereafter, the department's personnel formed the nucleus of the colonial IB, as the need for political intelligence grew in British India.
16. Bureau of Police Research and Development article entitled 'Intelligence Bureau', accessed online at http://www.bprd.gov.in/writereaddata/linkimages/104301563730.pdf, 30 August 2008.
17. An Opposition member in 1995 called the agency the 'Unintelligent Bureau'. Raman, B., *Intelligence: Past, Present and Future* (New Delhi, Lancer, 2002), p. 89.

18. Griffiths, Percival, *To Guard My People: The History of the Indian Police* (London: Ernst Benn Limited, 1971), pp. 344–345.
19. The British had felt that Indians in general were unsuited for the task of high-level intelligence management. When the IB did begin to take in a small number of Indians as analysts, it did so exclusively from the Muslim community. 'Minutes from military secretary W. Johnston – terrorism in Bengal, conference at Government House, etc.', IPI collection, IOR, File No. L/P&J/12/398, Document No. P&J(S) 907/34.
20. According to one observer, the Bureau was left 'in a tragic-comic state of helplessness', with just 'office furniture, empty racks and cupboards, and a few innocuous files dealing with office routine', Sen, L.P., *Slender was the Thread: Kashmir Confrontation 1947–48* (New Delhi: Orient Longman, 1969), p. 19.
21. Sainis, Sunil, 'Rameshwar Nath Kao (1918–2002)', *Bharat-Rakshak Monitor*, Vol. IV/5, (2002), accessed online at http://www.bharat-rakshak.com/Monitor/issue4–5/sainis.html, on 30 August 2008. Also, Narayanan, M.K., 'A spy and a gentleman', *Kashmir Sentinel*, accessed online at http://www.kashmirsentinel.com/jan 2003/20.html, on 30 August 2003.
22. The author was struck by the strong commitment which many Indian intelligence officers, both serving and retired, expressed for the defence of democratic values. Their views seem to derive from preference for a political system that allows the agencies to retain their professionalism and objectivity, which would be jeopardised under a totalitarian regime. Johnson, Loch K., 'Sketches for a theory of strategic intelligence', in Peter Gill, Stephen Marrin, and Mark Phythian eds., *Intelligence Theory: Key Questions and Debates* (Abingdon, Oxon: Routledge, 2009), p. 46.
23. Kulkarni, R.N., *Sin of National Conscience* (Mysore: Kritagnya, 2004), p. 54.
24. Interviews of two former Secretaries (Research). Both officers served directly under Mullik and reserved the highest praise for him. Admittedly, Mullik had a despotic streak, which led other officers who did not have direct dealings with him to allege that he was a petty tyrant.
25. Subramanian K.S., *Political Violence and the Police in India* (New Delhi: Sage, 2007), pp. 84–85. Interestingly, the 9/11 Commission report observed that the CIA director's 'real authority has been directly proportional to his personal closeness to the President, which has waxed and waned over the years'. It appears as though getting close to the political executive is the priority for most intelligence chiefs, irrespective of concerns about losing objectivity, *9/11 Commission Report,* p. 86.
26. This trend grew pronounced after 1974, as Prime Minister Indira Gandhi began to face challenges to her leadership. Interview of former IB agent – H, New Delhi, 28 March 2008.

27. 'Rajiv wants total subservience', *Frontline*, 2–15 April 1988, pp. 20–21.
28. The Henderson-Brookes Report, a still-classified analysis of Indian politico–military failures during the Sino–Indian war, commented briefly on the subject of intelligence. According to a statement issued by the government in 1963, the report found that acquisition and dissemination of intelligence information had been slow. Data passed on to decision makers had been vague and there was no clear estimate of the Chinese military build-up along the border. Bhargava, G.S., *The Battle of NEFA: The Undeclared War* (New Delhi: Allied Publishers, 1964), pp. 177–178.
29. Singh, V.K., *India's External Intelligence: Secrets of Research and Analysis Wing (R&AW)* (New Delhi: Manas, 2007), p. 30.
30. 'Out in the RAW', *India Today*, 1–15 April, 1977, p. 30.
31. 'The second oldest profession', *Sunday*, 18–24 September 1988, p. 39. A former R&AW officer who played a key role in events during this period told the author that R.N. Kao was not the kind of man to oppose Indira Gandhi once she had made up her mind about declaring the Emergency.
32. The well-known columnist B.G Verghese wrote in 1978 that the 'intelligence agencies have been used to place political opponents, ministers, officials, journalists, judges, businessmen and others under surveillance on oral instructions to further personal vendettas and partisan political interests without the slightest regard for established procedures, properties or the law'. His was a commonly held view. 'An open look at intelligence', *India Today*, 16–30 November 1978, p. 46.
33. These figures are cited from 'The sleuth's eye view', *Frontline*, 28 April-11 May 1990, p. 99.
34. According to former IB Joint Director Maloy Dhar, barely three per cent of the agency's Class Two employees get promoted to the rank of Deputy Director, which results in considerable frustration and demoralisation. Interview, New Delhi, 6 September 2008.
35. 'Bitterness at the top', *Sunday*, 23–29 January 1994, p. 20.
36. Interview of Indian defence analyst Air Commodore (retired) Jasjit Singh, New Delhi, 5 July 2008. Also see Bayley, C.A., *Empire and Information*, p. 19.
37. One former R&AW chief told the author that the Indian Army has little right to complain about the quality of military assessments it receives from the agency. This is because army officers seconded to R&AW usually produce such assessments. The agency itself does not have the prerogative of choosing who joins it – it has to accept whomsoever the army decides to send. This rarely includes the army's best officers. Interview of former Secretary (Research) – Vikram Sood, New Delhi, 4 September 2008.
38. 'Not a clue', *Outlook*, 5 February 2007, accessed online via www.outlookindia.com, on 6 June 2008.

39. Interview of former Secretary (Research) – A3, London, 25 July 2008.
40. 'RAW wounds', *India Today*, 28 August 2006, accessed online at http://www.indiatoday.com/itoday/20060828/cover-terror.shtml, on 16 June 2008.
41. Raman, B., *The Kaoboys of RAW: Down Memory Lane* (New Delhi, Lancer, 2007), p. 133.
42. Interview of former Secretary (Research) – PK Hormese Tharakan, Bangalore, 20 September 2008.
43. Dhar, Maloy, *Open Secrets: India's Intelligence Unveiled* (New Delhi: Manas, 2005), pp. 230–231.
44. 'Inside intelligence', *Times of India*, 15 July 2006.
45. 'New challenges', *Frontline*, 18–31 October 1986, p. 17.
46. EMS officers posted to the IB used to receive a deputation allowance of just Indian Rupees 200 during the 1960s. It is unthinkable to expect most currently serving Indian police officers to accept such terms. Rebuilding a professional officer cadre within Indian intelligence will therefore require massively increasing pay and perquisites. Interview of former Secretary (Research), Amarjit Singh Dulat, New Delhi, 28 December 2008.
47. 'Spy versus spy', *India Today*, 13 February 2009, accessed online at http://indiatoday.intoday.in/index.php?option=com_content&task=view&id=28860§ionid=40&secid=0&Itemid=1&issueid=102, on 15 March 2009.
48. Brooks, David, 'The Elephantiasis of reason', *Atlantic Monthly*, January–February 2003, accessed online at http://www.theatlantic.com/doc/200301/brooks, on 27 April 2009.
49. 'Out in the RAW', *India Today*, 1–15 April 1977, p. 30.
50. 'India rejects US offer of joint operations against LeT', *Times of India*, 21 March 2007.
51. 'Secrets for sale', *Frontline*, 15–28 July 2006, accessed online at http://www.flonnet.com/fl2314/stories/20060728002903900.htm, on 4 May 2008.
52. 'The vanished spies', *Outlook*, 2 August 2004, accessed online via www.outlookindia.com, on 3 June 2008.
53. 'Of political bondage', *India Today*, 15 August 1982, p. 75.
54. 'James Bond ki hartal', *Sunday*, 18–24 September 1988, pp. 38–39.
55. Interview of former Indian Chief of Army staff, General (retired) Ved Malik, New Delhi, 9 September 2008.
56. Saluja, A.R., 'Reorganizing Indian intelligence organization', *Indian Defence Review*, Vol. XIII/3, (1998), p. 37.
57. Palit, D.K., *War in the High Himalaya: The Indian Army in Crisis, 1962* (London: Lancer International, 1991), p. 85.
58. Kasturi, *Intelligence Services*, pp. 61–62.
59. Interview of Indian defence analyst Air Commodore (retired) Jasjit Singh, New Delhi, 5 July 2008.

60. Raman, B., 'After Mumbai: Points for action – international terrorism monitor–Paper No. 474', *South Asia Analysis Group*, 1 December 2008, accessed online at http://www.southasiaanalysis.org/papers30/paper2949.html, on 31 March 2009.
61. Malik, *Kargil*, pp. 78–79.
62. Subrahmanyam et al, *From Surprise to Reckoning*, p. 238 and p. 255.
63. 'The Pakistan connection', *Sunday*, 21–27 March 1993, p. 36.
64. 'Terror in Bombay', *India Today*, 31 March 1993, p. 40.
65. Singh, Satyindra, 'The Kargil Review Committee Report: Much to learn and implement', *Indian Defence Review*, Vol. XV/1, accessed online at http://satp.org.satporgtp/publication/idr/vol_15(1)/real_admiral_satyindra_singh.html, on 28 August 2008.
66. Singh Jafa, Vijendra, 'Ten O' clock to bed: Insouciance in the face of terror', *Faultlines: Writings in Conflict and Resolution*, Vol. V (2000), pp. 24–26.
67. Subrahmanyam, K., and Monteiro, Arthur, Shedding *Shibboleths: India's Evolving Strategic Outlook* (Delhi: Wordsmiths, 2005), p. 74.
68. Interview of K. Subrahmanyam, New Delhi, 7 September 2008.
69. Interview of former Secretary (Research) – A3, London, 25 July 2008.
70. The IB dealt with the professional dilemmas created by the Emergency in quite a shrewd manner. It mounted close surveillance on Mrs. Gandhi's political opponents, but fed her 'some correct, some incorrect and some fabricated information'. By not committing itself to the survival of her regime, the agency ensured that when she was voted out of power, it could execute a political about-turn and cozy up to her opponents. *The Shah Commission Report: Circumstances Leading to Declaration of Emergency* (New Delhi: Delhi Press, 1978), pp. 11–12 and interview of former IB Additional Director – B1, New Delhi, 8 September 2008.
71. 'Touching a RAW nerve', *India Today*, 16–30 June 1980, p. 29. 'There is a strong possibility that this story about Desai only meeting the R&AW chief thrice was incorrect, since B. Raman writes that the intelligence chief was able to build a "good personal equation" with the Prime Minister'. (Raman, *Kaoboys*, p. 62). However, there is no doubt that Desai's premiership continues to evoke visceral memories amongst those R&AW officers who served through it.
72. 'Tinker, tailor, soldier, spy', *Outlook*, 4 February 2002, accessed online via www.outlookindia.com, on 31 March 2009.
73. 'Taming the RAW', *Frontline*, 28 April-11 May 1990, p. 107.
74. Subrahmanyam et al, *From Surprise to Reckoning*, p. 159.
75. 'Given a RAW deal', *Outlook*, 21 June 1998, accessed online via www.outlook india.com, on 24 May 2008.
76. 'RAW on the rise', *India Today*, 1–15 March 1980, p. 9.
77. 'Of political bondage', *India Today*, 15 August 1982, p. 75.
78. 'Restive spies', *India Today*, 1–15 May 1981, pp. 25–26.

79. Dhillon, *Police and Politics in India*, pp. 303–304.
80. 'The sleuth's eye view', *Frontline*, 28 April-11 May 1990, p. 9.
81. Mullik, *The Chinese Betrayal*, pp. 133–134.
82. Interview of former IB Additional Director B-1, New Delhi, 8 September 2008.
83. 'Muslims and Sikhs need not apply', *Outlook*, 13 November 2006, accessed online via www.outlookindia.com, on 6 June 2008.
84. Telephonic interview of former IB Assistant Director R.N. Kulkarni, 21 July 2008.
85. 'Getting a RAW deal', *Sunday*, 23–29 January 1994, p. 21.
86. 'The military option', *Sunday*, 27 August-2 September 1995, p. 35.
87. 'Spies left out in the cold', *Outlook*, 7 February 1996, accessed online via www.outlookindia.com, on 10 May 2008.
88. 'Playing politics with intelligence', *Times of India*, 8 October 2007.
89. 'Spies left out in the cold', *Outlook*, 7 February 1996, accessed online via www.outlookindia.com, on 10 May 2008.
90. 'A RAW repast', *India Today*, 15 March 1984, p. 37.
91. Interview of former R&AW Joint Secretary Major General (retired) V.K Singh, New Delhi, 4 September 2008.
92. 'At their masters' beck and call', *The Statesman*, 3 December 2003, accessed online at http://www.thestatesman.net/page.arcview.php?clid=4&id=57794&usrsess=1, on 25 May 2008.
93. For instance, senior officials have commandeered surveillance aircraft to go sightseeing with their families. 'What's wrong with our Intelligence?' *Outlook*, 1 July 2002, accessed online via www.outlookindia.com, on 31 March 2009. Also, 'Special report: New era, new hope at India's intelligence agency', *Middle East Times*, 13 February 2009, accessed online at http://www.metimes.com/Politics/2009/02/13/special_report_new_era_new_hope_at_indias_intelligence_agency/1096/, on 31 March 2009.
94. One journalist suggested that the force be renamed 'the sexual freedom force'. 'Sexy spooks', *India Today*, 1–15 March 1981, p. 113.
95. 'School for scandal', *India Today*, 15 May 1982, p. 101.
96. *Official 1962 war history* prepared by the Indian Defence ministry and accessed online at http://www.bharat-rakshak.com/ARMY/History/1962War/PDF/1962Chapter10.pdf, on 31 March 2009, pp. 419–420.
97. Singh, R.K., Jasbir, *Indian Defence Year Book 2000* (Dehra Dun: Natraj, 2000), p. 111.
98. Interview of K. Subrahmanyam, New Delhi, 7 September 2008.
99. *Official 1965 War History*, prepared by the Indian defence ministry and accessed online at http://www.bharat-rakshak.com/ARMY/History/1965War/PDF/1965Chapter09.pdf, on 31 March 2009, p. 146 and p. 170.

100. Nair, K Sankaran, *Inside IB and RAW: The Rolling Stone that Gathered Moss* (New Delhi: Manas, 2008), pp. 152–153.
101. According to one IB agent who reported on insurgent groups, the Joint Director handling Naga affairs merely said 'Naga *ka baap bhi nahin jaa sakta*' (literally: Not even the Nagas' fathers will be able to go across). Interview of IB agent – H, New Delhi, 28 March 2008.
102. Raman, B., 'Dimensions of intelligence operations', *USI Journal*, April–June 2004, accessed online at http://www.usiofindia.org/subject_wise_index2004.htm, on 2 April 2009.
103. 'Security puzzles', *Frontline*, 22 June -5 July 1991, pp. 32–33.
104. According to journalist Manoj Joshi, in June 1987 the LTTE duped their R&AW handlers into providing them with 40 tons of armaments and high explosives. This hardware was soon put to devastating use against the Indian army. 'Supping with the enemy', *India Today*, 1 December 1997, accessed online at http://www.indiatoday.com/itoday/01121997/covltte.html, on 28 May 2008.
105. Interview of Indian defence analyst Dr. Bidanda Chengappa, Bangalore, 29 August 2008.
106. Quoted in 'Barrack room bonanza', *India Today*, 15 February 1983, p. 91.
107. Kitson, Frank, 'Low intensity operations: Subversion, insurgency and peacekeeping', (London: Faber and Faber, 1991), p. 96.
108. Saksena, N.S., *Law and Order in India* (New Delhi: Abhinav Publications, 1987), pp.181–185.
109. Rajagopalan, Rajesh, 'Restoring normalcy: The evolution of the Indian army's counterinsurgency doctrine', *Small Wars and Insurgencies*, Vol. XI/1, (2000), pp. 47–50.
110. Akbar, M.J., *Nehru: The Making of India* (London: Penguin, 1988), pp. 572–576.
111. Paper on 'Lessons from India for the war on terrorism', emailed by former IB Special Director, D.C. Nath, to this researcher on 4 July 2008.
112. Bureau of Police Research and Development article entitled 'Intelligence Bureau', accessed online at http://www.bprd.gov.in/writereaddata/linkimages/104301563730.pdf, 30 August 2008.
113. Bhaumik, Subir, 'Insurgencies in India's Northeast: Conflict, Co-Option and Change', accessed online at www.eastwestcenter.org/fileadmin/stored/pdfs/EWCWwp010.pdf, on 31 March 2009, p. 6.
114. 'Government of Bengal, political department, political branch, No.1065 PSD', Indian political intelligence collection, India office records, files no. L/P&J/12/398, document no. P&J(S) 907 1934.
115. Dennis, Mike, *The Stasi: Myth and Reality* (London: Pearson Education Limited, 2003), pp. 231, 242–246.

116. One police officer complained that during his twelve years' of service in a district, he never once received a specific threat assessment from the IB. All forecasts from the agency, according to him, were couched in open-ended language so as to cover all possibilities. Interview of Inspector General of Police, Sanjay Vir Singh, Bangalore, 28 August 2008.
117. Kasturi, Bhashyam, and Mehra, Pankaj, 'Geo-politics of south Asian covert action: India's experience and need for action against Pakistan', *Indian Defence Review*, Vol. XVI/2, accessed online at http://www.satp.org/satporgtp/publication/idr/vol_16(2)/kasturi.htm, on 31 March 2009.
118. 'Base camp India', *India Today*, 1 October 2001, accessed online at http://www.india-today.com/itoday/20011001/cover-outfits.shtml, and http://www.india-today.com/itoday/20011001/cover-outfits2.shtml, on 12 June 2008.
119. 'The spy trade', *India Today*, 31 December 1983, p. 15.
120. Kulkarni, *Sin of National Conscience*, p. 47.
121. 'The invisible forces', *India Today*, 16–31 December 1979, p. 16.
122. 'Damning disclosures', *India Today*, 30th November 1992, p. 97.
123. 'Ghost busting', *India Today*, 17 June 2002, accessed online at http://www.indiatoday.com/itoday/20020617/states2.shtml, on 12 June 2008.
124. Raman, *Kaoboys*, pp. 55–56. This coup by the R&AW was not fabricated, as some have alleged. One of the former intelligence officers interviewed for this thesis was intimately involved with the espionage operation that warned of the Pakistani air strike.
125. 'The secret state', *Sunday*, 30 March-5 April 1997, pp. 8–9.
126. According to one news report, as of 2006, 40 per cent of the R&AW's imagery intelligence aircraft were inoperable. 'There are no secrets here', *Outlook*, 13 November 2006, accessed online via www.outlookindia.com, on 6 June 2008.
127. Interview of former IB Special Director D.C Nath, New Delhi, 4 July 2008.
128. Monitoring the quality of governance has been an intelligence function in India since ancient times. Rohatgi, Manila, *Spy System in Ancient India: From the Vedic period to the Gupta period* (Delhi: Kalpa Publications, 2007), pp. 265–266.
129. 'Food police', *India Today*, 31 March 1997, p. 13.
130. Naipaul, V.S., *India: A Million Mutinies Now* (London: Minerva, 1991), pp. 517–518.
131. Institute of Conflict Management report entitled 'India Assessment – 2007', accessed online at http://www.satp.org/satporgtp/countries/india/index.html, on 31 March 2009. The Indian Home ministry estimated in 1998 that 40 per cent of the country's districts were affected by some measure of organized political violence. N.N. Vohra, 'Integrated management of

national security', in P.C Dogra, ed., *Changing Perspective on National Security* (New Delhi: Lancer's, 2004), p. 42.

132. 'Return of the veterans', *India Today*, 1–15 September 1981, p. 28.

2 The Strength of Terrorist Counterintelligence

1. Tomes, Robert, 'Schlock and Blah: counter-insurgency realities in a rapid dominance era', *Small Wars and Insurgencies*, Vol. XVI/1, (2005), p. 50.
2. Kumar, Suneel, 'Sikh Ethnic Uprising in India and Involvement of Foreign Powers', *Faultlines: Writings in Conflict and Resolution*, Vol. XVIII (2007), pp. 101–153.
3. 'Revisiting Punjab's secret search for peace', *The Hindu*, 1 October 2007, accessed online at http://www.hindu.com/2007/10/01/stories/2007100155861300.htm, on 17 March 2009.
4. Tellis, Ashley J., 'Pakistan's Record on Terrorism: Conflicted Goals, Compromised Performance', *The Washington Quarterly*, Vol. XXXI/2 (2008), p. 9.
5. Habibullah, Wajahat, 'The Political Economy of the Kashmir Conflict: Opportunities for Economic Peacebuilding and for U.S Policy', *United States Institute of Peace Special Report 121* (2004), p. 6.
6. Mahadevan, Prem, 'The November 2008 Fidayeen attack in Mumbai: origins and implications', *RIEAS Research Paper Number 127* (2009), accessed online via www.rieas.gr on 12 February 2009.
7. Soman, Appu, 'Keep the Pressure on Pakistan', 4 March 2009, accessed online at http://belfercenter.ksg.harvard.edu/publication/18875/keep_the_pressure_on_pakistan.html?breadcrumb=%2F%3Fprogram%3Denrp, on 10 December 2010.
8. According to a 1997 news report, 27 per cent of the Delhi police's total manpower had been allocated to protecting politicians from terrorist threats while only 24 per cent had been assigned to law and order duties. 'Security check', *Sunday*, 29 December 1996–4 January 1997, p. 39. Dr. Bidanda Chengappa, an Indian academic, specialising in strategic affairs, told the author that over-emphasis on VIP security has led to deterioration in public security. Interview, Bangalore, 29 August 2008.
9. Reno, William, 'Shadow states and the political economy of civil wars', in Mats Berdal and David Malone eds., *Greed and Grievance: Economic Agendas in Civil Wars* (Boulder, Colorado: Lynne Rienner Publishers, 2000), pp. 43–64.
10. Heymann, *Terrorism and America*, pp. 12–13.
11. 'Hitting deep', *India Today*, 31 October 1986, p. 19.

12. 'Poor catch', *India Today*, 31 May 1986, p. 13.
13. 'Hitting home', *India Today*, 15 November 1991, p. 46.
14. 'Ribeiro's challenge', *India Today*, 30 April 1986, p. 32.
15. 'Army versus state', *India Today*, 30 April 1991, pp. 48–49.
16. 'The Kashmir cauldron', *Frontline*, 23 December-5 January 1990, p.11.
17. 'Bloody April', *Sunday*, 23–29 April 1989, pp. 35–36.
18. 'Exploding security myths', *India Today*, 15 February 1995, p. 61.
19. 'The serpent in paradise', *Outlook*, 22 December 1997, accessed online via www.outlookindia.com, on 11 May 2008.
20. CIA world fact book – India, accessed online at https://www.cia.gov/library/publications/the-world-factbook/geos/in.html, on 3 April 2009.
21. 'Militancy on the move', *India Today*, 15 October 1986, p. 33.
22. 'Dark facts behind the men in khaki', *Outlook*, 24 August 1998, accessed online via www.outlookindia.com, on 13 May 2008.
23. 'Terror round-up', *Frontline*, 25 February 1994, p. 44.
24. Interview of former IB Deputy Director and Director, Central Bureau of Investigation, R.K Raghavan, London, 8 October 2008. Mr. Raghavan said that Muslims are understandably hesitant to come forward with information in the aftermath of communal tension, since they fear being further harassed by the police. Former Director IB, D.C. Pathak, told the author that 'since participation in terrorism is an individual decision, the entire Muslim community should not be assumed guilty just because some people do not volunteer information'. Interview, New Delhi, 27 December 2008.
25. 'Punjab: Poll games', *Frontline*, 29 April-12 May 1989, p. 20.
26. Informers in Punjab were easy to detect until the mid 1980s because they maintained an overt relationship with local policemen and were often seen in their company. 'Terror unlimited', *Sunday*, 14–20 December 1986, pp. 24–25.
27. 'Ribeiro's challenge', *India Today*, 30 April 1986, p. 32.
28. Interview of K.P.S Gill, New Delhi, 20 June 2007.
29. 'Punjab: March of militancy', *Frontline*, 19 March-1 April 1988, p. 13.
30. "In a war like this there are ups and downs', *Frontline*, 27 December-9 January 1986, pp. 7–9.
31. 'Punjab: the inevitable', *Frontline*, 14–27 November 1987, p. 16.
32. Marwah, Ved, *Uncivil Wars: Pathology of Terrorism in India* (New Delhi: Harper Collins, 1997), p. 371.
33. 'Flashpoint', *Sunday*, 28 January-3 February 1990, p. 15.
34. Behera, Navnita Chadha, *State, Identity and Violence: Jammu, Kashmir and Ladakh* (New Delhi: Manohar, 2000), p. 206.
35. 'J&K: the stick at work', *Frontline*, 1–14 September 1990, p. 105.
36. Singh, Tavleen, *Kashmir: A Tragedy of Errors* (New Delhi: Penguin, 1996), p. 115.

37. Warikoo, K., 'Islamist mercenaries and terrorism in Kashmir', *Himalayan and Central Asian Studies*, Vol. II/2, (1998), p. 37.
38. Menon, J.E., and Komerath, N.M.,'The Hizbul Mujahideen ceasefire: Who aborted it?', *Bharat-Rakshak Monitor*, Vol. III/2,(2000), accessed online at http://www.bharat-rakshak.com/MONITOR/ISSUE3–2/narayanan.html, on 29 March 2009.
39. 'Give voice to moderate Islam', op-ed by K.P.S Gill in *The Pioneer*, 20 December 2003, accessed online at http://satp.org/satporgtp/kpsgill/terrorism/03Dec20Pio.htm, on 27 April 2009.
40. 'Valley of gloom', *Frontline*, 8 October 1993, pp.120 and 'Invisible tragedies', *Frontline*, 9 August 1996, pp. 42–43.
41. 'Hired guns', *India Today*, 4 May 1998, pp. 26–27.
42. As if to emphasize the point, Pakistani mercenaries burnt down the second holiest Islamic shrine in Kashmir in May 1995. 'A shocking setback', *India Today*, 31 May 1995, pp. 31–41.
43. 'House in ruins', *Frontline*, 25 March-7 April 2006, accessed online at http://www.flonnet.com/fl2306/stories/20060407003202800.htm, on 29 April 2008.
44. 'Inhuman sacrifices', *Frontline*, 15–28 July 2006, accessed online at http://www.flonnet.com/fl2314/stories/20060728002104200.htm, on 4 May 2008.
45. Swami, Praveen, 'J&K: the Taliban take on Rajouri', *South Asia Intelligence Review* (hereafter abbreviated to *SAIR*), 6 January 2003, Vol. I/25, accessed online at http://satp.org/satporgtp/sair/Archives/1_25.htm#assessment3, and Swami, Praveen, 'J&K: Operation Sarp Vinash – The army strikes hard', *SAIR*, 2 June 2003, Vol. I/46, accessed online at http://satp.org/satporgtp/sair/Archives/1_46.htm#assessment2, on 3 April 2009.
46. Musharraf, Pervez, *In the Line of Fire: A Memoir* (London: Simon & Schuster, 2006), pp. 1–7.
47. Khetan, Ashish, 'Karachi to Mumbai: terror, step by step' in Harinder Baweja ed., *26/11: Mumbai Attacked* (New Delhi: Roli, 2009), p. 135.
48. Levy,Bernard-Henri, *Who Killed Daniel Pearl?* (London: Duckworth, 2003), p. 5.
49. 'Into thin air', *Newsweek*, 3 September 2007, p. 24.
50. Pachnanda, Ranjit K., *Terrorism and Response to Terrorist Threat* (New Delhi: UBSPD, 2002), p. 163.
51. Pathak, D.C., *Intelligence: A Security Weapon* (New Delhi: Manas, 2003), p. 125.
52. Interview of Bhashyam Kasturi, New Delhi, 1 September 2008.
53. *Review of Terrorist Activities in Punjab for the year 1993*, compiled by the office of the Additional Director General of Police (Intelligence), Punjab, pp. 128–129.

54. According to one IB veteran, Khalistani terrorists would talk very indiscreetly over the telephone. He estimates that 50 per cent of the agency's tactical intelligence was derived from technical sources. Interview of former IB Additional Director – B1, New Delhi, 8 September 2008.
55. Peter Chalk, 'Pakistan's Role in the Kashmir Insurgency', *Jane's Intelligence Review*, 1 September 2001, accessed online at http://www.rand.org/commentary/2001/09/01/JIR.html, 12 November 2009. Winchell, Sean P., 'Pakistan's ISI: The Invisible Government', *International Journal of Intelligence and CounterIntelligence*, Vol. XVI/3 (2003), pp. 380–381.
56. 'Wireless wars', *India Today*, 14 September 1998, accessed online at http://www.indiatoday.com/itoday/14091998/war.html, on 28 May 2008.
57. According to a former Indian-army officer who has experience of counterinsurgency in Jammu and Kashmir, military intelligence alone intercepts between fifteen and twenty thousand terrorist messages every month (averaging out to 600 per day). Triangulation and spectral analysis constitutes the bulk of its workload in counterterrorism. Interview of former Army officer – G, New Delhi, 2 September 2008.
58. Interview of former Director General, Border Security Force, E.N. Rammohan, New Delhi, 3 July 2008.
59. Interview of Praveen Swami, New Delhi, 10 September 2008.
60. 'Trail to Pakistan', *India Today*, 30 March 1998, pp. 32–35.
61. 'Chennai: in focus', *Frontline*, 14–27 January 2006, accessed online at http://www.flonnet.com/fl2301/stories/20060127005802200.htm, on 28 April 2008.
62. 'Terror module', *Outlook*, 20 October 2003, accessed online via www.outlookindia.com, on 2 June 2008.
63. Interview of former special Secretary R&AW, Kalyan Mitra, New Delhi, 4 September 2008 and interview of former IB Deputy Director and Director, Central Bureau of Investigation, R.K. Raghavan, London, 29 September 2008.
64. Chandra, Satish, cited in 'Chatroom shrapnel', *Outlook*, 14 November 2005, accessed online via www.outlookindia.com, on 4 June 2008.
65. Every intelligence report viewed by the author, whether of the Punjab police, or national intelligence agencies, identified the ISI as the coordinating influence on terrorist groups. Among the most detailed reports was the *Review of Terrorist Activities in Punjab for the year 1997*, complied by the office of the Additional Director general of Police (Intelligence), Punjab, pp. 18–22.
66. *Review of Terrorist Activities in Punjab for the month of May 1995*, compiled by the office of the Additional Director General of Police (Intelligence), Punjab, p. 21.
67. 'ISI spreads its net', *India Today*, 7 December 1998, accessed online at http://india-today.com/itoday/07121998/isi.html, on 30 March 2009.

68. One Indian diplomat asserted in 2003 that embassy-based espionage was all but impossible in Pakistan. Surveillance and intimidation of Indian diplomats was so pervasive that their sources of information did not extend beyond innocuous gossip picked up on the cocktail circuit. Given that Pakistan was waging a proxy war against India, he argued, it would make better sense to shut down diplomatic offices in both countries. By doing so, ISI operations in India would be curtailed while R&AW activities against Pakistan would suffer relatively little damage. 'Diplomacy past dinner time', *Outlook*, 3 February 2003, accessed online via www.outlookindia.com, on 1 June 2008.
69. 'Octopus reflexes', *Outlook*, 2 June 2008, accessed online via www.outlookindia.com, and Ajai Sahni, 'Jaipur: Get to the basics', *SAIR*, 19 May 2008, Vol. VI/45, accessed online at http://satp.org/satporgtp/sair/Archives/6_45.htm, on 24 May 2008.
70. *Review of Terrorist Activities in Punjab for the Year 1993*, p. 18.
71. Joshi, Manoj, *The Lost Rebellion: Kashmir in the Nineties* (New Delhi: Penguin, 1999), pp. 165–178.
72. 'Battered and Bruised', *Sunday*, 7–13 June 1992, p. 12.
73. The Indian journalist Harinder Baweja, who is one of the best informed writers on Pakistan, told the author that Pakistani counterintelligence had rendered the R&AW station in Islamabad ineffective. Interview, New Delhi, 22 July 2006.
74. Dhar, *Open Secrets*, p. 359.
75. Occasionally, the Pakistani embassy in New Delhi was caught out while trying to concoct evidence that its staff had been tortured by the IB. One hilarious case in August 1993 featured an embassy official furiously bickering with his colleagues over a bugged telephone. He urged them to retract a statement that the embassy had just made, admitting that Indian counterintelligence personnel had not tortured one of its spies. 'Spy snafu', *India Today*, 31 August 1993, p. 10.
76. 'Far from Normal', *Frontline*, 26 August 1994, pp. 36–37 and 'Unneighbourly ways', *Frontline*, 28 August 1994, pp. 38–39.
77. As one article observes, 'by knowledgeably moving agents and operations in and out of and across these artificial boundaries, hostile intelligence services enmesh ... CI agencies in cumbersome and complicated entanglements that usually defy disentanglement and coordination at least in time for the agencies to catch up with the action'. Kalaris, George, and McCoy, Leonard, 'Counterintelligence for the 1990s', *International Journal of Intelligence and CounterIntelligence*, Vol. II/2 (1998), p. 184.
78. 'Jinda: prize catch', *Frontline*, 19 September-2 October 1987, p. 29.
79. 'Turning the tide', *Frontline*, 19 September-2 October 1987, p. 30.

80. 'Turmoil in the valley', *Frontline*, 14–27 October 1989, p.112.
81. 'Mentors, monitors', *Outlook*, 17 June 2002, accessed online via www.outlookindia.com, on 29 May 2008.
82. The ISI has always been worried about the prospect of New Delhi being able to win over a sizeable chunk of the Kashmiri separatists. Accordingly, since 1990 it has followed a divide-and-rule strategy by promoting infighting between separatist groups and positioning itself as an arbiter. By 1991, there were approximately 150 terrorist groups of various sizes in Jammu and Kashmir. While most of them were only splinter groups of larger, more powerful terrorist organisations, all of them depended on the ISI for support. 'Back to basics', *India Today*, 15 September 1991, p. 34.
83. This term is derived from David Kahn, 'A Historical Theory of Intelligence', *Intelligence and National Security*, Vol. XVI/3 (2001), pp. 81–84.
84. Dolman, Everett Carl, 'Military intelligence and the problem of legitimacy: opening the model', *Small Wars & Insurgencies*, Vol. XI/1, (2000), p. 34.
85. 'Tunnel to "Khalistan", *Frontline*, 14–27 February 2004, accessed online at http://flonnet.com/fl2104/stories/20040227004303100.htm, on 3 April 2009.
86. Accessed online at http://www.theatlantic.com/doc/200405u/ss2004–05-27, on 12 April 2009, reprinted with permission.
87. 'Stretched to the limits', *India Today*, 31 May 1997, p. 40.
88. 'Intelligence failure', *India Today*, 14 June 1999, accessed online at http://www.indiatoday.com/itoday/14061999/cover.html, on 4 June 2008.
89. Derksen, Kevin Michael, 'Commentary: the logistics of actionable intelligence leading to 9/11', *Studies in Conflict & Terrorism*, Vol.XXVIII/3,(2005), pp. 255–256.
90. Interview of former Secretary (Research) Vikram Sood, New Delhi, 4 September 2008.
91. 'The elusive solution', *India Today*, 15 August 1984, p. 28.
92. 'New challenges', *Frontline*, 18–31 October 1986, p. 19.
93. 'Grasping at straws', *India Today*, 30 September 1985, p.16.
94. Malhotra, Inder, *Indira Gandhi: A Personal and Political Biography* (Boston: Northeastern University Press, 1989), pp. 17–19.
95. Interview of former IB Special Director D.C. Nath, New Delhi, 4 July 2008.
96. Interview of former IB officer and Director, Central Bureau of Investigation, R.K. Raghavan, London, 20 September 2008.
97. Interview of former R&AW Special Secretary – B2, Bangalore, 19 July 2008.
98. 'New challenges', *Frontline*, 18–31 October 1986, p. 18.

99. The Deputy Inspector General of Police who handled Rajiv Gandhi's security posted the R&AW warning on the notice board at Delhi police headquarters. He was later suspended for negligence and for potentially compromising sensitive information. Interview of former Indian Home Secretary C.G. Somaiah, Bangalore, 19 July 2008.
100. Interview of former Secretary (Research), P.K. Hormese Tharakan, Bangalore, 20 September 2008.
101. Interview of former Special Secretary R&AW, R.Swaminathan, Chennai, 15 July 2008.
102. For details on the SIB report and how it accurately forecasted that the security forces' confidence in their own alertness would prove misplaced, see 'A dubious document', *Frontline*, 25 November-8 December 2000, accessed online at http://flonnet.com/fl1724/17240230.htm, on 3 April 2009.
103. 'Stammer, and Speak', *Outlook*, 14 August 2000, accessed online at www.outlookindia.com, on 27 April 2009.
104. An example is the elimination of Hizb-ul Mujahiddin's most senior commander in Jammu and Kashmir, Ghulam Rasool Dar, on 16 January 2004. For several weeks prior to his death, R&AW had intercepted calls made by Dar on his satellite telephone. Analysis of these only told the agency that he was hiding somewhere in the town of Srinagar. Developing the lead was the responsibility of local security forces. On 15 January, they raided a Hizb-ul safe house, killing one of Dar's deputies. Follow-up raids were conducted on all the addresses which this man had been in contact with. Fearing that he would be located through these raids, Dar fled to a safe house on the outskirts of Srinagar. In the new neighbourhood, which was relatively less crowded, his arrival was noticed by an informer working for the army. Praveen Swami, 'J&K: Haze Shrouds the Hizb-ul-Mujahiddin', *SAIR*, 19 January 2004, Vol. II/27, accessed online at http://satp.org/satporgtp/sair/Archives/2_27.htm#assessment1, on 3 April 2009.
105. These differences were outlined in a lecture by David Hadley, Director of Group Strategic Analysis. The lecture was on 'Internationalizing intelligence sharing', delivered at the Royal United Services Institute (RUSI) in London on 10 November 2006.
106. The assassination of Rajiv Gandhi in May 1991 is a classic example of how police inaction on generic warnings from intelligence agencies hampers the production of more specific warnings. See *The Jain Commission report*, Vol. III, Ch.4, para 4.18–4.22, accessed online at http://www.india-today.com/jain/vol3/chap4.html, on 15 June 2008.
107. 'Passing the buck', *India Today*, 31 July 1984, p. 24. A former IB officer who was closely involved in 'Operation Blue star', told the author that when the agency formally confronted the Indian Army over the latter's accusations

of 'intelligence failure', the army withdrew its complaints. Interview of B1, New Delhi, 5 January 2005.

108. 'The Pakistan connection', *Sunday*, 3–9 April 1988, pp. 60–62.
109. *White Paper on the Punjab agitation*, pp.44, 56–57. The paper was released on 10 July 1984, by the Government of India, to explain the sudden militarisation of counterterrorist efforts in Punjab during the preceding month.
110. 'Is there a way out', *India Today*, 15 May 1984, p. 28.
111. For instance, there were strong suspicions that the Punjab police had penetrated terrorist leader Jarnail Singh Bhindranwale's inner circle through an informer codenamed 'Falcon'. It was speculated that Falcon might have been Harminder Singh Sandhu, the only senior Bhindranwale aide who survived 'Operation Bluestar'. Sandhu was killed by Khalistanis in 1991 on suspicion of being a government agent. See 'The spy in the Sant's camp', *Sunday*, 8–14 February 1987, pp. 26–27.
112. It appears that the army's complaint about 'intelligence failure' revolved mostly around the lack of tactical detail provided to its troops regarding weapon positions in the Golden Temple. The army did not know the precise location of machine-gun nests, which had been cut into the side of various Temple buildings and which would inflict heavy losses on the troops. One can dispute however whether responsibility for acquiring such information rested with the IB and R&AW in the first place. Kuldip Nayar and Khushwant Singh, *Tragedy of Punjab: Operation Blue star and After* (New Delhi: Vision Books, 1984), pp. 94–98.
113. Brar, K.S., *Operation Blue Star: The True Story* (New Delhi: UBSPD, 1993), pp. 45–46.
114. 'Diary of an extremist', *India Today*, 15 September 1985, p. 56.
115. 'Coping with terrorism', *India Today*, 15 September 1985, p. 21.
116. 'Pakistan connection', *India Today*, 15 October 1984, p. 34.
117. 'The Pakistan hand', *India Today*, 15 May 1986, p. 21.
118. Henceforth, Indian policy makers would remain suspicious of Pakistani dictator Zia Ul Haq's claims of goodwill. They would recall how he had constantly reiterated a desire for friendly relations with India, while proceeding to undermine those very relations by sponsoring Khalistani terrorism. 'The peace offensive', *Frontline*, 7–20 March 1986, pp. 26–28.
119. 'More saber-rattling', *India Today*, 15 November 1984, p.18.
120. *Review of Terrorist Activities in Punjab for the month of March 1995*, compiled by the office of the Additional Director General of Police (Intelligence), Punjab, p. 23.
121. Bamford, Bradley W.C., 'The role and effectiveness of intelligence in Northern Ireland', *Intelligence and National Security*, Vol. XX/4, (2005), pp. 587–588.

122. Grau, Lester W., 'Something old, something new: Guerrillas, terrorists, and intelligence analysis', *Military Review*, July–August 2004, p. 47.
123. Factional feuds appeared in the Khalistan movement as early as 1984, when it was relatively disciplined and had a pronounced ideological component. 'Escalating threat', *India Today*, 31 May 1984, p. 25.
124. The IB attempted to replicate the success of its Mizoram strategy. Accordingly, it propped up a relative of Bhindranwale's, in the hope that he could serve as a negotiating partner with New Delhi. The strategy failed in Punjab due to strong ISI interference, as well as the fact that it was too obvious. 'Madness without method', *India Today*, 15 November 1988, pp. 18–20 and 'Deadly spurt', *India Today*, 30 November 1988, p. 40.
125. Telephonic interview of former IB Additional Director Kalyan Rudra on 6 January 2005. Rudra said the IB had 'lumpenised' the Khalistan movement during the late 1980s.
126. Some commentators have suggested that the IB sponsored terrorist atrocities upon non-combatants with the express purpose of discrediting the Khalistan movement. See Kumar, Ram Narayan, *Terror in Punjab: Narratives, Knowledge and Truth* (Delhi: Shipra, 2008), p. 226. This view is incorrect. From conversations with agency officials who served in Punjab, a more nuanced picture begins to emerge. It appears that the IB was only focused on infiltrating the separatists' ranks by any means, and was not concerned one way or another about the number of deaths from terrorist violence. Khalistani groups were in any case so indiscriminate in their targeting strategy that they did not need help from the central government to defame the separatist struggle. For a profile of the terrorists' activities, see. Puri, Harish K., Judge,Paramjit Singh, and Sekhon, Jagrup Singh, *Terrorism in Punjab: Understanding Grassroots Reality,* (New Delhi: Har-Anand, 1999), pp. 59–87.
127. Pruthi, R.K, *An Encyclopedic Survey of Global Terrorism in the 21st Century* (New Delhi: Anmol, 2002), p. 173.
128. Interview of former Director IB – A1, New Delhi, 6 September 2008.
129. Ibid.
130. The ISI had contributed to criminalising the Khalistan movement by demanding that Sikh separatist groups pay in cash for the weapons they received from the Pakistanis. This forced the terrorists to raise finances through banditry and drug-smuggling, which over time, dominated the terrorists' activities to a greater extent than politically-subversive actions. With the Kashmiris, the ISI did not make the same mistake and supplied large numbers of weapons free of charge. Interview of former R&AW Additional Secretary B. Raman, Chennai, 28 December 2004.

131. "Mercenaries here are tough", *Outlook*, 21 June 1999 and 'The forgotten war', *Outlook*, 14 June 1999, accessed online via www.outlookindia.com, on 23 May 2008.
132. 'A spring too far', *Frontline*, 8 March 1996, p. 32 and 'An encounter at Hazratbal', *Frontline*, 14 June 1996, p. 121.
133. 'Villain No.1', *India Today*, 25 July 2005, accessed online at http://www.indiatoday.com/itoday/20050725/cs-attack.shtml, on 15 June 2008.
134. 'Willow wilt', *Outlook*, 28 April 2003, accessed online via www.outlookindia.com, on 2 June 2008.
135. Many of the intelligence professionals interviewed for this thesis agreed that there is a trade-off between timeliness and specificity in intelligence reporting. Since it is preferable for an intelligence agency to be 'vaguely right rather than precisely wrong', the four pillars of terrorist counterintelligence drive national-level agencies towards producing generic warnings or, in other words, strategic intelligence. Turner, Michael, *Why Secret Intelligence Fails,* (Washington D.C: Potomac, 2006), p. 175.
136. Interview of former Secretary (Research) – A2, New Delhi, 3 July 2008.
137. Laldenga came to terms largely because one of the IB's most brilliant officers had won over his entire top echelon of advisors, and left him facing the prospect of fighting the Indian government alone. Interview of former Director IB – A1, New Delhi, 6 September 2008.
138. 'Passage to nowhere', *India Today*, 1–15 August 1978, p. 5.
139. 'Killings with a message', *India Today*, 16–31 July 1980, p. 14–17.
140. 'No hostage-terrorist swap now', *Times of India*, 11 December 2006.
141. 'IB: Need to raise special forces', *Times of India*, 11 December 2006.
142. 'Existing laws enough to tackle terror', *Times of India*, 26 November 2006. Also see 'PM dodges IB demand for more teeth to fight terror', *Times of India*, 24 November 2006 and 'IB chief's call may spark political storm', *Times of India*, 24 November 2006.

3 A Lack of Political Consistency

1. Metz, Stephen, 'Insurgency and counterinsurgency in Iraq', *The Washington Quarterly*, Vol. XXVII/1, (2003), p. 25.
2. 'Ways to defeat ourselves', op-ed by Ajit Doval in *Indian Express*, 1 June 2006.
3. 'Politics of insecurity', *India Today*, 1–15 September 1980, pp. 17–18.
4. Swami, *India, Pakistan and the Secret Jihad*, p. 47.
5. 'The summer of discontent', *India Today*, 1–15 May 1978, pp. 42–48.

6. According to one media report, the attacks were carried out by former R&AW operatives angered by the Morarji Desai government's decision to downsize the agency. 'R&AW rides again', *Economic and Political Weekly*, 16 December 1978, pp. 20–24.
7. 'Cross fire: Punjab', *India Today*, 15 August 1991, p. 58.
8. 'Extreme Measures', *India Today*, 31 May 1982, pp. 19–20.
9. 'Embarrassing tale?', *India Today*, 15 February 1982, p. 24.
10. Congress patronage to Bhindranwale appears to have continued until at least late 1981, after which it seems to have tapered off. 'Rising Extremism', *India Today*, 30 April 1984, p. 14.
11. Raman, B., 'Pakistani sponsorship of terrorism', *South Asia Analysis Group*, 25 February 2000, accessed online at http://www.southasiaanalysis.org/papers2/paper106.html, on 3 April 2009.
12. 'Rising extremism', *India Today*, 30 April 1984, p. 19.
13. 'Harvest of hatred', *India Today*, 31 May 1982, p. 17.
14. 'A slow-burning fuse', *India Today*, 1–15 July 1981, pp. 76–79.
15. 'Talks and Terror', *India Today*, 15 November 1981, p. 31.
16. 'Tinderbox of religion and politics', *India Today*, 31 October 1981, pp. 36–37.
17. 'Rallying the faithful', *India Today*, 30 April 1982, p. 61.
18. 'The Pakistan hand', *India Today*, 15 May 1986, p. 23.
19. *White Paper on the Punjab Agitation*, pp. 32. The exact figure was 298 fatalities (between 1 January and 3 June).
20. 'Is there a way out?', *India Today*, 15 May 1984, p. 28.
21. Raman, B., 'Intelligence: As flawed as ever', *South Asia Analysis Group*, 20 July 2004, accessed online at http://www.southasiaanalysis.org/papers11/paper1060.html, on 2 April 2009.
22. 'Operation Blue Star', *India Today*, 30 June 1984, pp. 8–9.
23. Crelinsten, Ronald, *Counterterrorism* (Cambridge: Polity, 2009), pp. 78–79.
24. Interview of former IB officer and Director, Central Bureau of Investigation, R.K. Raghavan, London, 20 September 2008. Also, interview of former Indian Home Secretary C.G. Somaiah, Bangalore, 12 August 2004.
25. 'Operation crackdown', *India Today*, 15 November 1984, p. 32.
26. 'Held to ransom', *India Today*, 31 January 1987, p. 15.
27. 'The clouds darken further', *Frontline*, 5–18 April 1986, p. 9.
28. 'Extreme claims', *India Today*, 30 November 1985, p. 22.
29. 'Dangerous upsurge', *India Today*, 31 December 1990, pp. 17–18.
30. Interview of former Director IB – A1, New Delhi, 6 September 2008.
31. Ribeiro, Julio, *Bullet for Bullet: My Life as a Police Officer* (New Delhi: Penguin, 1998), p. 337.
32. 'Punjab: new dimensions', *Frontline*, 16–29 April 1988, p.19 and p. 22.

33. 'Punjab: a gory high', *Frontline*, 14–27 May 1988, p. 106.
34. 'An explosive phase', *India Today*, 15 July 1988, p. 28.
35. Gill, K.P.S., 'End game in Punjab: 1988–1993', *Faultlines: Writings on Conflict and Resolution*, Vol. I (1999), p. 38.
36. 'A new offensive', *Frontline*, 14–27 April 1990, p. 13.
37. 'Punjab: the lost hopes', *Frontline*, 14–27 April 1990, p. 7.
38. 'Punjab: issues and initiatives', *Frontline*, 20 January-2 February 1990, p. 14.
39. Joshi, Manoj, *Combating terrorism in Punjab: Indian democracy in crisis* (London: Research Institute for the Study of Conflict and Terrorism, 1993), p. 8.
40. Mullik, *Kashmir*, pp. 54–61.
41. 'Extreme claims', *India Today*, 30 November 1985, p. 22.
42. 'Kashmir: the autumn of the jihad?'*The Hindu*, 19 February 2008.
43. Interview of Major General (retired) Afsir Karim, New Delhi, 2 July 2008.
44. The MUF won four seats in the 75-seat state Assembly. An intelligence assessment compiled prior to the election had predicted that it would win 10 seats. The discrepancy was undoubtedly due to large-scale rigging but even otherwise, it is impossible to see how the Opposition could have toppled the National Conference government. 'A tarnished triumph', *India Today*, 15 April 1987, pp. 40–42.
45. 'Tackling Kashmir', *Frontline*, 20 January-2 February 1990, p. 21.
46. 'Troublesome links', *Frontline*, 2–15 July 2005, accessed online at http://www.flonnet.com/fl2214/stories/20050715001104900.htm, on 27 April 2008.
47. Interview of former IB Joint Director Maloy Dhar, New Delhi, 6 September 2008.
48. 'Losing control', *India Today*, 15 August 1982, p. 67.
49. Karim, Afsir, *Counter-terrorism: The Pakistan Factor* (New Delhi: Lancer, 1991), p. 116.
50. 'And unquiet lies the valley', *Sunday*, 9–15 July 1989, p. 48.
51. 'How green is his valley?' *Sunday*, 27 November-3 December 1988, pp. 33–34.
52. Interview of former Indian Home Secretary C.G Somaiah, Bangalore, 19 July 2008.
53. Praveen Swami has argued that the IB did not predict the outbreak of a terrorist movement in Jammu and Kashmir, citing the paralysis which struck its intelligence network during 1990. He asserts that the only service which warned of an imminent rebellion was the state-police intelligence wing. This claim has been disputed by former IB officer Maloy Dhar in an interview with the author. On the basis of available evidence, it is possible to conclude that the IB, R&AW and state police did in fact know that Pakistan was planning an insurrection, but they perhaps underestimated the scale it

would take. Interviews of Praveen Swami, New Delhi, 10 September 2008 and Maloy Dhar, New Delhi, 6 September 2008.

54. Raman, B., 'Psychological Warfare (Psywar) in the New Millenium', *South Asia Analysis Group*, 27 February 1999, accessed online at http://www.southasiaanalysis.org/papers/paper39.html, on 2 April 2009.
55. 'Flashpoint', *Sunday*, 28 January-3 February 1990, p. 17.
56. *Ministry of Home Affairs Annual Report 1990–91*, p. 9.
57. Malhotra, Jagmohan, *My Frozen Turbulence in Kashmir* (New Delhi: Allied Publishers, 1991), p. 342.
58. 'The valley of fear', *Frontline*, 28 April-11 May 1990, p. 16.
59. 'The politics of Kashmir', *Frontline*, 17 February-2 March 1990, p. 116.
60. 'Another winter of revolt', *Frontline*, 29 September-12 October 1990, pp. 13–16.
61. 'J&K: changing scene', *Frontline*, 26 May-8 June 1990, p. 18.
62. 'Back from the brink?' *Frontline*, 28 April-11 May 1990, p.20.
63. 'J&K: the stick at work', *Frontline*, 1–14 September 1990, p. 105.
64. 'Lives on the line', *India Today*, 15 August 1990, pp. 36–37.
65. One crucial question was how to prevent Pakistan from imposing the kind of costs on India that it had inflicted on Soviet forces in Afghanistan. The answer was straightforward: R&AW warned the ISI that if an aircraft within Indian airspace was shot down by surface-to-air missiles, the result would be an all-out war. Pakistan's nuclear weapons would have no deterrent effect under such circumstances. Islamabad got the message and did not supply the Kashmiri separatists with Stinger missiles. 'Covert contestation', *Frontline*, 10–23 September 2005, accessed online at http://flonnet.com/fl2219/stories/20050923004503000.htm, on 3 April 2009.
66. 'A shocking setback', *India Today*, 31 May 1995, p. 41.
67. 'A surprise in Kashmir', *Frontline*, 14 June 1996, p. 116.
68. Gregory, Shaun, 'The ISI and the War on Terrorism', *Pakistan Security Research Unit (PSRU) Brief No. 28* (2008), p. 7.
69. Interview of former R&AW Special Secretary R. Swaminathan, Chennai, 15 July 2008.
70. 'The Islamic conspiracy', *Sunday*, 12–18 July 1992, p. 13.
71. 'Valley of gloom', *Frontline*, 8 October 1993, p. 116.
72. 'The Pokhran-Kargil Connection', *Frontline*, 19 June-2 July 1999, accessed online at http://flonnet.com/fl1613/16130080.htm, on 3 April 2009.
73. 'War by proxy', *India Today*, 26 July 1999, accessed online at http://www.indiatoday.com/itoday/19990726/cover5.html, on 5 June 2008.
74. 'Unease in the Valley', *India Today*, 21 June 1999, accessed online at http://www.indiatoday.com/itoday/21061999/cover6.html, on 5 June 2008.
75. 'The Bin Laden factor', *Outlook*, 5 July 1999, accessed online via www.outlookindia.com, on 23 May 2008.

76. 'Next front in Kashmir', *Outlook*, 26 July 1999, accessed online via www.outlookindia.com, on 23 May 2008.
77. Lecture by Lieutenant General Vinayak Patankar (retired), at the Observer Research Foundation (ORF), New Delhi, 5 September 2008.
78. 'Kashmir's bloody puzzle: can it be solved', *India Today*, 14 August 2000, accessed online at http://www.indiatoday.com/itoday/20000813/cover.shtml, on 10 June 2008.
79. Unnamed intelligence officer quoted in 'Shadow boxing', *India Today*, 7 August 2000, accessed online at http://www.indiatoday.com/itoday/20000807/nation.html, on 10 June 2008.
80. 'Death in disguise', *India Today*, 3 April 2000, accessed online at http://www.indiatoday.com/itoday/20000403/nation.html, on 10 June 2008.
81. 'Shadow boxing', *India Today*, 7 August 2000, accessed online at http://www.indiatoday.com/itoday/20000807/nation.html, on 10 June 2008.
82. 'Peace act; scene two', *Outlook*, 28 August 2000, accessed online via www.outlookindia.com, on 26 May 2008.
83. 'The benefits of truce', *Outlook*, 11 December 2000, accessed online via www.outlookindia.com, on 26 May 2008.
84. 'An idea laid waste', *Outlook*, 19 March 2001, accessed online via www.outlookindia.com, on 26 May 2008.
85. 'The Kashmir checker board: the players and their game plans', *India Today*, 4 June 2001, accessed online at http://www.india-today.com/itoday/20010604/cover-box2.shtml, on 11 June 2008.
86. 'The next steps to peace', *Frontline*, 8–21 April 2006, accessed online at http://www.flonnet.com/fl2307/stories/20060421003503700.htm, on 29 April 2008.
87. 'Death in disguise', *India Today*, 3 April 2000, accessed online at http://www.indiatoday.com/itoday/20000403/nation.html, on 10 June 2008 and 'Lashkar moves to give struggle in "pure Kashmir colour"', *The Hindu*, 26 December 2001, accessed online at http://www.hindu.com/2001/12/26/stories/2001122601431200.htm, on 3 April 2009.
88. 'The new face of terror', *Frontline*, 17–30 December 2005, accessed online at http://www.flonnet.com/fl2226/stories/20051230003103300.htm, on 27 April 2008.
89. Hussain, Zahid, *Frontline Pakistan: The Path to Catastrophe and the Killing of Benazir Bhutto* (London, I.B Tauris, 2008), pp. 111–112.
90. This view was also held by independent analysts such as Loretta Napoleoni and Jason Burke, who argued that the spread of Al Qaeda's millennial worldview ('Al Qaedism') was what sustained regional jihadist groups like Lashkar-e-Toiba. 'Little Osamas', *Outlook*, 31 July 2006, accessed online via www.outlookindia.com, on 5 June 2008.

91. This view is shared by former Punjab Police chief K.P.S Gill. See his op-ed entitled 'Homegrown, yes, but ISI-inspired', *The Pioneer*, 24 September 2008, accessed online at http://satp.org/satporgtp/kpsgill/governance/08nov24Pio.htm, on 27 April 2009.
92. 'Bearded and tagged', *Outlook*, 31 July 2006, accessed online via www.outlookindia.com, on 5 June 2008.
93. Aisha Sultanat, 'Madrassas in India', *Institute of Peace and Conflict Studies Issue Brief*, 14 November 2003, accessed online at http://ipcs.org/pdf_file/issue/1850403881IB14-AishaSultanat-MadrassasInIndia.pdf, on 2 April 2009.
94. During the 1999 Kargil Crisis, Deobandi clerics in Delhi magnificently demonstrated their patriotism when they publicly lambasted Pakistan for its '*gaddari*' (treachery) in attacking India.
95. 'Made in India', *Outlook*, 31 July 2006, accessed online via www.outlookindia.com, on 6 June 2008.
96. 'The skyline from the roof', *Outlook*, 14 August 2006, accessed online via www.outlookindia.com, on 6 June 2008.
97. 'Shame at Ayodhya', *Frontline*, 1 January 1993, p. 7.
98. Khan, A.A., *Surrender* (Mumbai: Yogi Impressions, 2004), pp. 87–91.
99. 'The tangled web', *Frontline*, 23 April 1993, p. 28.
100. 'Hostile neighbour', *Sunday*, 10–16 January 1993, pp. 13 and 'Unneighbourly nexus', *India Today*, 15 July 1992, pp. 27.
101. 'The invisible forces', *India Today*, 16–31 December 1979, p. 9.
102. 'The tangled web', *Frontline*, 23 April 1993, p. 28.
103. Targeting a nuclear installation, particularly the Bhabha Atomic Research Centre, seems to be a long-term project that Pakistani jihadists have pursued with unwavering focus. In July 2006, a Lashkar-e-Toiba cell was neutralised in Mumbai while it was preparing to bomb BARC. This strengthens the argument that jihadism in India is nothing but a continuation of the ISI's K2M Plan, and that it is driven by strategic considerations, not merely religious ones. Kanchan, Lakshman: 'Pakistan: The ISI Exposed', *SAIR*, 2 October 2006, Vol. V/12, accessed online at http://satp.org/satporgtp/sair/Archives/5_12.htm#assessment1, on 3 April 2009.
104. 'The tangled web', *Frontline*, 23 April 1993, p. 28.
105. This is bound to happen whenever consumers depend heavily on intelligence agencies to provide specific warnings of terrorist attacks. Freedman, Lawrence, 'The politics of warning: terrorism and risk communication', *Intelligence and National Security*, Vol. XX/3, (2005), pp. 387–388.
106. The author asked Maloy Dhar, a former IB Joint Director who was handling counterterrorism against Islamist groups in the early 1990s, about this note of the DIB. Mr. Dhar said that although he could not

recall the specific note cited by *India Today*, several intelligence warnings issued during the first quarter of 1993 had clearly stated that jihadism posed a new long-term threat. Interview, New Delhi, 6 September 2008. Former R&AW Special Secretary S. Gopal told the author that available information indicated that ISI would use disaffected Indian Muslims to bomb sensitive military installations. Interview, Bangalore, 20 July 2008.

107. 'Exporting terror', *India Today*, 15 May 1994, pp. 26–27.
108. 'The deadly trail', *Frontline*, 7 May 1993, p. 116.
109. Pathak, *Intelligence*, p. 31.
110. 'Terror round-up', *Frontline*, 25 February 1994, pp. 41–42.
111. 'A war on many fronts', *Frontline*, 7 May 1989, pp. 118–119.
112. 'Trail to Pakistan', *India Today*, 30 March 1998, pp. 32–35.
113. Ibid.
114. 'How we bought RDX', *Outlook*, 2 October 2006, accessed online via www.outlookindia.com, on 6 June 2008.
115. For example, following the 1993 Mumbai blasts there were allegations in the press that the Chief Minister of Gujarat state had patronised some of the gangsters involved. Police action against smuggling networks suspected of bringing explosives into India could not go ahead, due to his interference. 'Failed equations', *Frontline*, 8 April 1994, pp. 25–26 and 'Baring a link', *Frontline*, 12 August 1994, pp. 31–32.
116. 'Not a tap, a river', *Outlook*, 9 October 2008, accessed online via www.outlookindia.com, on 6 June 2008.
117. *Reforming the National Security System – Recommendations of the Group of Ministers, Chapter V*, accessed online at http://mod.nic.in/newadditions/chapter-v.pdf, on 2 April 2009.
118. 'Playing with fire', *India Today*, 2 March 1998, pp. 34–35.
119. 'A time of troubles', *Frontline*, 20 March 1998, pp. 18–22.
120. Intelligence officials believed that the Al-Umma had links with the DMK government in Tamil Nadu. 'The serpent in paradise', *Outlook*, 22 December 1997, accessed online via www.outlookindia.com, on 11 May 2008.
121. 'Echoes of Bombay', *Outlook*, 2 March 1998, accessed online via www.outlookindia.com, on 12 May 2008.
122. According to one news report, Tamil Nadu police intelligence had dispatched 12 warnings to the Coimbatore authorities between 3 December 1997 and 10 February 1998. At least four of these were relays of IB assessments. They included lists of possible Al-Umma targets, and more importantly, specified that the organisation was planning to assassinate Hindu politicians. The DMK government publicised these warnings largely to shift blame from itself to the local police chief in Coimbatore, who it

alleged had been negligent. 'Human bombs and human error', *Frontline*, 22 May 1998, p. 33.

123. Otherwise, it is hard to reconcile the poor responsiveness of the Coimbatore authorities to intelligence reports prior to the 1998 blasts, with their excellent use of such reports subsequently. 'Behind the Coimbatore tragedy', *Frontline*, 20 March 1998, p. 16.
124. Interview of former R&AW special Secretary R. Swaminathan, Chennai, 15 July 2008.
125. For instance, the Indian security establishment has concluded that even the Coimbatore bombings (which were preceded by Hindu–Muslim communal riots) featured some degree of ISI involvement. Details on the depth of Pakistani involvement remain elusive. Sahni, Ajai, 'No surprises in Bangalore', *SAIR*, 2 January 2006, Vol. IV/25, accessed online at http://satp.org/satporgtp/sair/Archives/4_25.htm#assessment1, on 3 April 2009.
126. *Review of Terrorist Activities in Punjab for the year 1994*, compiled by the Office of the Additional Director General of Police (Intelligence), Punjab, p. 58.
127. *Review of Terrorist Activities in Punjab for the month of January 1994*, compiled by the office of the Additional Director-General of Police (Intelligence), Punjab, pp. 1–5.
128. 'A fatwa in reverse', *Outlook*, 8 October 2001, accessed online via www.outlookindia.com, on 27 May 2008.
129. 'The dons of terror', *India Today*, 25 February 2002, accessed online at http://www.indiatoday.com/itoday/20020225/cover.shtml, and http://www.indiatoday.com/itoday/20020225/cover2a.shtml, on 12 June 2008.
130. 'Bridging the gulf', *India Today*, 25 February 2002, accessed online at http://www.indiatoday.com/itoday/20020225/cover-box2.shtml, on 12 June 2008.
131. 'Jehad's dirty money', *India Today*, 14 January 2002, accessed online at http://www.indiatoday.com/itoday/20020114/crime.shtml, on 12 June 2008.
132. 'The new don', *India Today*, 11 February 2002, accessed online at http://www.indiatoday.com/itoday/20020211/nation.shtml, on 12 June 2008.
133. Pachnanda, *Terrorism and Response*, p. 197. Praveen Swami told this researcher that regardless of what they say in public, most Indian politicians admit in private that they do not consider terrorism a serious threat. They are more concerned with voting-winning issues, such as rural development and road-building projects. Interview of Praveen Swami, New Delhi, 10 September 2008.
134. Clausewitz has argued that the lower the stakes in a war, the less the common population is concerned about its outcome. Consequently, the war effort will be governed more by political considerations than by strictly military ones. Clausewitz, Carl Von, *On War*, (London: Everyman's Library, 1993), p. 91.

4 A Lack of Political Consensus

1. Kalaris and McCoy, 'Counterintelligence for the 1990s', p. 184.
2. Freeman, *Freedom or Security*, p. 29.
3. 'The mystery mission', *India Today*, 15 May 1983, p. 43 and Raman, *Kaoboys*, pp. 95- 96.
4. 'Operation Whitewash', *India Today*, 31 July 1984, p. 27.
5. 'Operation Blue Star', *India Today*, 30 June 1984, pp. 20–21.
6. 'A state of uncertainty', *India Today*, 15 July 1984, pp. 9–11.
7. "We will tackle the terrorists with love", *Sunday*, 13–19 October 1985, p. 31.
8. 'Punjab: now for action', *Frontline*, 19 April-2 May 1986, p. 23.
9. 'We are already doing a good job', *Frontline*, 6–19 September 1986, p. 11.
10. 'Girding the border', *Frontline*, 23 August-5 September 1986, p. 110.
11. 'The Punjab quagmire', *Frontline*, 4–17 March 1989, p. 9 and 'The lingering agony', *Frontline*, 4–17 March 1989, p. 13.
12. 'Punjab: perceptible change', *Frontline*, 27 June-10 July 1987, pp. 116–117.
13. 'Punjab: the inevitable', *Frontline*, 14–27 November 1987, p.16.
14. 'Lawless in Punjab', *Frontline*, 15–28 September 1990, p. 16.
15. 'Another step backward', *India Today*, 15 May 1989, pp. 36–37.
16. K.P.S. Gill told the author that whenever the Punjab police sought to set up village defence militias, they gave priority to those villages which sympathised with leftist politics. Interview, New Delhi, 20 June 2007.
17. 'Punjab: different task', *Frontline*, 2–15 September 1989, pp. 93- 94.
18. 'Punjab's winter of despair', *Frontline*, 8–21 December 1990, pp. 6- 7.
19. 'Life after terrorism', *Frontline*, 23 September 1994, p. 115.
20. Singh, Sarab Jit, *Operation Black Thunder: An Eyewitness Account of Terrorism in Punjab* (New Delhi: Sage, 2002), pp. 238–240.
21. One interviewee emphasised that the cooperation of US, UK and Canadian intelligence was central to defeating the Khalistan movement. The strategic-intelligence picture produced by the IB and R&AW drew heavily upon information obtained through foreign liaison. Telephonic interview of former IB Additional Director – B1, 19 March 2005.
22. Raman, B., 'The ISI bogey: really?'*South Asia Analysis Group*, 13 February 2000, accessed online at http://southasiaanalysis.org/notes/note69.html, on 12 April 2009. This issue of initial US support (which was mostly tacit rather than active) for the Khalistanis was confirmed to this researcher by a former Director IB. Interview of A1, New Delhi, 19 June 2007.
23. Raman, *Kaoboys*, p. 152.
24. Interview of former R&AW Additional Secretary B. Raman, Chennai, 28 December 2004.

25. 'Of spies and lies', *Outlook*, 5 March 1997, accessed online via www.outlookindia.com, on 10 May 2008.
26. 'Punjab: spreading war', *Frontline*, 3–16 February 1990, p.13.
27. 'Return of the prodigal', *India Today*, 31 January 1989, p. 47.
28. 'Old games', *India Today*, 15 October 1989, p. 33.
29. *Review of terrorist activities in Punjab for the month of May 1991*, compiled by the Office of the Additional Director General of Police (intelligence), Punjab, p. 36.
30. 'Fear in the fray', *Frontline*, 28 February 1992, pp. 5–9.
31. 'The turnaround', *Frontline*, 20 November 1992, p. 28.
32. Interview of former IB Joint Director Maloy Dhar, New Delhi, 6 September 2008.
33. 'Diplomatic shadowboxing', *Frontline*, 11 February 1994, p. 23.
34. 'Problems of policing', *Frontline*, 17–30 March 1990, p. 18.
35. Verghese, B.G., 'A Jammu and Kashmir primer: From myth to reality', Centre *for Policy Research Occasional Paper, June 2006*, accessed online at http://cprindia.org/papersupload/1215102284-Verghese_JK_Primer.pdf, accessed online at 27 April 2009, p. 23.
36. 'The war goes on', *Frontline*, 17 December 1993, p. 27.
37. 'Standing firm', *Frontline*, 28 January 1994, p. 23.
38. 'Facing third degree', *Frontline*, 11 September 1992, pp. 40–41.
39. 'Failed equations', *Frontline*, 8 April 1994, pp. 25–26.
40. 'Don't lose the momentum', *India Today*, 31 March 1994, p. 3.
41. The Pakistani delegation at the UNHCR ruined its own argument by resorting to crude hyperbole and outright fabrication. It compared the situation in Kashmir to the Nazi genocide against the Jews – a claim so outrageous that not even Pakistan's traditional allies could bring themselves to entertain it. Furthermore, many members of the Pakistani delegation claimed to be from Kashmir, but remained embarrassingly silent when asked to speak in Kashmiri. 'Triumph of diplomacy', *India Today*, 31 March 1994, pp. 26–33.
42. 'On a short fuse', *India Today*, 15 March 1994, p. 28.
43. 'Under fire', *Frontline*, 2 June 1995, p. 9.
44. 'A decisive phase', *Frontline*, 2 May 1997, pp. 37–38 and 'Blasts in the Valley', *Frontline*, 24 January 1997, p. 15. These successes were brought about after the IB posted its best counterintelligence expert as head of the Jammu and Kashmir Subsidiary Intelligence Bureau.
45. At a meeting in Geneva on 4 June 1998, the UN Security Council Permanent Five (P5) members indicated their intention to mediate on Kashmir. They pledged to 'actively encourage India and Pakistan to find mutually acceptable solutions, through direct dialogue, that address the root causes of the

tension, including Kashmir, and to try to build confidence rather than seek confrontation'. The thought that its sponsorship of terrorism was finally going to pay off thrilled Islamabad. Quoted from 'The rising costs of the BJP's *akrasia*', *Frontline*, 20 June- 3 July 1998, accessed online at http://www.flonnet.com/fl1513/15130080.htm, on 5 May 2008.

46. 'Grand designs', *India Today*, 6 July 1998, pp. 12–18.
47. During 1995, when five western nationals including an American were abducted by Pakistani mercenaries in Jammu and Kashmir, Washington sought permission to establish an FBI presence in the state. Since India was keen to retain American support for its policy of economic liberalisation, policy makers were inclined to accede to the request. However, spirited resistance from senior IB and army officers eventually led to permission being refused. This turned out to be a wise decision, since the US had wanted India to depart from its 'no compromise' hostage negotiations policy and do a deal with the terrorists. 'Clear and coherent', *Frontline*, 4 April 1997, p. 4, 'A "spy" hunt', *Frontline*, 7 February 1997, p. 24 and 'The ban on Harkat', *Frontline*, 31 October 1997, p. 132.
48. The pro-active policy was introduced because Advani expected that Islamabad would step up terrorist infiltration into Jammu and Kashmir after the nuclear tests. He also thought it likely that western governments would overlook Pakistani provocations, given their annoyance with India for conducting the tests. 'Advani draws a hard line', *Outlook*, 1 June 1998, accessed online via www.outlookindia.com, on 12 May 2008.
49. 'Exit, the last of the sahibs', *Outlook*, 17 August 1998, accessed online via www.outlookindia.com, on 13 May 2008.
50. 'What will they talk', *India Today*, 4 June 2001, accessed online at http://www.india-today.com/itoday/20010604/cover3.shtml, on 11 June 2008.
51. 'Kashmir on the mind', *India Today*, 16 July 2001, accessed online at http://www.india-today.com/itoday/20010716/cover.shtml, on 11 June 2008.
52. Raman, B., 'Terrorism: India should watch out', *South Asia Analysis Group*, 27 January 2005, accessed online at http://www.southasiaanalysis.org/papers13/paper1233.html, on 10 June 2009.
53. 'Back to the trenches', *India Today*, 6 August 2001, accessed online at http://www.india-today.com/itoday/20010806/nation2.shtml, on 11 June 2008.
54. Sood, V.K., and Sawhney, Pravin, *Operation Parakram: The War Unfinished* (New Delhi: Sage, 2003), pp. 9–10.
55. Lecture by Lieutenant General (Retired) Vinayak Patankar, at the Observer Research Foundation (ORF), New Delhi, 5 September 2008.
56. *Ministry of Home Affairs Annual Report 2002–2003*, p. 15.
57. 'Dining with Armageddon', *The Economist*, 18 May 2002, p. 71.

58. 'Terror on hold', *Outlook*, 17 June 2002, accessed online via www.outlook india.com, on 29 May 2008.
59. 'Mentors, monitors', *Outlook*, 17 June 2002, accessed online via www.outlook india.com, on 29 May 2008.
60. Mehta, Ashok K., 'J&K: The election body-count begins', *SAIR*, 16 September 2002, Vol. I/9, accessed online at http://satp.org/satporgtp/sair/Archives/1_9.htm#Assessment2, on 3 April 2009.
61. 'Now thrust, now parry', *Outlook*, 3 June 2002, accessed online via www.outlookindia.com, on 29 May 2008.
62. See *SAIR*, 22 July 2002, Vol.I/1, for the full table. Accessed online at http://satp.org/satporgtp/sair/Archives/1_1.htm, on 3 April 2009.
63. Lakshman, Kanchan, 'J&K: No respite from the Jehadis', *SAIR*, 25 November 2002, Vol. I/XIX , accessed online at http://satp.org/satporgtp/sair/Archives/1_19.htm#assessment2, on 3 April 2009.
64. 'Roar of silence', *Outlook*, 8 December 2003, accessed online via www.outlook india.com, on 3 June 2008.
65. Stephen Cohen has noted that it was the inability of terrorist and insurgent movements to come together and coordinate their activities, which allowed the Indian government to contain and crush them. He commented that if a multiple-front terrorist offensive could be organised, counterterrorism in India might prove to be a lot less effective than it has thus far been. Cohen, Stephen, *India: Emerging Power* (New Delhi: Oxford University Press, 2002), p. 113.
66. 'Shame at Ayodhya', *Frontline*, 1 January 1993, p. 9, 'The wrecking crew', *Frontline*, 1 January 1993, p. 15 and 'Games in UP', *Frontline*, 1 January 1993, p. 14.
67. 'Unease in the east', *Outlook*, 2 August 1999, accessed online via www.out lookindia.com, on 23 May 2008.
68. 'Terror's new dawn', *Outlook*, 4 February 2008, accessed online via www.outlookindia.com, on 28 May 2008.
69. 'Challenges in the east', *Frontline*, 14–27 January 2006, accessed online at http://www.flonnet.com/fl2301/stories/20060127006201100.htm, on 29 April 2008.
70. 'A quiet invasion', *India Today*, 15 September 1985, pp. 52–55.
71. Vohra, N.N., 'National governance and internal security', *Journal of Defence Studies*, Vol. I/2, (2008), pp. 2–3.
72. 'Land wars', *India Today*, 30 June 1994, p. 43.
73. 'Dawood Inc.', *Outlook*, 29 September 1997, accessed online via www.outlook india.com, on 11 May 2008.
74. In 2001, Indian intelligence gained surreptitious access to Dawood Ibrahim's email account. Through this penetration, they learnt that the ISI was using

his brother Anees as a conduit for smuggling weapons and ammunition into India. Furthermore, they also learnt that Dawood had developed contacts with insurgent groups in north-eastern India. By accessing the email account of Dawood's key associate 'Chhota' Shakeel, the agencies were also able to ascertain the identities of influential mafia supporters in Mumbai. Shakeel was being used to liaise with Indian journalists and political leaders on Ibrahim's behalf, gathering information which invariably found its way to the ISI. 'D'wood bum stead', *Outlook*, 28 January 2002, accessed online via www.outlookindia.com, on 28 May 2008.

75. 'Shake-up in intelligence set-up soon in state', *The Hindu*, 28 August 2007, accessed online at http://www.hindu.com/2007/08/28/stories/20070828 50100100.htm, on 3 April 2009.
76. 'Target Hyderabad', *Frontline*, 8–21 September 2007, accessed online at http://flonnet.com/fl2418/stories/20070921501902700.htm, on 3 April 2009.
77. 'Hyderabad blues', *Times of India*, 1 September 2007, accessed online at http://timesofindia.indiatimes.com/Hyderabad_Blues/articleshow/2328118.cms, on 3 April 2009.
78. Agraharkar, Vishal, 'Political incentives and Hindu-Muslim violence: a study of Hyderabad, India', Bachelor of Arts dissertation, submitted to Williams College, Williamstown, Massachusetts, in May 2005. Accessed online at http://library.williams.edu/theses/pdf.php?id=31, on 12 May 2008.
79. 'Charminar's curse', *Outlook*, 10 September 2007, accessed online via www.outlookindia.com, on 8 June 2008.
80. As one academic has noted, 'there is not an unlimited reservoir of people willing to replace those who are executed or imprisoned. There was no terrorism under fascism and communism'. Walter Laqueur, *The New Terrorism: Fanaticism and the Arms of Mass Destruction* (London: Phoenix Press, 1999), p. 252.
81. 'A state of fear', *Frontline*, 14–27 January 2006, accessed online at http://www.flonnet.com/fl2301/stories/20060127005301700.htm, on 28 April 2008.
82. 'Simmering fanaticism', *India Today*, 15 October 2001, accessed online at http://www.india-today.com/itoday/20011015/crime.shtml, on 12 June 2001.
83. 'Exporting terror', *India Today*, 15 May 1994, p. 25.
84. For instance, in May 2006 the Uttar Pradesh government, then led by the Samajwadi Party, announced that it would not support continuation of the nation-wide ban on the Students' Islamic Movement of India. Less than two months later, members of SIMI carried out a joint operation with Pakistani jihadists and bombed commuter trains in Mumbai. Routray, Bibhu Prasad, 'SIMI: steady subversion', *SAIR*, 10 July 2006, Vol. IV/52, accessed online at http://satp.org/satporgtp/sair/Archives/4_52.htm#assessment1, on 3 April 2009. Also Singh, Ajit Kumar, 'Uttar Pradesh: looming threat of subversion',

SAIR, 8 January 2007, Vol. V/26, accessed online at http://satp.org/satporgtp/sair/Archives/5_26.htm#assessment2, on 3 April 2009.

85. This incident has been referred to by former IB Joint Director Maloy Dhar in his book *Open Secrets*. His account differs from the media report cited by this thesis in only one sense: it says that the targets of the raid were foreign-born terrorists. Also, Mr. Dhar writes that the officer heading the SIB in Lucknow was hounded out of the agency. Dhar, *Open Secrets*, p. 367.
86. 'Wrong move', *India Today*, 15 December 1994, p. 14.
87. In January 2000, the United States and India set up a Joint Working Group on counterterrorism to facilitate information-sharing and investigative efforts. See statement by Indian Minister of State for Home Affairs, Mr. Vidyasagar Rao, in the Indian Parliament's Upper House (known as the 'Rajya Sabha') on 15 May 2002. Accessed online at http://164.100.47.5:8080/rsq/quest.asp?qref=66941, on 27 April 2009.
88. 'Lacking punch', *India Today*, 12 March 2001, accessed online at http://www.india-today.com/itoday/20010312/diplomacy.shtml, on 11 June 2008.
89. 'Raw deal', *Sunday*, 10–16 January 1993, pp. 10–13.
90. 'Target America', *India Today*, 2 July 2001, accessed online at http://www.india-today.com/itoday/20010702/crime.shtml, and http://www.india-today.com/itoday/20010702/crime2.shtml, on 11 June 2008.
91. 'The Armies of the Night', *Outlook*, 15 December 2008, accessed online via www.outlookindia.com, on 3 April 2009.
92. 'The asset managers', *Outlook*, 5 April 2010, accessed online via www.outlookindia.com, on 7 April 2010.
93. Raman, B., 'Headley's Case: Indian Distrust of FBI Will Increase – International Terrorism Monitor– Paper No. 685', *South Asia Analysis Group*, 18 October 2010, accessed online at http://southasiaanalysis.org/papers42/paper4102.html, on 18 October 2010.
94. Olson, James M., 'The Ten Commandments of Counterintelligence', *Studies in Intelligence*, Vol. XLV/5 (2001), accessed online at https://www.cia.gov/library/center-for-the-study-of-intelligence/kent-csi/vol45no5/html/v45i5a08p.htm, on 18 October 2010.
95. 'In a state of war', *Frontline*, 17–30 May 1986, p. 43.
96. Former Director IB, D.C Pathak described the central government as a 'notional' government, since it does not have direct jurisdiction over much of the territory where terrorist activity actually takes place. Interview, New Delhi, 27 December 2008.
97. This has been documented by Ujjwal Kumar Singh in his book *The State, Democracy and Anti-Terror Laws in India* (London: Sage, 2007), pp. 165–208.
98. 'Lethal weapon', *India Today*, 2 April 2002, accessed online at http://www.indiatoday.com/itoday/20020408/nation.shtml, on 12 June 2008.

99. *Ministry of Home Affairs Annual Report 1999–2000*, pp. 12–13.
100. 'Made in India', *Outlook*, 31 July 2006, accessed online via www.outlook india.com, on 6 June 2008.
101. Mahadevan, Prem, 'The Gill Doctrine: A Model for 21st Century Counterterrorism?, *Faultlines: Writings on Conflict and Resolution*, Vol. XIX (2008), p. 29.
102. 'A stiff, formal handshake', *Outlook*, 2 October 2006, accessed online via www.outlookindia.com, on 6 June 2008.
103. Gill, K.P.S., 'Gujarat: New theatre of Islamist terror', *SAIR*, 30 September 2002, Vol. I/11, accessed online at http://satp.org/satporgtp/sair/Archives/1_11.htm#assessment1, on 3 April 2009.
104. 'The age of violence', *Outlook*, 17 January 2000, accessed online via www.outlookindia.com, on 24 May 2008.

5 A Lack of Operational Capacity

1. Interview of former Delhi Police Joint Commissioner, Maxwell Pereira, New Delhi, 8 September 2008.
2. During the early 1980s, when the rebellion in Mizoram was starting to wind down, the insurgents created numerous 3–4 man attack cells to keep the movement alive. They hoped that these cells could carry out attacks in urban areas, while relying on good operational security to avoid detection by the security forces. Such hopes were belied due to the active participation of the Mizoram police criminal investigation department in the counterterrorist effort. The CID included among its ranks a large number of former rebels who had defected to the government side. Using information obtained through local contacts and community liaison, they unravelled the rebels' urban infrastructure. 'Laldenga's legacy', *India Today*, 30 June 1982, pp. 39 and 'The ambushers ambushed', *India Today*, 31 July 1982, p. 33.
3. Kitson, Frank, *Bunch of Five* (London: Faber and Faber, 1977), pp. 33–35.
4. Interview of former Director IB – A1, New Delhi, September 6, 2008. However, this officer felt that the advantage of faster response times to intelligence reports is cancelled out by the resentment which army-led counterterrorist operations generate.
5. There is a counter-argument to this point, which is that prolonged deployment of soldiers in internal security duties/counterterrorism could lead to them becoming corrupt as well. However, at least in the short-term, commentators seem to agree that soldiers are less prone to extorting money from members of the public than policemen are. Sonal, Ashish, *Terrorism and Insurgency in India: A Study of the Human Element* (New Delhi: Lancer, 1994), pp. 97–99.

6. Freeman, *Freedom or Security*, pp. 124–125.
7. 'A turning point', *India Today*, 31 October 1983, p. 14.
8. Marwah, *Uncivil Wars*, p. 173.
9. Brar, *Operation Blue Star*, pp. 65–67.
10. Telephonic interview of former IB Additional Director Kalyan Rudra, 6 January 2005.
11. 'The spy trade', *India Today*, 31 December 1983, p. 15.
12. 'Rebel rousing', *India Today*, 29 February 1984, p. 30.
13. 'The elusive solution', *India Today*, 15 August 1984, p. 28.
14. 'Is there a way out', *India Today*, 15 May 1984, p. 28.
15. 'Coping with terrorism', *India Today*, 15 September 1985, p. 25.
16. 'The hit men', *India Today*, 31 August 1984, p. 15 and 'Coping with terrorism', *India Today*, 15 September 1985, p. 19.
17. Interview of former IB Additional Director – B1, New Delhi, 5 January 2005.
18. "In a war like this there are ups and downs", *Frontline*, 27 December–9 January 1986, p. 9.
19. Mahadevan, Prem, 'Counterterrorism in the Indian Punjab: assessing the "cat" system', *Faultlines: Writings on Conflict and Resolution*, Vol. XVIII (2007), pp. 24–25.
20. Interview of former Director IB – A1, New Delhi, 6 September 2008.
21. 'In sheer terror', *Frontline*, 4–17 March 1988, p. 11.
22. 'Punjab: what can be done', *India Today*, 31 December 1986, p. 28.
23. 'Slush funds: pay-off secrets', *India Today*, 15 February 1995, pp. 52–53.
24. 'Paws and claws', *Outlook*, 1 October 2007, accessed online via www.outlookindia.com, on 8 June 2008.
25. 'Getting messier', *India Today*, 31 December 1987, pp. 16–18 and 'Playing to a new plan', *India Today*, 15 January 1988, pp. 16–18.
26. The main attraction of the 'cat' system was that it reduced the Punjab police's dependence on the IB and R&AW, whose tactical intelligence was unsatisfactory. 'To bottle the genie', *Frontline*, 18 November 1994, p. 42.
27. Interview of former IB Additional Director – B1, New Delhi, 5 January 2005.
28. Telephonic interview of former Additional Director IB, Mr. Kalyan Rudra, 6 January 2005.
29. 'Remote control terrorism', *India Today*, 15 July 1988, pp. 31–32.
30. Interview of Ajai Sahni, New Delhi, 3 September 2008.
31. Gill, 'Endgame', pp. 20–21.
32. Interview of K.P.S Gill, New Delhi, 3 January 2005.
33. Gill, K.P.S., 'Technology, terror and a thoughtless state', *Faultlines: Writings on Conflict and Resolution*, Vol. III (1999), p. 6.

34. "Pakistan has lost", *India Today*, 15 April 1993, pp. 42–43.
35. Marwah, *Uncivil Wars*, pp. 218–219.
36. Singh, Prakash, *Kohima to Kashmir: On the Terrorist Trail* (New Delhi: Rupa, 2001), p. 128.
37. Gill, 'Endgame', p. 29.
38. Singh, Sarab Jit, *Operation Black Thunder*, p. 287.
39. The academic Manoj Joshi emphasised that the sheer number of troops employed in Rakshak II was crucial to its success. The Khalistanis were outnumbered and outgunned in virtually every engagement they fought with the security forces. Previously, this had not been the case, since manpower and firepower shortages had dogged police operations. Interview, New Delhi, 26 March 2008.
40. 'Policing Punjab', *Frontline*, 17 July 1992, p. 60.
41. 'For another round', *Frontline*, 20 December 1991, p. 11.
42. 'Fear in the fray', *Frontline*, 28 February 1992, p. 9.
43. Marwah, *Uncivil Wars*, p. 217.
44. 'Life after terrorism', *Frontline*, 23 September 1994, p. 114.
45. 'A double edged sword', *India Today*, 15 February 1992, pp. 14–15.
46. Interview of former Indian Home Secretary, C.G Somaiah, Bangalore, 12 August 2004.
47. Interview of K.P.S Gill, New Delhi, 3 January 2005.
48. 'Military moves', *Sunday*, 22–28 April 1990, p. 37.
49. The IB had previously maintained an extensive network of agents in Jammu and Kashmir, owing to the state's sensitivity. However, the assassinations of IB operatives in early 1990 led to demands that the agency provide better physical security to its employees. Until this could be done, intelligence production naturally suffered. 'Tackling Kashmir', *Frontline*, 20 January–2 February 1990, p. 19.
50. 'A troubled force', *Frontline*, 3 – 16 February, p. 9.
51. 'On battle stations', *India Today*, 30 June 1990, pp. 36–38.
52. 'Challenge in the mountains', *India Today*, 30 June 1991, p. 27.
53. 'A deceptive calm', *India Today*, 30 June 1991, p. 28.
54. 'Passing the baton', *Frontline*, 16 December 1994, p. 106.
55. Bammi, Y.M., *War Against Insurgency and Terrorism in Kashmir* (Dehra Dun: Natraj Publishers, 2007), pp. 52–57 and p. 155.
56. 'Changing strategy', *Frontline*, 31 January 1992, pp. 86–87.
57. 'Problems of policing', *Frontline*, 17–30 March 1990, p. 18.
58. 'Turmoil in the valley', *Frontline*, 14–27 October 1989, p. 112.
59. 'Kashmir: perilous turn', *India Today*, 30 April 1990, p. 16.
60. 'Tackling terror', *Frontline*, 22 May 1998, pp. 66–69.
61. 'Attack on secularism', *Frontline*, 18 April 1997, p. 29.

62. 'A decisive phase', *Frontline*, 2 May 1997, pp. 37–38.
63. Ibid.
64. 'Changing slowly', *Frontline*, 27 June 1997, p. 37.
65. 'Tackling terror', *Frontline*, 22 May 1998, p. 69.
66. 'Setting free the bugbear', *Outlook*, 25 November 2002, accessed online via www.outlookindia.com, on 1 June 2008.
67. Wirsing, Robert G., *India, Pakistan and the Kashmir Dispute: On Regional Conflict and its Resolution* (Basingstoke, Hampshire: Macmillan, 1994), p. 143 and 'Terror sets off khaki craze in Kashmir', *The Telegraph*, 18 January 2008, accessed online at http://www.telegraphindia.com/1080118/asp/nation/story_8796031.asp, on 5 April 2009.
68. 'The RDX files', *India Today*, 1 February 1999, pp. 14–18.
69. 'J&K confidential', *Outlook*, 30 June 2003, accessed online via www.outlookindia.com, on 2 June 2008.
70. Joshi, *Lost Rebellion*, pp. 429–432.
71. 'Hostile neighbour', *Sunday*, 10–16 January 1993, p. 13.
72. 'The battle spills over', *India Today*, 30 September 1992, pp. 42–43.
73. 'The spiral of terrorism', *India Today*, 15 November 1992, p. 19.
74. 'The Doda deathtrap', *India Today*, 15 May 2006, accessed online at http://www.indiatoday.com/itoday/20060515/state-kashmir.shtml, on 15 June 2008.
75. 'A charged atmosphere', *India Today*, 30 June 1994, p. 51.
76. 'Valley's wounds', *Frontline*, 23 February 1996, pp. 35–36.
77. 'The Mullah's monologue with the Buddha', *Outlook*, 12 November 2001, accessed online via www.outlookindia.com, on 5 April 2009.
78. 'A warning signal', *India Today*, 31 July 1995, p. 33.
79. 'Resounding rebuff', *India Today*, 30 November 1995, p. 32.
80. 'Whatever happened to Mr. Tough', *India Today*, 17 August 1998, p. 13.
81. 'Reaction plans', *India Today*, 31 January 2000, accessed online at http://www.indiatoday.com/itoday/20000131/nation.html, on 10 June 2008.
82. 'It's overt combat now', *Outlook*, 23 August 1999, accessed online via www.outlookindia.com, on 23 May 2008.
83. 'Invasion of the hordes', *Outlook*, 17 April 2000, accessed online via www.outlookindia.com, on 25 May 2008.
84. "We should now target India", *India Today*, 4 October 1999, accessed online at http://www.indiatoday.com/itoday/19991004/cover.html, on 5 June 2008.
85. 'The new vigilantes', *India Today*, 11 October 1999, accessed online at http://www.indiatoday.com/itoday/19991011/defence.html, on 5 June 2008.
86. 'A jehad against militancy', *Frontline*, 1–14 January 2005, accessed online at http://www.flonnet.com/fl2201/stories/20050114003603300.htm, on 27 April 2008.

87. 'The new vigilantes', *India Today*, 11 October 1999, accessed online at http://www.indiatoday.com/itoday/19991011/defence.html, on 5 June 2008.
88. 'Valley's wounds', *Frontline*, 23 February 1996, p. 36.
89. 'A livewire boundary', *Outlook*, 23 April 2001, accessed online via www.outlookindia.com, on 27 May 2008.
90. 'Another winter of revolt', *Frontline*, 29 September-12 October 1990, pp. 16–17.
91. 'The forgotten war', *Outlook*, 14 June 1999, accessed online via www.outlookindia.com, on 23 May 2008.
92. Sinha, S.K., 'Jammu and Kashmir: past, present and future', *USI Journal*, April-June 2005, accessed online at http://www.usiofindia.org/article_apr_jun05_1.htm, on 2 April 2009.
93. 'Somewhere in the west ...', *Outlook*, 17 November 2003, accessed online via www.outlookindia.com, on 3 June 2008.
94. 'K for conciliation', *Outlook*, 2 May 2005, accessed online via www.outlookindia.com, on 4 June 2008.
95. Interview of former Delhi Police Joint Commissioner, Maxwell Pereira, New Delhi, 13 January 2006.
96. 'Lashkar's new wave of recruits from Indian expatriates', *The Hindu*, 2 January 2004, accessed online at http://www.hinduonnet.com/2004/01/02/stories/2004010203071200.htm, on 10 June 2009.
97. For an illustration of how battlefield intelligence gained in Kashmir could yield counterterrorist success elsewhere in India, 'Terrorism: the wages of hate', *Frontline*, 3–16 July 2004, accessed online at http://flonnet.com/fl2114/stories/20040716004101800.htm, on 6 April 2009.
98. Dhar, Maloy Krishna, *Fulcrum of Evil: ISI-CIA-Al Qaeda Nexus* (New Delhi: Manas, 2006), pp.191–192.
99. Interview of former IB Assistant Director K.S Subramanian, New Delhi, 9 September 2008. Dr. Subramanian worked in the IB during the 1960s and therefore did not handle jihadist terrorism. He did however, point out to the author that the IB's heavy dependence on state-police intelligence branches has the potential to corrupt its own products.
100. According to one news report, police in the state of Gujarat took the help of military intelligence personnel in analysing mobile phone records and tracking down suspected terrorists in July-August 2008. If true, it signifies a rare instance of police–army collaboration in counterterrorism in the Indian heartland. 'Cracking the case was Herculean effort', *DNA*, 18 August 2008, accessed online at http://www.dnaindia.com/report.asp?newsid=1184029, on 30 January 2009.
101. 'Making India safe', *India Today*, 28 August 2006, accessed online at http://www.indiatoday.com/itoday/20060828/cover-terror.shtml, and 'Terror

percolating', *India Today*, 4 December 2006, accessed online at http://www.indiatoday.com/itoday/20061204/crime.shtml, on 16 June 2008.

102. Dhar, *Fulcrum of Evil*, pp. 191–192.
103. 'CT scan', *Defence and Security of India*, 3 December 2008, accessed online at http://satp.org/satporgtp/ajaisahni/index.htm, on 6 April 2009.
104. 'Botched Mumbai arrest highlights India's Intel failures', *Time*, 10 December 2008, accessed online at http://www.time.com/time/world/article/0,8599,1865554,00.html, on 4 April 2009.
105. 'About 175 terror groups active in India', *Times of India*, 13 April 2009, accessed online at http://timesofindia.indiatimes.com/175_active_terror_groups_in_India/articleshow/2948867.cms, on 6 April 2009.
106. 'Intelligence gap', *DNA*, 12 August 2008, accessed online at http://www.dnaindia.com/report.asp?newsid=1182985&pageid=2, on 6 April 2009.
107. Interview of Praveen Swami, New Delhi, 10 September 2008.
108. Bureau of Police Research and Development report entitled 'Data on police organization as on 01/01/07', accessed online at http://www.bprd.gov.in/writereaddata/linkimages/All%20Chapters5598831415.pdf, on 6 April 2009, p. 1.
109. 'Makeover a must', *Deccan Herald*, 30 November 2007, accessed online at http://www.deccanherald.com/Content/Nov302007/editpage2007112938507.asp, on 5 April 2009.
110. Khan, M. Shamsur Rabb, 'Poor policing and weak intelligence gathering', *Institute of Peace and Conflict Studies*, 10 October 2007, accessed online at http://ipcs.org/article_details.php?articleNo=2391, on 5 April 2009.
111. 'Making India safe', *India Today*, 28 August 2006, accessed online at http://www.indiatoday.com/itoday/20060828/cover-terror.shtml, on 16 June 2008.
112. 'The mirror cracked', *Outlook*, 8 September 2003, accessed online via www.outlookindia.com, on 2 June 2008 and 'When the quiet one weaves a web', *Outlook*, 8 September 2003, accessed online via www.outlookindia.com, on 2 June 2008.
113. 'A tragedy foretold', *The Hindu*, 12 June 2006, accessed online at http://www.hindu.com/2006/07/12/stories/2006071208921100.htm, on 5 April 2009.
114. 'Maximum terror and its mechanics', *Frontline*, 15–28 July 2006, accessed online at http://flonnet.com/fl2314/stories/20060728004600400.htm, on 5 April 2009.
115. The precise date when the warning was sent is not clear. One source cites it as 26 May, another as 1 June and yet another as 27 June. In all probability, multiple missives were dispatched, whose contents were later leaked out by the IB to different journalists, in order to clear the agency of blame for

'intelligence failure'. In any case, the Mumbai police acknowledged that prior warnings had been received from the central government, so the date is actually a moot point. 'Fog on the Monocles', *Outlook*, 10 September 2007, accessed online via www.outlookindia.com, 'State had 40-day warning about 7/11', *DNA*, 22 July 2006, accessed online at http://www.dnaindia.com/report.asp?NewsID=1043104, 'Mumbai police tipped off on June 27!', *Express India*, 15 July 2006, accessed online at http://www.expressindia.com/news/fullstory.php?newsid=71127#compstory, and 'Mumbai blasts: conspiracy or blind spot?', *DNA*, 24 July 2006, accessed online at http://www.dnaindia.com/report.asp?newsid=1043468, on 5 April 2009.

116. 'Riding a miracle', *Outlook*, 24 July 2006, accessed online via www.outlookindia.com, on 5 June 2008.
117. 'A city keeps its cool', *Outlook*, 31 July 2006, accessed online via www.outlookindia.com, on 5 June 2008.
118. 'Why does Indian intelligence fail?', 17 August 2006, accessed online at http://www.rediff.com/news/2006/aug/17guest1.htm?zcc=rl, on 5 April 2009. The writer is former IB Joint Director Maloy Dhar.
119. 'A mindset of insecurity', *Tehelka*, 13 December 2008, accessed online at http://tehelka.com/story_main40.asp?filename=Ne131208a_mindset.asp, on 5 April 2009.
120. *Ministry of Home Affairs Annual Report 2007–08*, p. 33.
121. 'IB warned terrorists would intrude by sea', *India Today*, 28 November 2008, accessed online at http://indiatoday.digitaltoday.in/index.php?option=com_content&task=view&id=21192§ionid=19&Itemid=1&issueid=86, on 5 April 2009.
122. Swami, Praveen, 'Mumbai: the road to maximum terror', *SAIR*, 15 December 2008, Vol. VII/23, accessed online at http://satp.org/satporgtp/sair/Archives/7_23.htm#assessment1, on 6 April 2009.
123. 'The Armies of the Night', *Outlook*, 15 December 2008, accessed online via www.outlookindia.com on 22 January 2009.
124. 'Wanted: total overhaul', *India Today*, 4 December 2008, accessed online at http://indiatoday.digitaltoday.in/index.php?option=com_content&task=view&id=21778&Itemid=1&issueid=87§ionid=30&limit=1&limitstart=1, on 6 April 2009.
125. Unnamed intelligence officer cited in 'Made in India', *Outlook*, 31 July 2006, accessed online via www.outlookindia.com, on 6 June 2008.
126. 'A mindset of insecurity', *Tehelka*, 13 December 2008, accessed online at http://tehelka.com/story_main40.asp?filename=Ne131208a_mindset.asp, on 5 April 2009.
127. Sahni, Ajai, 'Jaipur: get to the basics', *SAIR*, 19 May 2008, Vol. VI/45, accessed online at http://satp.org/satporgtp/sair/Archives/6_45.htm#assessment1, on

5 April 2009. Sahni's argument is buffered by the writings of Israeli scholars like Schlomo Gazit. According to the latter, the quality of output produced by intelligence agencies is directly related to the amount of data that is available. Gazit, Schlomo, 'Estimates and fortune-telling in intelligence work', *International Security*, Vol. IV/4, (1980), p. 40.

128. 'Wake-up call', *India Today*, 19 June 2000, accessed online at http://www.indiatoday.com/itoday/20000619/neighbours.html, on 10 June 2008.
129. 'Smuggler's paradise', *India Today*, 30 June 1988, p. 82.
130. 'Corridor of doubt', *India Today*, 3 July 2000, accessed online at http://www.indiatoday.com/itoday/20000703/neighbours.html, on 10 June 2008.
131. 'Intelligence failure', op-ed by K.P.S Gill in *Outlook*, 26 November 2007, accessed online via www.outlookindia.com, on 5 April 2009.
132. 'India lacks capability to win terror war', *Hindustan Times*, 11 September 2007, accessed online at http://www.hindustantimes.com/StoryPage/StoryPage.aspx?id=33f35579–1a90–426d-b924–4df83ede8122, on 5 April 2009.
133. 'Indian intelligence lost in translation', *Hindustan Times*, 23 October 2006, accessed online at http://www.hindustantimes.com/StoryPage/StoryPage.aspx?id=20f26bff-b856–4494-b8a4–0d4b9c7aa02d, on 6 April 2009.
134. 'And, life goes on', *Frontline*, 17 July 1992, p. 66. Also 'Peace in peril', *Frontline*, 8 October 1993, p. 25. Person quoted is Praveen Swami.
135. 'Area of darkness', *India Today*, 15 July 1992, p. 25.
136. According to a former Indian Chief of Army staff, credit for the early counterterrorist successes of 1990 should go to a military-intelligence unit, which was rushed directly to Jammu and Kashmir from Sri Lanka. Provided with massive funds, it built up a tactical-intelligence network to replace the losses suffered by the IB in January-February 1990. Sharma, V.N., 'Whither India?', in P.C Dogra ed., *Changing Perspective on National Security* (New Delhi: Lancer's, 2004), p. 56.
137. 'The battle for the mind', *Sunday*, 5–11 June 1994, p. 24.
138. For example, the Rashtriya Rifles' Kilo Force, responsible for counterterrorism in the highly disturbed districts of Kupwara, Baramulla and Srinagar, divided up its operational time as follows: 55 per cent on aggressive patrolling and hunter-killer operations, 35 per cent on running local HUMINT networks and the rest (10 per cent) on civic action. Bammi, *War Against Insurgency and Terrorism*, p. 171.
139. Interview of former Joint Director IB Maloy Dhar, New Delhi, 6 September 2008.
140. One example is the town of Meerut in Uttar Pradesh, which has a history of communal violence. During 1992, local police officials established a three-tiered surveillance network to pre-empt terrorist activity. First, a

thousand special police officers were recruited from both the Hindu and Muslim communities. Their recruitment and tasking were complete by August 1992, four months before the destruction of the Ayodhya mosque. Second, 'peace committees', consisting of a total of 1,250 members were created, many of whom were either former or currently active criminals. Their job, and that of the SPOs, was to identify individuals seeking to incite communal riots and inform the police about them immediately. To keep both sets of informers focused on their task, weekly meetings were held at police stations and updates on the communal situation submitted. A third initiative involved monthly interactions between community leaders and intellectuals, and civil administration officials. Complaints against corrupt or unresponsive officials were noted, and grievances about the quality of governance discussed. Owing to these measures, it proved difficult for religiously-motivated terrorists to operate in the town, even after the events at Ayodhya. When on 26 January 1993, a group of miscreants launched a grenade attack on a police camp; they were swiftly identified on the basis of information volunteered by local Muslims. Regrettably, such initiatives have not been widely copied elsewhere in India. 'Message from Meerut', *India Today*, 31 March 1993, pp. 58–59.

141. According to one former R&AW officer, the intelligence agencies can generate 'actionable' intelligence for immediate use by security forces in only two instances out of every hundred. For the rest of the time, independent follow-up on intelligence reports is mandatory if terrorist plots are to be thwarted. Interview of B2 – Bangalore, 19 July 2008.

6 A Lack of Operational Coordination

1. Raman, B., *Kaoboys*, p. 97.
2. 'Spies left out in the cold', *Outlook*, 7 February 1996, accessed online via www.outlookindia.com, on 10 May 2008.
3. 'Misreading the message', *India Today*, 15 June 1982, p. 8.
4. 'The spy trade', *India Today*, 31 December 1983, p. 17.
5. 'Communication issues', *Frontline*, 28 February 1992, p. 80.
6. Most criticisms of Indian intelligence in light of recent counterterrorist failures have hinged on this presumption: 'actionable' information is always available; it only needs to be pieced together. Ghosh, Samarjit, 'Mumbai terror attacks: an analysis', *Institute of Peace and Conflict Studies Special Report, February 2009*, accessed online at http://ipcs.org/pdf_file/issue/SR660Samarjit-Final.pdf, on 2 April 2009.
7. Kasturi, *Intelligence Services*, p. 47.

8. 'Passing the buck', *India Today*, 31 July 1984, p. 25.
9. This charge was levelled by General Krishnaswami Sundarji, who was closely involved in planning 'Operation Bluestar'. Sundarji was known within the army for disregarding intelligence data and emphasising the need for speed and aggression during military exercises. 'Disputed legacy', *India Today*, 15 May 1988, p. 37 and 'I had to aim for the moon', *India Today*, 15 May 1988, p. 39.
10. Chowdhary, R.S., *A Short History of the Intelligence Corps* (Pune: Military Intelligence Training School, 1985), p. 43.
11. Interview of Lieutenant General (Retired) V.K Nayyar, New Delhi, 5 July 2008.
12. 'Night of blood', *India Today*, 15 August 1984, pp. 32–33.
13. 'Coping with terrorism', *India Today*, 15 September 1986, p. 19.
14. 'The Pakistan hand', *India Today*, 15 May 1986, p. 22.
15. 'Rebeiro's challenge', *India Today*, 30 April 1986, p. 33.
16. 'Catching smugglers and spies', *Sunday*, 10–16 February 1985, p. 58.
17. 'Punjab: state of flux', *Frontline*, 3–16 October 1987, p. 9.
18. 'A state of desolation', *India Today*, 15 July 1986, p. 15.
19. Gill, 'Endgame', p. 23.
20. 'Punjab: changing strategies', *Frontline*, 30 September-13 October 1989, p. 106.
21. 'A dramatic success', *India Today*, 15 June 1988, p. 38.
22. Interview of former Indian Home Secretary C.G Somaiah, Bangalore, 12 August 2004.
23. Interview of former R&AW Additional Secretary B. Raman, Chennai, 28 December 2004.
24. *A Status Paper on Punjab Terrorism*, dated 3 July 1998 and compiled by the Office of the Additional Director General of Police (Intelligence), Punjab, p. 19.
25. Gill, 'Endgame', p. 59.
26. 'Fear in the fray', *Frontline*, 28 February 1992, p. 9.
27. *A Status Paper on Punjab Terrorism,* p. 26.
28. Interview of K.P.S Gill, New Delhi, 20 June 2007.
29. Interview of former IB Additional Director – B1, New Delhi, 5 January 2005.
30. Dhar, *Open Secrets,* p. 385. The Babbar Khalsa, a Khalistani group that was especially close to the ISI, suspected that Manochahal was negotiating with New Delhi. In 1991, it formed a 15-member squad to assassinate him. *Review of Terrorist Activities in Punjab for the month of May 1991*, compiled by the Office of the Additional Director General of Police (intelligence), Punjab, p. 37.

31. 'Anatomy of terror', *Frontline*, 19 June 1992, pp. 89–93.
32. 'Expanding turf', *India Today*, 30 September 1991, p. 42.
33. 'Wild goose chase', *India Today*, 31 October 1986, p. 40.
34. 'Terror in the Terai', *Frontline*, 13–28 May 1989, pp. 36, 41–42.
35. Rudra, Kalyan, *Rise and Fall of Punjab Terrorism 1978–1993* (New Delhi: Bright Law House, 2005), pp.100–101.
36. 'No soft options', *India Today*, 7 October 2002, accessed online at http://www.indiatoday.com/itoday/20021007/cover3.shtml, on 13 June 2008.
37. 'The Terai's horror', *Frontline*, 26 October-8 November 1991, p. 21. 'Army again', *Frontline*, 20 December 1991, p.13 and 'Spreading fear', *Frontline*, 2 January 1992, p. 22.
38. 'Coping with terrorism', *India Today*, 15 September 1986, p. 19.
39. 'The VIP scare', *India Today*, 15 May 1984, p. 32 and 'A desperate dilemma', *India Today*, 15 September 1986, p. 45.
40. 'Startling revelation', *India Today*, 15 October 1987, p. 62 and 'Puja killings', *India Today*, 15 November 1987, p. 35.
41. 'In a communal tinder box', *Frontline*, 9–22 August 1986, p. 110.
42. 'Another killing field', *India Today*, 15 July 1992, p. 26.
43. 'A plot unearthed', *Frontline*, 7 February 1997, pp. 31–32.
44. 'Flawed approach', *Frontline*, 4 June 1993, p. 116.
45. 'A troubled force', *Frontline*, 3–16 February 1990, p. 9.
46. In one particularly outrageous incident, BSF personnel went on a rampage in the town of Sopore on 6 January 1993, killing at least 45 people and injuring 300, besides causing an estimated INR 1 billion worth of damage to property. The cause of the onslaught was a surprise attack on a BSF picket earlier in the day that left two troopers injured. Reacting in frustration, the force carried out an act of reprisal which even its own officers subsequently deemed indefensible. 'Terror in Sopore', *Frontline*, 12 March 1993, pp. 58–60.
47. Karim, *Counter-terrorism*, pp. 126–127.
48. 'Lives on the line', *India Today*, 15 August 1990, pp. 36–38.
49. Subramanian, L.N., 'CI operations in Jammu & Kashmir', *Bharat-Rakshak Monitor*, Vol. III/2, (2000), accessed online at http://www.bharat-rakshak.com/MONITOR/ISSUE3–2/lns.html, on 5 April 2009.
50. 'Seesaw battle', *India Today*, 31 August 1990, p. 29.
51. 'Hour of the gun', *Sunday*, 22–28 April 1990, pp. 30–31.
52. 'Jammu and Kashmir: contours of militancy', *Frontline*, 30 September-13 October 2000, accessed online at http://flonnet.com/fl1720/17200800.htm, on 6 April 2009.
53. 'A deceptive calm', *India Today*, 30 June 1991, pp. 26–27.
54. Thakur, Pradeep, *Militant Monologues: Echoes From the Kashmir Valley* (New Delhi: Parity Publishers, 2003), pp. 84–95.

55. 'Cut and thrust', *Frontline*, 3 November 1995, p. 20.
56. An example was the abduction and murder of two teenage boys and their 24-year old friend from the remote village of Thijiwara in December 1994. For 17 months, the boys' families pleaded for their release but were told they had voluntarily joined the separatist movement. Only in June 1996 did a captured terrorist reveal during his interrogation what had happened to them. The boys had been killed because they had found out that the terrorists were forcing a local girl to serve as their collective mistress. The girl's family had been too scared to come forward and the boys had unwisely withheld the information from the rest of the village when they interceded on her behalf. Their unmarked graves were soon discovered as a result of the captured terrorist's information. 'Invisible tragedies', *Frontline*, 9 August 1996, pp. 42–43.
57. 'The bogeyman', *Frontline*, 3 November 1995, pp. 22–23.
58. 'An untold story', *Frontline*, 15 November 1996, p. 48.
59. 'Carving up the Valley', *Outlook*, 18 October 1995, accessed online via www.outlookindia.com on 10 May 2008.
60. 'New straws in the wind', *India Today*, 30 June 1994, p. 47.
61. 'Will polls bring peace?', and "We are against polls", *Outlook*, 3 April 1996, accessed online via www.outlookindia.com on 10 May 2008.
62. 'Growing disillusionment', *Frontline*, 12 July 1996, p. 51. The journalist Harinder Baweja emphasised to the author that the petty-mindedness of some local commanders had severely hampered counterterrorist efforts. Interview, New Delhi, 29 March 2008.
63. 'Blasts of terror', *Frontline*, 6 October 1995, p. 142.
64. 'In the shadow of the gun', *Outlook*, 17 April 1996, accessed online via www.outlookindia.com, on 10 May 2008.
65. 'Guns and votes', *Frontline*, 14 June 1996, p. 124.
66. Kasturi, Bhashyam, 'Unified command HQ in counter insurgency and role of intelligence in J&K', *India Defence Review*, Vol.XVI/1, accessed online at http://www.satp.org/satporgtp/publication/idr/vol_16(1)/bhashyam.htm, on 5 April 2009.
67. 'Taking on the ISI', *Frontline*, 15 July 1994, pp. 17–18 and 'Faltering steps', *Frontline*, 22 April 1994, p. 6.
68. 'Taking on the ISI', *Frontline*, 15 July 1994, pp. 17–18.
69. The IB had assessed that the ISI's strategy in Kashmir would closely follow the strategy it had used against the Soviets in Afghanistan, and based its predictions of Pakistani moves on this paradigm. Interview of former Director IB, D.C Pathak, New Delhi, 27 December 2008.
70. 'Taking on the ISI', *Frontline*, 15 July 1994, pp. 17–18.
71. 'Whatever happened to Mr. Tough', *India Today*, 17 August 1998, p. 13 and 'In the frontline of fire', *India Today*, 23 November 1998, pp. 36–38.

72. 'On a short fuse', *India Today*, 15 March 1994, p. 30.
73. 'Fighting insurgency', *Frontline*, 31 January 1992, p. 61.
74. 'Sliding into gloom', *India Today*, 31 January 1997, pp. 32–34.
75. 'For an effective counter-terrorist organization', *Frontline*, 21 February 1997, p. 35.
76. *Ministry of Home Affairs Annual Report 2003–2004*, p. 16.
77. *Ministry of Home Affairs Annual Report 2000–2001*, pp. 29–30.
78. 'Security challenges', *Frontline*, 24 September–7 October 2005, accessed online at http://www.flonnet.com/fl2220/stories/20051007005103000.htm, on 27 April 2008.
79. The colonial IB was in fact, keen to limit the expectations of its consumers. Towards this, it was even prepared to forego the opportunity for organisational expansion, if this portended a transformation from its role as a coordination agency to a collection one. For instance, see letter entitled 'Superior staff in the Intelligence Bureau', India Office Records, Indian Political Intelligence Collection, File Number J&P(S) 243 1924, Document Number L/P&J/12/181.
80. Interview of former IB Special Director D.C Nath, New Delhi, 4 July 2008.
81. 'The spy trade', *India Today*, 31 December 1983, p. 15. The R&AW was given a written charter in 1990. Since then, the general consensus among informed commentators is that it has stayed out of domestic affairs and concentrated on foreign intelligence.
82. 'A force under pressure', *Frontline*, 18 June 1993, p. 116. Also see 'New challenges', *Frontline*, 18–31 October 1986, p. 18 and 'A screenfull of holes', *Frontline*, 18–31 1986, p. 9.
83. 'The Intelligence Bureau: India's prime intelligence agency', accessed online at http://frontierindia.net/the-intelligence-bureau-india%E2%80%99s-prime-intelligence-agency, on 5 April 2009. This article has been deemed a reliable source because it has been written by former IB officer Maloy Dhar, who was interviewed for this book.
84. 'Steps to counter the threat', *Frontline*, 22 April 1994, p. 118.
85. 'Taking on the ISI', *Frontline*, 15 July 1994, p. 18.
86. Joshi, *Lost Rebellion*, p. 93 and p. 174.
87. A minor point of nomenclature: by 1995, numerous low-ranking defections from the IuM had forced the group's leaders to rename and restructure it. When the May 1996 bombings took place, it was calling itself the Jammu and Kashmir Islamic Front (JKIF). 'Extending terror', *Frontline*, 13–26 March 1999, accessed online at http://flonnet.com/fl1606/16060160.htm, on 6 April 2009.
88. 'Another round', *Frontline*, 14 June 1996, pp. 110–111.

89. 'A surprise in Kashmir', *Frontline*, 14 June 1996, p. 119 and 'Trail of two blasts', *Frontline*, 28 June 1996, pp. 54–55.
90. 'Guns and votes', *Frontline*, 14 June 1996, p. 124.
91. 'The Kashmir connection', *Frontline*, 14 June 1996, p. 112.
92. 'Two blasts in Delhi', *Frontline*, 28 November 1997, p. 39.
93. Dhar, *Open Secrets*, p. 449 and 'Intelligence unit to monitor terrorists needed', *The Hindu*, 9 March 2005, accessed online at http://www.hindu.com/2005/03/09/stories/2005030914320300.htm, on 6 April 2009.
94. 'Ceasefire and peace drama', *Frontline*, 6–19 January 2001, accessed online at http://flonnet.com/fl1801/18010190.htm, on 5 April 2009.
95. 'The one man army', *India Today*, 26 February 2001, accessed online at http://www.india-today.com/itoday/20010226/neighbours3.shtml, on 11 June 2008.
96. By all accounts, physical security was quite poor at Parliament prior to 13 December 2001, even though intelligence agencies had warned of a terrorist threat. Security personnel stationed at the outer perimeter of the complex merely waved the terrorists through. Only sheer luck led to the latter being discovered before they could enter the Parliament building itself. Of a total of 1,050 armed policemen in the area, only two opened fire on the terrorists without waiting for orders. Between them, they killed all the attackers. Other policemen merely took cover and waited for senior officers to arrive and take charge. 'Price of openness', *India Today*, 24 December 2001, accessed online at http://www.indiatoday.com/itoday/20011224/cover-box3.shtml, on 12 June 2008 and interview of Maxwell Pereira, New Delhi, 22 July 2006.
97. 'Piecing the 13/12 jigsaw', *India Today*, 24 December 2001, accessed online at http://www.indiatoday.com/itoday/20011224/cover-res.shtml, on 12 June 2008. It was partly due to prior warning from the intelligence agencies that the Delhi police were able to swiftly identify and apprehend the perpetrators. The force pooled together information on all possible suspects and zeroed in on those most likely to be involved in the Parliament attack. Thereafter, IB and Jammu and Kashmir police helped track their movements. Interview of former IB Special Director D.C Nath, New Delhi, 4 July 2008.
98. 'Security policy', *Frontline*, 31 March-13 April 2001, accessed online at http://flonnet.com/fl1807/18070220.htm, on 27 April 2009.
99. 'The intelligence secret', *Strategic Affairs*, July 2001, accessed online at http://www.stratmag.com/issue2July-1/page05.htm, on 4 June 2008.
100. 'Why our spies fail us', *Tehelka*, 19 February 2005, accessed online at http://www.tehelka.com/story_main10.asp?filename=ts021905Why_our.asp, on 5 April 2009.

101. 'The new order', *India Today*, 4 June 2001, accessed online at http://www.india-today.com/itoday/20010604/defence.shtml, on 11 June 2008.
102. 'Low on the IQ', *Outlook*, 4 July 2005, accessed online via www.outlookindia.com, on 4 June 2008. This was also confirmed to the author by Bhashyam Kasturi. Interview, New Delhi, 1 September 2008.
103. *Ministry of Home Affairs Annual Report 2002–2003*, p. 41.
104. 'India's stalled intelligence war', *The Hindu*, 12 February 2008, accessed online at http://www.hindu.com/2008/02/12/stories/2008021255320900.htm, on 5 April 2009.
105. 'Handicapped intelligence', *Frontline*, 3–16 July 2004, accessed online at http://www.flonnet.com/fl2114/stories/20040716001204900.htm, on 5 April 2009.
106. 'Terror in Delhi', *India Today*, 14 November 2005, accessed online at http://www.indiatoday.com/itoday/20051114/cover2.shtml, on 15 June 2008. The author was not able to get independent corroboration for this piece of information, because he did not have access to anyone who dealt with the case in question.
107. 'Terror trail', *India Today*, 28 November 2005, accessed online at http://www.indiatoday.com/itoday/20051128/crime2.shtml, on 15 June 2008.
108. 'There are no secrets here', *Outlook*, 13 November 2006, accessed online via www.outlookindia.com, on 6 June 2008.
109. Ibid.
110. 'Transform, not reform', op-ed by Ajit Doval in *Hindustan Times*, 31 December 2006, accessed online at http://www.hindustantimes.com/news/specials/emotion2006/Index/middle_transform.shtml, on 5 April 2009.
111. *Review of Terrorist Activities in Punjab for the Year 1993*, p. 11.
112. 'Terrorism: groping in the dark', *Frontline*, 24 May-6 June 2008, accessed online at http://flonnet.com/fl2511/stories/20080606251113000.htm, on 6 April 2009.
113. Lecture by Niki Tompkinson, Director, Transport Security and Contingencies Directorate, Department for Transport, at RUSI on 29 May 2007.
114. Lakshman, Kanchan, 'The expanding jihad', *SAIR*, 18 February 2008, Vol. VI/32, accessed online at http://satp.org/satporgtp/sair/Archives/6_32.htm, on 6 April 2009.

7 Reflections and Conclusions

1. Shulsky and Schmitt, *Silent Warfare*, p. 63.
2. There is a methodological issue with this view; with some scholars arguing that intelligence performance should not be judged by the outcome of

particular crises. These outcomes may have resulted from factors unconnected with the quality of intelligence support provided to decision-makers. However, in the absence of a suitable substitute which can be empirically tested, there is little alternative but to use events themselves as a guide to interpreting intelligence performance. This book has matched retrospective knowledge of events with what was known of them at the time. It has thus sought to ascertain how much Indian intelligence agencies knew about developing threats and how accurately these were assessed. Merom, Gil, 'The 1962 Cuban intelligence estimate: a methodological perspective', *Intelligence and National Security*, Vol. XIV/3, (1999), pp. 50–51.

3. Garthoff, Raymond L., 'US intelligence in the Cuban missile crisis', *Intelligence and National Security*, Vol. XIII/3, (1998), pp. 20–21.
4. Interview of General (Retired) Ved Malik, New Delhi, 9 September 2008.
5. Wolhstetter, Roberta, *Pearl Harbour: Warning and Decision* (Stanford, California: Stanford University Press, 1962), p. 387. Marrin, Stephen, 'Preventing intelligence failures by learning from the past', *International Journal of Intelligence and CounterIntelligence*, Vol. XVII/4, (2004), pp. 663–664.
6. Crenshaw, Martha, 'Terrorism, strategies and grand strategies', in Audrey Kurth Cronin and James M. Ludes eds., *Attacking Terrorism: Elements of a Grand Strategy* (Washington D.C: Georgetown University Press, 2004), pp. 79–80.
7. 'Coping with terrorism', *India Today*, 15 September 1985, p. 19.
8. Singh, Sarab Jit, *Operation Black Thunder*, p. 118.
9. Gill, 'Endgame', p. 37.
10. 'Losing battle', *India Today*, 30 April 1990, pp. 18–19.
11. For instance, in early 1992 the districts of Ludhiana and Sangrur were the two most heavily affected in the state by terrorism. Over a six month period, security forces broke the terrorists' psychological stranglehold over the population. By August, the largest flow of community intelligence came from these districts, with many locals wanting to avenge themselves on the terrorists by helping the police. "Terrorism has been contained", *India Today*, 15 September 1992, pp. 32–33.
12. Narayanan, V.N., *Tryst with Terror: Punjab's Turbulent Decade* (Delhi: Ajanta, 1996), pp. 56–57.
13. The 'theory of decompression' has been referred to by Dr. Ajai Sahni, in light of the civil disturbances in the Kashmir Valley during 2008. Dr. Sahni is highly critical of the idea that allowing terrorists to run riot through a war-torn society can help the government eventually re-establish control. 'J&K: idiot philosophies', *SAIR*, 25 August 2008, Vol. VII/7, accessed online at http://satp.org/satporgtp/sair/Archives/7_7.htm#assessment1, on 6 April 2009.

14. Interview of former Director IB – A1, New Delhi, 6 September 2008.
15. Thompson, Robert, *Defeating Communist Insurgency: Experiences from Malaya and Vietnam* (London: Chatto and Windus, 1966), pp. 55–57.
16. 'The war within', *India Today*, 31 October 1992, p. 15.
17. *Review of Terrorist Activities in Punjab for the Year 1993*, p. 11.
18. 'Punjab's progress', *Frontline*, 23 April 1992, p. 63.
19. E-mail correspondence with Dr. Ajai Sahni, 24 June 2007.
20. 'The Pakistan connection', *Sunday*, 28 March – 3 April 1993, pp. 36–37.
21. "Pakistan has lost", *India Today*, 15 April 1993, pp. 42–43.
22. 'A golden opportunity', *India Today*, 30 November 1992, p. 38.
23. Mahadevan, 'Gill Doctrine', p. 22.
24. 'New dimensions', *Frontline*, 22 September 1995, p. 15, 'Complacence shattered', *Frontline*, 22 September 1995, p. 16 and 'On the killer's trail', *Frontline*, 6 October 1995, pp. 21–22.
25. 'Terror revisited', *Outlook*, 23 July 1997, accessed online via www.outlookindia.com, on 11 May 2008.
26. Dash, Sandipani, 'Trouble-makers abound, but fail', *SAIR*, 14 January 2008, Vol. VI/27, accessed online at http://satp.org/satporgtp/sair/Archives/6_27.htm#assessment2, on 6 April 2009.
27. Sahni, Ajai, 'Punjab: terror in the wings', *SAIR*, 25 June 2007, Vol. V/50, accessed online at http://satp.org/satporgtp/sair/Archives/5_50.htm#assessment1, on 6 April 2009.
28. Raman, B., 'India's national security management & cross-border terrorism', in Lakshmi Krishnamurti, R.Swaminathan and Gert W. Kueck eds., *Responding to Terrorism: Dilemmas of Democratic and Developing Societies* (Madras: Book venture, 2003), pp. 58–59.
29. This book does not consider lack of domestic consensus to be a constraining factor on counterterrorist operations in Jammu and Kashmir. It takes this view because successive state governments have closely adhered to the overarching counterterrorist policy set out by New Delhi during the early 1990s. Although the two main political parties in the state, the National Conference and the People's Democratic Party, tend to be soft towards indigenous separatist groups, this is within the bounds of the central government's own policy. By relentlessly hunting down foreign mercenaries and showing leniency towards local terrorists, New Delhi has limited the intensity and spread of terrorist violence. Significantly, no political party in Jammu and Kashmir has asked for non-Kashmiri terrorists to be treated leniently. 'An outrage in Jammu', *Frontline*, 7–20 December 2002, accessed online at http://flonnet.com/fl1925/stories/20021220009812100.htm, on 6 April 2009.
30. 'Double deception', *India Today*, 28 May 2001, accessed online at http://www.india-today.com/itoday/20010528/state-kashmir.shtml, on 11 June 2008.

31. Lakshman, Kanchan, 'J&K: financing the terror', *SAIR*, 23 June 2008, Vol. VI/50, accessed online at http://satp.org/satporgtp/sair/Archives/6_50.htm#assessment1, on 6 April 2009.
32. Swami, Praveen, 'Kashmir's waning jihad', *SAIR*, 7 April 2008, Vol. VI/39, accessed online at http://satp.org/satporgtp/sair/Archives/6_39.htm#assessment1, on 6 April 2009.
33. It has been noted by some scholars that the very act of conducting peace negotiations with terrorists can yield long-term dividends. This is not because the negotiations themselves are likely to resolve intractable differences, but because they provide a window into the terrorists' mindset. By temporarily suspending hostilities, governments can periodically assess if their chosen policies are delivering the desired results or not. Picco, Giadomenico, 'The challenges of strategic terrorism', *Terrorism and Political Violence*, Vol. XVII/1, (2005), p. 12.
34. Sahni, Ajai, 'The arc of terror crystallizes again', *SAIR*, 12 August 2002, Vol. I/4, accessed online at http://satp.org/satporgtp/sair/Archives/1_4.htm#assessment1, on 6 April 2009.
35. Lakshman, Kanchan, 'J&K: a violent peace', *SAIR*, 10 January 2005, Vol. III/26, accessed online at http://satp.org/satporgtp/sair/Archives/3_26.htm#assessment1, on 6 April 2009.
36. Lakshman, Kanchan , 'Jammu and Kashmir: respite from a proxy war', *SAIR*, 4 February 2008, Vol. VI/30, accessed online at http://satp.org/satporgtp/sair/Archives/6_30.htm, on 6 April 2009.
37. Interview of Pakistan studies expert, Sushant Sareen, New Delhi, 3 September 2008.
38. Swami, Praveen, 'J&K's party of exiles', *SAIR*, 9 June 2008, Vol. VI/48, accessed online at http://satp.org/satporgtp/sair/Archives/6_48.htm#assessment1, on 6 April 2009.
39. Swami, Praveen, 'J&K: experiments with terror', *SAIR*, 3 July 2006, Vol. IV/51, accessed online at http://satp.org/satporgtp/sair/Archives/4_51.htm#assessment1, on 6 April 2009.
40. Gill, K.P.S, 'Diplomatic tourism: Powell in South Asia... again', *SAIR*, 29 July 2002, Vol. I/2, accessed online at http://satp.org/satporgtp/sair/Archives/1_2.htm#assessment1, on 6 April 2009.
41. Lakshman, Kanchan ,'J&K: troop withdrawal – Musharraf's bid to re-open terror routes', *SAIR*, 10 October 2005, Vol. IV/13, accessed online at http://satp.org/satporgtp/sair/Archives/4_13.htm#assessment1, on 6 April 2009.
42. Swami, Praveen, 'Fresh fears in Kashmir', *SAIR*, 2 July 2007, Vol. V/51,accessed online at http://satp.org/satporgtp/sair/Archives/5_51.htm#assessment2, on 6 April 2009.

43. According to one estimate by the New Delhi-based Institute of Defence Studies and Analyses (IDSA), since 2001 annual fatalities from jihadism in India have increased at a rate of 628 per cent, if averaged out. Mathew, Thomas, 'India's confrontation with terror: need for bold initiatives', *IDSA Policy Brief, 25 February 2009*, accessed online at http://www.idsa.in/policy_briefs/ThomasMathewIndiaConfrontationwithTerror.pdf, on 27 April 2009.
44. 'Deoband first: a fatwa against terror', *Times of India*, 1 June 2008, accessed online at http://timesofindia.indiatimes.com/India/Deobands_first_A_fatwa_against_terror/articleshow/3089161.cm, on 11December 2008.
45. Sahni, Ajai, 'A tide of terror', *SAIR*, 1 September 2003, Vol. II/7, accessed online at http://satp.org/satporgtp/sair/Archives/2_7.htm#assessment1, on 6 April 2009.
46. "Releasing Masood Azhar was a political decision", *Tehelka*, 29 April 2006, accessed online at http://tehelka.com/story_main17.asp?filename=Ne042906Releasing_CS.asp&id=2, on 6 April 2009.
47. Lakshman, Kanchan, 'The expanding jihad', *SAIR*, 18 February 2008, Vol. VI/32, accessed online at http://satp.org/satporgtp/sair/Archives/6_32.htm, on 19 January 2009.
48. Swami, *India, Pakistan and the Secret Jihad*, p. 46.
49. 'Shackled by a doctrine', *Outlook*, 16 March 2009, accessed online at www.outlookindia.com, on 27 April 2009.
50. Interview of Indian defence analyst Air Commodore (retired) Jasjit Singh, New Delhi, 4 July 2008.
51. Sahni, Ajai ,'Augmenting threat, sclerotic responses', *SAIR*, 26 November 2007, Vol. VI/20, accessed online at http://satp.org/satporgtp/sair/Archives/6_20.htm#assessment1, on 6 April 2009.
52. One example was the disruption of a 2004 plot by the Lashkar-e-Toiba and Hizb-ul Mujahiddin, which aimed to bomb the Mumbai Stock Exchange. The initial leads for the security forces came through communications intelligence. Swami, Praveen, 'J&K: An abortive revival', *SAIR*, 3 October 2005, Vol. IV/12, accessed online at http://satp.org/satporgtp/sair/Archives/4_12.htm#assessment2, on 6 April 2009.
53. Interview of former Director IB – A1, New Delhi, 6 September 2009.
54. Parthasarathy, G., 'A Prime Minister surrenders', *SAIR*, 25 September 2005, Vol. V/11, accessed online at http://satp.org/satporgtp/sair/Archives/5_11.htm#assessment1, on 6 April 2009.
55. Mullik, B.N., *My Years With Nehru: The Chinese Betrayal* (New Delhi: Allied Publishers, 1971), p.514.
56. Even during the 1971 Indo–Pakistani war, intelligence support to the armed forces proved unsatisfactory. The R&AW swiftly disseminated reports to the concerned user, thereby flooding the latter with information which could not

be contextualised in time and thus made 'actionable'. It was only because the armed forces were fighting offensively – for once – that these handicaps did not matter. Knowledge gaps were filled up by battlefield intelligence. *Official 1971 War History*, prepared by the Indian Defence Ministry and accessed online at http://www.bharat-rakshak.com/ARMY/History/1971War/PDF/1971Chapter19.pdf, on 31 March 2009, pp. 797–798.

57. Interview of former Delhi police Joint Commissioner Maxwell Pereira, New Delhi, 8 September 2008.
58. ISI officials based out of the Pakistan High Commission in Delhi are known to provide generous 'donations' to terrorist groups active in Kashmir and elsewhere in India. Kanchan Lakshman, 'J&K: Losing the war against terrorist financing?', *SAIR*, 11 November 2002, Vol. I/17, accessed online at http://satp.org/satporgtp/sair/Archives/1_17.htm#assessment1, on 6 April 2009.
59. Interview of former Director IB – A1, New Delhi, 6 September 2009. Also, interview of former Indian army brigadier involved in military intelligence and counterterrorism operations – V, 3 January 2011. Also see Indranil Banerjie, 'Kashmir–Deciphering Islamabad's Signals', 8 February 2011, accessed online at http://www.vifindia.org/article/2011/february/8/Kashmir%E2%80%93Deciphering-Islamabads-Signals, on 9 February 2011.
60. *The National Investigation Agency Bill 2008*, pp.3, accessed online at www.prsindia.org/docs/bills/1229428259/1229428259_The_National_Investigation_Agency_Bill__2008.pdf, on 12 April 2009.
61. Das, Pushpita, 'National investigation agency: A good start but not a panacea', *IDSA Strategic Comments*, 12 January 2009, accessed online at http://www.idsa.in/publications/stratcomments/PushpitaDas120109.htm, on 12 April 2009.
62. Sahni, Ajai, 'Strategic vastu shashtra', *SAIR*, 22 December 2008, Vol. VII/24, accessed online at http://satp.org/satporgtp/sair/Archives/7_24.htm#assessment1, on 6 April 2009.
63. Interview of former IB officer and Director General, Border Security Force (BSF) Prakash Singh, New Delhi, 1 September 2008.
64. A former Directorate of Revenue Intelligence (DRI) senior officer told the author that coordination meetings between intelligence agencies take place even at present. These are a complete waste of time since very little information is shared. Interview of DRI – R, Bangalore, 15 September 2008. A former R&AW chief argued strongly for the introduction of parliamentary oversight of intelligence agencies on the grounds that this would reduce popular misconceptions about their role. While this might be desirable, it is unlikely to make any difference to their effectiveness in counterterrorism. Interview of former Secretary (Research) N. Narasimhan, Bangalore, 27 August 2008.

65. Pillar, Paul, 'Intelligence' in Audrey Kurth Cronin and James M. Ludes, eds., *Attacking Terrorism: Elements of a Grand Strategy* (Washington D.C: Georgetown University Press, 2004), p.117.
66. Stempel, John D.,'Error, folly, and policy intelligence', *International Journal of Intelligence and CounterIntelligence*, Vol.XII/3, (1999), p. 278.
67. Miliband's trip to India `a disaster', after Kashmir gaffe', *The Independent*, 18 January 2009, accessed online at http://www.independent.co.uk/news/world/politics/milibands-trip-to-india-a-disaster-after-kashmir-gaffe-1418914.html, on 20 October 2010. Also see Mathew, Thomas, 'David Miliband is not right', *IDSA Strategic Comment*, 22 January 2009, accessed online at http://www.idsa.in/idsastrategiccomments/DavidMilibandisnotRight_TMathew_220109, on 20 October 2010.
68. Black, Crispin, 7–7*: The London Bombs – What Went Wrong?* (London: Gibson Square, 2005), p. 31.
69. Pathak, D.C, 'Internal Security and Foreign Policy', *Eternal India*, Vol. II/4 (2010), p. 98.
70. Acharya, Asutosha, `Afghanistan-India-Pakistan: Troubled Triad', *SAIR*, 29 March 2010, Vol. VIII/38, accessed online at http://www.satp.org/satporgtp/sair/Archives/sair8/8_38.htm#assessment1, on 20 October 2010.
71. A November 2010 lawsuit filed in New York by relatives of American victims of the Mumbai 2008 terror attacks squarely accuses the Pakistani intelligence service of having 'purposefully engaged in the direct provision of material support or resources' to the attackers. American officials allege that Pakistan retaliated to this development by exposing the CIA station chief in Islamabad, thus placing him at risk of elimination by terrorists and compelling him to leave the country. 'Pakistani Role Is Suspected in Revealing U.S. Spy's Name', *New York Times*, 17 December 2010, accessed online at http://www.nytimes.com/2010/12/18/world/asia/18pstan.html?_r=1, on 20 December 2010.
72. Singh, Ajit Kumar, 'LeT: Spreading Menace', *SAIR*, 5 July 2010, Vol. VIII/52, accessed online at http://www.satp.org/satporgtp/sair/Archives/sair8/8_52.htm#assessment1, on 20 October 2010.
73. 'The Karachi Project', *India Today*, 18 February 2010, accessed online at http://indiatoday.intoday.in/site/Story/84662/cover-story/The+Karachi+project.html, on 15 March 2010.
74. Jamwal, Ajaat, 'From Terrorism to "Agitational Terrorism" in Kashmir, *SAIR*, 8 March 2010, Vol. VIII/35, accessed online at http://www.satp.org/satporgtp/sair/Archives/sair8/8_35.htm#assessment1, on 20 October 2010.
75. Doval, Ajit 'Need for a National Response on Security', *Eternal India*, Vol. II/9 (2010), p. 8.

76. Singh, Ajit Kumar, 'J&K: Surging Shadows', *SAIR*, 19 April 2010, Vol. VIII/41, accessed online at http://www.satp.org/satporgtp/sair/Archives/sair8/8_41.htm#assessment1, on 20 October 2010.
77. Singh, Ajit Kumar, 'Kashmir: Orchestrated Rage', *SAIR*, 23 August 2010, Vol. IX/7, accessed online at http://www.satp.org/satporgtp/sair/Archives/sair9/9_7.htm#assessment1, on 20 October 2010.
78. Sharma L.N, and Kumar, Umesh, 'A Need for Cogent Counter-Terror Doctrine', *Eternal India*, Vol. I/11 (2009), p. 88.
79. Kalkat, A.S, 'Aspects of Internal Security', *Eternal India*, Vol. II/8 (2010), pp. 27–28.
80. Doval, Ajit, 'Terrorism: The Response Strategy for India', *Eternal India*, Vol. I/4 (2009), p. 56.
81. Sahni, Ajai, `Counter-Terrorism and the Flailing State', *Eternal India*, Vol. I/5 (2009), p. 39.

INDEX